CHRISTIAN THEOLOGIES OF THE SACRAMENTS

Christian Theologies of the Sacraments

A Comparative Introduction

Edited by
Justin S. Holcomb and David A. Johnson

NEW YORK UNIVERSITY PRESS
New York

NEW YORK UNIVERSITY PRESS
New York
www.nyupress.org

© 2017 by New York University
All rights reserved

A portion of Chapter 6 was published in *Duns Scotus*, by Richard Cross, Oxford University Press, 1999:135–145; copyright 1999, Oxford University Press (global.oup.com); reprinted by permission

References to Internet websites (URLs) were accurate at the time of writing. Neither the author nor New York University Press is responsible for URLs that may have expired or changed since the manuscript was prepared.

ISBN: 978-0-8147-2432-3 (hardback)
ISBN: 978-0-8147-7010-8 (paperback)

For Library of Congress Cataloging-in-Publication data, please contact the Library of Congress.

New York University Press books are printed on acid-free paper, and their binding materials are chosen for strength and durability. We strive to use environmentally responsible suppliers and materials to the greatest extent possible in publishing our books.

Manufactured in the United States of America

10 9 8 7 6 5 4 3 2 1

Also available as an ebook

CONTENTS

Introduction: Mapping Theologies of Sacraments   1
Justin S. Holcomb and David A. Johnson

PART I. PATRISTIC AND MEDIEVAL

1. Patristic and Medieval Theologies of Sacraments   15
Ryan M. Reeves

2. St. Basil the Great   24
Jacob N. Van Sickle

3. St. Augustine of Hippo   41
Thomas L. Humphries, Jr.

4. Peter Lombard   59
Philipp W. Rosemann

5. Aquinas on the Sacramental Life   81
Matthew Levering

6. John Duns Scotus   100
Richard Cross

PART II. REFORMATION AND CATHOLIC COUNTER-REFORMATION

7. Theologies of Sacraments in the Reformation and Catholic Counter-Reformation   119
Michael S. Horton

8. Martin Luther   132
Robert Kolb

9. Huldrych Zwingli   152
Bruce Gordon

10. Menno Simons   175
Scot McKnight

11. John Calvin 191
    Randall C. Zachman
12. Thomas Cranmer 209
    Ashley Null
13. The Catholic Reform 233
    Donald S. Prudlo

PART III. EIGHTEENTH TO TWENTY-FIRST CENTURIES

14. Theologies of Sacraments in the Eighteenth to
    Twenty-First Centuries 261
    James R. Gordon
15. John and Charles Wesley 271
    Paul W. Chilcote
16. Friedrich Schleiermacher 295
    Paul T. Nimmo
17. Karl Barth 314
    John Yocum
18. Edward Schillebeeckx and Louis-Marie Chauvet 333
    Joseph C. Mudd
19. Feminism and Womanism 352
    Mary Veeneman
20. Liberation Theology 366
    Mario I. Aguilar

About the Contributors 383
Index 387

Introduction

Mapping Theologies of Sacraments

JUSTIN S. HOLCOMB AND DAVID A. JOHNSON

In the prologue of the Gospel According to John the apostle writes about the incarnation of the Word of God, Jesus Christ, that "from his fullness we have all received, grace upon grace" (1:16). One of the means by which Christians believe we receive the grace of God in Christ is the sacraments. But what are the sacraments? As many Christians know, Augustine of Hippo succinctly defined a sacrament as being "an outward and visible sign of an inward and invisible grace." However, throughout church history there has been little agreement about the means by which this grace is given and received in the sacraments. For example, the catechism in the *Book of Common Prayer* defines sacraments as "outward and visible signs of inward and spiritual grace, given by Christ as sure and certain means by which we receive that grace" (857). The first half of that definition—"outward and visible signs of inward and spiritual grace, given by Christ"—is a nearly verbatim echo of Augustine, and something about which most Christians can agree. The second half of that definition, which identifies sacraments as "sure and certain means by which we receive that grace," is something about which many Christians disagree.

And while definitions of sacraments all emphasize their function in ministering the grace of God in Christ to Christians, throughout church history there have emerged a wide variety of approaches to the sacraments. Since the doctrine of grace rests at the heart of the Christian faith, it stands to reason that disagreement over the means of grace has been a recurring theme throughout church history. While in some ways the inherent divine mystery of how the grace of God in Christ is communicated through the sacraments defies human efforts of definition, classification, or explanation, many different approaches to sacramental theology have still emerged in church history. This book provides an introduction and map to many of these differing approaches to the sacraments.

Sacramental theology is a complex and multilayered discipline with numerous implications for both the corporate church and the individual believer, a discipline that generates a myriad of questions. How do you define "sacrament"? How many sacraments are there? Are sacraments necessary for salvation? What is their function? What do they do, symbolize, or represent? Do they convey grace? Strengthen faith? Enhance unity and commitment within the church? Reassure Christians of God's promises? What are the conditions necessary for sacraments to be efficacious? Who is authorized to administer the sacraments? What is required to receive the sacraments? How does one prepare oneself to receive the sacraments? In what manner are the sacraments to be administered? In what context are the sacraments to be administered? How often are the sacraments to be administered? How do the sacraments relate to the Old Testament? How do the sacraments relate to the incarnation, death, resurrection, and ascension of Jesus Christ? What is the connection between Baptism and repentance, or Eucharist and sanctification? What is the role of the Holy Spirit in the administration of the sacraments? How is God present in the administration of the sacraments? Is Jesus present in some way in the Lord's Supper? Does Baptism save? Who should/can be baptized? Under what circumstances can the sacraments be restricted or withheld? How do sacraments "strengthen and confirm our Faith in" God? How are the sacraments related to other aspects of worship, like preaching, music, prayer, and confession?

To ask these questions about sacraments is to set forth on a dark and winding path—there seems no end to the list of questions. But we are not the first to ask them; in fact, two thousand years of Christian tradition provides guideposts to mark our way and lampposts to illuminate our path. This book traces what the preeminent Christian theologians have said about sacraments. Its goal is to map the terrain of the Christian tradition on sacraments and let the contours speak for themselves. This is not a work of dogmatic or systematic theology that posits a specific doctrine of scripture that must be rigidly followed. Nor is this a work of religious history that records the transmission of Bible texts or the development of the canon; it does not enter into debates about how the Bible was formed, compiled, and preserved. Rather, this book investigates the history of Christian thought by looking at major figures in the tradition and describing their unique contributions to the lingering and overarching questions about sacraments.

In this book the phrase "theologies of the sacraments" is used to refer to these expressions of sacramental theology throughout church history. There has been a wide range of theologies of the sacraments that have emerged throughout church history, new theologies of the sacraments continue to emerge today, and even more theologies of the sacraments will likely emerge in the years to come.

Our investigation will find that different theologies of sacraments exist not because the Christian tradition is inherently contentious and Christians cannot reach a consensus, but because each moment, era, and epoch raises different questions about the nature, efficacy, and purpose of sacraments. In this book, contributors address various theologies of the sacraments, each bringing his or her own expertise to bear on theologies of the sacraments as expressed in the work of specific theologians and in historical periods of church history, as well as cultural and sociological perspectives of the present.

* * *

This book has three parts. Each part presents key theologies of sacraments developed by important Christian figures in a different historical era. Each part begins with an introductory chapter that presents an overview of the theologies of sacraments in that era. The goal of the overview chapters is to provide readers with a broader context for understanding the more specialized studies of individual theologians that follow, and also to identify the concerns that bind their work together.

Part I, on patristic and medieval theologies of sacraments, covers Basil, Augustine, Peter Lombard, Thomas Aquinas, and Duns Scotus. Ryan M. Reeves begins Part I with the overview chapter. He addresses the sacraments in patristic and medieval theology, how the "mysteries" of the Christian faith were understood and incorporated into the life of the early and medieval Christians with emphasis on "the unity of the church in the life of the Eucharist, as it was the definitive mark of grace upon a church that had been graced with the presence of the Spirit." He describes Augustine's focus on sacraments as expressions of the grace of God, the importance of sourcebooks compiled in the Early Middle Ages by the likes of Isidore of Seville, the impact of the Fourth Lateran Council (1215) on sacramental theology, and Thomas Aquinas's scholastic approach to the sacraments. Reeves also touches on how John Wycliffe and Han Hus responded, and how their response set the stage for the Reformation.

Jacob N. Van Sickle writes about the sacramental theology of St. Basil, who insisted that proper understanding of the sacraments must be rooted in Scripture, adhere to orthodox Christianity as it emerged from the Council of Nicaea (325), and address the pastoral issues of a fourth-century culture in which sacred and secular societies were increasingly merging. His theology of Baptism highlighted the role of the Trinity, and his theology of the Eucharist was "oriented toward the message of Scripture and the inspiration of faith." Readers are also reminded of the contextual nature of theology, such that studying the theology of someone like St. Basil must be accompanied by studying the various cultural influences of the time.

Thomas L. Humphries, Jr. examines St. Augustine of Hippo, whose sacramental theology emphasized the mystery of God and the fruit of love, and identified sacraments as "visible signs that symbolize and connect us to the mystery of our saving God." Baptism was to occur only once in a believer's life and marked not only the entrance of the believer into the church but also the believer's identity with the death and resurrection of Jesus Christ. Augustine encouraged infant Baptism and considered marriage and ordination to be sacraments as well. In addition, for Augustine, "the Eucharist is the summit of sacramental theology because it is so obviously and closely connected to the Incarnate Christ himself and because it is a visible sign that connects us to the mystery of salvation in Christ which is fulfilled in love." Augustine's work on the sacraments was in many ways seminal and has continued to influence Christian sacramental theology ever since.

Philipp W. Rosemann covers the theology of the sacraments of the scholastic theologian and bishop Peter Lombard. Lombard's *Book of Sentences* of the mid-twelfth century defined a sacrament as "a sign of God's grace and the form of invisible grace, in such a way as to carry its image and be its cause," and included seven sacraments: Baptism, Eucharist,

Confirmation, Marriage, Ordination, Confession (Penance), and Extreme Unction. Rosemann discusses how two sacraments reveal unique aspects of Lombard's sacramental theology: Marriage—an expression of Christ's union with the church—and Confession (Penance)—contrition caused by grace being poured into the hearts of believers that leads to penance.

Matthew Levering describes how Thomas Aquinas's theology of the sacraments is connected to Christ's mission of reconciliation for humanity, a mission in which human beings are invited to participate. Aquinas's theology of the sacraments also included the seven sacraments mentioned above. Various aspects of this mission as related to the sacraments include love, holiness, evangelism, refraining from sin, and the vanquishing of death. Moreover, Aquinas viewed sacraments as gifts of grace from the risen Christ that aid in this mission of reconciliation for humanity.

Richard Cross examines the theologies of the sacraments of John Duns Scotus. Scotus viewed sacraments as "signs of God's salvific activity" in the lives of believers and fascinatingly asserted that "the seven sacraments—baptism, Eucharist, confirmation, confession, unction, marriage, and ordination—correspond supernaturally to the seven requirements of natural life, individual and social: birth, nutrition, physical exercise, healing after illness, preparation for death, procreation, and the creation of spiritual leaders." The grace communicated to believers through the seven sacraments fosters the growth of Christian character in believers, evident in their growth in grace. Regarding the Eucharist, like his contemporary Aquinas, Scotus believed in transubstantiation, although there are complicated nuances with the concept of "real presence." He also asserted "that Christ somehow offers himself in the Eucharist."

Part II covers the era of the Reformation and Catholic Counter-Reformation and includes chapters on Martin Luther, Ulrich Zwingli, Menno Simons, John Calvin, Thomas Cranmer, and the Catholic Reform. In the overview chapter, Michael S. Horton recounts how the theologies of the sacraments in the Reformation era differed from those of the Catholic Counter-Reformation. Salvation in the Protestant view means believers are "justified by grace alone, through faith alone, in Christ alone." This differed significantly from the Roman Catholic position in which "'created' grace is a substance infused into the sinner to bring spiritual and moral healing." For the Reformers grace was not a created substance but God's attitude or disposition of favor toward sinners. This dependency on grace alone involved both preaching as a means of grace in its own right and the divine activity that gives efficacy to Baptism and Communion. While they differed somewhat in their theologies of the sacraments, Luther, Calvin, Zwingli, Cranmer, and other Reformers were in agreement that the grace of God in Jesus Christ is presented in the Word preached and the sacrament administered.

Robert Kolb examines Martin Luther's theology of the sacraments. Luther maintained that sacraments were a form of the Word that conveyed the forgiveness of sins, was instituted by Christ, and connected with an external sign—and as such were a powerful way for believers, many of whom were illiterate, to experience firsthand and personally the grace of God. He identified Baptism and Eucharist as sacraments, and occasionally Confession (Penance) as well, not as a separate sacrament but as an extension of the sacrament of Baptism. Baptism marked not only the establishment of one's relationship with God but also identification as part of the church community and was therefore a sign of oneness in God. Regarding Eucharist, Luther rejected transubstantiation and the idea of Christ being "re-sacrificed" at the Mass, and yet he took Christ's words of institution literally in identifying the bread and wine as the Body and Blood of Christ, and thus "food of the soul." As connected to Luther's "theology of the cross," by which believers are utterly dependent upon the grace of God in Jesus Christ, sacraments are a means by which believers can receive and be nourished by that grace.

Bruce Gordon covers Huldrych Zwingli's theology of the sacraments. Zwingli viewed spirit and material as being utterly separate and therefore deemed it impossible for material objects to be conduits of spiritual blessing. He defined a sacrament as "a sign of a sacred thing, i.e., of grace that has been given." Sacraments are signs of the work of grace done by God in Christ through the power of the Holy Spirit, not the means of that work of grace. Baptism is a sign of the regenerative work of the Holy Spirit and Eucharist a sign memorializing the redemptive death of Jesus Christ. While agreeing with Luther in his opposition to transubstantiation, Zwingli could not agree with him on the nature of Christ's presence in the sacraments; Gordon recounts the specifics of their disagreements.

Scot McKnight addresses the Anabaptist theology of the sacraments of Menno Simons. He demonstrates that Anabaptists' observance of the sacraments in their way took considerable courage because it could be life-threatening and lead to their martyrdom. Simons advocated personal conversion and regeneration versus simply participating in the institutional church, believers' Baptism versus infant Baptism, and all believers receiving both the bread and wine at Eucharist, versus only clergy receiving the wine. Baptism "accomplished nothing in sacramental terms" but was rather an act of obedience to Jesus's command and example. Eucharist in his view did not involve any "re-sacrificing" of Christ, nor did the bread and wine undergo transubstantiation into the Body and Blood of Christ—rather, Eucharist was an expression of the love of God for the church. In short the sacramental theology of Menno Simons and the Anabaptists was essentially non-sacramental.

Randall C. Zachman presents the recurring connection and interplay between word and image in John Calvin's theology of the sacraments— that is, that both the Law and the Gospel are portrayed in a way that connects with the physical senses in the image of the sacraments. Sacraments for Calvin are connected to the self-manifestation of God in creation and in Christ as well as the self-revelation of Christ in word and sacrament. An intriguing aspect of Calvin's sacramental theology is his view that Christ initially gave himself through the "sacrament of the Law" and later gave himself through the "sacraments of the Gospel"—Baptism and the Lord's Supper, the latter being a ladder ascending to heaven.

Ashley Null examines the sacramental theology of the leading figure of the English Reformation, Thomas Cranmer. According to medieval Scholasticism, Jesus had established the church as the intermediary between God and his people. The bishops served as the administrators of saving apostolic spiritual power, and the sacraments were the effective means of dispensing that heavenly grace to the people. However, during the 1530s Thomas Cranmer chose to embrace justification by faith, which completely rejected that narrative. He believed that Jesus had come to preach a saving message, which had supernatural power to create a community linking God to his elect by inspiring trust in his divine promises. The question that would occupy Cranmer for the remainder of his life was how exactly the sacraments of the church fit into this new narrative.

Donald S. Prudlo describes the theologies of the sacraments as expressed in the Council of Trent (1545–63) and the subsequent "Catholic Reform." Sacraments were reaffirmed as "channels of grace" available to believers through the medium of material things like bread, wine, and oil. Moreover, the validity of the seven sacraments—Baptism, Eucharist, Confirmation, Marriage, Ordination, Confession (Penance), and Extreme Unction—as instituted by Christ himself was also reaffirmed. While only Baptism and Eucharist are explicitly instituted by Christ in Scripture, church history and leadership (primarily bishops) were cited as advocating that the other five sacraments were ultimately also instituted by Christ. The Mass as a real sacrifice of Christ was also reaffirmed. Prudlo also addresses how the sacramental theology that emerged from the Council of Trent made an impact on Catholic architecture, music, and devotional life.

Part III, on theologies of sacraments from the eighteenth to the twenty-first centuries, covers John and Charles Wesley, Friedrich Schleiermacher, Karl Barth, Edward Schillebeeckx, Louis-Marie Chauvet, and feminist and womanist theologies. James R. Gordon's overview chapter covers theologies of sacraments in the context of the development of modernity in the eighteenth to twenty-first centuries. He explores the relationship of sacraments to the ideas of conversion and regeneration, particularly in the ministries of eighteenth-century pastors Jonathan Edwards and John and Charles Wesley. Sacramental theology in the nineteenth century is addressed in relation to the First Vatican Council (1868), the Oxford Movement, and the writing of Friedrich Schleiermacher. Twentieth-century theologies of the sacraments are described in terms of what transpired at the Second Vatican Council (1962) and the 1982 document *Baptism, Eucharist, and Ministry* from the World Council of Churches, as well as the work of theologians Henri de Lubac, Hans Urs von Balthasar, and Alexander Schmemann. All these perspectives contribute to what is often emphasized in theologies of the sacraments in the twenty-first century, that "the things the church does in the liturgy, including the sacraments, *already implicitly contain* the things we believe about God and therefore should be a foundational starting point for thinking about who God is."

Paul W. Chilcote examines the theologies of the sacraments of the eighteenth-century brothers John and Charles Wesley. Based on the synergistic relationship between worship and theology, and combining the evangelical experience and sacramental grace, the Wesley brothers asserted that God in Christ initiates the work of grace in believers through Baptism and sustains it through Eucharist. Believers receive inward grace through the outward means of the sacraments. In their theological writings and hymns, the grace-focused sacramental theology of the Wesley brothers found vigorous and creative expression.

Paul T. Nimmo recounts the theology of the sacraments of the post-Enlightenment Reformed theologian and pastor Friedrich Schleiermacher. Rather than rooting his theologies of the sacraments in a "magical" or "empirical" approach, Schleiermacher advocated a "mystical" approach, grounded in "the religious affections of the Christian community" united in its redemption through Jesus Christ. Baptism and Eucharist are "actions which establish and preserve communion of life with Christ in the present day." His approach to the theology of the sacraments was quite ecumenical, for while disagreeing with Luther, Calvin, and Zwingli he accepted their views as equally valid, rather than reasons for division in the church.

John Yocum traces Karl Barth's theology of the sacraments regarding Baptism and Eucharist as addressed in Barth's magnum opus, *Church Dogmatics*. Sacraments along with preaching are the two primary ways the church proclaims Jesus Christ as the Word of God. Barth emphasizes sacraments as signs of the "secondary objectivity of God," signs of receiving the self-giving God. While linking Christian Baptism with the Baptism of Jesus, fascinatingly Barth eventually argues that Baptism is not an actual sacrament—and eventually Barth actually denies any sacrament except Jesus Christ.

Joseph C. Mudd argues that Edward Schillebeeckx and Louis-Marie Chauvet formulate their theologies of sacraments to intentionally counter the negative influences of Neo-Scholasticism, which created too much separation between the natural and supernatural, theology and life. Schillebeeckx, building on his interpretation of Thomas Aquinas, emphasized that sacraments are instances of personal encounter grounded in the saving work of God in the incarnation and therefore proper to a distinctly human world. Throughout his work on the topic, Schillebeeckx reorients sacramental theology in order to take the human world of history and subjectivity seriously. Chauvet describes this theology as "objectivist." It was a theology concerned with the objective effects of sacraments in terms of the production of grace in the individual recipient. He proposes a theology of sacramentality grounded in contemporary explorations into the nature of language and culture. Schillebeeckx and Chauvet are two of the most innovative, and sometimes controversial, voices in Catholic sacramental theology in the past fifty years. They share a common concern that contemporary sacramental theologies take the concrete historicity of human subjects seriously rather than rely on abstract philosophical categories.

Mary Veeneman investigates feminist and womanist approaches to theologies of the sacraments in which sacraments are "events in the church in which God's grace is made present to the community." Citing the work of Susan Ross, Elizabeth Johnson, and others, she posits the need for theologies of the sacraments to be reworked in light of the experience of women, particularly regarding the sacraments of Ordination and Eucharist. Ordained clergy should relate the Eucharist to ministry to the poor and hungry. In addition, the patriarchal framework that undergirds male privilege in the Catholic Church has resulted in misunderstanding both the maleness of Jesus and the possible role of women to serve as ordained clergy. Ultimately reevaluating theologies of the sacraments from a feminist and womanist perspective is for the sake of empowering worship and furthering mission in the world.

Mario I. Aguilar identifies theologies of sacraments in the context of liberation theology, rooted primarily in work among poor Christians in 1960s Latin America. In doing so he addresses the "first step" ("the experience of God through the poor and the marginalized") and the "second step" ("the historical and theological developments that led to the beginnings of liberation theology as a reflection on Christian experience"). The seminal work in liberation theology developed by Gustavo Gutiérrez and Juan Luis Segundo is described, as is the impact of the 1968 Latin American Bishops Conference in Medellín. In addition, the work of Ernesto Cardenal, a Nicaraguan Catholic priest, poet, and politician, in viewing the Eucharist in connection to the prophetic work of Jesus Christ among the poor is examined—specifically in the context of celebrating Eucharist in the Nicaraguan peasant communities of the archipelago of Solentiname.

* * *

In mapping the theologies of sacraments, this book serves as a guide to the variety of views about sacraments found throughout the Christian tradition, and it can also assist us in developing theologies of sacraments for our present and future contexts.

Sacramental theology relates to and overlaps with other loci of theology—Christology, soteriology, pneumatology, ecclesiology, eschatology—as well as other aspects of the Christian life—sanctification, reconciliation, holy orders, worship, and mission. Sacramental theology is therefore not an esoteric enterprise, but a critical one for the life of the church and the academic discipline of theology.

Certainly there are many different perspectives regarding theologies of the sacraments, and yet the recurring unifying theme is their role in connecting the grace of God with believers in a meaningful way. While this book does not advocate one theology of the sacraments above any other, it offers readers an opportunity to gain further knowledge about the sacramental theology with which they are familiar, and also to become further informed about other theologies of the sacraments, which in turn may foster a deeper sense of humility and respect.

PART I

Patristic and Medieval

1

Patristic and Medieval Theologies of Sacraments

RYAN M. REEVES

Introduction

It takes hubris to attempt a history of the patristic and medieval views of the sacraments. Here be dragons. Scholarly debates over theologians, or on the major turning points over the centuries, can bewilder as much as they can clarify. The risk is creating genealogies that stretch over fourteen hundred years, giving the impression that doctrine is driven by great figures adding their perspective at regular intervals. Still the fear of anachronism need not paralyze us. We must begin somewhere, and color is best to add to a portrait only after the broad strokes are applied.

Christian history is marked by a commitment to the sacraments and their importance in the life of the church. We look in vain for influential examples of theologians in the patristic and medieval eras who place little emphasis on the rites of the church—especially in the initiation of Christians in Baptism and the spiritual feeding of Christians in the Eucharist. For centuries, a church without sacraments is either oxymoronic or so inconceivable that theologians devote none of their writings to refuting Christians who denigrate the role of the sacraments in the church.

Still the patristic and medieval eras were woven into the fabric of the wider theological controversies of various stages in time. Just as it would be improper to describe them as being unconcerned with the sacraments, it also would be improper to describe their reflections using modern rubric of a "theology of the sacraments." The modern desire for such precision was not the virtue (or vice) of earlier centuries. There were tensions over issues related to sacramental power, grace, and practice, but these should not be confused with controversies over a standard theological framework that was enshrined from the very beginning.

Our task in this introduction, therefore, is to sketch the broad contours of these eras on the subject of the sacraments. The period runs from the murky days just after the passing of the disciples (approx. AD 100) until the period just before the dawn of the Reformation (AD 1500). Though these centuries share a commitment to the bedrock necessity of the sacraments, they differ in the way they explore certain facets of the church's teaching and practice in their own day.

The Earliest Church and the Sacraments

The earliest language of the sacraments nearly always reverts to the earliest phase associated with the life of the church: the mysteries (τὰ μυστήρια). These mysteries should be confused not with something exotic or strange, but rather with the inner life of God as revealed in Christ. The mysteries are wrapped up in the Gospel and salvation through the cross, as they were lived out in the life of the church in the witness of redemption.

In general, the witness of the earliest patristic writers on the sacraments, then, was both fervent and imprecise. The fervor of devotion to the sacraments from the earliest witnesses is overwhelming from the sources that describe early Christian life. The church affirmed in particular the unity of the church in the life of the Eucharist, as it was the definitive mark of grace upon a church that had been graced with the presence of the Spirit.[1]

The imprecision of the patristic witness, though, is often underappreciated. This is due largely to the hefty debates in medieval and Reformation contexts on the sacraments, which occasionally create an echo chamber of their own concerns. In the first centuries of the church, however, controversies related to the grammar of the faith—how the sacraments will be taught to the laity and practiced by the clergy—had not arisen to any significant level. For this reason later Christian writers of such depth as Basil the Great (AD 330–79) still do not have specific language about what constitutes a "sacrament," preferring instead to reflect on the broader "mysteries" of the faith.[2] Basil as frequently refers to the Gospel itself as a mystery as he does the Eucharist, and he does not refer to Baptism or other rituals in this same way. This case serves as a microcosm of the kind of careful reflection needed by modern readers of patristic writers: the lack of sophistication in Basil's writings should not force us to conclude he held no real conviction about the sacraments themselves.

Augustine and the Sacraments

The patristic teachings on the sacraments were crowned by the teachings of Augustine.[3] Augustine was born into the context of the intense faith of North Africa, a church context that rarely spoke of compromise.[4] Augustine was a precocious child, uniquely gifted in the art of rhetoric. He was also a Manichean heretic during his youth and early adulthood, finding the materialism of the Manichean faith preferable to the spiritual faith of Christianity. When he did find faith, Augustine brought with him the arsenal of his rhetorical education, and given his unique position during several key early controversies, he shaped the vocabulary of the church that was emerging in the Western Latin half of the Christian world.

In Augustine, the very nature of the sacraments find their definitive early expression. Augustine wove the concept of the sacraments, not merely into the rites of the church, but into the fabric of the Christian life itself. As with earlier writings on the sacraments, Augustine's theology is hard to categorize according to modern standards. He, too, shares the earlier flexibility in sacramental language. There is no single definition, for example, of Augustine's idea of what constitutes a sacrament (*sacramentum*). But the driving force behind Augustine's teachings is his commitment to the mystery of God's grace in the life of the church and his commitment to the life-giving love of God through the rites of the church.

The crux of Augustine's teachings on the sacraments is his thinking on the difference between a sign and the thing signified. His writings on this difference became more than a theological trope: they became the grammar of sacramental teaching in the West.[5] In this language Augustine managed to do justice to the outward life of creation, for example in the bread and wine, while also distinguishing the inward grace of God that nourishes, cleanses, and draws the Christian into the life of God. The intention here is not to separate the two, as one might see today in the difference between an advertisement (sign) and the offer of a product for purchase (thing signified). Augustine has in mind more of an intimate relationship that we see between sex and love: the physical union and the expression of love are intertwined, though we can speak of them each separately.

In this conceptualization of the sacraments, Augustine provided the West with a language that could develop a "sacramentalist" view of the entire world, rather than merely function within the rites of the church. The entirety of creation is seen as the sign of God's work that is united to the grace of God in the soul. From Augustine, then, there arose a deeper reflection on the sacraments that rested upon a simple yet compelling theological structure.

The Sacraments during the Medieval Period

Moving out of the patristic age there arose the period we today call the Early Middle Ages, an age that spans from Late Antiquity to the High Middle Ages (ca. 500–1000). Historians have not always been kind to this period of time. The number of myths surrounding this time, dubbed by Petrarch as the "Dark Ages," can bewilder: heroic sagas, unwashed peasants, and plague-infested cities are common in popular novels and movies—almost to the point of canonization. These enduring myths prove the point that good slogans die slowly. It was the Renaissance, too, that categorized one thousand years of church history as being a "middle age" between the glories of the classical and Renaissance periods.

If there is anything dark about this period, it is the relative lack of theological material compared with the patristic and scholastic periods. The fall of the Western half of the Roman Empire between AD 410 and 476 drove European kingdoms to sprout up across the West. The most pivotal of these was the Carolingian dynasty, springing out of the Merovingian dynasty, which would eventually come to dominate much of modern Germany and France. The Gothic and Visigothic tribes swept down into the Mediterranean regions, and not a few became devotees to the Arian faith, putting them at odds with later Nicene Christians who proselytized in these same regions. Much of Northern Europe was still pagan. The Vikings of the Scandinavian regions began their expansion of raids and resettlements, while the burgeoning kingdoms within the Anglo-Saxon regions of modern Britain began to form their own identity. During this same time, too, there arose the rapid expansion of Islam, which quickly took North Africa and broke into the lands of modern Spain, making their way to the Pyrenees, just south of France. These were hot-blooded times.

Still the Early Middle Ages were not irrelevant to sacramental theology. This period provided the West with the documents that began, in time, to shape the formation of scholastic theology: sourcebooks on theological topics. These were perhaps the most important texts when it comes to shaping later theological method. Isidore of Seville (ca. 560–636), for example, compiled his *Etymologiae*, an extensive sourcebook of anything Isidore felt was worth preserving for the Latin-speaking world, from geography, food, and medicine to the structure of education (*Trivium* and *Quadrivium*), a list of church offices and rules, and finally lengthy descriptions of patristic writers on theological subjects.

What these sourcebooks managed, intentionally or not, was to press home the reality that a great deal of time had passed since the patristic age. The passage of time brought with it the need for reflection on how the church maintained its fidelity to the biblical and patristic witness—and more importantly how it resolved tensions within patristic writings. A great concern of men like Isidore was to stifle sloppy thinking and half-remembered sources. What these patristic writings created, though, was a collection of the primary sources and quotations, on which the majority of subsequent theological debate would rest.

The Sacraments and Scholasticism

One of the most notable changes in the life of the Western church occurred at the Fourth Lateran Council (1215).[6] Though earlier writers had little problem using "realist" language when describing the presence of Christ in the Eucharist, the Fourth Lateran Council took the step of clarifying how this reality was to be articulated in the life of the church. They chose philosophical language related to the form and substance of a thing to come up with the language of transubstantiation. Today in English we are familiar with the language of something transforming—its external shape changes into something else. The analogy is that, according to the council, it is not the outward form that changes, but rather its inner essence (trans-substance) is changed to be the body and blood of Christ. Christians taste bread and wine, but they can, by this doctrine, be affirmed that they are partaking in Christ.

The issues of the Fourth Lateran Council arose within to a wider set of reflections on theology, the sacraments, and the appropriate method of determining truth. Beginning in AD 1000, there arose a set of competing perspectives, loosely committed to distinctive approaches to the relationship of faith and reason. On either extreme we find examples of those who, on the one hand, radically embrace the use of reason and its claims over traditional doctrine and who, on the other, embrace a more obscurantist position that reason has no role in testing revealed dogma. Between these poles developed a spectrum of theologians who strove to find a dialectical tension between faith and reason, and from whom flowed the rise of Scholasticism.

The tension within scholastic theology, though, brought a new urgency to the discussion on the sacraments. Berengar of Tours (ca. 999–1088) was perhaps the most well-known defender of a stronger form of rationalism. The result was a controversy in the run-up to the Fourth Lateran Council related to Berengar's rejection of materialist language in descriptions of the Eucharist. His rejection of traditional sacramental language sparked the ensuing debates as to the limits of theological language in describing the mysteries of the faith. In the end, the Fourth Lateran Council was left to decide the appropriate language of the sacramental understanding of grace in the Eucharist.

During this early flowering of scholastic reflection there came the influential figure of Peter Lombard (1100–1160). Lombard served most of his life in the intoxicating world of Paris, where Abelard lusted after Heloise and quarreled with Bernard of Clairvaux over the limits of reason, while students debated Anselm's ontological arguments for the existence of God. Lombard's principal work is the *Book of Sentences* (*Libri Quatuor Sententiarum*), a collection of biblical and patristic sources that would become the standard theology textbook for nearly five hundred years.[7] The book has appeared to moderns as merely a collection of source material, making Lombard seem to be an academic bean counter—more interested in appropriate citation of sources than with rich reflection on biblical themes. But this is to get the history wrong. Lombard's principal goal in the development of the *Sentences* was to provide students with a complete theological companion—a master sourcebook—that would advance the questions of theology in a way that was based on a strong method.[8]

Standing tall among the scholastic theologians is Thomas Aquinas. There is virtually no doctrine on which Aquinas is not considered a supreme authority, with some who rival his importance but none who surpass it.[9] On the sacraments, too, Aquinas is a pivotal figure. Born just twelve years after the Fourth Lateran Council, Aquinas addressed the need for a fuller articulation of the connection between earlier patristic reflections on the sacraments and the medieval articulation of a mature language the church felt was necessary to articulate its belief in the grace given to Christians in the sacramental life.

One of the most important approaches Aquinas used in his theological writings is the concept that "Grace perfects Nature." Aquinas intends by this concept the biblical reality that we are created in God's image (Nature), though our natures are obscured by the ongoing effects of sin and rebellion. Christ, then, comes not to obliterate who we are but to draw us into the Trinitarian life (Grace) in such a way that makes us, in this life and culminating in heaven, the full embodiment of our purpose as God's image. By this balancing of nature and grace, Aquinas repeatedly in his theological writings is able to affirm elements that are ours by human nature without describing the created order as being merely the expression of sin. He also is able to affirm a commitment to the infusion of grace, by Christ in the power of the Spirit, yet not in a way that suggests that salvation is intended to make us less than fully human. Aquinas affirms that human nature was created good, yet because of sin it requires the grace of salvation and the sacraments to nourish us to new life. If grace perfects nature, then already we can see the pivotal role the sacraments will play in Aquinas's theology. The role of the sacraments in the mission of God, lived in the church, is to sanctify us and make us holy—not in terms of making us other than human, but to cleanse us of sin and so unite us to Christ, in order that we might be made more fully human.

Conclusion

It would be a mistake to believe that medieval theologies of the sacraments end with Aquinas. There were a few influential reactions against the development of medieval sacramental teachings—especially in the writings of John Wycliffe and Jan Hus. Both Wycliffe and Hus assaulted the medieval church for what they felt were errors introduced into Christian orthodoxy, though both chose as their central criticism the teachings and practice of the Eucharist. Hus battered the church for its practice of withholding the cup from the laity during communion, calling for a restoration of communion in "both kinds" (later called Utraquism). Wycliffe focused instead on the teachings of the Fourth Lateran Council as to the nature of transubstantiation, arguing that such ideas were smuggled in by philosophers and not from scripture. In the end these protests failed to carry significant weight in changing the medieval church, and their teachings were considered heretical until the Reformation revived several of these same criticisms.

Perhaps the most long-lived debate for modern Christians is whether these changes reflect the deepening awareness of the Catholic Church's own reflection on the sacraments or whether they constitute significant changes within the life of the church. Protestant theology has almost always been unanimous in its hostility to medieval sacramental thinking and practice, though of course ongoing Roman Catholic reflection on patristic and medieval sources emphasizes the unity of the church's mission as it is grounded in the sacramental life of the church. Despite these debates, the roots of sacramental thinking, even today, come from the important theological teachings of the patristic and medieval eras.

NOTES

1. See John D. Zizoulas, *Eucharist, Bishop, Church: The Unity of the Church in the Divine Eucharist and the Bishop during the First Three Centuries* (Brookline, MA: Holy Cross Orthodox Press, 2001).
2. On this feature of Basil's teachings, see chapter 2.
3. For Augustine's views on the sacraments, see chapter 3.
4. Historians have at times described North Africa as the "Bible Belt" of the late Roman world. For Augustine's life, see Peter Brown, *Augustine of Hippo: A Biography*, new ed. (Berkeley: University of California Press, 2000).
5. It must always be stressed that Augustine has virtually no influence on the Eastern Church (i.e., Eastern Orthodoxy), though it would be erroneous to suggest his teachings on the sacraments are antithetical to Eastern theology. Rather, Eastern Orthodox reflections on the sacraments do not share the same Augustinian categories, and so are removed from later developments in the West along Augustinian lines.

6. The decrees of the council can be found in Norman P. Tanner, ed., *Decrees of the Ecumenical Councils*, 2 vols. (Washington, DC: Georgetown University Press, 1990). For a brief history, see also Tanner, *The Councils of the Church: A Short History* (New York: Crossroad, 2001).
7. A modern English translation is now available in Giulio Silano, trans., *The Sentences*, 4 vols. (Toronto: Pontifical Institute of Mediaeval Studies, 2008).
8. The purpose and context of Lombard's *Sentences* are discussed in chapter 4.
9. See, for example, Michael Dauphinais and Matthew Levering, eds., *Knowing the Love of Christ: An Introduction to the Theology of St. Thomas Aquinas* (Notre Dame, IN: University of Notre Dame Press, 2002).

2

St. Basil the Great

JACOB N. VAN SICKLE

St. Basil (329/330–79) was born to wealthy Christian parents in Caesarea, Cappadocia, in Asia Minor. Early in his childhood the family moved to the estate of his paternal grandmother, St. Macrina the Elder, in Pontus near the southern coast of the Black Sea. Basil grew up learning the faith from his grandmother, who had learned from St. Gregory the Wonderworker, a disciple of Origen and the first bishop of Caesarea. In 346 Basil left home to begin his formal studies—the finest of his day—which took him from Caesarea to Constantinople and finally to Athens, where he remained until 355. After returning to Caesarea to take up a teaching post, Basil had an epiphany: "I awoke as out of a deep sleep. I beheld the wonderful light of the Gospel truth, and I recognized the nothingness of the wisdom of the princes of this world."[1] He quit his position and commenced a two-year tour of the famous religious establishments of Egypt, Palestine, and Syria. He then returned to Caesarea to be baptized before taking up a life of asceticism at the family estate in Pontus alongside his sister, St. Macrina the Younger. Theological controversy eventually pulled him out of his retreat, and in 360 he was ordained presbyter by Eusebius of Caesarea. By 365 he was already, in the words of his biographer, the de facto "chief pastor of Caesarea."[2] It became official when Eusebius died in 370 and Basil was promptly elected to his post, which he held until his own death on 1 January 379.

St. Basil made many significant contributions to the Church and society, which are still felt today. He was the leading figure of Nicene Christianity during the brief but crucial period between the death of St. Athanasius (†373) and the second Ecumenical Council at Constantinople in 381, which affirmed the Trinitarian theology Basil helped to craft. His *Asketikon* or monastic Rule established a form of monasticism in community that spread throughout the Greek-speaking world and was an important source for St. Benedict of Nursia, whose own Rule did the same for the Latin West. He invented the modern inpatient hospital as part of a nexus of philanthropic institutions that he established outside the city of Caesarea. Finally, he composed many occasional prayers and a Eucharistic liturgy that are still in use today among many Christians. Apart from his liturgical contributions and the aforementioned *Asketikon*, his more famous writings include the treatises *On the Holy Spirit* and *To the Youth, On How They Might Benefit from Pagan Literature*, another treatise, *On Baptism*, a collection of *Ethics* or moral rules gathered from Scripture to govern the Christian life, a wealth of correspondence, and a number of sermons, including the well-known series *On the Six-Day Creation*.

Introduction

To attempt a treatment of Basil's "theology of sacraments" is already to risk anachronism, for even to posit such a thing as a theology of sacraments presupposes certain developments in theological enquiry that occurred after Basil's time. And yet, a thorough understanding of Christian sacramental theology would lack historical foundation if it did not reach back to the "pre-sacramental" foundations of Christian reflection on the grace-filled rites that have always been at the center of Church life. The most obvious example of our distance from Basil on the question of sacraments is the fact that he has no word for "sacrament" as such. The term usually applied by later Greek writers to the sacred rites of the Church that would come to assume the technical meaning of "sacraments" is "the mysteries" (τὰ μυστήρια). However, Basil's use of this term is not technical and is by no means consistent. It can refer to the Gospel message revealed in Christ (the "mystery of Christ" in Eph. 3:4) as easily as it can baptism or the Eucharist. In one place, a "steward of the mysteries of God" (quoting 1 Cor. 4:1) is anyone in a position of spiritual authority who teaches others the will of God from Scripture,[3] while later in the same work Basil identifies a steward of God's mysteries as one who administers baptism.[4] In his treatise *On Baptism*, Basil refers to the Eucharist as "a mystery" or "the mysteries" no fewer than five times,[5] but nowhere in that work is baptism itself so designated. Basil also knows of the practices of confession, marriage, ordination, and anointing, though he does not call these "mysteries," nor, as we will see, does he consider them in the same light as he does the former two. What Christians today know as confirmation or chrismation he did not distinguish from baptism, which was in his practice always accompanied by the seal (in the form of *chrism*) of the gift of the Spirit and followed immediately by regular participation in the Eucharist.

There is then some uncertainty about what does or does not count as a "sacrament" for Basil, and thus whether he can be said to have a "sacramental theology" at all. This reality undermines any attempt to look backward to Basil in search of ideas or definitions that appear to confirm or contradict aspects of current thinking about the sacraments. What we can do is attempt to appreciate Basil's thought, as much as we are able, on its own terms. Then we can put his ideas into dialogue with our own. Such an approach to the past has the benefit of forcing us to cast our inquiry in a somewhat different light. It puts assumptions to the test and opens up the possibility that we will learn something genuinely new about Christian theology. For such a method, context is key. Just as the questions and assumptions of our day govern the direction of our theology, Basil's thinking grows distinctly out of his own pastoral context. There is also in our case a pressing question of content. If we are not permitted to assume even the notion of "sacraments" in Basil, then where can we begin to place his theology in dialogue with our own on this issue? The answer to which Basil's own works point is in the rites of baptism and the Eucharist. These two rites, which we now call sacraments, occupy a uniquely prominent place in his thinking about Christian life as enlightened and nourished by God Himself. And there are three features of Basil's context that played a formative role in what we might, with care, call his "sacramental theology." These are (1) his insistence that the Scriptures must be the first principles of Christian thought, (2) the pressing need to articulate and defend Nicene orthodoxy, and (3) the pastoral crisis brought about by a narrowing of the gap between Christian and civic society in the fourth century.

Revelation of Mystery

One of Basil's better known legacies in the Church today is his succinct, oft-remarked defense of "unwritten" tradition:[6]

> Of the dogmas and proclamations that are guarded in the Church, we hold some from the teaching of the Scriptures, and others we have received in mystery as the teachings of the tradition of the apostles. Both hold the same power with respect to true religion. . . . If we attempt to reject non-scriptural [literally: "unwritten"] customs as insignificant, we would, unaware, lose the very vital parts of the Gospel.[7]

The renown of Basil's teaching in this passage has led to the common notion that Basil held "tradition" as a second source of Christian theology that sits alongside Scripture and rivals it in authority. But that is a misunderstanding. First of all, the examples he gives of such traditions fall entirely into the category of ritual: the sign of the cross, customs for prayer—standing on the Lord's Day, at various times kneeling, and always toward the East—the prayers used to consecrate the bread and cup of the Eucharist, and the waters of baptism.[8] Other features of baptism are also mentioned: the anointing (*chrism*), triple immersion in water, the renunciation of Satan and his angels, and the form of the confession of faith recited by the convert. For Basil, it is true, these traditions are no more to be tampered with than are the words of the Bible. However, when it comes to explaining the *meaning* of these practices, to articulating the theology behind them, he relies entirely upon Scripture. Prayer is made to the East because, as the Scripture says, paradise was planted there. Standing on the Lord's Day reminds us of the grace of the resurrection (literally in Greek [and in Latin]: "standing again") proclaimed in the Gospel. Even the confession of faith, which he invokes as an unwritten tradition in support of his teaching about the Holy Spirit, is "unwritten" only in the sense that it is not found in Scripture word-for-word in its entirety. In fact, Basil elsewhere devotes a short essay to demonstrating that every line of the confession used in his church (which closely resembled the Nicene Creed as we have it today) can be traced to one passage or another in Scripture.[9] This is in keeping with his insistence that all matters of faith must be rooted in holy writ, insofar as Christian faith itself is nothing other than absolute trust in the inspired Scripture: "For if 'all that is not from faith is sin,' as the Apostle says, and 'faith is from hearing, and hearing is through God's Word,' then everything outside the God-breathed Scripture, being not from faith, is sin."[10]

Basil's teaching about baptism and the Eucharist is no different. He knows of many unwritten traditions governing their ritual performance, but the function of these is to reiterate and reinforce the teaching of Scripture rather than supplement or qualify it. His most direct and summary statements about baptism and the Eucharist come from his *Ethics* (also known as the *Moralia*), a work in which he summarizes all of the directives he has found in the New Testament for leading a Christian life. Citing the Great Commission and Christ's words to Nicodemus in addition to several passages of Paul,[11] he finds that "it is necessary for those who believe in the Lord to be baptized in the name of the Father and of the Son and of the Holy Spirit," so that "the one baptized is changed according to mind and reason and activity and becomes, by the power given, that very thing [i.e., "spirit"] from which he was born."[12] Immediately after his remarks on baptism, he adds on the strength of John 6:53–58, "that necessary also for eternal life is partaking of the body and blood of Christ,"[13] and he repeats Paul's warning to receive communion not unworthily but with "consideration for the reason why the participation of the flesh and blood of Christ is given,"[14] which is to be reminded of "the Lord's obedience until death: so that the living no longer live for themselves but for the one who died and was raised on their behalf."[15]

Basil's uncompromising view of Scripture leads him to affirm a high estimation of the rites of the Church as both necessary and effectual.[16] Of course, this has largely to do with the fact that he reads John chapters 3 and 6 in the traditional way as references to baptism and Eucharist, respectively, readings that have been contested along denominational lines since the sixteenth century. The alternative reading of these passages typically advanced is that Jesus is speaking not of the visible rituals of the Church, but of the invisible movements of the Spirit and the Word of God in the heart of the believer, because faith is what guarantees salvation, as the Scripture says elsewhere. Basil does not take such an "either . . . or" approach to the question. If the natural readings of two (or more) passages of Scripture say different things, his instinct is rather to find a way to affirm both at once: "Faith and baptism are two ways of salvation that are naturally united with each other and indivisible. While faith is perfected by baptism, baptism is established by faith. . . . The confession that brings salvation comes first and there follows baptism which seals our assent."[17] Basil discerns that the reason Scripture maintains in some places that baptism and the Eucharist are necessary for salvation, while in others only faith in Christ is mentioned, is because there is an inseparable relationship between faith in Christ and participation in the rituals Christ commanded. When Scripture speaks of faith in Christ, baptism and the Eucharist, like all works that spring from a living faith,[18] are presumed.

However, the connection of faith with baptism and Eucharist goes beyond even the obvious affirmation that trusting Christ entails doing as he says, even if we may not understand the reason. What the rites of baptism and the Eucharist actually do, according to Basil, is instill faith in the Word of God like nothing else can. When Basil reflects on John the Baptist's remark that the baptism of Christ is "in the Holy Spirit and fire,"[19] he likens the person being baptized to "iron dipped in fire whose flames are fanned by the wind (or 'Spirit': πνευμα)." He explains,

> After the iron is transformed not only in color but also in texture, its hardness and rigidity are rendered pliant, so that it becomes very malleable in the hands of the artisan and wonderfully adapts itself to the will of its master. . . . It necessarily follows, then, that he who has been baptized in fire, *that is, in the word of doctrine* which overcomes the malice of sin and makes manifest the grace of righteousness, hates and abominates iniquity, as it is written, and desires to receive purification through faith in the power of the blood of our Lord Jesus Christ.[20]

The fire in Basil's image, that which actually transforms the individual in baptism, is "the word of doctrine." The grace received is not some ephemeral divine favor that bestows salvation apart from faith, but it is the teaching of that faith itself, which in baptism is aided, or "fanned," by the Holy Spirit.

The operation of the Eucharist is similarly oriented toward the message of Scripture and the inspiration of faith. Its "power" is, at first glance, even less mysterious than that of baptism. Regular communion in the body and blood of the Lord keeps alive and immediate the memory of what Christ did for us in the flesh, which inspires us to live not for ourselves, but for Him. The apparent modesty of this "remembrance" seems at first to be on the same order as a simple retelling of Christ's passion and resurrection. And yet, it is not a reading of the Gospel narrative that Christ commands but a regular commemorative meal in which his body and blood are consumed.[21] To account for this, Basil again points to a mysterious connection between rite and Word. After we have been baptized into Christ, he says, "We require to be nourished with the food of eternal life." What is this food? He quotes a long list of Scriptures, beginning with two sayings of Christ that identify heavenly food with the word and will of the Father: "Not in bread alone does man live, but in every word that proceeds from the mouth of God";[22] "My meat is to do the will of him that sent me: the Father."[23] Then, without preamble, he quotes Christ's discourse in John 6 (mentioned already above) about the necessity of consuming his flesh and blood, which he concludes by recounting the words of institution at the Last Supper.[24] Finally, he offers the following rationale for joining all these texts together in his account of the Eucharist:

> [These words just quoted] help us, when eating and drinking, always to remember Him who died for us and rose again; thus, we are certain to learn how to follow before God and His Christ the teaching handed down by the Apostle, in the words: "For the love of Christ presses us; judging this, that if one died for all, then all were dead; and Christ dies for all, that they also who live may not now live to themselves, but unto him who died for them and rose again."[25]

The memory of Christ's death and resurrection brought to the fore with each celebration of the Eucharist "presses" us (in the sense of being pressed into service: συνέχει) to live the life of faith. This effect of the rite is what lies at the heart of the obvious, if somewhat mysterious, continuity between the nourishment of hearing and fulfilling the Word of God and the nourishment of eating the body and drinking the blood of the Lord in the Eucharist. Basil sees this continuity manifest in the very language of the Scriptures, and that is enough for him to be sure it exists even if he is unable to fully explain it.

Heavenly Mysteries

The foremost theological concern of Basil's career was to defend the Trinitarian faith as codified at the Council of Nicaea. Basil unsurprisingly, therefore, develops his understanding of the two rituals of salvation, baptism and the Eucharist, in terms of the God who saves as Trinity. The Trinitarian formula of baptism delivered by Christ to the apostles in the Great Commission is his starting place. Invocation of the three persons at the moment of the saving ritual, Basil contends, is simply shorthand for the entire Trinitarian confession of faith into which believers in that faith are baptized and to which they must adhere in order to retain the grace of their adoption: "How are we saved? Clearly we are regenerated through the grace of baptism. How else? So then knowing that this salvation is established through the Father and the Son and the Holy Spirit, should we cast away the 'standard of teaching' which we have received?"[26] Just as the saving confession of faith is inseparable from the saving act of baptism, inseparable too is the Triune God who is confessed and who alone saves. "If, living in the Spirit, we also walk in the Spirit, thus becoming receptive of the Holy Spirit [in baptism], we shall be enabled to confess Christ, because 'no one can say the Lord Jesus but by the Holy Spirit.'"[27]

The Holy Spirit is present in baptism in a unique and powerful way by enabling the confession and accomplishing the rebirth of the sinner into new life in Christ. Basil is emphatic that the power of baptism is not something granted by God to the water, but it is the very presence of the third person of the Trinity in every baptism: "The water furnishes the image of death, just as the body is received in burial, but the Spirit infuses life-giving power, renewing our souls from the death of sin to their original life. . . . Thus, if there is some grace in the water, it is not from the nature of the water, but from the presence of the Spirit."[28] This does not become for him an excuse for skirting the ritual, since we have it on Christ's command. Rather his point is to rule out any "magical" understanding of what takes place in baptism, as though the form or matter of the rite had any power in and of itself, and highlight the direct presence and activity the Holy Spirit as God, who in accordance with the will of the Father accomplishes his greatest works through this rite: "Through the rebirth from above . . . the Spirit enlightens all, inspires prophets, gives wisdom to lawmakers, consecrates priests, empowers kings, perfects the just, exalts the prudent, is active in gifts of healing, gives life to the dead, frees those in bondage, turns foreigners into adopted sons."[29]

If the Spirit is present as agent in baptism, the Lord is also present as its efficient and final cause:

> It would be impossible to be born anew unless the grace of God had first been vouchsafed to us, as the Apostle himself shows. . . . "But God commended his love for us, because when we were yet sinners, Christ dies for us. . . . For if, when we were enemies, we were reconciled to God by the death of His Son, much more, being reconciled, shall we be saved by his life."[30]

It is the death in the flesh of the second person of the Trinity, suffered for all, in which all those who are baptized continue to participate. Christ's death once and for all was the first and lasting grace, which is made available to all in baptism through the ongoing activity of the Holy Spirit. Christ's activity in the flesh consecrated baptism, as it were, and caused it to be the vehicle of the Spirit unto sanctification. And the end result of the Spirit's work in baptism is that the one baptized is "clothed" in Christ.[31]

This interaction between the Son and Spirit in baptism accords with a fundamental tenet of Basil's Trinitarian theology. The Son of God is the image of the Father, who came to reveal the Father and accomplish his will. The Spirit both cooperated in Christ's work in the flesh (beginning in his virginal conception) and continues it by making Him always present to everyone who believes. One of Basil's predecessors, St. Irenaeus of Lyon, spoke of the Son and the Spirit as the "two hands of the Father," which always cooperate in doing His work. The activity of the Spirit is the same as the Son's, and vice versa. This dictum holds true also for the Eucharist. It was a universal feature of early Greek Eucharistic prayers, of which Basil composed at least one, that the minster who made the invocation would call down the Holy Spirit "upon us and upon these gifts here offered"[32] to consecrate the bread and wine to become the body and blood of Christ. Whereas in baptism the Spirit is present through the initial work of the Son, in the Lord's Supper it is Christ who is present in his body and blood, through the consecratory activity of the Spirit. In each rite the Son and the Spirit make one another present in turns, so that the end result is that a believer is transformed by the Spirit into the image of Christ. The parallel of baptism with the Eucharist holds also for the source of their efficacy. The power of the Eucharist lies not in bread and wine, nor is to do even with the human flesh of Christ that these become, "for the flesh profits nothing."[33] Instead its power comes from His divinity, which is most clearly manifest in his voluntary death and resurrection in perfect obedience to the Father's will.

Dread Mysteries

One of the more curious features of life in a fourth-century Church is that a great many of those who professed belief in Christ and who attended services on a regular basis were not baptized and communing members. Often these were "converts" to the faith, who had become convinced of the truth (or, for the more cynical, the usefulness) of Christianity but had not yet steeled themselves for the whole-life commitment that baptism into membership in Christ was understood to entail. In the aftermath of the conversion of the Emperor Constantine in 313 and his subsequent patronage of the Church, Christianity became mainstream. It attracted many adherents whose commitment was less than absolute and who elected to live their lives on the periphery of the Church looking in, postponing baptism until death was imminent. Constantine himself had taken this route. Perhaps the most well-known example of a deferred baptism in the fourth century is that of St. Augustine of Hippo, who gives us the reason. Though his mother Monica was a Christian, she chose to defer his baptism "on the assumption that . . . I would be sure to soil myself, and after that solemn washing the guilt would be greater and more dangerous if I then defiled myself with sins."[34] As already mentioned, Basil himself did not receive baptism until about the age of twenty-seven, and by his own account he "was raised by Christian parents from the very first."[35] It was only after he determined to commit himself to living out the will of God in all things that Basil sought out baptism for himself. Christian children were not, as a rule, denied baptism by the Church. By the fourth century, the practice of infant baptism was well-known,[36] but Basil's parents, like Augustine's mother, made a conscious choice not to have him baptized. In the fourth century even those who considered themselves faithful to Christ might defer baptism for themselves or their children for fear that life in the world would lead them to betray their baptismal promise. Baptism was a very serious affair.[37]

As a bishop, Basil struggled to convince those sitting on the fence of his congregation to receive baptism and be brought into the full communion of the Church. In a sermon preached on this topic, we get a sense of Basil's appreciation for the awesomeness of the rite—both what it has to offer, and what it demands of a newly minted Christian. He perceives that those he addresses, many who, like himself, had "received Christian teaching since childhood,"[38] are procrastinating mainly because they dread the obligation it entails. Our participation in the death and resurrection of Christ in baptism is not simply something done for us once and for all, as Basil explains elsewhere; we also promise to remain dead to sin and alive to Christ by fulfilling the hard commands of the Gospel.[39] Such fear was born of two things: a healthy respect for the high calling of holiness but also a lack of faith in the power of God to assist us in living up to it. Some saw only their own deficiencies and spurned the gift from a misguided humility. "Do not despair," he implores, "if you find you have many sins, for 'where sin increased, grace abounded all the more,' if, that is, you receive grace."[40] That grace that abounds is not merely the forgiveness of past sins, nor even the promise of forgiveness for sins to come, but also the power to actually reform a sinful life. Basil encourages those who now feel as though they are under the sway of sin and cannot hope to begin living a life of holiness with the promise that the power of baptism is real and effectual and that those who are assisted by its power can "experience the promised miraculous transformation"[41] of their lives. All that is required is their willingness to submit to grace.

But this does not mean that the Spirit saves us in baptism apart from our own effort. Salvation for Basil is not accomplished by divine fiat but is the end result of our actual transformation into the human beings we are intended to be. Baptism does not benefit the unrepentant. Rather, the grace of baptism must be nurtured and protected.[42] This demands discipline, service, humility, purity, turning from anger, forgoing vengeance, meeting hatred with love, in a word—death to sin. All this is hard, Basil acknowledges, but it is possible with the aid of the Spirit, and righteousness is far more rewarding and far less exhausting than the life of sin.[43]

In *On Baptism*, Basil dwells at greater length on the obligations that attend the reception of grace. He begins, of course, with an appeal to

Scripture. His recipient had asked simply for an explanation of baptism, no doubt anticipating an explanation of all the good things it bestows. But Basil, taking his cue from Matthew 28:19 ("Go, therefore, and make disciples of all nations, baptizing them in the name of the Father and of the Son and of the Holy Spirit"), insists that baptism (the second part of the verse) is comprehensible only as a follow-up to discipleship (the first part). A person must already be a disciple before coming to baptism, and when we turn to the Gospels for an account of discipleship, the standard, it turns out, is quite high. It is death to sin and death to this world with all of its attachments, however natural these might seem. We must "care nothing for our possessions and for the necessities of this life . . . [and] make no account of just claims"[44]—even those of our closest relations, for "He who loves father or mother more than me is not worthy of me."[45]

Basil identifies four stages through which a person who is converted to Christ must proceed *before* coming to baptism. First comes the profession of faith in Jesus Christ, which secures pardon for sins (note that this is prior to baptism). Second, the new believer is "delivered from his sinful state," which means that he is empowered to live a life of flight from sin. Now he is prepared for the third stage, to receive instruction (be catechized). But even after instruction he is still like the rich young man, who had kept all the commandments from his youth but still was unable to follow Christ because of an attachment to his wealth. Therefore the final stage, Basil says, before one is truly prepared for baptism, is complete detachment from worldly goods and sole adherence to the Lord.[46]

Such a high call to discipleship may seem a strange expectation for those who have not even been admitted into the Church through baptism. Today we are accustomed to receiving baptism either in infancy or later childhood on the strength of a profession of faith alone, whether our own or our sponsors', while the struggle to attain anything like the Gospel standard of discipleship remains with us throughout our lives, and precious few are those who approach a real imitation of it. Basil is well aware that we all sometimes fail to live up to the ideal of Christ.[47] In that sense, no one is "perfect." But at the same time, Basil speaks of baptism as "the final and perfect stage," of which we become worthy "when the soul has [already!?] been clothed with the Son of God."[48] What kind of perfection can he mean? We have already seen that the assistance of the Spirit granted in baptism is necessary for the Christian life. Necessary likewise is the "grace of our Lord Jesus" present especially in the Eucharist, "through [which] we successfully accomplish that command which is added to the precept of baptism by the same Jesus Christ."[49] Elsewhere he says more clearly that baptism is "the great, ineffable benevolence of God in freely pardoning our sins and *granting us the means and the power of performing righteous acts* for the glory of God and His Christ in the hope of gaining eternal life."[50]

We are forced to conclude therefore that there is not a strictly sequential relationship between discipleship and baptism.[51] Rather, authentic discipleship must begin before baptism and continue with renewed vigor in the fullness of grace after it. But the "perfection" of discipleship is, we might say, a perfection of form rather than a necessarily perfect execution. Basil does not mean to suggest that only those who have ceased stumbling along the way are worthy of baptism. But it is for those who have made a definitive change of heart and mind toward God and toward obedience of His commandments. And this singleness of purpose must remain with them for their whole lives if their baptism is to have any lasting consequence. A baptized Christian cannot simply rest on her laurels:

> As he who is poor in spirit cannot, by reason of the decree, enter into the kingdom of heaven unless he has been born of water and the Holy Spirit, so, on the other hand, unless the justice of that man "abound more than that of the scribes and Pharisees," or if any other requirement be unfulfilled, he is not accounted worthy of the kingdom.[52]

Basil agrees with those who fear that baptism entails a lofty obligation. The bar has indeed been set high once the utmost grace has been given: "To whom they have committed much, of him they will demand the more."[53]

The Eucharist, as another vehicle of divine grace, likewise bears a promise that is also from another perspective, a threat. "So great a blessing" as the Eucharist, "a mystery so sublime," Basil says, must be received worthily, by proceeding to maintain the memory of Christ's loving sacrifice by striving to live no longer for ourselves.[54] One who fails to do so is in no way benefitted but "eats and drinks judgment on himself."[55] Basil likens such a negligent participation in the mysteries to the action of the idle servant who buried his talent in the ground and returned it to his master without interest.[56] But at the same time, rejecting the grace of baptism and subsequent participation in the Eucharist does not free a person from the universal human obligation, which exists regardless. The only difference is perhaps the immediacy with which it is felt by the individual. Participation in the divine life is the high calling for which humankind was created, and as such it is the greatest tragedy if those to whom potential has been given fail to realize it. However, it is no less tragic if, for fear of failure, human beings do not even venture to acquire the potential. For in both cases the end is the same.

Conclusion

Though there are marked differences, Basil's understanding that the rites of baptism and the Eucharist constitute inimitable manifestations of the Triune God, participation in which both produces and perfects the Christian person, has much in common with the sacramental theology of Christians of different denominations today. However, his theology also poses a number of challenges to the entrenched positions of polemicists on all sides. I have remarked on but a few of these along the way in my analysis of Basil, but the reader will no doubt have recognized more. One of the benefits of studying a figure like Basil is that precisely because he is a man of his own times and his theology derives from his particular historical and ideological context, taking the time to appreciate the contours of his thought can help us to ferret out the unhelpful assumptions we fall into when we focus solely on our own. When we not only know what theologians of the past have said but also understand their driving concerns, and when we appreciate the contextual nature of all theology, we are in an ideal position to do theology in and for our context even as we strive to remain faithful to the "faith once delivered to the saints."[57]

NOTES

1. St. Basil of Caesarea, *Epistle* 223.2 (hereafter cited as *Ep.*), Roy J. Deferrari, trans., *Basil: Letters 59–185*, Loeb Classical Library 215 (New York: G.P. Putnam's Sons, 1928), 145, quoted in Johannes Quasten, *Patrology III: The Golden Age of Greek Patristic Literature* (Allen, TX: Christian Classics, 1995), 205.

2. Philip Rousseau, *Basil of Caesarea* (Berkeley: University of California Press, 1994), 133.
3. St. Basil of Caesarea, *Reg. br.* 98.1, English translation in Anna M. Silvas, *The Asketikon of St Basil the Great* (Oxford: Oxford University Press, 2005), 327. (Basil citations are formatted as standard Latin title references.)
4. *Reg. br.* 288.4–5, translation in *Asketikon*, 431–32.
5. St. Basil of Caesarea, *Bapt.* 1.3, 2.2, 2.3, 2.8. This work has very large chapters, which makes reference to them alone insufficient. Therefore, references to this work include page numbers to the most recent critical edition: Umberto Neri, ed., *Basilio di Cesarea: Il Battesimo* (Brescia: Paideia Editrice, 1976), here 296, 316, 318, 362, 364, English translation in M. Monica Wagner, *Saint Basil: Ascetical Works*, The Fathers of the Church 9 (Washington, DC: Catholic University of America Press, 1999), 339–430, here 390, 394–95, 409.
6. The bibliography on this idea in Basil is quite large. The main study is still Emmanuel de Mendieta, *"Unwritten" and "Secret" Apostolic Traditions in the Theological Thought of St. Basil of Caesarea* (Edinburgh: Oliver and Boyd, 1965). But see also Jaroslav Pelikan's brief but necessary critique of Mendieta in "The 'Spiritual Sense' of Scripture," in *Basil of Caesarea: Christian, Humanist, Ascetic*, ed. Paul J. Fedwick (Toronto: Pontifical Institute of Mediaeval Studies, 1981), 358–59.
7. St. Basil of Caesarea, *Spir.* 66, Stephen Hildebrand, trans., *St Basil the Great: On the Holy Spirit*, Popular Patristics Series 42 (Yonkers, NY: St Vladimir's Seminary Press, 2011), 104.
8. That is, in addition to Christ's own words, "This is my body . . . ," which he also includes.
9. St. Basil of Caesarea, *De fide*, Greek text and English translation in Jacob N. Van Sickle, trans., *St Basil the Great: On Christian Ethics*, Popular Patristics Series 51 (Yonkers, NY: St Vladimir's Seminary Press, 2014), 68–89. Compare the statement of Basil's contemporary, St. Cyril of Jerusalem: "For where the divine and holy mysteries of the Creed are concerned, one must not teach casually without reference to the sacred Scriptures, or be led astray by persuasive and elaborate arguments. Do not simply take my word when I tell you these things, unless you are given proof for my teaching from Holy Scripture" (*Catechetical Lectures* 4.17, translation in E. J. Yarnold SJ, *Cyril of Jerusalem* [New York: Routledge, 2000], 56).
10. St. Basil of Caesarea, *moral.* 80.22; *On Christian Ethics*, 323; quoting Rom. 14:23 and 10:17.
11. Matt. 28:19; John 3:3–8; Rom. 6:3–11; Gal. 3:27–28; and Col. 2:11–12; 3:9–11.
12. *Moral.* 20.1–2; *On Christian Ethics*, 151.
13. *Moral.* 21.1; *On Christian Ethics*, 153.
14. *Moral.* 21.2; *On Christian Ethics*, 155; citing 1 Cor. 11:27–29 and John 6:61–63.
15. *Moral.* 21.3; *On Christian Ethics*, 155; citing Luke 22:19–20; 1 Cor. 10:16–17; 11:23–26; 2 Cor. 5:14–15.
16. He does make the traditional allowance for those who are martyred for the faith before receiving baptism (and, by extension, the Eucharist) since in their imita-

tion of the death of Christ they are effectively "baptized in their own blood," but he hastens to add, "I say this not to reject baptism in water," which remains the norm (*On the Holy Spirit* 36; Hildebrand, 69).

17. *Spir.* 12.28; Hildebrand, 59.
18. See James 2:26.
19. Matt. 3:11.
20. *Bapt.* 1.2; 202–4; *Ascetical Works*, 361–62.
21. Basil writes in one place that his own practice was to commune four or more times per week (*Ep.* 93; Deferrari, 145).
22. Matt. 4:4.
23. John 4:34.
24. Matt. 26:26–28; 1 Cor. 11:23–26.
25. *Bapt.* 1.3; 292–94; *Ascetical Works*, 388–89; quoting 2 Cor. 5.14–15.
26. *Spir.* 26; Hildebrand, 56–57; quoting Rom. 6.17.
27. *Bapt.* 1.2; 256–58; *Ascetical Works*, 378; quoting 1 Cor. 12.3.
28. *Spir.* 35; Hildebrand, 67–68.
29. St. Basil of Caesarea, *hom.* 3, trans. Mark DelCogliano, *St Basil the Great: On Christian Doctrine and Practice*, Popular Patristics Series 47 (Yonkers, NY: St Vladimir's Seminary Press, 2013), 238.
30. *Bapt.* 1.2; 194; *Ascetical Works*, 359–60.
31. *Bapt.* 1.2; 264; *Ascetical Works*, 379.
32. *Anaphora of St Basil the Great*. Though many Greek editions are available for this text, none may be called critical. The text of an eleventh-century manuscript was published in C. A. Swainson, ed., *Greek Liturgies* (Cambridge: Cambridge University Press, 1884), 161 (public domain); English translations both in print and online are innumerable. A convenient one is the *Service Book of the Holy Eastern Orthodox Catholic and Apostolic Church* (Englewood, NJ: Antiochian Orthodox Christian Archdiocese of New York and All North America, 2002), 138. Scholars are in general agreement that this prayer can be traced to Basil, though we may not have it entirely in its original form. These uncertainties do not touch the point I am making, however, since it was universal among Eastern anaphoras to ask for the Spirit to consecrate the gifts.
33. John 6:63; quoted by Basil to make this point in *Bapt.* 1.3; 294; *Ascetical Works*, 389.
34. Augustine of Hippo, *Confessions*, 1.11.17, trans. Henry Chadwick (Oxford: Oxford University Press, 1991), 13–14.
35. *Jud.*; Greek text with facing translation in *On Christian Ethics*, 38/39.
36. Infant baptism was a widespread practice at least as early as the beginning of the third century. Its origins, however, are lost to history. It may be that it was practiced going back to the apostles in the first century, but we simply have no solid evidence to say one way or another.
37. On this point see further Stephen Hildebrand, *Basil of Caesarea* (Grand Rapids, MI: Baker Academic, 2014), 113–16.

38. *Hom.* 1; *On Fasting and Feasts*, 42.
39. *Bapt.* 1.1; 146–48; *Ascetical Works*, 346–47.
40. *Hom.* 4; *On Fasting and Feasts*, 46, quoting Rom. 5:20.
41. *Hom.* 5; *On Fasting and Feasts*, 47.
42. *Hom.* 3; *On Fasting and Feasts*, 46.
43. *Hom.* 7; *On Fasting and Feasts*, 51–52.
44. *Bapt.* 1.1; 140; *Ascetical Works*, 344.
45. Matt. 10:37, quoted by Basil in *On Baptism* 1.1; 142.
46. *Bapt.* 1.1; 140–42.
47. This is evident from his many prescriptions for confession and repentance in the *Asketikon*.
48. *Bapt.* 1.2; 268; *Ascetical Works*, 380.
49. *Bapt.* 1.2; 268; *Ascetical Works*, 381.
50. *Bapt.* 1.2; 194; *Ascetical Works*, 360.
51. The reader will have already noted that Basil's approach to baptism does not seem capable of accounting for the practice of baptizing infants (he nowhere addresses the practice directly either to forbid or encourage it). However, widespread acceptance of the irrelevance of the timing of baptism led ultimately to infant baptism becoming the nearly universal practice of the Church already in the sixth century. There is a hint of that idea here in Basil, though he obviously does not develop it in that direction.
52. *Bapt.* 1.2; 170–72; *Ascetical Works*, 353.
53. Luke 12:48, quoted by Basil in *On Baptism* 1.2; 196; *Ascetical Works*, 360.
54. *Bapt.* 1.3; 296–98; *Ascetical Works*, 390.
55. *Bapt.* 1.3; 294; *Ascetical Works*, 389; quoting 1 Cor. 11:29.
56. *Bapt.* 1.3; *Ascetical Works*, 390. See Matt. 25:25–29.
57. Jude 1:3.

3

St. Augustine of Hippo

THOMAS L. HUMPHRIES, JR.

St. Augustine was born to a Christian mother, St. Monica, and a pagan father, Patricius, in a part of North Africa dominated by the Mediterranean at the edge of the desert (modern Souk Ahras, Algeria) in 354. He grew up in a relatively rural part of the Roman Empire. When he fell ill with a fever and stomach pain, he begged to be baptized in the Catholic Church, but he recovered before the sacrament could be celebrated, and his baptism was postponed until he was in his early thirties. By that time, he had become a professional orator, a formal speaker who acted as a lawyer and teacher, and had moved from his birthplace, Thagaste, to Carthage (for studies), to Rome (for work), and to Milan (again for work and then to retire from formal teaching). He was baptized in Milan in 387 by the bishop, St. Ambrose, after exploring many paths to truth, including the Manichee sect, and after fathering a son, Adeodatus, with his common-law wife. Augustine was terribly close to his mother, who had come with him to Italy. She died in Ostia (the port of Rome) shortly after Augustine was baptized and right after they had a mystical experience of spiritual ascent. He returned to North Africa in 388 and was ordained a priest in 391 and then made bishop of Hippo Regius in 395. He served as bishop for thirty-five years, dying in 430. He is hailed as an official doctor of the Church, and his feast day is celebrated on 28 August, the day he entered eternal life. As priest and bishop, Augustine was a celebrated preacher, a noted author, and a frequent participant in Church councils. He corresponded with theologians locally and on different continents and was exceptionally well read.

Augustine wrote many "best-sellers," the most famous of which is his *Confessions*, which has been translated into nearly every language and read continuously for sixteen hundred years. His *Sermons* (homilies preached on the assigned liturgical text) and *Tractates* (homilies preached *lectio continua*) continue to be inviting and meaningful today. His Letters are studied for their pastoral concern and theological insight. His responses to various theological controversies, heresies, and schisms are still bound together topically and republished frequently. Among "the Fathers," Augustine stands as a giant. Students are drawn to his honesty. Augustine was not afraid to change his mind in light of new information and dedicated himself to refining his arguments in light of what was revealed in Scripture, celebrated in the sacraments, experienced in prayer, and developed in mental reflection. It is sometimes difficult to follow his thought as it develops because we must often separate his initial position from his more mature position. But it is also challenging because Augustine's honesty about his own struggles invites us to a similar honesty and humility about ours. We not only read, but find ourselves praying with Augustine, "grant me chastity and self-control, but please not yet."[1] We find in ourselves the same longing for God to be our "all in all" (1 Cor. 15:28). We lament only recently having come to a deeper awareness of God in our lives and wonder if it will be enough: "Late have I loved you, Beauty so ancient and so new, late have I loved you! You were with me, but I was not with you. . . . You called, shouted, broke through my deafness; you flared, blazed, banished my blindness; you lavished your fragrance, I gasped, and now I pant for you; I tasted you, and I hunger and thirst."[2] We, too, long to taste and see, to drink, and to be at peace. Augustine found food for his hunger and drink for his thirst in the sacraments, the sacred mysteries, of the Catholic Church, which nourished him and allowed him to nourish others as a celibate priest and pastor of a diocese. He found fulfillment in conforming himself to the humility of Christ and in loving his neighbor and God with all his heart, all his soul, and all his mind (Matt. 22:34–40; Deut. 6:5). Studying his theology should be an invitation for us to do the same.

Introduction

At the end of the fourth century, halfway through his life, St. Augustine reflected on the nature of time. He admitted that he was puzzled: "We surely know what we mean when we speak of it. We also know what is meant when we hear someone else talking about it. . . . Provided that no one asks me, I know. [But] If I want to explain it to an inquirer, I do not know."³ Modern theologians often feel the same when reflecting on Augustine's theology of sacraments. We are puzzled because so much seems familiar, and yet so much seems odd. Augustine's work has been foundational for Protestant and Catholic sacramental theology. We share many of his sensibilities about Baptism, Marriage, and Communion even a millennium and a half after he died. Augustine's arguments and conclusions are ubiquitous in our contemporary theology. But not all of Augustine has been absorbed over the centuries. He freely refers to Old Testament events as sacraments. Scripture itself seems to be a sacrament for Augustine, as do many objects and seasons associated with Christian worship. Put simply, Augustine means more by *sacramentum* than we usually mean by "sacrament." We wonder if there is a single definition of *sacramentum* for Augustine, or even a unifying theme that can help us piece together what we want to call "Augustine's sacramental theology." While many famous and useful formulas derive from Augustine's theology of sacraments, he resists a simple definition for "sacrament." Not only do modern students face the challenge of understanding a topic about which we already have strong preconceived ideas, we also face the challenge of understanding a system that is subtle and complex. In a way, then, we all know roughly what we mean when we refer to Augustine's sacramental theology, but we are all surprised about the difficulties we encounter when speaking about it.

Augustine's Sacramental Theory

It is helpful to consider three fundamental elements of Augustine's sacramental theory. First, the theological concept of mystery lies at the foundation of Augustine's theology of sacraments. Second, sacraments bear fruit and are fulfilled in love. Third, sacraments are visible signs that symbolize and connect us to the mystery of our saving God. Mystery, in the theological sense, is not something we can figure out, but rather is something that can be known only by being loved. Other humans are mysteries in this theological sense, not because they are puzzling or irrational, but because they cannot be completely known through reason alone. The understanding of mystery or sacrament as that which connects us to salvation is common to theologians of Augustine's era. It also belongs to the language used in sacred Scripture. The Latin *mysterium* is a transliteration of the Greek *mysterion*; they sound almost the same in either language. But the Latin *sacramentum* often translates the Greek *mysterion*. This is the case in Latin versions of Scripture (e.g., 1 Cor. 13:2 and Eph. 5:31–32) that Augustine and other Latin-speaking Christians used.[4] For example, where the Letter to the Corinthians reads "If I have the gift of prophecy and comprehend all *mysteria*," the Latin reads, ". . . and comprehend all *sacramenta*." This is not an error in translation, but rather an overlap of the meaning of terms that is not always familiar to modern English speakers. In Augustine's Latin vocabulary *mysterium* and *sacramentum* are closely related.[5] Augustine can just as easily speak of the "sacred mysteries" as he can speak of the "holy sacraments." Attempts to divide mystery and sacrament fail to understand Augustine's theology.

When fully realized, sacraments connect us to the mystery of salvation in love. Augustine teaches that the fundamental mystery of existence is God's love. God's love is a key to Trinitarian theology and is expressed most visibly in the Incarnation of the Word. All sacraments point to the Incarnate Christ as God's love for us and help us return that love for God and neighbor.[6] In the sacramental economy (the total operation of all sacraments), God reaches out to humanity with His salvific love and humans are transformed in order to respond in love.[7] Again, this is mysterious not so much in the sense that we cannot figure it out, but in that it connects us to salvation in love.

Sacraments are also visible signs; they are symbolic of the salvific mystery of God.[8] This means sacraments point to and can even make present the reality they signify. A kiss between lovers is a human parallel; it not only expresses their love, but also stimulates and deepens it. For Augustine, a sacrament is both the mystery that is revealed and the manner in which that mystery is revealed or takes effect in our lives. Sacraments are the language by which God communicates His love to us. As with any language, it is possible for us to overhear a conversation and not understand what is being communicated, as when we listen to a conversation in a language we do not speak or we cannot make out all the words in a muffled conversation in a language we do speak. As with other conversations, we may observe a sacrament without it "speaking" to us. We need to be trained in and attentive to the sacraments. Signs are flexible. As a sign, a sacrament can indicate more than one thing. A single sacrament can connect us to multiple aspects of the mystery of God, just as words often have multiple senses. Furthermore, multiple sacraments can point to the same reality, just as we may use different words to express the same idea. "Reading" the sacramental signs is both an art and a science that Christians must learn, according to Augustine.[9] Historically, Augustine was a pioneer in intellectual treatment of the sacraments as signs, and so, this aspect of his thought receives considerable attention from other scholars. One needs to be trained not only in reading the sacramental signs, but also in reading Augustine reading the sacramental signs.

There is a deep link between prophecy and sacraments in Augustine's theology. "Reading" or understanding the sacraments is related to reading or understanding Sacred Scripture. The depth of this connection comes from the sense in which God is the author of the story of salvation. God writes the story of salvation first in human lives. These events are later recorded in Sacred Scripture as inspired text. But the first level of inspiration is the level of God working in and among humans. To fully "read" the symbolism of the sacraments includes "reading" God's saving work in the lives of humans (something akin to prophecy) as well as "reading" the meaning of various material signs (something akin to reading words on a page). Events themselves can be sacraments and the stories told about them can include additional literary devices and inspiration that further reveal the mystery of God and salvation, according to Augustine. When Paul teaches that "all these things . . . happened among them in figure," Augustine argues that Paul is explaining exactly this point about sacramental activity.[10] The events themselves prophetically point to and sacramentally make present some aspect of the mystery of God. Marriage and Eucharist are two key examples in this regard. Old Testament marriages and meals serve not only as types or prefigures of New Testament marriages and Eucharist; in some cases they already pointed to Christ and made certain graces available even before the Incarnation. The connection goes beyond literary structures (though Augustine is sensitive to those, as well) because Augustine teaches that God was active in the lives of Old Testament figures, inspiring them even then to be conformed to Christ.

Nearly every detail of salvation history points to Christ. All of Scripture is, broadly speaking, a sacrament, in the sense of both the stories in their written form and the original events that took place throughout time. Augustine, for example, puzzles over the details of the woman being formed from the rib of the man.

> It was surely not without reason that she was made like that—it must have been to suggest some hidden truth. Was there any shortage of mud, after all, for the woman to be from, or couldn't the Lord . . . have painlessly removed the man's rib from him while he was still awake? . . . It was certainly not pointlessly that it was said or done like this. No, it is all assuredly pointing to mysteries and sacraments.[11]

The use of the rib with flesh and bone, and not some other material, is also a detail worth meditation, according to Augustine, as is the use of the verb "to build" instead of "fashion" or "make." "These things were done . . . to signify something, with God in his foreknowledge already mercifully foretelling in his actual works the fruit to be derived in the age to come from the very origins of the human race."[12] There is the moral lesson we are to learn that man and woman should live side by side as partners, and not head to foot as master and servant. The details of our creation teach us that men and women stand face-to-face in a mutual relationship. The rib is a "sign of the strength of their union. For those who walk together, and look ahead together to where they are walking, do so at each other's side."[13] The creation of Eve from Adam is also a sacrament of the Church. "[Christ] too was put to sleep, falling asleep in death, in order that his consort the Church might be formed for him."[14] Marriage is also an eschatological sign: "the sacrament of monogamous marriage . . . is a symbol that in the future we shall all be united and subject to God in the one heavenly city."[15] The very first marriage of Adam and Eve points not only to the ideal for all other marriages, but also to the relationship between Christ and the Church now and in eternity. Had there been a third human person there who was skilled in reading the sacraments, she would have seen not only Adam and Eve, but also Christ and the Church; she would have seen the entire plan of salvation unfolding. The events and relationships of the Old Testament can all be considered sacraments when they unite us to the mystery of salvation, according to Augustine. Nearly seven hundred years later, especially with the arguments of Peter Lombard, Catholic

Christians would tighten the definition of "sacrament" to include only seven specific rituals. Nearly four hundred years after that, Protestant Christians would limit the definition of sacrament primarily to Baptism and the Lord's Supper. For Augustine, though, much more of the world points to redemption as a sign, and many of those signs make God's grace present.

Specific Sacraments
Baptism

Perhaps the sacrament most familiar to all Christians is Baptism. As is often the case today, the fifth-century celebration of Baptism involved water and reference to the Trinity, following the command given in Matthew's Gospel: "Go therefore, and make disciples of all nations, baptizing them in the name of the Father, and of the Son, and of the Holy Spirit."[16] Though Augustine argues that grace can operate before Baptism (i.e., in moving an adult to seek Baptism), the sacrament is a definitive moment in a person's salvation that offers forgiveness of sins and the virtue of faith.[17] The graces of Baptism are necessary for salvation, and those graces are normally given through the sacramental rite involving water and the Church.[18] Baptism allows us to participate in the paschal mystery, the saving death and resurrection of Christ. "The sacrament of the font . . . baptism . . . has the same value as being buried with Christ, as the apostle says: 'For we have been buried with Christ through baptism into death, so that just as he has risen from the dead, so we too may walk in newness of life.'"[19] As a sacrament, Baptism forgives sins, brings about our justification, and anticipates our own resurrection. "Baptism in Christ is nothing but an image of Christ's death, and . . . Christ's death on the cross is nothing but an image of the remission of sin. Just as his death was real, so also the remission of our sins is real; and just as his resurrection was real, so also our justification is real."[20] Baptism incorporates new Christians into the Body of Christ, weaving them into the mystery of salvation. Much of Augustine's theology of Baptism continues to operate in modern understandings of Baptism and is familiar to Christians of the third millennium.

There are less familiar aspects of the sacrament of Baptism in Augustine's teaching, including its relationship with other sacraments. Augustine celebrated the ritual of Baptism most often at the Easter Vigil with a variety of small rites, ascetic practices, and meditations on Scripture. There were minor exorcisms, various anointings, signing with the cross, and objects like the font and the oil associated with baptism. All of these were also considered sacraments since they all signify and unite us to God's saving plan.[21] After the Baptism in water, Augustine speaks of a "sacrament of chrism" that involved invoking the sevenfold gifts of the Holy Spirit and a separate anointing.[22] Since this anointing was the special prerogative of the bishop, later theologians separated it into the sacrament of Confirmation (distinct from Baptism), though Augustine seems to have always celebrated the two together. Augustine also firmly believed in the efficacy of infant Baptism. Because sacraments involve Christ's action through the Church, infant baptism is legitimate. Christ can forgive the sins of any human, regardless of age or mental ability. Some later Christians understood Baptism as a kind of human action in which a new believer declares his or her status as a Christian. For Augustine, Christ incorporates new members into his body in Baptism; Christ acts in the sacraments. The later sense of Baptism reverses the direction of action (a human claiming Christ instead of Christ claiming a human), and so infant Baptism and Baptism as a unique forgiveness of sins fell out of some later theological systems. For Augustine, the sacrament of Baptism is not dependent on the age of those to be baptized and shares sacramental signs with the Easter Liturgy and with the sacrament of chrism (Confirmation).

Following the creedal statement "one baptism for the forgiveness of sins," Augustine taught that Baptism could be celebrated only once. A separate set of rituals provide for post-baptismal penance and reconciliation.[23] Ordination as a sacrament runs parallel to baptism in that it transforms a man and imparts a character that cannot be removed.[24] The related beliefs that the Church has power to forgive sins and exercises this through the sacraments landed him in the middle of a thorny controversy with heretical Christians. Two sacramental principles helped him steer through this thorny issue: (1) defining Christ as the agent or principal actor in sacraments and (2) distinguishing the validity and practice of a sacrament from its effect in the life of a Christian. What to do with those baptized in a separated community becomes a difficult issue when baptism cannot be repeated. We must either recognize the baptism of separated Christians or deny that their baptism has any value. The Donatists of Augustine's day posed exactly this dilemma. They believed that the power of baptism was related to the holiness of the minister and the purity of the Church. They believed that the Catholic Church had lost its purity during the Diocletian persecution and its priests were no longer holy, and they questioned the ability of any Church to forgive sins committed after one was baptized. Thus, Donatists did not recognize Catholic baptism. But Augustine argued that Catholics should recognize Donatist baptism; when Donatists want to become Catholic, they should not be baptized a second time. Augustine teaches that the Lord Jesus Christ Himself baptizes through the ministers (priests) of the Church. "The quality of the baptism is commensurate with the quality of the person [Christ] by whose power it is given, not with the quality of the person through whose ministry it is given."[25] The grace of baptism passes like water through a stone, and is "like light in this way: it is both received pure by those to be enlightened, and if it passes through the impure, it is not defiled."[26] Ministers should be virtuous, but baptism comes from Christ, not from the ministers who perform it. This principle has been favored by Catholic theologians, especially under the technical term *ex opere operato* (literally "from the action having been done," as opposed to *ex opere operantis*, "from the action of the worker"). Sacraments happen even when the human ministers are flawed. In this way Augustine separates the validity of the baptism (which can happen even with heretical and schismatic ministers) from the full effect of the sacrament. Recall Augustine's point about sacraments as a kind of language. He argues that the Donatists are speaking the right language (the baptism is valid), but they do not grasp its full meaning (the baptism either has no effect or has a negative effect). Later theologians will make a technical distinction that follows Augustine's point when they separate the *sacramentum tantum* ("the sacrament itself" or the sign considered separately from the spiritual reality or grace it brings), the *res tantum* (the thing signified considered separately from the sacramental sign), and the *sacramentum et res* (the sacrament and the inner reality made present by the sign considered together). On this analysis, the Donatists have the *sacramentum* (the sign), but not the *res* (grace of faith and union with Christ and the Church). While helpful, this distinction sometimes allows us to ignore the theology of signification involved and focus instead on the abstract definitions of the parts of what should be a unified whole. Similarly, the distinction between validity and effect or practice of the sacrament and grace of the sacrament sometimes hides Augustine's deeper theological point about love. In Augustine's analysis, separated Christians say all the words of love, but ultimately fail to become lovers.

Augustine's sense that sacraments reveal and make present the mystery of salvation is intrinsically connected to love in his theological system. The mystery of God is the mystery of the divine lover, beloved, and love-by-which. The entire Law is summarized in the twofold love of God and love of neighbor. The Law and faith are both fulfilled in love. Love is the capstone of Augustine's sacramental theology, especially amid the thorny issues of separated Christians. To those baptized outside the Catholic Church, he says,

> The sacrament is divine; you have baptism, and I admit it. But what does the same Apostle say? "If I know all the sacraments, and have prophecy and all faith so as to move mountains," perhaps to prevent you from also saying, "I have believed and that is enough for me." But what does James say? "The demons believe and tremble." Faith is great, but it gives no benefit at all if it should lack love. Even the demons confessed Christ. . . . They had faith; they did not have love.[27]

Because love seeks unity, and schism is the opposite of unity, those who are baptized in a schismatic congregation are baptized, but to no benefit or even to their detriment. This is akin to forcing a kiss. Schismatics do not have genuine Christian love. Outside the Church, people participate in the sacraments to their ruin. Because the sacrament cannot be fulfilled in love when celebrated outside the Church, Augustine teaches that baptism does not come to fruition and does not bring about salvation. Instead, it brings about judgment and condemnation. "Even holy things can injure; for in good men holy things exist for their salvation, but in evil men for their judgment."[28] This danger exists categorically for those outside the Church, but it also exists for those baptized within the Catholic Church. The ritual of Baptism is not some mechanistic guarantee of salvation. Preaching to fellow Catholics, Augustine reminds them, "Question your heart, in case you have the sacrament and do not have the power of the sacrament. Question your heart. If love of a brother is there, be free of anxiety. There cannot be love without the Holy Spirit."[29] The danger that one would participate in the ritual and observe the sacramental signs but not be transformed, that one would hear the sacramental language but not listen to the mystery, that one would be washed in the water but not be washed in the Spirit exists for those inside the Church as well as those outside the Church. The sacraments celebrated inside the Church promise God's saving action, but they are not magic incantations. They require the participation of the faithful in love.

Marriage

In the Letter to the Ephesians, Paul references Genesis 2:24 and makes a connection between marriage and the Body of Christ: "For this reason a man shall leave father and mother and stick to his wife; and they shall be two in one flesh. This is a great sacrament; but I mean in Christ and in the Church."[30] Though some modern theologians deny that there was a historical Adam and Eve, Augustine thinks Scripture records historical persons. "So then, what as a matter of history was fulfilled in Adam, as a matter of prophecy signifies Christ."[31] Adam and Eve are not simply literary types or patterns for future human marriages and for Christ and the Church; they are also living prophetic symbols of the salvation offered in the Incarnation. For Augustine, every time "a man leaves his father," this points to and is fulfilled in Christ "leaving" his Father to become flesh (e.g., John 16:28). Every time a man "leaves his mother," this points to and is fulfilled in Christ leaving his mother "from the seed of David according to the flesh," that is, Judaism.[32] Every time a man clings to his wife and becomes one flesh with her, this points to and is fulfilled in Christ's relationship with the Church. The events of the first "marriage" that are recorded in Genesis not only speak to the original story that they recount (e.g., Adam and Eve), but point to their fulfillment in Christ and to the possibility that every other married man and woman can also be a sign of and participate in the mystery of the Incarnate Christ.

Marriage, while being continuously lived throughout human existence, also had a temporary sacramental expression. Augustine argues that polygamous marriage was a sacrament that was appropriate in the past, though is no longer appropriate in the present. His argument is sometimes awkward, if not troubling, for modern Christians, but it reveals the connections between sacraments and the mystery of salvation and between sacraments and virtuous love that are important for Augustine's sacramental theology. Augustine argues that the creation accounts in Genesis 1 and 2 reveal that marriage and sexuality are fundamentally good. The creation of humanity as male and female reveals that social union, fidelity to relationships in chastity, procreation of children, and the value of marriage as a sign of salvation in Christ are fundamental to human existence.[33] Both Marriage and Ordination are sacraments that form the community of the faithful.[34] In addition, after the Fall, through which sinfulness and punishment enter the world, marriage helps to redeem and tame wayward desires by giving us appropriate ways to express our love and to forgive certain sins.[35] This means that marriage is good for individuals and for society as a whole and that marriage should be monogamous and indissoluble until death. Much of this is familiar to modern Christians because Augustine's arguments were repeated in medieval Scholasticism and shaped modern Christianity. But when arguing for a "biblical" notion of marriage, there are obvious counterexamples to the teaching that marriage is fundamentally good, monogamous, and indissoluble and exists for procreation of children. Many of the Old Testament Patriarchs (e.g., Abraham, Sarah, and Hagar) present a stumbling block for the exegetical arguments about monogamous marriage as a sacrament. Augustine argues that polygamous marriage was appropriate at certain times because it fulfilled a role in the divine plan of salvation and those who participated in it were pure and virtuous.

Augustine's argument about the temporary polygamous form of the sacrament of marriage is illustrative of the connection between sacraments, the plan of salvation, and love. Abraham was not at all lustful for his wife, Sarah, or their slave, Hagar, but rather they

> had intercourse because it was their duty, and their natural enjoyment of it was never let go to the point of becoming irrational or sinful passion. Children have had to be provided for our mother Jerusalem, now spiritually and at that time physically, but always from the same

source, love. The deeds of the fathers were different only because the times were different.³⁶

The virtues of chastity and love remain crucial for the sacrament of marriage. Though polygamy is no longer possible today, in the past it was possible for polygamous marriage to virtuously provide children, unite human society, and function as a sacrament bringing about and pointing to God's plan of salvation. "Out of many souls there will arise a city of people with a single soul and single heart turned to God. . . . Just as the sacrament of polygamous marriage of that age was a symbol of the plurality of people who would be subject to God in all nations of the earth, so too the sacrament of monogamous marriage of our time is a symbol that in the future we shall all be united and subject to God in the one heavenly city."³⁷ Now that Christ has come in the Incarnation and established other sacraments, people can belong to the New Covenant of salvation by baptism, and so polygamous marriage has lost its role in the divine plan of salvation. "For this reason in our age the sacrament of marriage has been restored to being a union between one man and one woman."³⁸ The marriage of Abraham, Sarah, and Hagar was a sacrament. It expressed the virtues of charity, chastity, and obedience, and it brought about God's plan of salvation. It was also a sign of the eschatological fulfillment when people from all nations will belong to the same body that worships the one, true God. But his sacramental theology also allows him to argue that polygamous marriage is not normative for Christian marriage. The demands of chastity and obedience and God's plan of salvation no longer allow for marriage to involve polygamy. Christ has taught us to return to the beginning, and Paul reminds us that this beginning is a great and fundamental sacrament.³⁹

Eucharist

The Eucharist is the simplest of the sacraments because it is directly rooted in the Last Supper as narrated in various New Testament passages and explained in John's Gospel.⁴⁰ Christians have celebrated this sacrament for more than two millennia, consistently repeating the declaration, "This is the Body of Christ." And yet, because the "Body of

Christ" is itself a complex and dense theological subject, the Eucharist is the most complex and controversial sacrament.[41] For Augustine, the Eucharist is the summit of sacramental theology because it is so obviously and closely connected to the Incarnate Christ himself and because it is a visible sign that connects us to the mystery of salvation in Christ that is fulfilled in love.

The Eucharist involves many layers of signification, and so is a sacramental sign par excellence. The bread and wine signify unity. Augustine uses the Pauline imagery: "Because the loaf of bread is one, we, though many, are one body."[42] The unity of this body has two poles. Just as the many individual grains form a new thing, individual believers are united with Christ as the Body *of Christ*. Just as the grains are united as a whole, the baptized are united with each other in the Church as the *Body* of Christ, who is the Head. This unity is fulfilled in charity as love of God and love of neighbor. In that they are made from many parts, the bread and wine signify the Body of Christ understood as the Church in harmony with itself and with Christ. As food, the visible bread and wine also signify the invisible spiritual food of truth and faith. We should "'not labor for the food that perishes, but for that which endures unto life everlasting.' . . . Why . . . make ready your teeth and stomach? Believe, and you have eaten."[43] Physical nourishment signifies spiritual nourishment. The action of offering the bread and wine (celebrating Eucharist, Mass, or the Lord's Supper) is "a daily sign of [the Sacrifice of the Word made flesh] in the . . . Church, which, being His body, learns to offer herself through Him."[44] The ritual of the Eucharistic Liturgy is sacramental because it signifies the self-sacrifice of Christ. The Eucharist is the sacramental symbol of the "mystery of true faith . . . [the] sign of unity . . . [and the] bond of love."[45]

According to John's Gospel, Jesus connects the manna that Moses ate in the desert to the Eucharist Jesus would offer in his own body.[46] Augustine argues that those who ate manna and died did so "not because the manna was an evil thing, but because they ate it evilly. . . . Manna signified this bread [which Christ says he is]; the altar of God signified this bread. Those were mysteries [*sacramenta*]; in signs they are different, in the thing which is signified they are alike."[47] Here we have an example of Augustine's sensibility that more than one sacramental sign can point to the same sacramental reality. The manna of Moses's day and the Eucharist of Augustine's day are both sacraments of Christ's Body. Augustine quotes 1 Corinthians 10:1–3 to make the argument that all those who lived under Moses were baptized and ate the same spiritual food as Christians do at the Eucharistic Liturgy. "The same spiritual food, of course; for corporeally it was another thing, because they ate manna, we something else, but [they ate] the spiritual [food] which we [eat]."[48] As with the creation of Adam and Eve, Augustine thinks the manna is not a fiction or simple literary device used in sacred Scripture, but rather an event that God orchestrated for His people. This event, the actual manna, was itself a sacrament that not only pointed to the future sacrament of the Eucharist, but even made present the same spiritual effect (union with Christ). Part of Augustine's sacramental theology hints that Moses was somehow connected to Christ through sacraments like the manna. Manna was a temporary sacramental sign that lasted only a generation. The Eucharist as a sacrament will last until we are with Christ in eternity.

Augustine teaches that the Eucharistic bread and wine are the Body and Blood of Christ. Addressing the newly baptized before the Eucharistic prayers have begun, Augustine preaches, "it's still . . . as you can see, bread and wine; come the consecration, and that bread will be the body of Christ, and that wine will be the blood of Christ."[49] The prayers of the Eucharistic Liturgy effect a change in the bread and wine. "What you can see here . . . is bread and wine; but . . . when the word is applied to it, [it] becomes the body and blood of the Word."[50] Following Paul's teaching that those who eat and drink without recognizing the Body and Blood, eat and drink judgment upon themselves, Augustine taught that sinners and those outside of the Church should not receive the sacrament.[51] As with baptism, it is dangerous to ignore the reality of the mystery presented in the sacrament of the Eucharist. "Recognize in the bread what hung on the cross, and in the cup what flowed from his side."[52] More than one theological controversy has been rooted in attempting to read the real presence of Christ over and against the symbolism or figurative meanings of the sacrament as if Augustine's sacramental theology allowed for only one layer of signification. When such controversies appeal to Augustine, they present only a partial reading of his theology. The bread and wine are signs not to the exclusion of the Body of Christ, but rather to the inclusion of the wonderful depth and richness of the Body of Christ.

Conclusion

For Augustine, there is no salvation apart from participating in the paschal mystery, the saving death and resurrection of Christ, which is also to say there is no salvation apart from genuine love. The sacraments allow Christians to mature as better lovers of God and neighbor. In the broad sense of a "signs of divine things," key moments within salvation history are sacraments that we can study in Scripture.[53] They teach us to love.[54] The liturgical seasons allow us not only to reflect upon, but also to experience the plan of salvation. Specific sacraments like Baptism and Marriage recapitulate Creation, forgive sins, heal vice, and anticipate our eschatological fulfillment. Having been baptized and anointed, Christians are incorporated into the Body of Christ, and so we can offer ourselves as the Body of Christ. Liturgically, this happens most directly in the sacrament of the Eucharist, but it provides the basic pattern for Christian life in general. Sacraments teach Christians to repeat the pattern of Christ on the Cross, the pattern of self-sacrifice or self-gift. Thus, sacraments allow Christians to love genuinely and to participate in the mystery of salvation until that day when we shall see no longer dimly in a mirror, but face-to-face with the mysteries—the sacraments unveiled.

NOTES

1. St. Augustine, *Confessions* 8.7.17 (hereafter cited as *Conf.*), trans. Henry Chadwick (Oxford: Oxford University Press, 1991), 230; Works of Saint Augustine 1.1.149 (hereafter cited as WSA).
2. *Conf.* 10.27.38, WSA 1.1.203.
3. *Conf.* 11.14.17.
4. St. Augustine, *Tractates of the Gospel of John* 6.21.1 and 13.16.4 (hereafter cited as *Jo. ev. tr.*, where the numbers refer to chapter and verse in the work). On sacraments in Augustine and this period in general, see Lewis Ayres and Thomas Humphries, "Augustine and the West to AD 650," in *The Oxford Handbook of Sacramental Theology*, ed. Hans Boersma and Matthew Levering (Oxford: Oxford University Press, 2015), 156–69.
5. See Cutrone, "Sacrament," in *Augustine through the Ages: An Encyclopedia*, ed. Allan Fitzgerald, OSA (Grand Rapids, MI: Eerdmans, 1999), 741–42. The terms are not exact synonyms. *Sacramentum* also refers to a military oath taken by a soldier. *Mysterium* does not. In the context of Christianity, the religious ritual includes the notion of promise or oath, in the sense both that God promises to save and that Christians pledge to remain part of God's chosen people.

6. E.g., *Jo. ev. tr.* 80.3, 15.3.2, *Tractates on the First Letter of John* 4.12 (hereafter cited as *ep. Jo.*).
7. E.g., *ep. Jo.* 2.9, *Jo. ev. tr.* 6.14.
8. E.g., St. Augustine, *Against Faustus* 19.11–16 and *Letter* 138.7 (hereafter cited as *ep.*).
9. Augustine's most famous treatment of signs is *De Doctrina Christiana* (*On Christian Teaching*).
10. St. Augustine, *Literal Meaning of Genesis* 1.1.1 (hereafter cited as *Gn. litt.*) (WSA 1.13.168). Cf. *ep.* 55.10.18–11.21.
11. St. Augustine, *On Genesis: A Refutation of the Manichees* 2.12.17 (hereafter cited as *Gn. adv. Man.*) (WSA 1.13.83).
12. *Gn. litt.* 9.13.23 (WSA 1.13.389).
13. St. Augustine, *Excellence of Marriage* 1.1 (hereafter cited as *b. cong.*) (WSA 1.9.33). Cf. *Gn. adv. Man.* 2.12.16.
14. *Gn. adv. Man.* 2.24.37 (WSA 1.13.97).
15. *B. cong.* 18.21 (WSA 1.9.49).
16. Matt. 28:19 (New American Bible, NAB). There is evidence that fifth-century liturgical celebration of baptism preferred posing three questions with an immersion following each answer instead of a simple declaration. See William Harmless, "Baptism," in Fitzgerald, *Augustine through the Ages*, 84–87, and Harmless, *Augustine and the Catechumenate* (Collegeville, MN: Liturgical Press, 1995).
17. St. Augustine, *The Gift of Perseverance* 13.23 and St. Augustine, *Sermons* (hereafter cited as *serm.*) 213.9, *Jo. ev. tr.* 11.4.
18. St. Augustine, *On the Merits and Forgiveness of Sins and on Infant Baptism* 1.26.39ff.; St. Augustine, *Grace and Rebuke*; St. Augustine, *The Grace of Christ and Original Sin* 8.19, 2.5.5. The notable exceptions to baptism in water are baptism "in blood" or martyrdom, and the more controversial baptism "in desire." St. Augustine, *On Baptism* 4.14.22; St. Augustine, *Explanations of the Psalms* 57.5; *Jo. ev. tr.* 4.13.2.
19. *Serm.* 229A.1 (WSA 3.6.256), quoting Rom. 6:4.
20. St. Augustine, *Enchiridion*, or *Handbook of Faith, Hope, and Love* 8.25.
21. See Harmless, "Baptism," 86.
22. St. Augustine, *Against the Letters of Petilianus* 2.104.237–2.105.239.
23. See Fitzgerald, "Penance," in Fitzgerald, *Augustine through the Ages*, 640–46.
24. See Joncas, "Ordination, Orders," in Fitzgerald, *Augustine through the Ages*, 599–602.
25. *Jo. ev. tr.* 5.6.2 (FOTC 78.113).
26. *Jo. ev. tr.* 5.15.3 (FOTC 78.123).
27. *Jo. ev. tr.* 6.21.1–2 (FOTC 78.149), quoting 1 Cor. 13:2 and Jas. 2:19.
28. *Jo. ev. tr.* 6.15.1 (FOTC 78.143).
29. *Ep. Jo.* 6.10.2 (FOTC 92.209).
30. Eph. 5:31–32, quoting Gen. 2:24. The translation can be found in *Gn. adv. Man.* 2.13.19 (WSA 1.13.84).
31. *Gn. adv. Man.* 2.24.37 (WSA 1.13.96).
32. *Gn. adv. Man.* 2.24.37 (WSA 1.13.96), quoting Rom 1:3.

33. E.g., *b. cong.* 24.32. See also Hunter, "Marriage," in Fitzgerald, *Augustine through the Ages*, 535–37, and Philip Reynolds, *Marriage in the Western Church* (Boston: Brill, 1994).
34. *B. cong.* 24.32.
35. *B. cong.* 6.6.
36. *B. cong.* 16.18 (WSA 1.9.47).
37. *B. cong.* 18.21 (WSA 1.9.49).
38. *B. cong.* 18.21 (WSA 1.9.49).
39. Matt. 19:8, Mark 10:5, and Eph. 5:32.
40. 1 Cor. 11:23–34, Mark 14:22–26, Matt. 26:26–30, Luke 22:14–20, John 6:22–71.
41. There are numerous studies of the Eucharist and history of reflection on the Body of Christ. Henri DeLubac, *Corpus Mysticum: The Eucharist and the Church in the Middle Ages*, trans. Gemma Simmonds (South Bend, IN: University of Notre Dame Press, 2007) is a fantastic place to begin study of this history. On Augustine more specifically, see Pamela Jackson, "Eucharist," in Fitzgerald, *Augustine through the Ages*, 330–34; Patout Burns, "The Eucharist as the Foundation of Christian unity in North African Theology, *Augustinian Studies* 32, no. 1 (2001): 1–24; and Thomas Humphries, "These Words Are Spirit and Life: Thomas' Use of Augustine on the Eucharist in ST 3.73–83," *Recherches de Théologie et Philosophie Médiévales* 78, no. 1 (2011): 59–96.
42. 1 Cor. 10:17 (NAB); cf. Augustine, *serm.* 228B.4, 229A.
43. *Jo. ev. tr.* 25.12.1 (FOTC 79.249).
44. St. Augustine, *City of God* 10.20, trans. Marcus Dods (New York: Modern Library, 1993), 325.
45. *Jo. ev. tr.* 26.13.3 (FOTC 79.271).
46. John 6:22–59, esp. 32, 49, and 58.
47. *Jo. ev. tr.* 26.12.1 (FOTC 79.269–70). Cf. *Tr. Ev. In.* 25.12–13.
48. *Jo. ev. tr.* 26.12.1 (FOTC 79. 270).
49. *Serm.* 229A.1 (WSA 3.6.256). Cf. *serm.* 228B.2.
50. *Serm.* 229.1 (WSA 3.6.252).
51. 1 Cor. 11:29. E.g., *Ep.* 153.21, *Jo. ev. tr.* 26.11.2ff.
52. *Serm.* 228B.2 (WSA 3.6.249).
53. Cf. *ep.* 138.7.
54. *Doct. Chr.* 1.35.40.

BIBLIOGRAPHICAL NOTE

A key resource for students of St. Augustine is *Augustine through the Ages: An Encyclopedia*, ed. Allan Fitzgerald, OSA (Grand Rapids, MI: Eerdmans, 1999). Two modern translation series have become the standard not only for contemporary English, but for their introductions and notes to the texts: "FOTC" refers to the Fathers of the Church series published by the Catholic University of America Press; "WSA" refers to the Works of Saint Augustine series published by New City Press.

4

Peter Lombard

PHILIPP W. ROSEMANN

As his name suggests, Peter Lombard hailed from the northern Italian region of Lombardy, where he was born in the village of Lumellogno around 1095/1100. His early years cannot be reconstructed with much detail or certainty, but chroniclers report that he was of humble origins, his mother sometimes being depicted as a washerwoman. His early studies most likely occurred at the cathedral school of nearby Novara. Later he was associated with Lucca, in Tuscany, whose bishop recommended him to St. Bernard of Clairvaux for further studies in France. In the early 1130s, therefore, we find him at Rheims, in the north of France, which together with Laon was an important center for biblical studies. These were the years when Anselm of Laon and his school created the *Glossa ordinaria*, a standard biblical commentary that incorporated explanations from the entire Western Christian tradition. In 1136, St. Bernard issued a letter of recommendation on Peter Lombard's behalf to Abbot Gilbert, of the famous abbey of Saint-Victor in Paris. His move to Paris placed Lombard in contact with some of the leading theologians of his day, including Hugh of Saint-Victor and Peter Abelard, both of whom influenced his thought.

Peter Lombard soon established himself as a master at the cathedral school of Notre-Dame, where he taught in the 1140s and 1150s, becoming a canon around 1145. He prepared glosses on the Psalter and the Pauline epistles, which because of their respective moral and doctrinal content were regarded as the central books of the Old and the New Testament. The Lombard's so-called *Magna Glosatura* quickly superseded the corresponding portions of the *Glossa ordinaria*—a fact that testifies to the authority he enjoyed. Pope Eugene III sought his advice in 1147, in 1148 he participated in the Council of Rheims, and in 1154 he accompanied the bishop of Paris on a trip to Rome. The stay there enabled him to consult a new translation of St. John Damascene's *On Orthodox Faith*. Extracts from the latter appear in the *Book of Sentences*, Peter Lombard's chef d'oeuvre, on the basis of which he started teaching theology in the years 1156 to 1158. He also delivered Latin sermons to the community of Parisian scholars and students; thirty-six of them have survived.

In 1159, Peter Lombard was appointed bishop of Paris. He had a powerful contender for this prestigious position, namely, Philip, the brother of King Louis VII. But Philip withdrew from the election in recognition of Peter Lombard's authority and fame. Peter Lombard died in 1160, after only one year in office, of unknown causes. He was buried in the church of Saint-Marcel, but his grave was desecrated in 1796, and the church itself was demolished in 1806.

Introduction: The *Book of Sentences* in the History of Christian Theology

The *Book of Sentences* belongs to a literary genre that served a crucial role in the development of Western theology, but is difficult to understand for the modern reader, whose criteria for the value of a written work include originality and a clearly discernible authorial voice. The term *sententia*, "sentence," designates a short quotation from an authoritative source.[1] (The verb *sentire* means "to feel" or "to perceive"; so a *sententia* is a mental perception of a state of affairs.) Collections of sentences were compiled dating to patristic times; in the Latin West the first such collection, which was prepared by Prosper of Aquitaine (ca. 390–463), brought together sentences from the works of St. Augustine. The goal of these compilations was to reduce large bodies of text to a manageable size. Soon, the scope of these "executive summaries" extended beyond the writings of a single author; thus, Isidore of Seville (ca. 560–636) had already composed *Sentences* that included quotations from Scripture, Augustine, and Gregory the Great, among other sources.

Despite their seemingly simple approach, collections of sentences gave rise to a number of important methodological questions. The first of these was what to include from the growing body of theological literature; resolving this question involved judgments of authority and importance. Second, in what order was the excerpted material to be presented? This question points to the difficulty of establishing the succession of topics in a comprehensive theological discourse. Is it best, following the narrative order of Scripture, to begin with the creation account, or should the anthology of sentences—considering the fact that there has to *be* a God before creation can occur—start with texts regarding God's existence and nature? Third, once extracts are assembled from a variety of texts by a number of authoritative writers—Eastern and Western, biblical, patristic, and medieval—tensions and contradictions will become apparent in their juxtaposition. What is the status of these tensions? How can they be resolved?

Their importance notwithstanding, these questions did not become truly pressing until the twelfth century, which saw the rise of the first accounts of the Christian faith in the Latin West that can be called "systematic." Departing from the narrative order of Scripture, a theological system requires a logical framework in which every aspect of dogmatic belief finds its place. The existence of unresolved contradictions among the authoritative statements on which it draws threatens the coherence of a theological system. During the patristic period and the Early Middle Ages, however, Christian theologians in the West did not make the step from "story" to "system."[2] The time was not ripe—for a number of reasons, one of which was the fact that there were no professional theologians yet. The authors of theological texts were typically monks and bishops, whose primary interests were contemplative and pastoral. They composed scriptural commentary, on the one hand, and treatises devoted to particular, well-defined topics, on the other. This changed in the course of the so-called Renaissance of the twelfth century, when the growth of towns and cities created an educational environment in which a new type of theologian arose: the "master."[3] The master could be attached to a cathedral school, as Peter Lombard was, but he could teach independently as well. Teaching was his primary vocation, and just as his social role as an intellectual came to be detached from other functions in the Church, so the theological project gained a new autonomy and coherence.[4]

It was in this environment that masters of theology began to experiment with different types of theological syntheses. "To experiment" is the appropriate term here, as more than one theologian failed in the attempt to render a coherent account of the Christian faith as a whole. Peter Abelard (ca. 1079–1142), for example, published several books titled *Theologia*, which he planned to structure in accordance with the virtues of faith, hope, and charity, but in none of them did he manage to move beyond the Trinity. Hugh of Saint-Victor (1096–1141) meanwhile published *On the Sacraments of the Christian Faith*. While the work was comprehensive in its scope, its presentation followed the chronological order of salvation history, rather than attempting a more logical arrangement. There was, moreover, no effort to compare and reconcile conflicting sentences, which—as we have seen—was an important task in the eyes of contemporary theologians. Robert of Melun (ca. 1100–1167), who taught in and around Paris during roughly the same period as Peter Lombard, had the ambitious plan of merging Peter Abelard's and Hugh's approaches; yet this project proved beyond his powers, as his *Sentences* also remained incomplete.[5]

The *Book of Sentences*: Structure and Method

The *Book of Sentences*, then, stands out among similar contemporary endeavors by offering all the basic elements of a complete systematic theology. Building upon the foundation of tradition, Peter Lombard's work brings together thousands of sentences from authoritative sources. Although many other Church Fathers, canonists, and theologians are represented, together with material from the *Glossa ordinaria*, the *Sentences* give pride of place to Augustine, whose stature as a theological authority was unparalleled. Scripture is, of course, constantly present as well, indeed so much so that Peter Lombard describes his project as nothing but a "treatment of the sacred page" (*sacrae paginae tractatum*).[6] Nevertheless, he usually quotes the Bible through the writings of the Church Fathers—an approach that reflects the conviction that Scripture is polysemous and requires interpretation.[7]

In the opening pages, Lombard explains the principle used to structure the material that he has gathered in the *Book of Sentences*. It is an Augustinian principle, based upon the famous division of reality into things and signs in the treatise *On Christian Doctrine*: a "thing" is an element of reality that does not point beyond itself, whereas a "sign" is characterized by its reference to another. One way to understand this distinction is to say that all of reality is a sign of its Creator, so that there is ultimately only one "thing," namely, God himself. But that is not what

Peter Lombard has in mind. He is already thinking specifically of the sign-character of the sacraments and announces that he is first going to treat things and then signs. This gives us the division of the *Sentences* into a "thing" part (Books I–III) and a "sign" part (Book IV).

As for the "thing" part, Lombard continues to apply the analysis of *On Christian Doctrine*. There, Augustine distinguishes things to be enjoyed from things to be used. "Enjoyment" is a very specific term indicating rest in an object loved for its own sake. The Trinity alone is properly to be enjoyed. The created world should only be an object of use, although again distinctions are necessary. Human beings and the virtues are not used in the same way in which we use inanimate objects or even animals—that is, as mere means toward the end of enjoyment. They occupy a position somewhere in between use and enjoyment. This further set of distinctions allows us to infer the structure of the remaining books of the *Sentences*: Book I is devoted to God as the object of enjoyment; Book II deals with creation, the object of use, also including a treatment of human beings and of the virtues, with their intermediate status; and Book III contains Peter Lombard's Christology: this makes sense since, in Christ, the means and the end have become one.

Peter Lombard breaks each of these books down further into chapters and paragraphs, which often carry headings that identify the subject matter under consideration. In the thirteenth century, the Parisian master Alexander of Hales (ca. 1185–1245) bundled the chapters into what he called "distinctions": larger groups of chapters devoted to a particular topic.[8]

We have now discussed the nature of the *Book of Sentences* as a sentences collection as well as its structure. A word about its method is in order because, as pointed out earlier, any collection of sentences is sooner or later confronted with the question of how to reconcile tensions and even contradictions among the authoritative statements that it has assembled. In this respect, just as in its other characteristics already mentioned, the success of the *Book of Sentences* was not due to its author's originality in inventing methods and procedures never heard of. The dialectical problem of the reconciliation of authorities was well known. Peter Abelard composed a book under the telling title *Sic et non* (Yes and no), in which he juxtaposed contradictory authorities without any resolution, with the goal to make material available to his students on which they could exercise their dialectical skills. The preface to *Sic et non* contained an outline of the methods germane to the task at hand. In the *Sentences*, Peter Lombard applies these dialectical rules thoroughly and patiently to the vast corpus of quotations that make up the four books of his work. Sometimes, in particularly difficult contexts, he follows Peter Abelard's example of laying out only the options while declaring himself incapable of a solution. He then states something like, "this question is insoluble, surpassing human understanding" or "this question as well is inexplicable, since it rises beyond the weaknesses of man."[9] The most famous example of such doctrinal restraint is the Lombard's Christology: he sketches out three possible theories of the hypostatic union (concerning the union of the two natures in the one person of Jesus Christ) without making it clear which one he considers preferable.[10]

Peter Lombard's humility was a key factor in the spectacular success that the *Book of Sentences* enjoyed as it became the standard theology textbook used in the medieval theology faculties until the time of the Council of Trent—and in some cases beyond then. Since every aspiring medieval master of theology had to lecture on the *Sentences* as part of his training, there is no work of Christian literature, except for Scripture itself, that was commented upon more frequently.[11] How could the *Sentences* remain a viable basis for theology lectures over several centuries, amid sometimes virulent disputes among different schools in a continuously evolving doctrinal landscape? The answer lies in the kind of system Peter Lombard presents in his work. A system can be rigid and closed, claiming to offer a definitive account of the truth. Such a system forces the one contemplating it either to subscribe to it as a whole or to reject it with equal determination, in favor of an alternative account. Peter Lombard's system is not of this kind. While comprehensive, it frequently remains open, time and again inviting the reader not to consider "our disputation to be sufficient; rather, he should read other, perhaps better considered and treated [positions]."[12]

In sum, the *Book of Sentences* places at its reader's disposal the materials from Scripture and the tradition necessary to arrive at thoughtful and orthodox theological views; it teaches him (or, nowadays, her) methods that can be used to adjudicate among competing claims and synthesize them; and it does so in the context of a well-structured doctrinal whole. Peter Lombard does have a theological vision of his own (one of his famous claims is the identification of charity with the Holy Spirit),[13] but it is not so rigid as to exclude alternative accounts. This is why the *Book of Sentences* found admiring readers in generations of theologians, ranging from Thomas Aquinas to Martin Luther, who even later in life found him to be a "great man."[14]

The Sacraments: Definition and General Traits

While there were theological discussions of individual sacraments before the time of Peter Lombard—one can think of the Eucharistic controversy of the eleventh century, for example—the *Book of Sentences* has been called "the first treatment of the sacraments in general."[15] Such a claim may seem surprising. For, we have already noted that Peter Lombard's teacher Hugh of Saint-Victor authored a book with the title *On the Sacraments of the Christian Faith*. Not unexpectedly, the work includes a discussion of the seven sacraments—but it goes far beyond that. Hugh writes before the time when the seven sacraments would be singled out as special among other possible candidates for sacramental status (such as religious vows); he does not distinguish clearly between sacraments and sacramentals either. The bulk of the work is a sweeping theological synthesis divided into matters pertaining to the Old Testament (Book I) and subjects arising in connection with the New Testament (Book II). For Hugh all these topics, from creation to eschatology, fall under the rubric of sacraments.

This is because, in *On the Sacraments of the Christian Faith*, Hugh of Saint-Victor was still working with an older, very broad notion of sacrament. If, as Augustine had it, a sacrament is "a visible sign of an invisible grace," then the entire created universe can be understood as a vast sacramental system that points to its Creator. This sacramental view of reality has never become obsolete; the twentieth century, in fact, rediscovered it in the writings of Father Alexander Schmemann and others.[16] Still, such a broad conception of sacramentality is insufficient to grasp exactly what occurs in a rite such as baptism or penance.

Peter Lombard clarified the debate, first, by narrowing the concept of sacrament, which he applied only to baptism, confirmation, the Eucharist, penance, unction of the sick, ordination, and marriage. Second, he developed a definition that, by emphasizing their causal power, managed to demarcate these seven sacraments from other forms of sacramentality:

> *What is properly called "sacrament."* We therefore properly call "sacrament" that which is a sign of God's grace and the form of invisible grace, in such a way as to carry its image and to be its cause. Therefore, the sacraments were instituted not only for the sake of signifying, but of sanctifying as well.[17]

This definition makes the seven sacraments into very specific kinds of signs: signs that not only signify God and God's grace, but carry the image of divine grace and even cause it. In this manner, they possess a sanctifying or justifying power.

Several elements of this definition call for clarification. The word "form" does not have the Aristotelian connotations that it would acquire later on, in the theology of the thirteenth century; in the *Book of Sentences*, it means simply "visible appearance."[18] Each of the sacraments resembles God's grace because of the particular symbolism of its material support. Water, for example, is a most suitable medium for baptism because even in its daily use it serves a cleansing function; in baptism, too, a cleansing occurs, although not of our bodies but of our souls. In this way, the sacraments teach us to develop something like a "deep reading" of the world, that is to say, to penetrate from the surface of things to their inner power, and thence to their Maker. It requires humility for man to submit himself to elements of the material universe, even to venerate them, in seeking salvation.[19] As one can see, the larger sacramental character of the created world is not lost on Peter Lombard, even if he gives the term "sacrament" a more specific focus than did his predecessors.

The power of the sacraments to confer grace, or to cause justification, allows Master Peter to distinguish the seven sacraments of the New Covenant from Old Testament sacrifices and ceremonial observances, "which could never render those offering them just."[20] The only exception to this strict distinction is circumcision. The *Book of Sentences* quotes statements from Saints Augustine and Bede acknowledging the ability of circumcision to remit sin, just as baptism does. The difference, explains the Lombard, lies in the fact that baptism also confers a fortifying grace and strengthens the virtues. The sacraments of the New Covenant of course derive their remarkable power from Christ's saving work; that is why they could not have been given to the people of the Old Law.[21]

One further point needs to be added to complete the initial definition. While a sacrament, as the "form of invisible grace," is en-mattered, so to speak, in the things of this world, it cannot perform its function without the addition of words, such as the invocation of the Trinity in baptism.[22] Peter Lombard does not pursue an important question that would occupy many a commentator on his work, namely, whence exactly the words spoken as part of a sacramental rite derive their power to transform a particular element of creation into an efficacious sign of God's grace. What makes a phrase or expression so powerful that it can change reality? Such lack of speculative depth is evident in other parts of the *Sentences* as well. In the history of the reception of the *Sentences*, however, Peter Lombard's often elementary accounts enabled different commentators to develop their own ideas.[23]

Since we are talking about weaknesses in the *Book of Sentences*, here is another: Master Peter's treatment of the sacraments is not always completely coherent. In other words, he strives to reconcile and synthesize the sentences that he has discovered in his sources, but does not always fully succeed. Historical distance now permits us to see these inconsistencies, some of which are striking. For example, before embarking on his treatment of the individual seven sacraments, the Lombard offers the following typology:

> *On the sacraments of the New Law.* Let us now approach the sacraments of the New Law, which are baptism, confirmation, the bread of benediction (that is, the Eucharist), penitence, extreme unction, ordination, [and] marriage. Some of these offer a remedy for sin and confer helping grace, like baptism; others are just for remedy, like marriage; [yet] others strengthen us through grace and virtue, like the Eucharist and ordination.[24]

This list makes marriage appear like a second-class sacrament, comparable to circumcision in its inability to bestow any additional grace or virtue beyond the remission of sin. As we will discover, the Lombard's treatment of marriage is conflicted about precisely this matter.

Instead of providing an overview of all seven sacraments in the *Book of Sentences*, we will focus on two that are particularly revealing of Peter Lombard's sacramentology: penance and marriage.[25]

Penance

One of the points that Master Peter establishes early on in his treatment of penance is that this sacrament can be celebrated more than once.[26] The fact that he considers this question points to the historical context in which he was writing. In the middle of the twelfth century, sacramentology was still in flux in the Latin Church. Not only was there doubt about the precise number of sacraments (Hugh of Saint-Victor, as we have seen, did not limit himself to seven); the exact nature of the sacraments that made Peter Lombard's list was also not a settled question.

Two forms of penance, both of which the *Book of Sentences* recognizes as legitimate, coexisted in the practice of the twelfth-century Church. One, which was indeed not repeatable, was a solemn, public form of penance, reserved for particularly heinous crimes, such as family violence (parricide, uxoricide, rape of one's daughters) or the murder of a priest. Presided over by a bishop, it involved the symbolic expulsion of the sinner from the Eucharistic community on Ash Wednesday, followed by a period of isolation (or imprisonment), and then the reconciliation with the Church on Holy Thursday. Men in holy orders were not eligible for public penance. This *paenitentia publica* had its roots in the even more severe canonical penance that was practiced in the early Church.

But there also existed a second, private form of penance, which developed in the twelfth century from the so-called "tariff penance" of the Early Middle Ages. The latter already included an acknowledgment of one's sins in a personal conversation with a confessor. The name "tariff penance" was derived from the practice of imposing acts of atonement like ransoms for sins: for example, as atonement for a sin, the confessant was required to release a female serf or donate twelve pieces of fowl to the confessor's monastery. By the twelfth century, however, this *paenitentia taxata* was disappearing in favor of the kind of private penance that still exists today, that is to say, one in which the formation of conscience in dialogue with a confessor is emphasized over mechanically imposed fines. The Fourth Council of the Lateran in 1215 codified the *paenitentia privata* in its canon 21, mandating that every Christian be given the opportunity once a year to confess his or her sins privately to a priest.[27] Some scholars, such as Marie-Dominique Chenu, have interpreted these developments as the "awakening of conscience in medieval civilization."[28]

But let us return to Peter Lombard. After spending a few paragraphs on the solemn and public rite of penance, he devotes the majority of his long discussion to private penance. How "private" exactly is private penance? In other words, does it necessarily involve a priest, or is inner contrition sufficient for the forgiveness of sins? Gratian, the famous canonist on whom the *Book of Sentences* draws frequently, presented arguments in favor of both possibilities and then left the answer open to further discussion.[29] Peter Lombard, too, is open to both sides of the argument, although he shows a preference for confession to a priest, albeit with some caveats. The first caveat, which the Lombard emphasizes several times, is that a priest has to be available for confession in the first place. This could not at all be taken for granted, according to the historian Joseph Goering: "Provisions were available, by means of traditional public penance, for confessing grave sins and for reconciling public sinners, but lesser sinners would not have had easy access to a priest for confession."[30] Peter Lombard's position that sins should be confessed to a priest is therefore tempered by a certain pastoral realism—one cannot demand the impossible. He writes,

> For what the second question contained—namely, whether it might be sufficient to confess to God alone, without confession [to] and judgment of a priest—has been disclosed, and it has been established by the aforementioned testimonies that it does not suffice to confess to God without a priest; neither is the penitent truly humble if he does not desire and seek out the judgment of a priest. But is it equally valid for someone to confess to a companion or to his neighbor, at least when a priest is not available?
>
> *Solution.* It can soundly be said about this [matter] that the examination of a priest should be sought out eagerly, since God has granted

priests the power to bind and loose; and therefore those whom they forgive, God too forgives. Should, however, a priest not be available, confession should be made to a neighbor or companion.[31]

There is a second caveat. Since private confession as a kind of soul searching with the goal to form the penitent's conscience was still a relatively new practice, not every priest was trained to perform the required function of spiritual advisor. In one of the few passages of the *Book of Sentences* where Peter Lombard displays emotion, he bemoans the low personal quality of many men who "presume to receive the position of the priesthood, being unworthy of it in knowledge and life," and from there concludes that if one cannot find an ordained confessor who exhibits wisdom and good judgment, it is better to make one's confession to a layperson.[32]

The priest, however, is not just a spiritual advisor; he also possesses the power "to bind and loose," that is to say, to forgive sins. What exactly does this mean? According to Master Peter, it would be a serious mistake to believe that God follows the judgment of the Church, especially since the Church "sometimes judges with dishonesty and ignorance."[33] Thus, he interprets the power of binding and loosing as the power to *show* that God has, or has not, forgiven a sinner:

> We can soundly say and teach this, that God alone forgives and retains sins, and [that] nonetheless he has granted the Church the power of binding and loosing. But he himself binds and looses in one way, the Church in another. For he, through himself only, forgives sin in such a way as to cleanse the soul from its inner stain and to free it from the debt of eternal death.
>
> *How priests loose and bind from sins.* However, he has not granted this [power] to priests. Rather, he has assigned them the power of binding and loosing, that is, of showing that people are bound or loosed.[34]

The very fact that a penitent feels compunction already shows that he or she is filled with charity. True charity, however, means belief in Christ; and a true believer in Christ is not subject to God's wrath. The function of the priest, then, is only to confirm God's forgiveness of sins, which has preceded the external act of confession, and to help the penitent in the formation of conscience and in deciding on appropriate acts of satisfaction for his or her misdeeds.

Penance, then, comprises three elements. There is the need (in ideal circumstances) to confess one's sins to a priest in order to receive confirmation that they have been forgiven, together with spiritual advice on a how best to atone. There is, second, the penitent's contrition, which must precede the confession; otherwise the latter is empty and meaningless. Finally, there is God's remission of sins. To put this in the terminology that Master Peter has developed for his sacramentology, the sacrament of penance has a twofold *res*. *Res* is a very broad term in Latin, meaning anything that has any kind of reality, even something just imagined. We could translate it as "thing," but "reality" may be closer to what Peter Lombard has in mind (and "reality" derives from the Latin *realis*, an adjective formed from *res*). So, the sacrament of penance has a twofold reality, understood as that which, according to the Lombard's definition, it indicates as an efficacious sign. The first reality that the confession of one's sins indicates is one's contrition. This contrition, in turn, indicates God's forgiveness of one's sins.

According to Peter Lombard's definition of sacrament ("that which is a sign of God's grace and the form of invisible grace, in such a way as to carry its image and to be its cause"), one would expect the sacramental rite of confession to cause God's forgiveness of sins. However, as we have just seen in our discussion of the role of the confessor, it is in fact the other way around: we confess because we feel contrition; we feel contrition because God has already poured his charity into our hearts. Peter Lombard does not seem to be troubled by this difficulty: "If the exterior penance," he writes, "is the sacrament and the interior [penance] the reality of the sacrament, then the reality precedes the sacrament more often than the sacrament the reality." "But this is not problematic," we learn, "because in other sacraments too, which bring about that which they indicate, this is often the case."[35] Depending on how one views the matter, this inconsistency is a sign either of Master Peter's openness to discussion or of his lack of rigor.

Marriage

Peter Lombard's presentation of marriage begins in a way that, from a contemporary perspective, can only appear to be dated—and perhaps more than that, misguided.

First, the *Book of Sentences* suggests a distinction between marriage before and after the Fall. In paradise, marriage was a duty, as is evident from God's scriptural command to "increase and multiply" (a command that the Lord repeated later, after the flood, to ensure the survival of the human race). In the prelapsarian state, the sexual union occurred without concupiscence, while women gave birth without pain. The whole thing was an "honorable" affair. After the Fall, marriage turns from duty into remedy—namely, a remedy for sin. Since the multiplication of the human race that was necessary in the beginning is now completed, marriage is no longer a duty. It is a "concession" made to account for human weakness. At most, it is possible to consider it a "minor good" insofar as it prevents us from committing worse transgressions; but the sexual part of it remains a "minor evil": it is "permitted, that is, tolerated, such that it is not prohibited."[36]

Now one might expect Master Peter to expatiate on the dangers of sex—but that is not the path he chooses. In the very next paragraph, immediately after the sentence quoted, he suddenly declares,

> *That marriage is good.* However, there were not a few heretics detesting marriage, who have been called the "Tatians."[37]

The astonished reader might ask him- or herself if the Lombard himself is not among those "heretics detesting marriage"! However, in the *Sentences* there now follow many pages devoted to the goods and the sacramentality of marriage, pages that demonstrate a genuine appreciation of the value, indeed beauty, of the marital bond. So, what should we think of the strange opening pages?

In the Western Christian tradition, Peter Lombard was far from alone in his reservations regarding marriage, especially in its physical aspects. There existed a long-held belief that the sexual act constituted the very occasion for the transmission of original sin: that it was the paradigm of all "incontinence" that characterizes sin. *Incontinentia* was a technical term that designated the inability to "contain oneself" morally: to eat too much, drink too much, be attached to luxuries and pride—in short, to love the world too much, more than its Creator. Because of the ecstatic character of sexual enjoyment, intercourse was considered to be the "tinder of sin," that is to say, the root cause of the body's inability to remain subject to the soul and obey its rational commands. Peter Lombard echoes this standard teaching of the patristic and early medieval tradition in Book II of the *Sentences*, in the context of his treatment of original sin.[38]

This long-standing Christian teaching on sexuality is usually dismissed as a Platonic and Neoplatonic accretion foreign to the spirit of Scripture.[39] The embarrassment of Christian scholars is understandable, yet we should not forget another, deeper reason as to why early Christianity regarded the celibate "way of life of the priest or monk as the authentic Christian way of existence, by comparison with which the way of life of the layperson—marriage in particular—count[ed] as a concession to human weakness."[40] For a long time, the expectation that the first Christian communities had of an imminent Second Coming remained paradigmatic, so that Christians viewed themselves as living at the end of history. It was not until the thirteenth century that, following the prophecies of Joachim of Fiore, theologians fundamentally rethought the structure of salvation history.[41] But what is the point of getting married if the end of the world is nigh? Why raise children?

Furthermore, Christian communities and thinkers for a long time remained profoundly skeptical of the values of the world, which they viewed as hostile to authentic Christian living. Again, this attitude was inherited from antiquity, when the early Christian communities were marginal and imperiled phenomena in a pagan environment. If the Kingdom had come, surely it had to be sought within the Church, not in the world at large. In this situation, it made sense to retreat to one's "parish"—a word that, understood from its etymological roots in the Greek *paroikia*, designates "a colony of resident aliens."[42] Again, the best such colony was the monastery, with the relative insulation it afforded from strife and temptation. Only the thorough Christianization of all aspects of life, which in Western Europe did not even begin until the Carolingian foundation of the Holy Roman Empire, made it possible to imagine the world as a place of salvation, and thus the lay state as possessing a dignity of its own.

To view marriage as a sacrament—a twelfth-century innovation—was a step in precisely this direction. This step involved a "spiritualization" of marriage, that is to say, a recognition of its spiritual value not only in the face of possible Christian reservations, but also because for medieval society the marital bond was usually a means for decidedly secular ends, such as ensuring the integrity of a family's possessions in the marriages of its heirs. Endogamous marriages were arranged to pursue this goal. Thus, parents exerted strong influence on their children's marital choices, while lords could, in order to protect their "property," force serfs into marriage and prevent marriages of serfs with partners from outside the manor.[43] It is not difficult to find traces of this feudal conception of marriage in the *Book of Sentences*; for instance, Peter Lombard devotes a couple of (inconclusive) paragraphs to the question of whether marriages between serfs from different manors are valid without the lord's consent.[44] How "medieval" the *Book of Sentences* is also appears clearly from other passages, such as one where Master Peter decides that marriages are valid even if "less honorable causes" have contributed to their contraction—causes such as the bride's beauty, not to mention love (*amor*)![45]

Despite this difficult historical context, a clear picture of the positive core of marriage emerges in the course of the discussion. Peter Lombard defines marriage as follows:

> *What marriage is.* A marriage consists in the marital union of a man and a woman, between legitimate persons, [a union] that maintains an undivided manner of life.—To the "undivided manner" it pertains that, without the consent of the other, neither of them may profess continence or devote him- or herself to prayer [i.e., choose the religious life]; and also that the marital bond endures while they are alive, so that it is not licit for them to have intercourse with others; and that they treat each other the way in which each would treat him- or herself.—Under this description, however, only the marriage of legitimate and faithful people is included.[46]

Note the repeated emphasis on the need for the partners in marriage to be "legitimate." Peter Lombard is aware of the fact that polygamy was acceptable under the Old Law, but of course now, "in the time of grace," the criteria of legitimacy have changed. Among those completely ineligible for marriage, he counts those who have made religious vows, have received holy orders, are too closely related, or belong to different faiths. (Later on in the *Sentences*, the Lombard attenuates the prohibition against interreligious marriage.)[47] Given the medieval preference for endogamous marriages, there is a detailed treatment of both "carnal" and "spiritual" consanguinity and how to calculate its degrees.

The phrase "undivided manner of life" from the excerpt just quoted represents a rather negative description of what constitutes marriage. Peter Lombard finds a way to speak of the marital relationship in more positive terms by referring to the mutual care that the spouses should show for each other's well-being. Along the same lines, he declares marriage to be a "conjugal fellowship," in which the husband takes a woman "not as a boss nor as a servant, but as a wife."[48] The relationship between husband and wife is well illustrated, Master Peter explains, by the biblical image of the woman being made from the man's side—rather than from his upper or lower body. The Lombard also emphasizes that although the production of offspring is one of the principal goals of marriage, marriage is constituted not by consent to engage in sexual relations, but by the agreement to live together in fellowship. The personal commitment that is at the heart of marriage also dictates that the marital vows must be made freely; any form of pressure invalidates them. Invalid, too, are promised marriages: "*I will take you as my husband*, and *I will [take you] as my wife*, that is not the consent which brings about marriage." The vow must be formulated in the present tense. It must also be made explicit "in words or other certain signs."[49]

These, then, are some important aspects of the human dimension of marriage. Its sacramental character will become manifest if we consider the reality, the *res*, that it causes as a sign and image of God's grace:

> *Of what reality marriage is the sacrament*. Since, therefore, marriage is a sacrament, it is also a sacred sign and [the sign] of a sacred thing, namely, of the union of Christ and the Church, as the Apostle says. It is written, he says [i.e., St. Paul says, quoting Gen. 2:24]: "'For this cause shall a man leave his father and mother, and shall cleave to his wife, and they shall be two in one flesh.' This is a great sacrament; but I speak in Christ and in the Church" [Eph. 5:31]. For, just as between the spouses there is a union according to a consent of souls and according to a mingling of

bodies, so the Church is joined to Christ (*Ecclesia Christo copulatur*) by will and by nature: because she wills the same as he, and [because] he took a form from the nature of man. Therefore, the bride is joined (*copulata*) to the bridegroom spiritually and corporeally, that is, by charity and by a conformity of nature.—The symbol of both these unions (*copulae*) is in marriage: for the consent of the spouses signifies the spiritual union (*copulam*) of Christ and the Church that comes about through charity; but the intermingling of the sexes signifies that [union] which comes about through a conformity of nature.[50]

Given Peter Lombard's ambivalence regarding the value of sexuality—we have heard him denounce it as the "tinder of sin" and quintessence of incontinence—it is striking that he has no hesitation to employ sexual imagery in order to capture Christ's union with the Church. The terms *copula* and *copulare* occur four times in the passage just quoted. Nor does he have qualms about considering the sexual union between husband and wife as an image of the union of Christ's divine and human natures.

The passage also sheds more light on the Lombard's conception of the conjugal fellowship that characterizes the spouses' "undivided manner of life." Ultimately, what animates this fellowship, which as we already know requires mutual respect and concern for each other's well-being, is charity. This means nothing less than that, just as the Holy Spirit dwells in the Church, so he dwells in marriage—in a very strong sense, because Peter Lombard identifies charity with the Holy Spirit. Charity is not an "infused virtue" for him, as it would be for Thomas Aquinas and later Scholasticism.[51] In the spouses' love for each other (*caritas*, not *amor*!), the Holy Spirit is therefore immediately present. One could hardly frame the sacramentality of marriage in more powerful terms.

A final difficulty remains, analogous to the one that we encountered in the Lombard's discussion of penance. A sacrament, we recall, is "a sign of God's grace and the form of invisible grace, in such a way as to carry its image and to be its cause." Peter Lombard has impressively demonstrated how both the spiritual and the physical aspects of marriage mirror God's grace; but how could marriage be the *cause* not only of the harmony of will between Christ and his Church, but even of the Incarnation itself? Clearly, the causal relationship operates the other way around: it is because

Christ has assumed human flesh and suffused the Church with his charity that the union of husband and wife, partaking of that charity, is able to reflect the marriage between Christ and the Church.

Conclusion

The *Book of Sentences*, then, raises not a few questions. Is penance public or private? Does private confession require a priest, or is it sufficient to confess one's sins to a lay Christian? What is the status of marriage, as it hovers between a concession to human weakness and a great sacrament that mirrors the union of Christ with his Church? Finally—and, for the theory of the sacrament, most important—in what sense does a sacrament "cause" divine grace?

Remarkably, the tradition did not view Peter Lombard's loose answers to these questions as defects that would have disqualified the *Sentences* from performing its function as the fundamental theological textbook of the medieval universities. This situation suggests that medieval theologians expected their standard textbook not to present them with a finished doctrinal system, but rather to provide something much less ambitious: food for thought. Theological doctrine did not come "from above," but was made by the masters of the theology faculties by their careful examination and scholarly discussion of difficult questions in light of the great "sentences" of the tradition.[52]

NOTES

1. See Mariken Teeuwen, *The Vocabulary of Intellectual Life in the Middle Ages* (Turnhout: Brepols, 2003), 336–39.
2. The expression "from 'story' to 'system'" comes from my book *Peter Lombard* (New York: Oxford University Press, 2004), chap. 1. Describing the same historical development, Aloys Grillmeier used the phrase "from symbol to *summa*"; see his article, "Vom Symbolum zur Summa. Zum theologiegeschichtlichen Verhältnis von Patristik und Scholastik," in *Kirche und Überlieferung*, ed. Johannes Betz and Heinrich Fries (Freiburg im Breisgau: Herder, 1960), 119–69.
3. The idea of a cultural renaissance that occurred in the twelfth century gained popularity in the wake of the book by Charles Homer Haskins, *The Renaissance of the Twelfth Century* (Cambridge, MA: Harvard University Press, 1927). Another well-known title in the long bibliography on the phenomenon is *Renaissance and Renewal in the Twelfth Century*, ed. Robert Benson and Giles Constable (Cambridge, MA: Harvard University Press, 1982).

4. On the genesis and role of the medieval intellectual, one may read the classic study by Jacques Le Goff, *Intellectuals in the Middle Ages*, trans. Teresa Lavender Fagan (Oxford: Blackwell, 1993). More specifically on the theological dimension of the changes in the educational landscape of the twelfth century, see Marie-Dominique Chenu, "The Masters of the Theological 'Science,'" in *Nature, Man, and Society in the Twelfth Century: Essays on New Theological Perspectives in the Latin West*, trans. Jerome Taylor and Lester K. Little (Chicago: University of Chicago Press, 1968), 270–309.
5. For more detail on each of these three thinkers, see my *Peter Lombard*, chap. 1. For an in-depth presentation of the *Book of Sentences* in the context of twelfth-century theology, one should turn to the magisterial two-volume study by Marcia L. Colish, *Peter Lombard* (Leiden: Brill, 1994).
6. Peter Lombard, *Sententiae in IV libris distinctae*, 3rd ed., 2 vols. (Grottaferrata: Editiones Collegii S. Bonaventurae Ad Claras Aquinas, 1971–81), book I, dist. 1, chap. 1, no. 1, 1:55. A complete English translation has recently become available: Peter Lombard, *The Sentences*, trans. Giulio Silano, 4 vols. (Toronto: Pontifical Institute of Mediaeval Studies, 2007–10). Silano's translation is reliable, but as a Lombard scholar, I have made my own translations for the quotations included in this chapter.
7. For a more complete account of Peter Lombard's sources, see Rosemann, *Peter Lombard*, 55–57.
8. Thus, standard references to the *Book of Sentences* are by book, distinction, chapter, and paragraph; see the example in note 6. More information on the structure of the *Sentences* is available in Rosemann, *Peter Lombard*, 57–61.
9. Respectively *Sentences*, book I, dist. 32, chap. 1, no. 2, 1:233 and book I, dist. 32, chap. 6, no. 2, 1:239.
10. See Rosemann, *Peter Lombard*, 124–30.
11. On the role of the *Book of Sentences* in shaping later medieval theology, I have written *The Story of a Great Medieval Book: Peter Lombard's "Sentences"* (Toronto: University of Toronto Press, 2007). For a more in-depth treatment, see the three-volume handbook *Mediaeval Commentaries on the "Sentences" of Peter Lombard*, ed. Gillian R. Evans (vol. 1) and Philipp W. Rosemann (vols. 2 and 3) (Leiden: Brill, 2002–15).
12. *Sentences*, book III, dist. 7, chap. 3, no. 3, 2:66.
13. On this point, see Rosemann, "Fraterna dilectio est Deus: Peter Lombard's Thesis on Charity as the Holy Spirit," in *Amor amicitiae—On the Love That Is Friendship: Essays in Medieval Thought and Beyond in Honor of the Rev. Professor James McEvoy*, ed. Thomas A. F. Kelly and Philipp W. Rosemann (Louvain: Peeters, 2004), 409–36.
14. "Ist ein grosser man gewesen," Luther remarked on Peter Lombard in a table talk dated 1532 (*D. Martin Luthers Werke. Kritische Gesammtausgabe* [Weimar: Böhlau, 1883–], TR 2:2544B). On Luther's glosses on the *Sentences*, one may read Pekka Kärkkäinen, "Martin Luther," in Rosemann, *Mediaeval Commentaries on the "Sentences" of Peter Lombard*, 2:471–94.

15. A. Michel, "Sacrements," in *Dictionnaire de théologie catholique*, vol. 14/1 (Paris: Letouzey et Ané, 1939), 485–644, at 530.
16. See Alexander Schmemann, *For the Life of the World: Sacraments and Orthodoxy*, 2nd ed. (Crestwood, NY: St. Vladimir's Seminary Press, 1973).
17. *Sentences*, book III, dist. 1, chap. 4, no. 2, 2:233: "Quid proprie dicitur sacramentum. Sacramentum enim proprie dicitur, quod ita signum est gratiae Dei et invisibilis gratiae forma, ut ipsius imaginem gerat et causa exsistat. Non igitur significandi tantum gratia sacramenta instituta sunt, sed et sanctificandi." The Latin edition employs bold characters to indicate chapter and paragraph headings that appear as rubrics (that is, in red ink) in the manuscripts.
18. See Joseph de Ghellinck, "Un chapitre dans l'histoire de la définition des sacrements au XIIe siècle," in *Mélanges Mandonnet. Études d'histoire littéraire et doctrinale du moyen âge*, 2 vols. (Paris: Vrin, 1930), 2:79–96, at 88.
19. See *Sentences*, book IV, dist. 1, chap. 5, nos. 2 and 3, 2:235.
20. Ibid., book IV, dist. 1, chap. 4, no. 3, 2:233.
21. See ibid., book IV, dist. 1, dist. 2, chap. 1, no. 2, 2:240.
22. See ibid., book IV, dist. 1, chap. 5, no. 6, 2:235.
23. In a study of remarkable depth and scope, Irène Rosier-Catach has used the commentary tradition on the *Book of Sentences* to find answers to the question of the efficaciousness of sacramental formulae: *La parole efficace. Signe, rituel, sacré* (Paris: Seuil, 2004).
24. *Sentences*, book IV, dist. 2, chap. 1, no. 1, 2:239–40.
25. For a complete account of the seven sacraments, see my *Peter Lombard*, chap. 7.
26. See *Sentences*, book IV, dist. 14, chap 5, 2:322–24.
27. For an overview of these developments, see the excellent entry "Buße (liturgisch-theologisch)," in *Lexikon des Mittelalters*, 9 vols. (Stuttgart: Metzler, 1980–99), 2:1123–44, esp. 1131–35 (by Cyrille Vogel). This can be supplemented by Karen Wagner, "*Cum aliquis venerit ad sacerdotem*: Penitential Experience in the Central Middle Ages," in *A New History of Penance*, ed. Abigail Firey (Leiden: Brill, 2008), 201–18.
28. Thus the title of Marie-Dominique Chenu's lecture, *L'éveil de la conscience dans la civilisation médiévale* (Montreal: Institut d'études médiévales, 1969).
29. Little is known about Master Gratian of Bologna. His famous legal textbook, *Harmony of Discordant Canons*, was completed around 1140. It enjoyed a status in canon law comparable to the role that the *Book of Sentences* played in theology. For a summary of Gratian's presentation, see Joseph Goering, "The Scholastic Turn (1100–1500): Penitential Theology and Law in the Schools," in Firey, *New History of Penance*, 219–38, esp. 221–25.
30. Ibid., 227.
31. *Sentences*, book IV, dist. 17, chap. 4, nos. 1 and 2, 2:351.
32. Ibid., book IV, dist. 19, chap. 1, no. 3, 2:365.
33. Ibid., book IV, dist. 18, chap. 6, no. 3, 2:361.
34. Ibid., book IV, dist. 18, chap. 5, no. 5 and chap. 6, no. 1 (2:360–61).

35. Ibid., book IV, dist. 22, chap. 2, no. 4, 2:389.
36. Ibid., book IV, dist. 26, chap. 4, 2:419.
37. Ibid., book IV, dist. 26, chap. 5, no. 1, 2:419.
38. See ibid., book II, dist. 30, chap. 8, 2:499–dist. 31, chap. 7, 2:510.
39. This is the position Hans Zeimentz takes in his study of the treatment of marriage in early scholasticism; see his *Ehe nach der Lehre der Frühscholastik* (Düsseldorf: Patmos-Verlag, 1973), 64–65.
40. Ibid., 238.
41. The new theology of history of the thirteenth century was the topic of Joseph Ratzinger's *Habilitationsschrift*; see *The Theology of History in St. Bonaventure*, trans. Zachary Hayes (Chicago: Franciscan Herald Press, 1971).
42. John Paul Vandenakker, *Small Christian Communities and the Parish: An Ecclesiological Analysis of the North American Experience* (Kansas City, MO: Sheed & Ward, 1994), 17.
43. On the status and development of marriage in medieval society, see Walter Prevenier and Thérèse de Hemptinne, art. "Ehe (in der Gesellschaft des Mittelalters)," in *Lexikon des Mittelalters*, 3:1635–40.
44. See *Sentences*, book IV, dist. 36, chap. 2, 2:474.
45. See ibid., book IV, dist. 30, chap. 3, nos. 2 and 3, 2:441.
46. Ibid., book IV, dist. 27, chap. 2, 2:422. In my book, *Peter Lombard*, 176, I mistranslated a crucial phrase in this definition. Giulio Silano's translation (cited in note 6) avoids the mistake (see *Sentences*, 4:161).
47. See *Sentences*, book IV, dist. 39, chap. 2, 2:484–87.
48. Ibid., book IV, dist. 28, chap. 3, no. 2, 2:435.
49. Ibid., book IV, dist. 27, chap. 3, 2:422.
50. Ibid., book IV, dist. 26, chap. 6, no. 1, 2:419–20.
51. See note 13.
52. On the status of magisterial authority in early scholasticism, one may read the fine study by Cédric Giraud, *Per verba magistri. Anselme de Laon et son école au xiie siècle* (Turnhout: Brepols, 2010). I have reviewed this book in *Speculum* 88 (2013): 520–21.

5

Aquinas on the Sacramental Life

MATTHEW LEVERING

Thomas was a master in theology (Magister in Sacra Pagina) at the University of Paris, engaged in the tasks of teaching (primarily commenting on Sacred Scripture), leading public disputations, and preaching.

Thomas Aquinas was born circa 1225 in the castle of Roccasecca. His parents were of noble lineage, and were kin to the Emperors Henry VI and Frederick II. As a young boy, he was sent to the care of the monks at the Benedictine monastery at Monte Cassino, where he displayed an unusual precocity in intellectual and spiritual matters, not to mention a mastery of the liberal arts. Around 1236 he began study in the University of Naples, where he became acquainted with the nascent Order of Preachers. Despite the attempts of his aristocratic family (two of his brothers were soldiers of Frederick's army) to dissuade him from a life of voluntary poverty, he joined the Dominican order in the early 1240s. In fact, at his mother's behest, Thomas's brothers kidnapped him and held him under house arrest, even tempting him by, as legend has it, introducing into his chamber prostitutes, whom he chased away with a firebrand. Undeterred, Thomas was allowed to return to Naples and pursue the religious life among the friars, among whom he studied the works of Aristotle, recently reintroduced to the Latin West through the work of Arabic commentators and translators, the *Sentences* of Peter Lombard, and the Holy Scriptures.

In the first of several sojourns in Paris, Thomas came under the tutelage of the eminent Dominican thinker Albertus Magnus, with whom he traveled in 1248 to establish a new studium generale in Köln. His early academic life was taken up, as was typical, with lecturing on the Lombard's *Sentences*, then the classic textbook of medieval theology, and on the Scriptures. From 1252 until his death in 1274, Thomas produced a range of works extraordinary in both number and ingenuity that display a mind of the highest conceivable order, brilliance, and devotion to Christ's Church. These include the two great Summae: the *Summa Contra Gentiles*, and his crowning achievement, the *Summa Theologiae*, left unfinished at the time of his death. Among his many other works are commentaries on several Old Testament books, on the Pauline epistles and two gospels, numerous commentaries on works of Aristotle, a commentary on Lombard's *Sentences*, *Quaestiones* on truth, evil, the virtues, and others, the liturgy for the Feast of Corpus Christi, and other works far too numerous to mention.

According to tradition, in December 1273, while en route to the Council of Lyons, called to resolve some theological disputes between the Eastern and Western churches, Thomas experienced a vision of such overwhelming power that he resolved never again to write another word, declaring everything he had written as "so much straw" compared to what he had seen. It was in fact a vision that ultimately cost him his life, for he became increasingly debilitated, and by January 1274 he was no longer able to travel, and died in the Cistercian monastery at Fossanova on 7 March. After a series of controversies regarding the interpretation of some of his theses, he was canonized in 1323, and later declared, by Pius V in 1567, a "doctor of the universal church." His feast is celebrated on 28 January.

Introduction

In accord with his Pauline understanding of the Church as Christ's Body, Aquinas conceives of the sacraments as a unified "organism" whose purpose is the healing and deification of individual and social life through participation in Christ's sacrificial mission. Ascended to the right hand of the Father, Jesus unites us to his salvific Pasch (his death, Resurrection, and Ascension) through his teachings and sacraments, which we receive in the Holy Spirit. The sacraments befit our nature as rational animals called to be united with the holy Trinity. Rather than serving an individualistic notion of salvation or a privatized notion of the Church, the sacraments heal and perfect humans individually and socially, drawing every area of our lives into the movement of deification. This can be seen most clearly in the Eucharist, where Christ makes his sacrificial Passion present sacramentally so that the community of believers comes to share in his perfect act of love and worship.

Since the sacraments must be understood in light of Aquinas's entire theology of the salvation wrought by Christ, I begin this chapter by examining Aquinas's reasons for the fittingness of Christ's Passion and Ascension, since it is from the right hand of the Father that Christ, through the Holy Spirit, sends his sacramental gifts upon the Church. I emphasize that Aquinas contemplates these mysteries of Christ's life—his Passion and Ascension—always with the Church in view. For Aquinas, the Church's sacramental mediation of the saving power of his Cross is always envisioned by Christ.[1] Yet, Aquinas makes clear that Christ never cedes his primacy to the Church but instead retains his active headship in the entirety of the Church's mission.[2] After examining why Aquinas considers that Christ's Passion and Ascension should consistently be understood in reference to the Church, I then turn explicitly to the sacraments as a central way in which Christ enfolds his Church within his salvific Pasch.

Christ's Mission and Ours: Why Sacraments Are Needed

Why did God redeem us by sending his innocent Son to die freely for our sins? Aquinas's answer tightly connects Christ's mission with ours—and thus with the Church and the sacraments. The way that God redeemed us is supremely fitting because it corresponds to what we need for following Christ on his passage into eternal life through self-giving love. From this perspective, Aquinas gives five reasons for the fittingness of the bloody way in which God redeemed the human race.

First and foremost, Christ's Passion reveals the love of God for us. Aquinas observes that "man knows thereby how much God loves him, and is thereby stirred to love Him in return, and herein lies the perfection of human salvation."[3] In his Passion, Christ fully reveals God to be love and thereby inspires our mission of love. The second reason is that Christ thereby showed us how to live in a holy manner. Aquinas notes that Christ "set us an example of obedience, humility, constancy, justice, and the other virtues displayed in the Passion, which are requisite for man's salvation."[4] Aquinas's reasoning here follows that of the entire New Testament, but he cites in particular 1 Peter 2:21, "For to this you have been called, because Christ also suffered for you, leaving you an example, that you should follow in his steps." Christ's mission reveals to us our mission: we "have been called" to "follow in his steps."

Aquinas's third reason has to do with the way in which Christ's mission fuels ours. By his Passion, Christ merited a glorious reward; and since he merited for all the members of his Mystical Body, he merited this reward for us. The fourth reason is that the revelation of God's love in Christ's Passion makes us "all the more bound to refrain from sin"; in this regard, Aquinas quotes Paul's exhortation to the Corinthians, "you were bought with a price. So glorify God in your body" (1 Cor. 6:20).[5] Last, the fifth reason is that "it redounded to man's greater dignity, that as man was overcome and deceived by the devil, so also it should be a man that should overthrow the devil; and as man deserved death, so a man by dying should vanquish death."[6] The point here is that God includes humanity in his mission to save humanity from sin. God works through the human soul and flesh of Jesus. The fact that humans have a mission is not negligible: in Christ, God gives us a part in our own salvation.

To sum up these five reasons for the fittingness of the Cross of Christ as the mode of our salvation: Love is the very center of everything, and Christ not only reveals God's superabundant love for us, but also enables us to turn away from sin, to follow him by imitating his example of perfect holiness, to rejoice that our human nature is included in so great a victory, and to share in Christ's reward that otherwise we could not have obtained. The point is that the Cross always has in view our participation in it as the Church.

As Aquinas writes, therefore, "Christ's action is our instruction."[7] He says this in the context of a discussion of Christ's manner of life, and he relates it in particular to preaching (Christ's and that of his disciples). Christ preached to the Jewish people as their Messiah.[8] But by his Cross, he became king of the Gentiles as well. Aquinas interprets Philippians 2:8–11 as speaking of this extension of Christ's kingship. Christ humbled himself even to death on a Cross, and in reward "God has highly exalted him and bestowed on him the name which is above every name, that at the name of Jesus every knee should bow, in heaven and on earth and under the earth, and every tongue confess that Jesus Christ is Lord, to the glory of God the Father" (Phil. 2:8–11).[9] The mission of the ascended Christ is not only to the people of Israel, among whom Christ spent his earthly life, but to the whole world.

As the risen and ascended Lord, Jesus calls humanity to himself, to an existence with the Father through the Holy Spirit, in a life of perpetual praise. Jesus's Ascension to the right hand of the Father reminds us that we are made for a spiritual communion that far exceeds what we can experience here and now. The ascended Jesus strengthens our faith, which is a faith in things unseen. In this regard Aquinas quotes Jesus's words in John 16:29, "Blessed are those who have not seen and yet believe."[10] Jesus's Ascension should also increase our hope, because we are made to dwell with God. Aquinas again quotes the Gospel of John, this time John 14:3, where Jesus tells his disciples, "When I go and prepare a place for you, I will come again and will take you to myself, that where I am you may be also."[11] Jesus's Ascension draws our love toward himself and the Father and thereby helps us not to cleave to the things of this world. In this vein, Paul instructs the Colossians to "seek the things that are above, where Christ is, seated at the right hand of God. Set your minds on things that are above, not on things that are on earth" (Col. 3:1–2).[12] Christ sends his Holy Spirit to lead our minds and hearts to the "things that are above."

At the right hand of the Father, says Aquinas, the ascended Jesus does three things: he opens the way, as the head of his Mystical Body, for us to join him; he "lives to make intercession" (Heb. 7:25) for us as the true high priest who has entered the divine sanctuary; and he "[sends] down gifts upon men."[13] But what kind of gifts are these? Aquinas explains that the ascended Christ sends down gifts of grace, the grace of the Holy Spirit.[14] It is these gifts of grace that establish our diverse missions in the Church. Aquinas cites Ephesians 4:10, "He who descended is he who also ascended far above all the heavens, that he might fill all things." In this passage from Ephesians, Paul goes on to say that Christ's gifts, by which he fills all things, are our missions that build up the Body of Christ. Paul states,

> And his gifts were that some should be apostles, some prophets, some evangelists, some pastors and teachers, for the equipment of the saints, for the work of ministry, for building up the body of Christ, until we all attain to the unity of the faith and of the knowledge of the Son of God, to mature manhood to the measure of the stature of the fullness of Christ. (Eph. 4:11–13)

By the gifts of grace sent by the ascended Christ through his Spirit, "we are to grow up in every way into him who is the head, into Christ, from whom the whole body, joined and knit together by every joint with which it is supplied, when each part is working properly, makes bodily growth and upbuilds itself in love" (Eph. 4:15–16). Christ cleanses and sanctifies the Church sacramentally, "by the washing of water with the word" (Eph. 5:26).[15]

This extension of Christ's salvific mission to the whole world is accomplished through his apostles and through all believers, as Christ enables us to participate in his mission and thereby to work out our salvation (won by Christ) in imitation of his love. In this participation, we do not of course become equal to Christ. This participation has various dimensions.

First, there is the extension of Christ's salvific mission to the whole world first with respect to Christ's prophetic mission—namely, his teaching. Christ's teaching, Aquinas says, was uniquely powerful and inexhaustibly rich in meaning. Aquinas quotes Matthew 7:29, "for he [Jesus] taught them as one who had authority, and not as their scribes"; and John 21:25, "But there are also many other things which Jesus did; were every one of them to be written, I suppose that the world itself could not contain the books that would be written." As Aquinas explains, "If Christ had committed his doctrine to writing, men would have had no deeper thought of his doctrine than that which appears on the surface of the writing."[16] Instead, Christ imprinted his doctrine in the minds and hearts of his hearers, especially his disciples. In Aquinas's view, this mediation of Christ's teaching (through the Church's mission) is more suitable than if Christ's teaching reached everyone "immediately," that is, without mediation.[17]

Why so? It would seem that if everyone heard Christ's teaching directly, without the mediation of the Church's mission (and thus without needing preachers or priests), everyone could be assured of hearing the correct teaching in its fullness. But in fact the mediation of Christ's revelatory mission is precisely what makes the Church, as willed by Christ, to be the Church.[18] Christ communicates himself not only in his earthly ministry, but also by allowing each of us to have a mission of proclamation to others.[19] Thus Christ's apostolic "members," inspired by the Spirit, write the texts of the New Testament. Guided by the Spirit, the successors of the apostles—the Catholic episcopacy—assemble the canonical books of Scripture, debate and define the doctrine of the Church. We learn about Christian faith through hearing the testimony of Christ's members, both priest and lay.

The Sacraments of Jesus Christ

Second, there is our sharing in Christ's priestly mission, his mission of sanctifying. This occurs through the sacraments. The sacraments that the ascended Christ bestows are bodily signs whose intention is made known by words.[20] Aquinas defines sacraments as signs not simply of any sacred thing, but of a sacred or "holy thing insofar as it makes us holy."[21] The sacraments that Christ institutes—the sacraments of the New Law—unite us to Christ by making us holy.[22] These sacraments cause and foster the life of grace in us, in a range of ways that accord with the missions that God has given us.[23]

For three reasons Aquinas considers that the bodily mode of the sacraments is the most fitting way of communicating grace to human beings—that is to say, of the ascended Christ giving us his gifts.

The first reason is that sacraments fit with our historical and corporeal mode of life. In particular, we learn not in a spiritually direct manner, as angels do, but in a manner that is mediated by our senses. Human nature, Aquinas observes, "has to be led by things corporeal and sensible to things spiritual and intelligible."[24] God therefore enriches us spiritually in a manner that fits with our nature.

Second, as fallen creatures, we tend to cleave to created things rather than to God. Aquinas reasons, then, that God fittingly gives us grace through bodily sacraments because "the healing remedy should be given to a man so as to reach the part affected by disease."[25]

Third, we are accustomed to undertaking bodily actions as part of everything that we do, including worship, and so it is helpful for us to receive Christ's gifts sacramentally.

Aquinas describes the sacraments as ordered to healing us from sin and perfecting us so that we come to share in the divine life. Since these things are precisely what Christ's Passion accomplished, "the sacraments of the Church derive their power specially from Christ's Passion, the virtue [or power] of which is in a manner united to us by our receiving the sacraments."²⁶ When Aquinas treats baptism, for example, he connects it with Christ's Passion through various biblical texts, including Romans 6:3: "Do you not know that all of us who have been baptized into Christ Jesus were baptized into his death?" He pairs such sacramental texts with others that emphasize faith, such as Romans 3:24–25 and Ephesians 3:17. The reception of the sacraments does not bear spiritual fruit without faith: "the power of the sacraments which is ordained unto the remission of sins is derived principally from faith in Christ's Passion."²⁷ Our mission in Christ is thus constituted by faith and the sacraments, not by one to the exclusion of the other.

In spelling out sacramentally our mission in Christ, Aquinas notes that "spiritual life has a certain conformity with the life of the body."²⁸ In the life of the body, we grow and thrive as individuals within societies. There are no pure individuals, since humans are made for social life. The sacraments that correspond to human perfection in society are holy orders and marriage. Holy orders gives certain members of Christ's Body the "power to rule the community and to exercise public acts," and especially "to consecrate the body and blood of Christ."²⁹ This power has its center in the Eucharist, and so it is power rooted in sharing in Christ's Passion. Ordained priests are called not simply to provide order to the Christian community in an extrinsic way, but to root that order intrinsically in Christ's sacrificial Passion and the Church's Eucharistic participation in it. The sacrifice that priests offer throughout the Church's generations is none other than Christ's sacrifice (sacramentally represented). So, Aquinas is not denying the observation in Hebrews that Christ "has no need, like those high priests [of Israel], to offer sacrifices daily, first for his own sins and then for those of the people; he did this once for all when he offered up himself" (Heb. 7:27).³⁰

The sacrament of marriage is the second sacrament that pertains to human perfection in society. How does marriage relate to the Church's mission of extending Christ's revelatory and salvific mission in the world? Aquinas remarks that marriage is a natural institution; the sacrament brings this natural institution within the sphere of Christ and the Holy Spirit.³¹ The sacrament of marriage enables the couple to live out their mission in Christ in three ways in particular: the "sacrament," children, and fidelity. Aquinas calls these three elements the "goods" of marriage, and he identifies the most essential good as the "sacrament." The good of the "sacrament" consists in marriage's indissolubility and the other ways in which marriage mirrors the permanent union of Christ and the Church. The central biblical texts here are Matthew 19:6, where Jesus says, "So they are no longer two but one. What therefore God has joined together, let no man put asunder"; and Ephesians 5:31–32, "'For this reason a man shall leave his father and mother and be joined to his wife, and the two shall become one' [Gen. 2:24]. This is a great mystery, and I mean in reference to Christ and the church." Witnessing in the world to the union of Christ and the Church is thus the primary mission of sacramental marriage. Husbands must give up their lives in loving (Eucharistic) service to their wives, and vice versa.[32]

The Church and the Christian family are public, social manifestations of Christ's ongoing mission in the world. The five sacraments that correspond to the perfection of the individual begin with the fact that in bodily life, we find generation, growth, and nourishment. These three aspects correspond in the sacramental life to baptism, confirmation, and the Eucharist. How so?

First, we are born into Christ through baptism, "by the washing of regeneration" (Titus 3:5). Baptism gives us a new birth and makes of us a new creation, able to share in the Church's worship and called to grow to maturity in Christ. Second, the sacrament of confirmation helps us in the process of growing into maturity in Christ. It does this by sealing us with the Holy Spirit, in a manner that strengthens the healing and elevating grace that we receive at baptism. Here Aquinas quotes the risen Jesus's words to his disciples before Pentecost: "I send the promise of my Father upon you; but stay in the city, until you are clothed with power from on high" (Luke 24:49). Confirmation, then, is our experience of a Pentecostal grace, strengthening us to go forth and evangelize as full members of the Body of Christ. Third, through the Eucharist we are daily nourished in Christ, so as to be strong in faith, hope, and love: "Unless you eat the flesh of the Son of man and drink his blood, you have no life in you; he who eats my flesh and drinks my blood has eternal life, and I will raise him up at the last day" (John 6:53–54).

Just as there are sacraments that correspond (in the spiritual life) to the body's generation, growth, and nourishment, so are there two sacraments that mirror our need to be restored to health from bodily illness. In this way, Christ applies the power of his Cross to give us, indeed, the full power of new birth and new creation. The sacrament of penance restores our spiritual health. Aquinas cites the plea from the psalm, "heal me, for I have sinned against you [God]!" (Ps. 41:4). The sacrament of extreme unction or anointing of the sick can be likened to the way in which, once our disease has been healed, we still need to be nursed back to health by diet and exercise. Extreme unction "removes the remainder of sin, and prepares man for final glory."[33] It underscores that in Christ, we are saved as body-soul unities. Like Christ, we are anointed (by Christ's own power) for our final passage.

Thus, through the sacraments that give us spiritual life and strength in Christ, we share ever more deeply in Christ's mission for the salvation of the world. We receive the grace of the Holy Spirit in a manner that fully accords with our embodied and historical condition, so much so that the sacraments imitate the central aspects of the generation and perfection of our bodies. Aquinas also points out that since human history is a history of sin (and not only a history of the development and flourishing of individual and social life), it is fitting that each of the sacraments applies the power of Christ's Passion to the healing of sin. The ascended Christ provides the sacraments not least to heal us from the defect of sin:

> Baptism is intended as a remedy against the absence of spiritual life; Confirmation, against the infirmity of soul found in those of recent birth; the Eucharist, against the soul's proneness to sin; Penance, against actual sin committed after baptism; Extreme Unction, against the remainders of sins.[34]

Even holy orders and marriage fight against sin: holy orders strengthen the Church "against divisions in the community" and marriage serves "as a remedy against concupiscence in the individual, and against the decrease in numbers that results from death."[35]

Aquinas considers that the Eucharist is the greatest sacrament. The Eucharist contains Christ, and therefore makes present even now, in the Church, God's revelation in Christ.[36] The Eucharistic liturgy, of course, includes the proclamation and preaching of the gospel, and so Aquinas does not thereby demote the imitation of Christ through preaching. The fact that Christ waited until his Last Supper to institute the Eucharist shows its centrality, "because last words, chiefly such as are spoken by departing friends, are committed most deeply to memory; since then especially affection for friends is more enkindled, and the things which affect us most are impressed the deepest in the soul."[37] The Eucharist also fulfills God's earlier signs or sacraments, including Melchizedek's offering of bread and wine, the sacrifice of atonement offered annually at Yom Kippur, the manna, and the Paschal Lamb.

Fueled by the Eucharist, the historical mission of Christians is an eschatological mission, one that already shares in the ascended Christ and that propels us toward the perfect communion that we will have with him in eternal life. Aquinas notes that the bread and water that Elijah miraculously receives from an angel of God, and that enable Elijah "on the strength of that food" to journey "forty days and forty nights to Horeb the mount of God" (1 Kgs. 19:8), prefigure the sacrament of the Eucharist and its eschatological power. Other effects of the Eucharist in those who receive it worthily have to do with the forgiveness of sin. Desire for the Eucharist is part of the experience of the grace of conversion. God turns us from sin and justifies us in Christ, and in this experience we come to desire deeper union with Christ.

Most important, Christ works through the Eucharist to increase our fervor of charity, and thereby to turn us away from venial sins and to heal the spiritual damage they cause in us. The Eucharist strengthens our "spiritual life, as spiritual food and spiritual medicine," and it thereby strengthens our charity and our ability to resist sin in the future.[38] Since the Eucharist is a sacrament-sacrifice—a real sharing in Christ's sacrificial Passion by sacramental representation of Christ's Passion—the offering of the Eucharist benefits all people "who are united with this sacrament through faith and charity."[39] The liturgy of the Eucharist is the supreme act by which the Church shares in Christ's mission for the sake of the salvation of the world.

Conclusion

For Aquinas, the sacraments are Christ's way of uniting the people of God to the healing and transforming power of the Cross and Resurrection. The first half of this chapter, therefore, addressed Christ's mission of salvation and how Christians are called to participate actively in it. If there were no need for mediation, no possibility of sharing in Christ's mission, then the Church would have no real role, and historical time after Christ would be deprived of real meaning. Aquinas explains that "by his Resurrection Christ entered upon an immortal and incorruptible life. But whereas our dwelling-place is one of generation and corruption, the heavenly place is one of incorruption."[40] It would have made a mockery of human history to have the risen Christ continually present in his incorrupt flesh in Jerusalem or Rome. In his Body the Church, however, Christ is intimately present in our world of generation and corruption, even though he has ascended in his glorified humanity (see Matt. 28:20). He is present most importantly through his sacraments.

The sacraments empower us, by the grace of the Holy Spirit, to share in the working out of our salvation. Thus the second half of the chapter dealt with how the sacraments are a fitting way of drawing us into Christ as individuals and a communal body, so that we are born into Christ and grow in Christ, being healed and strengthened for our mission of evangelization and our passage to eternal life. By his Passion, Jesus offers a sacrifice of perfect praise to the Father in the Holy Spirit. The sacraments unite us to Jesus's self-offering so that we, too, can offer his perfect praise.

As befits Jesus's status as the Messiah of Israel, the sacraments of the Church have their roots in God's covenantal relationship with Israel, which is defined by the need for right worship of God. In a passage noted by Aquinas, Paul tells the Corinthians, "I want you to know, brethren, that our fathers were all under the cloud, and all passed through the sea, and all were baptized into Moses in the cloud and in the sea, and all ate the same supernatural food and all drank the same supernatural drink. For they drank from the supernatural Rock which followed them, and the Rock was Christ" (1 Cor. 10:1–4).[41] Aquinas also pays attention to Hebrews 10:1, which states that "the law has but a shadow of the good things to come instead of the true form of these realities."[42] Are the sacraments of the Church, then, our final end?

Of course, the answer is no. Aquinas is well aware that the new covenant itself, despite its greatness, merely foreshadows "the glory to come, which is not yet revealed."[43] In accord with 1 Corinthians 13:12, "For now we see in a mirror dimly, but then face to face," Aquinas affirms that "as the first state [the Old Law] is figurative and imperfect in comparison with the state of the Gospel, so is the present state figurative and imperfect in comparison with the heavenly state."[44] To appreciate fully Aquinas's sacramental theology, therefore, we must recognize that it is thoroughly eschatological, ordered to the consummation of all things in the new creation.

Indeed, from this eschatological perspective, the sacraments should inform all of Christian teaching. *Sacra doctrina* is "a sacred *scientia* learned through revelation," taught by Christ Jesus who "showed unto us in his own person the way of truth, whereby we may attain to the bliss of eternal life by rising again."[45] To study Christ and the sacraments cannot be separated from this purpose of the attainment of eternal life. Since it is the Eucharist that "bestows on us the power of coming unto glory," we must study the Eucharist (and the other sacraments) for the same reason that we liturgically consume the Eucharist: deification.[46]

NOTES

1. Can this be held even in light of the historical development of the sacraments in the life of the Church, including the gradual affirmation of seven distinct sacraments? Here Colman O'Neill points us in the right direction:

    It is only if Christ is tacitly assumed to be a purely historical figure of the past, one who is no longer exercising saving mediation within the church, that the question of the "institution" of the sacraments will be understood in a juridical fashion and the attempt will be made to make its answer depend entirely on historical research. That the sacraments are instituted by Christ is, first of all, a Christological statement about his unique mediation. Its historical implications cannot, in every case, be documented by a specific or detailed ordinance given by Christ. Nor will it do to make a verbal distinction between the church as "fundamental sacrament" and its manifestation in the particular sacraments, with the implication that purely historical developments in the liturgy receive "ratification" from Christ. This will not do because the church is the sacrament of the life of the Blessed Trinity and not a continuation of the Incarnation, disposing of an authority that belongs to Christ alone. (Colman E. O'Neill OP, *Sacramental Realism: A General Theory of the Sacraments* [Chicago: Midwest Theological Forum, 1998], 73)

    The key is the "present mediatorial activity of the risen Christ" (ibid., 70). O'Neill adds,

    There was no really systematic attempt made before the twelfth century in the Western church to draw up a full list of seven sacraments. This was precisely because it required a very considerable effort of reflection on the symbolic structure of church life before the community's awareness of the

presence within it of the risen Lord could be scrutinized and made the subject of more precise conceptual distinctions. (Ibid., 71–72)
2. O'Neill's words in this regard should be underscored:
In sacramental practice the salient aspect of faith that is brought to light in prayer is the church's total dependence on Christ, the mediator who holds from the Father the mission of sending the Spirit on mankind to draw it away from sin and into the mystery of the Trinity. In a living refusal of all forms of Pelagianism, the church affirms in the sacraments that faith itself is a gift of the Spirit, awakened by the word of the gospel in the heart of the individual. Because there is faith, there is worship in union with Christ, and a pleading for grace to preserve the union. (Ibid., 208)
3. Aquinas, *Summa Theologiae*, part III, question 46, article 3 (hereafter cited as *Summa*). I employ the 1920 translation of the Fathers of the English Dominican Province, reprinted as Thomas Aquinas, *Summa Theologica*, 5 vols. (Westminster, MD: Christian Classics, 1981). Romanus Cessario comments that
the love and obedience of the Incarnate Son inaugurates the new dispensation. Christ reveals the perfection of the beatitude that he himself teaches as constitutive of the new law: "Blessed are those who are persecuted for righteousness' sake, for theirs is the kingdom of heaven" (Matt. 5:10). . . . In sum, the heart of Aquinas' salvation theology lies in the loving service of a priest-Son to God. (Romanus Cessario OP, "Aquinas on Christian Salvation," in *Aquinas on Doctrine: A Critical Introduction*, ed. Thomas G. Weinandy OFM Cap., Daniel A. Keating, and John P. Yocum [London: T&T Clark, 2004], 117–37, at 124–25)
See also Romanus Cessario OP, *The Godly Image: Christ and Salvation in Catholic Thought from Anselm to Aquinas* (Petersham, MA: St. Bede's Publications, 1990).
4. *Summa*, III, q. 46, a. 3. The breadth of virtues here would expand and enrich the argument of Michael Gorman's valuable *Cruciformity: Paul's Narrative Spirituality of the Cross* (Grand Rapids, MI: Eerdmans, 2001).
5. See, for further discussion, Karl Olav Sandnes, *Belly and Body in the Pauline Epistles* (Cambridge: Cambridge University Press, 2002).
6. *Summa*, III, q. 46, a. 3. For background see Saint Augustine, *The Trinity*, trans. Edmund Hill OP, ed. John E. Rotelle OSA (Brooklyn, NY: New City Press, 1991), book IV, chap. 3.
7. *Summa*, III, q. 40, a. 1, ad 3. See Richard Schenk OP, "*Omnis Christi Actio Nostra Est Instructio*: The Deeds and Sayings of Jesus as Revelation in the View of Thomas Aquinas," in *La doctrine de la revelation divine de saint Thomas d'Aquin*, ed. Leo J. Elders SVD (Vatican City: Libreria Editrice Vaticana, 1990), 104–31.
8. See *Summa*, III, q. 42, a. 1.
9. For further analysis, see my chapter on Aquinas's use of Philippians 2:5–11 in my forthcoming *Paul in the Summa Theologiae*.
10. *Summa*, III, q. 57, a. 1, ad 3.

11. Ibid.
12. Ibid. The historical-critical debates over who wrote such letters as Colossians are best left to biblical scholars (who seem to be evenly divided regarding Colossians). For background, see Margaret Y. MacDonald, *Colossians and Ephesians* (Collegeville, MN: Liturgical Press, 2008), 6–9; N. T. Wright, *The Epistles of Paul to the Colossians and to Philemon: An Introduction and Commentary* (Grand Rapids, MI: Eerdmans, 1986), 31–34. Wright helpfully cautions,

> We are able to chart changes in (say) Calvin's mind by studying the differences between successive editions of the *Institutes*, and it might appear easy to do the same with Paul and his letters. But this appearance is deceptive. The greater historical distance between us and him; the very small amount of relevant comparative material; the "occasional" nature of the letters—all these warn us to be on our guard against over-hasty conclusions. (Wright, *Epistles of Paul to the Colossians and to Philemon*, 33)

MacDonald argues that Colossians 3:1 evidences a realized eschatology, in which believers in the present are already united with the ascended and enthroned Christ. See MacDonald, *Colossians and Ephesians*, 130–33.
13. *Summa*, III, q. 57, a. 6.
14. For the bond between Aquinas's Christology, sacramental theology, and pneumatology, see Kimberly Hope Belcher, *Efficacious Engagement: Sacramental Participation in the Trinitarian Mystery* (Collegeville, MN: Liturgical Press, 2011), 160–62, although Belcher argues, mistakenly in my view (even if understandably given Aquinas's way of speaking about grace), that Aquinas's theology of sacramental "signification and causality" is not "as pneumatologically driven as one might wish" (ibid., 162). Belcher's theology of the Holy Spirit needs a much clearer elaboration: see ibid., 181, where she summarizes that

> [t]he Spirit is fissure, fracture, and generating space in the world and in God. He unites what has been divided—most shockingly spirit and body—and by this highlights the differentiation of what has been made whole. The infinite distance between Son and Father, he becomes also the generative distance between Christ and the church, between the world and God. This distance is essential to recognize difference, but difference is only recognized by being bridged. The Holy Spirit unites Son and Father in love by being the generative distance of the Son's procession from the Father. The Holy Spirit is the givenness of the Son, not only in his being given for the world, but even in his being given for himself. The Holy Spirit is the result of the generation of the Son, but the unity of Father and Son is not additive but results in the element of surprise: the Spirit, more than any expectation, is able to fracture every boundary and unite across any divide. In the incarnation, the Spirit is the unity of body and soul, the meetinghouse for the divine and the human. In the church, the Spirit is the givenness of the Gift of Christ, the givenness of the divine nature.

15. For the baptismal reference, see MacDonald, *Colossians and Ephesians*, 328.
16. *Summa*, III, q. 42, a. 4.

17. For discussion see Leo J. Elders SVD, "Aquinas on Holy Scripture as the Medium of Divine Revelation," in *La doctrine de la revelation divine de saint Thomas d'Aquin*, 132–52; J. Mark Armitage, "Why Didn't Jesus Write a Book? Aquinas on the Teaching of Christ," *New Blackfriars* 89 (2008): 337–53; Serge-Thomas Bonino OP, "The Role of the Apostles in the Communication of Revelation according to the *Lectura super Ioannem* of St. Thomas Aquinas," in *Reading John with St. Thomas Aquinas: Theological Exegesis and Speculative Theology*, ed. Michael Dauphinais and Matthew Levering (Washington, DC: Catholic University of America Press, 2005), 318–46.

18. Indeed, Richard Hays observes that for Paul, "The apocalyptic turn of the ages has created a new Spirit-inspired ministry," so that "Paul and his contemporaries are among those who have turned to the Lord and had the veil lifted" (Richard B. Hays, *The Moral Vision of the New Testament: Community, Cross, New Creation: A Contemporary Introduction to New Testament Ethics* [New York: HarperCollins, 1996], 24). Indeed, "Paul's defense of his own apostolic ministry turns out to be inextricably fused with the proclamation that the church community is a sneak preview of God's ultimate redemption of the world" (ibid., 24). Although the eschatological age has in this sense arrived in "the Spirit-empowered transforming effects of the gospel," nonetheless in another sense the eschaton is still awaited, because in the present time the Church "participates in the suffering of Christ" (ibid., 24, 25). The question then is to what degree we can expect to receive the truth of Christ, and the fullness of life in Christ, from the Church. Hays states that

    Paul's eschatology locates the Christian community within a cosmic, apocalyptic frame of reference. The church community is God's eschatological beachhead, the place where the power of God has invaded the world. All's Paul's ethical judgments are worked out in this context. The dialectical character of Paul's eschatological vision (already / not yet) provides a critical framework for moral discernment: he is sharply critical not only of the old age that is passing away but also of those who claim unqualified participation already in the new age. To live faithfully in the time between the times is to walk a tightrope of moral discernment, claiming neither too much nor too little for God's transforming power within the community of faith. (Ibid., 27)

    We know that we are still sinners. Does this mean that the Church, too, is sinfully weak in its participation in Christ's revelatory mission, so that the Church fundamentally obscures what it should have mediated? Given that the Church "is God's eschatological beachhead," we should expect that Christ's sending of the Holy Spirit ensures that the Church will not fail in its mediation of Christ's truth and grace, even though the sins of the Church's members make this mediation not as clear as it should be. The guidance of the Holy Spirit does not spare the Church, at any time in history, what Luke Timothy Johnson calls the "difficult and delicate process of disagreement, debate, and the discernment of Scripture" (Johnson, *The Acts of the Apostles* [Collegeville, MN: Liturgical Press, 1992], 16). But, while avoiding idealizing the eschatological community of the Church, we should also avoid domesticating or marginalizing it by supposing that it could carry out its eschatological mission while burdened, as a merely human institution would be, by an increasing weight of false teaching and practice. This problem plagues Johnson's *Scripture and Discernment: Decision Making in the Church* (Nashville, TN: Abingdon Press, 1996).

19. Bernd Wannenwetsch, in a discussion of holy orders and the male-only priesthood, rightly makes the point that all Christians, not only ordained priests, are called to the proclamation of the gospel: see Wannenwetsch, *Political Worship*, trans. Margaret Kohl (Oxford: Oxford University Press, 2004), 167–68. Wannenwetsch, however, rejects the significance of Christ's choosing of twelve males as his disciples. Catholics and Orthodox take Christ's deliberate choice very seriously, in part because of the role that sacramental representation plays in the Eucharist, the consecration of which is the central task of the ordained priest.

20. On the sacraments as the work of the ascended Christ, to whom we are personally united through the sacraments, see O'Neill, *Sacramental Realism*, 62, 72, 120–28, 215; Thomas G. Weinandy OFM Cap., "The Human Acts of Christ and the Acts That Are the Sacraments," in *Ressourcement Thomism: Sacred Doctrine, the Sacraments, and the Moral Life: Essays in Honor of Romanus Cessario, O.P.*, ed. Reinhard Hütter and Matthew Levering (Washington, DC: Catholic University of America Press, 2010), 150–68.

21. *Summa*, III, q. 60, a. 2. For a succinct discussion, see Belcher, *Efficacious Engagement*, 159.

22. The sacraments of the Mosaic Law, by contrast, are signs but not causes of grace (at least not direct causes of grace) according to Aquinas. For discussion, see John P. Yocum, "Sacraments in Aquinas," in Weinandy, Keating, and Yocum, *Aquinas on Doctrine*, 159–81, at 160–68. See also Benoît-Dominique de La Soujeole OP, "The Importance of the Definition of Sacraments as Signs," in Hütter and Levering, *Ressourcement Thomism*, 127–35.

23. See Bernhard Blankenhorn OP, "The Place of Romans 6 in Aquinas's Doctrine of Sacramental Causality: A Balance of History and Metaphysics," in Hütter and Levering, *Ressourcement Thomism*, 136–49; Bernhard Blankenhorn OP, "The Instrumental Causality of the Sacraments: Thomas Aquinas and Louis-Marie Chauvet," *Nova et Vetera* 4 (2006): 255–93. See also Liam G. Walsh OP, "The Divine and the Human in St. Thomas's Theology of the Sacraments," in *Ordo sapientiae et amoris: Image et message doctrinales*, ed. Carlos-Josaphat Pinto de Oliveira OP (Fribourg: Editions Universitaires, 1993), 321–52.

24. *Summa*, III, q. 61, a. 1.

25. Ibid., III, q. 61, a. 1.

26. Ibid., III, q. 62, a. 5. As A. N. Williams observes, Aquinas
    maintains that every sacrament makes the human person a participant in Christ's priesthood since every sacrament confers some effect of that priesthood (III.63,6 ad 1). Through the sacraments, then, one both participates in Christ and receives the benefits of Christ's priesthood, both of which are

deifying.... The sacraments themselves, then, are means, not just to sanctification in general, but of deification in particular. (Williams, *The Ground of Union: Deification in Aquinas and Palamas* [Oxford: Oxford University Press, 1999], 93)

27. *Summa*, III, q. 62, a. 5, ad 2. Given the role of faith, even people who lived before Christ or who have not heard of Christ can be united to his Passion, even simply by faith that God exists and providentially cares for us so as to reconcile us to himself (see Heb. 11:6). See ibid., II-II, q. 2, a. 7, ad 3.
28. Ibid., III, q. 65, a. 1.
29. Ibid., III, q. 65, a. 1; Suppl., q. 37, a. 5. For exploration of the priesthood in relation to the sacrament of penance, which helps to clarify the precise role of the ordained priesthood, see Thomas Joseph White OP, "The Priesthood Makes the Church: Ecclesial Communion and the Power of the Keys," *Nova et Vetera* 9 (2011): 209–36; Gilles Emery OP, "Reconciliation with the Church and Interior Penance: The Contribution of Thomas Aquinas on the Question of the *Res et Sacramentum* of Penance," in *Trinity, Church, and the Human Person: Thomistic Essays* (Naples, FL: Sapientia Press, 2009), 173–92.
30. See Mary Healy, "Christ's Priesthood and Christian Priesthood in the Letter to the Hebrews," *Nova et Vetera* 9 (2011): 395–410.
31. For discussion, see Joseph W. Koterski SJ, "Aquinas on the Sacrament of Marriage," in *Rediscovering Aquinas and the Sacraments: Studies in Sacramental Theology*, ed. Matthew Levering and Michael Dauphinais (Chicago: Hillenbrand Books, 2009), 102–13; Peter Kwasniewski, "St. Thomas on the Grandeur and Limitations of Marriage," *Nova et Vetera* 10 (2012): 415–36.
32. See Paul Gondreau, "The Redemption and Divinization of Human Sexuality through the Sacrament of Marriage: A Thomistic Approach," *Nova et Vetera* 10 (2012): 383–413.
33. *Summa*, III, q. 65, a. 1. See John F. Boyle, "Saint Thomas on the Anointing of the Sick (Extreme Unction)," in Levering and Dauphinais, *Rediscovering Aquinas and the Sacraments*, 76–84.
34. *Summa*, III, q. 65, a. 1. For a brief, helpful reflection on sin, see Jeremy Holmes, "Weight on the Lord: Sin as Burden in the New Testament and Beyond," *Nova et Vetera* 9 (2011): 123–31.
35. *Summa*, III, q. 65, a. 1.
36. See ibid., III, q. 65, a. 3.
37. Ibid., III, q. 73, a. 5.
38. Ibid., III, q. 79, a. 6. See Gilles Emery OP, "The Ecclesial Fruit of the Eucharist in St. Thomas Aquinas," in *Trinity, Church, and the Human Person*, 155–72.
39. *Summa*, III, q. 79, a. 7, ad 2. For a classic account of the Eucharist as sacrament-sacrifice, see Anscar Vonier OSB, *A Key to the Doctrine of the Eucharist* (Bethesda, MD: Zaccheus Press, 2003). See also Bruce D. Marshall, "The Whole Mystery of Our Salvation: Saint Thomas Aquinas on the Eucharist as Sacrifice," in Levering and Dauphinais, *Rediscovering Aquinas and the Sacraments*, 39–64; Richard Schenk

OP, "*Verum sacrificium* as the Fullness and Limit of Eucharistic Sacrifice in the Sacramental Theology of Thomas Aquinas," in Hütter and Levering, *Ressourcement Thomism*, 169–207. Underscoring the value of Aquinas's balance between negative and positive senses of sacrifice, Schenk addresses a criticism to Balthasar:

> Despite his attempt to thematize a theology of suffering that could better address the situation of humanity than had the best-known forms of transcendental theology, despite his keen sense of the need for salvation from above, Balthasar's divinization of suffering and sacrifice threatens to make suffering normative and thereby obscures its character as a *vitandum*. What had been thought to be God's antecedent, absolute, and unconditioned will for his and our complete happiness is replaced here by his fully originary desire for the beauty of suffering love, where the component of suffering is no longer merely tolerated and transformed but has been revealed as what constitutes the very Trinity itself. The sense that suffering ought not to be is obscured here. The anti-divine dimensions of literal sacrifice disappear behind the ultimate sanction. (Schenk, "*Verum sacrificium* as the Fullness and Limit of Eucharistic Sacrifice," 202–3)

40. *Summa*, III, q. 57, a. 1, ad 3.
41. Cf. I-II, q. 102, a. 2, *sed contra*; I-II, q. 102, a. 6; I-II, q. 103, a. 1. See also my "Readings on the Rock: Typological Exegesis in Contemporary Scholarship," *Modern Theology* 28 (2012): 707–31.
42. *Summa*, I-II, q. 101, a. 2; cf. I, q. 1, a. 10.
43. Ibid., I-II, q. 101, a. 2.
44. Ibid., I-II, q. 106, a. 4, ad 1. See also I-II, q. 103, a. 3 and III, q. 47, a. 2, ad 1 with regard to why Christians do not practice the Torah's laws regarding worship. Aquinas rejects Joachim of Fiore's view that the sacraments of the New Law will be displaced in history by the reign of the Holy Spirit. For discussion of Aquinas's critique of Joachim, see Henri de Lubac SJ, *La postérité spirituelle de Joachim de Flore*, vol. 1: *De Joachim à Schelling* (Paris: Éditions Lethielleux, 1979), 140–60. For further discussion of the topics treated in the present chapter, see my *Christ's Fulfillment of Torah and Temple: Salvation according to Thomas Aquinas* (Notre Dame, IN: University of Notre Dame Press, 2002) and my *Sacrifice and Community: Jewish Offering and Christian Eucharist* (Oxford: Blackwell, 2005).
45. *Summa*, I, q. 1, a. 1; III, Prologue.
46. Ibid., III, q. 79, a. 2, ad 1. At the conclusion of his "The Theology of Worship: St. Thomas," Avery Dulles SJ observes,

> Saint Thomas remains a valuable resource for situating worship within a theocentric, Christological, and ecclesial framework. Only if this is done can liturgy perform its healing and sanctifying task, bringing the Christian community together in union with its divine founder and preparing it for the perfect worship of the new Jerusalem. (Dulles, "The Theology of Worship: St. Thomas," in Levering and Dauphinais, *Rediscovering Aquinas and the Sacraments*, 1–13, at 13)

6

John Duns Scotus

RICHARD CROSS

John Duns Scotus (ca. 1266–1308) was the foremost philosopher-theologian of the medieval Franciscan order.[1] He was fiercely independent and highly original in both his theological and philosophical thought. But of course he had influences. His principal scholastic sources, for example, are earlier Franciscans (in particular Bonaventure), and the theologians of the twelfth century (in particular Richard of St. Victor). Of far greater intellectual significance for him, however, are the philosophers Aristotle and Avicenna. Among the Church Fathers, Augustine and John of Damascus are preeminent: but in this, Scotus is simply typical of his age. In any case, none of this earlier thought comes close to explaining the explosive intellectual novelty that is the philosophical theology of John Duns Scotus. He single-handedly set the agenda for almost all Franciscan (and subsequently Jesuit) theology in the Late Middle Ages and early modernity. Even thinkers who disagreed with him profoundly on questions of metaphysics—notably, William of Ockham—generally accepted his theological insights.

In philosophy, characteristic Scotist positions include an account of individuation via particular forms or thisnesses (*haecceities*); a defense of contra-causal freewill; a logical, not merely nomological or statistical, understanding of modalities (notions of possibility, necessity, and contingency); an understanding of the core concepts of metaphysics (*being, unity, goodness*) as univocal concepts, applying in the same sense across and outside the Aristotelian categories; strong epistemological empiricism grounded on systematic anti-skeptical arguments; a constructivist metaethic (such that many moral norms are determined merely by divine will); and an acceptance of the intellectual cognition of particulars (against Aristotelian accounts that restrict singular cognition to the senses). It is fair to say that in many ways he set the agenda for both rationalists and empiricists in early modern philosophy.

In theology, Scotus is notable for using accounts of sameness and identity that he holds to apply unproblematically in the created realm to clarify the doctrines of the Trinity and divine simplicity (his so-called "formal" distinction); for stressing the concrete individuality of Christ's human nature; for holding that justification at root consists simply in an extrinsic relation to the divine will; for defending the immaculate conception of Mary; and for defending the view that God's plan to become incarnate is independent of the Fall. As we shall see, Scotus's innovations in sacramental theology are less startling, and his position owes much to Bonaventure. But what is notable about it is the capacity of his metaphysics to accommodate seemingly intractable mysteries such as transubstantiation.

Introduction

Scotus's intense academic career lasted little more than a decade. In that time he commented on Peter Lombard's *Sentences* twice (first at Oxford—the *Ordinatio*—and then at Paris—the *Reportatio*, following his move from Oxford to Paris in or around 1302). (In addition we have an earlier version of the Oxford lectures for the first two books [the *Lectura*].) After he became doctor of theology at Paris, probably in 1305, he presided at one quodlibetal disputation, probably in 1306 or 1307. In addition, he wrote various sets of questions on Aristotelian logical works, as well as on the *Metaphysics* and *De anima*. None of these works was complete by the time of his death—probably at the age of forty-two—in Cologne, where Scotus had been moved to teach at that city's Franciscan *studium*. The works are all in greater or lesser states of disarray. And Scotus's tremendously supple and active mind was often more productive than systematic, making it difficult sometimes to piece together his final views on a particular matter, or even the sequence of the various views he proposed. But on some matters—most notably, many issues in metaphysics—he remained consistent and systematic; and, as far as I can see, sacramental theology is, in its small way, a case in point.

According to Scotus, the human condition makes it appropriate (*congruum*) that there be signs of God's activity.[2] In the time of the New

Covenant wayfaring humanity is in its closest state to beatitude. In this state, it consequently requires the most perfect signs of God's salvific activity.[3] The sacraments are such signs. They signify most appropriately the grace God confers through them. And the seven sacraments—baptism, Eucharist, confirmation, confession, unction, marriage, and ordination—correspond supernaturally to the seven requirements of natural life, individual and social: birth, nutrition, physical exercise, healing after illness, preparation for death, procreation, and the creation of spiritual leaders.[4] According to Scotus, citing the standard scriptural texts, these seven sacraments were instituted by Christ himself.[5]

In this chapter, I look at three features of Scotus's sacramental teaching in more detail: first, his account of the way in which the sacraments have a role in the causation of grace; second, his account of sacramental grace, and the indelible character given by three of the sacraments (baptism, confirmation, and ordination); third, his account of the Eucharist.

Sacramental Causality

Scotus's definition of "sacrament" weaves together several patristic themes: "A sacrament is a sensible sign, ordered to the salvation of the wayfaring human being, efficaciously signifying—by divine institution—the grace of God, or a gratuitous effect of God."[6] There is nothing much original about this. But the term "efficaciously" requires comment. In what sense are the sacraments "efficacious"—in what sense do they *cause* grace? One powerful tradition, represented in the thirteenth century most typically by Bonaventure, argues that the reception of a sacrament is no more than an *occasion* for a merely divine action.[7] On this view, the reception of a sacrament has no *causal* role in the divine gift of grace. There is another view in the thirteenth century too, best represented by Aquinas. On this view, God uses the sacraments in the process of imparting grace. The sacraments have some sort of causal role: they are *instrumental causes* of grace. Aquinas argues that if Bonaventure's view is correct, the sacraments are no more than signs of grace; they do not in any sense convey grace.[8]

Now, the medievals often analyze cause-effect relationships in terms of causal powers. An agent has certain active powers in virtue of which it can produce an effect; and the corresponding patient has certain passive powers in virtue of which it can be affected or effected. Aquinas believes that every member of a casual chain has active causal powers. Consistent with this, he believes that if the sacraments are instrumental causes of grace, then they must have certain active causal powers in virtue of which they can have a role in the process of conferring sacrament grace. He holds that such "instrumental" powers are caused by the motion of the principal agent, and presumably that they exist for only as long as the principal agent acts.[9] In the case of the sacraments, Aquinas is quite happy to claim that a supernatural power—the sort of power that could bring about a supernatural effect such as grace—could be given to a creature (in this case, to the sacrament).[10]

Scotus believes that Aquinas's view of sacramental causality is open to insuperable objections, and he much prefers the sort of occasionalist account defended by Bonaventure.[11] Scotus agrees with Aquinas that agents have casual powers. He also agrees with Aquinas that instrumental causes do not have intrinsic causal powers. Just like Aquinas, he believes that the causal powers in virtue of which an instrumental cause has a role in the production of an effect are caused in it by the motion of the principal agent.[12] But, against Aquinas, Scotus believes that it would be logically contradictory that a material object have a *supernatural* causal power. So not even God could give such an object a supernatural power. The reason is that a supernatural form cannot be extended to exist throughout a material agent; and any causal power of a material object must be so extended.[13] Worse still, a sacrament is an aggregate of words, substances, and actions, and so in any case is not the sort of thing that could be an agent, or in which any sort of casual power could inhere.[14]

On Scotus's account, no natural agent could have a supernatural causal power. Could a sacrament, however, be an instrumental cause of grace without its having any supernatural powers? (For example, could it be an instrumental cause of grace in virtue of its own natural powers?) Scotus thinks not, claiming that it is impossible for a sacrament to be an instrumental cause of grace. First, no creature can be an instrumental cause of a supernatural effect.[15] Second, a sacrament is a temporally extended aggregate—it takes time to say all the required words. The infusion of grace by God is instantaneous. And no temporally extended aggregate can be in any sense the cause of an instantaneous action.[16]

Scotus's arguments against Thomas rely on philosophical premises. In effect, Scotus is claiming that we can demonstrate that Aquinas's view is false. So the occasionalist option—the only other alternative—must be correct. Scotus thus argues that a sacrament is a noncausal "necessitating condition."[17] It does not *cause* God's action—after all, it has no causal powers, intrinsic or instrumental, in virtue of which it could bring about a divine action. God has decided, however, that *whenever* a sacrament is received, he will give the appropriate supernatural gift.[18] Indeed, this divine decision has been formalized in a covenant (*pactio*) made by God with the Church.[19] This does not commit Scotus to denying the reliability of sacramental grace. God's covenant guarantees sacramental reliability.[20]

Scotus argues similarly with regard to the consecration of the elements in the Eucharist. The priest's celebration of the Mass is an occasion for the conversion of the bread and wine into Christ's body and blood. But this conversion is not caused by the priest's words and actions in the Mass. The priest's words and actions are a noncausal necessitating condition of a divine action. And all of this is the result of "the ordering of God making a covenant with the Church."[21]

One advantage of the Thomist account rejected by Scotus is that it allows a clear distinction between the sacraments of the New Covenant and the ceremonies of the Old. According to Aquinas, the sacraments have instrumentally causal powers; the Old Testament ceremonies are just *occasions* for divine grace. This way of distinguishing the sacraments from the Old Testament ceremonies is not open to Scotus's occasionalist account of sacramental causality. He therefore distinguishes the sacraments from the Old Testament ceremonies rather differently. He holds that Christ's life and death is the meritorious cause of God's salvific action exhibited in both the New Testament sacraments and the Old Testament ceremonies. But the Old Testament ceremonies owe their efficacy to Christ's *foreseen* merits; the New Testament sacraments owe their efficacy to the *actual* merits of Christ. But in things that owe their efficacy to merits in this way, greater efficacy is received in virtue of actual merits than of foreseen merits. So the New Testament sacraments are more effective in the conferring of grace than are their Old Testament precursors.[22]

Grace and Character

Scotus is clear that the effect of the sacraments—which as we have seen is brought about the merits of Christ—is the gift of grace.[23] One and the same grace, existing in the soul, has various different effects; and the sacraments are distinguished from each other in virtue of their relations to these different effects.[24] Thus, for example, God by means of baptism causes the remission of original sin and actual sin,[25] without the need for penance,[26] remitting both the guilt of sin and the punishment due for it;[27] he gives spiritual birth,[28] adoption as sons of God,[29] and Church membership.[30] Confession brings about the remission of sins and the restoration of grace after its loss.[31] The Eucharist increases the force of the Christian's incorporation into Christ.[32]

Some sacraments—baptism, confirmation, and ordination—also confer some sort of indelible "mark" on their recipient. This mark is known technically as "character." Scotus provides a detailed description of the nature and effects of character. It is "an unrepeatable ... spiritual form impressed by God."[33] It in some way makes those who possess it conform to Christ,[34] and it places those who have it under some sort of obligation to Christ.[35] It also places us in communion—here, a sort of family relationship—with others who have this character.[36]

According to Aquinas, this character is a quality—a nonrelational perfection.[37] This quality inheres in the intellect, configuring the threefold structure of the mind to its Trinitarian model.[38] Furthermore, Aquinas sees character as an instrumental cause in the process of receiving sacramental grace.[39] Scotus disagrees with these claims of Aquinas. He argues that character is a relational property; that it inheres in the will; and that it functions merely as an occasion for God's giving us grace—it has no causal role, instrumental or otherwise.

According to Scotus, the very way in which character is defined involves relations to other items: conformity to Christ, and communion with other Christians. So character must in essence be a relation, not an absolute property.[40] Equally, character inheres in the will, not the intellect. Scotus's reason is that character places us under an obligation to God; and being obliged belongs to us in virtue not of our intellect but of our will.[41] Grace inheres in the will; and character, which is the occasion for the reception of grace, thus appropriately inheres in the will too.[42]

Scotus distinguishes the different characters of baptism, confirmation, and ordination in terms of their effects. Baptismal character incorporates us into the family of Christ; confirmation gives us a role in the defense of the Church militant; the character of ordination allows us to lead others as parent and shepherd.[43] Notably, Scotus believes that, were it not for a divine decision, the Church's restriction of ordination to the male sex (as Scotus believed) would constitute something "of the greatest injustice, not only to the whole [female] sex, but to individual persons too"[44]—although he concedes (without giving reasons) that the restriction is nevertheless "consonant with natural law."[45] The discussion is a very nice case of the application of Scotus's constructivist metaethic to theological doctrine.

Eucharist: Transubstantiation and Sacrifice

According to Lateran IV (1215), in the Eucharist the bread and wine are transubstantiated into the body and blood of Christ.[46] The school men understood this to entail that the *substance* of the consecrated bread and wine no longer exists, while the *accidents* of the bread and wine remain. Accidents are nonessential properties, paradigmatically analyzed by Aristotle as quantity, quality, relation, place, time, position, state, action, and passion.[47]

This doctrine raises three distinct problems. What sort of change is transubstantiation? How could the accidents of anything exist without their substance? How could Christ's body and blood be really present on the altar? I will look at these problems in turn, trying to see how effective Scotus's proposed solutions are. Scotus's major opponent here is Aquinas. So I will look briefly at Aquinas's view too.[48]

What Sort of Change Is Transubstantiation?

Aquinas and Scotus agree that the Eucharistic change—transubstantiation—is best defined as "the conversion of one whole substance into another."[49] Both men understand this to entail that the matter and form of the bread are converted into the matter and form of Christ's body. Aquinas believes that this sort of change is the only way to explain how Christ's body can be really present in the Eucharist. He argues that there are only two ways in which a body can begin to be present at a place: (1) by local motion from place to place and (2) by transubstantiation. (In the first of these, the body undergoes a change; in the second, something else changes into the body.) The first of these changes, according to Aquinas, cannot explain Christ's real presence. For a body to move from place a to place b, it must cease being at a; it must travel through all the places between a and b; and if it is in place b it cannot be in any other place c. Christ's body in the Eucharist can satisfy none of these conditions: it remains in heaven while present on the altar; it does not travel from heaven to earth; and it can be present on more than one altar at the same time. So the only way to explain presence must be transubstantiation: the complete change of the bread into Christ's body.[50]

It is in fact difficult to see how Christ's body can begin to be present without it undergoing some sort of change, and Scotus attacks Aquinas's account for just this sort of reason. He argues that transubstantiation, as understood by Aquinas, is in fact no help in explaining how Christ's body begins to be present in the Eucharist. Transubstantiation is a doctrine about *substances*, not about the *places* they occupy; and to explain the presence of a material substance, we need to be able to talk about the place it occupies. As Scotus understands Aquinas's theory, it entails that the bread is transubstantiated into Christ's body; but it also entails that Christ's body remains in heaven—and so is not really present at all.[51] In order to explain how Christ's body begins to be present in the Eucharist, we need to appeal to something like local motion. Christ's body begins to be present in the Eucharist because it has in some sense *moved*.[52]

Aquinas's objections (just outlined) to this sort of account look formidable. Scotus answers them by appealing to an Aristotelian account of place that both he and Aquinas share. According to Aristotle, being in a place is a relation: a body is in a place if and only if it is contained by its immediate surroundings.[53] On this account, moving from place to place involves gaining and losing successive relations to different surroundings. In answering Aquinas's objections, Scotus appeals to various features that he believes all categorical relations share. One such feature is that, in general, a substance can have more than one relation of the same sort. Suppose I am the same height as my two friends. "Being the same height as" is a relation; and according to Scotus, I have two such relations, one to each of my two friends. Furthermore, I can gain and lose such relations: perhaps one of my friends grows a little hunched as he gets older, or I gain another friend of the same height. Scotus argues that place relations are like this. God could give me, simultaneously, the relation of being in place *a* and being in place *b*. If this were to happen, there would not, despite appearances, be two substances: just one substance in two places.[54]

On this account of place, it is easy to see how God could bring it about both that Christ's body is present in the Eucharist without his leaving heaven, and that his body is present on other altars at the same time. And presumably, since Christ's body does not lose its first place—in heaven—there is no reason to suppose that it has to *travel* from heaven to earth, as Aquinas supposes would have to happen on this sort of scenario.

On Scotus's account, it is this change to Christ's body—and *not* transubstantiation—that properly explains the presence of Christ's body in the Eucharist. Scotus consequently thinks—unlike Aquinas—that there is no pressing theological reason for wanting to accept transubstantiation. He believes that consubstantiation—the doctrine that Christ's body comes to exist in the same place as the substance of the bread—is in principle preferable. It is simpler,[55] it is easier to understand (because it does not involve the claim that, despite appearances, the substance of the bread has changed),[56] and it is more scriptural.[57] However, Scotus believes that the doctrine of transubstantiation, despite its intrinsic undesirability, is true. His reason for this is just that it was taught "by the Roman Church" at Lateran IV.[58]

The Separated Accidents

The most telling objection to the doctrine of transubstantiation is that the existence of accidents without their substance is just impossible—the sort of absurdity satirized by Lewis Carroll in the Cheshire Cat's grin. Clearly, if it is impossible for accidents to exist without their substance, then transubstantiation is false. But, as I have tried to show elsewhere, Scotus argues on straightforwardly *philosophical* grounds, without invoking any theological principle, that accidents can exist without their substances.

Scotus argues that for substance and accident to form an accidental whole *w*, it is necessary that none of the parts of *w* are essentially parts of *w*. On this account of the nature of an accidental whole, it is possible either that accidents exist without any substance at all, or that they can "migrate" from substance to substance. Scotus believes (mistakenly) that this is a principle espoused by Aristotle.[59] Scotus (again mistakenly) argues that on his account of accidental unity, it follows that an accident can exist apart from any substance at all.[60] And this allows for the possibility of the separated accidents required for transubstantiation.

Presupposed to this argument is the claim, explicitly defended by Scotus, that accidents are individuated independently of their substances. (If they were not, it would be difficult to see how they could possibly exist without their substances.) Scotus argues that the individuation of something belonging to one of Aristotle's categories—e.g., an accident—cannot be explained by something existing in another of the categories—e.g., a substance.[61] Aquinas tries to give an account of transubstantiation that will be consistent with the claim that accidents are individuated by their substances. He claims—without making any attempt to justify his position—that an item can exist at a time t_N without its individuating feature if it was united to its individuating feature at t.[62] Scotus's attempt to find a stronger philosophical underpinning for the doctrine makes his account far more intellectually satisfying than Aquinas's more agnostic one.

Not all of the separated accidents in the Eucharist lack a subject. In fact, Scotus believes—adopting the standard thirteenth-century opinion—that it is most likely that only the quantity of the bread lacks a subject; the remaining accidents inhere in this quantity. His basic reason is Aristotelian: quality is extended by being received into quantity.[63] On this account, the subject of—say—the color, or taste, of the consecrated host is its extension. What we see on the altar is in essence the *size* of the bread and wine.

The Real Presence

The claim that Christ's body is *present* in the Eucharist is itself problematic. Christ's body, after all, includes flesh, organs, bones, and so on; and it is much bigger than the consecrated bread on the altar. Furthermore, does talk of Christ's body being present entail that his *blood* is, or his *soul*, or—perhaps more important still—his *divinity*?

Aquinas develops a doctrine to answer all of these questions: the doctrine of *concomitance*. Aquinas argues that Christ's body and all of its natural parts are really present; but that its quantity is present only "concomitantly": "after the manner of substance," and not as it would be naturally. Aquinas understands this to mean that the various parts of Christ's body are not *distant* from each other.[64] We could think of Aquinas as holding that there is breakdown in the spatial relations between the various parts of Christ's body.[65]

Being present "concomitantly" seems to have another, more basic, meaning too for Aquinas. The Eucharistic change in itself is just from bread/wine to body/blood. So, in itself, only the body and blood come to be present properly in virtue of the change. But those things that are joined to the body come to be present concomitantly—that is, as a natural result of the change to Christ's body/blood, as well as quantity, this includes Christ's soul and his divinity.[66] Equally, Christ's blood is concomitantly included in his body, and his body concomitantly in his blood.[67]

Scotus believes that Christ's body cannot be present in the way Aquinas describes. Scotus holds that it is a necessary feature of a body that it is physically extended. Specifically, he holds that the parts of a human body must be distant from each other if that body is to be the sort of body that could be the subject of an intellectual soul.[68] Equally, Scotus does not see how the fact of Christ's body coming to be present could in itself entail that Christ's body lacks any of its intrinsic natural properties—such as its spatial extension.[69]

Scotus argues instead that the body of Christ present on the altar includes its proper extension, and has organs that are spatially distant from each other. But Scotus argues that there is a breakdown in the relation between the different parts of Christ's body and the parts of the place that contains this body. Each part of Christ's Eucharistic body is spatially distant from all other parts of this body, and the whole of this body is spatially related to the whole of the place that contains it; but there are no spatial relations between the *parts* of Christ's body and the *parts* of the place that contains it. Rather, the whole body is present each part of its place.[70]

One obvious objection to any doctrine of real presence is that Christ's body seems to be present in the same place as the bread, or at least the same place as the accidents of the bread. Scotus, as we might expect, does not believe that this dual presence offers any real difficulties. Being the place of a body—containing this body—is an extrinsic relational property, and such relations can be multiplied, allowing one place to contain two bodies.[71]

Scotus believes, then, that the quantity of Christ's body is present naturally, not merely concomitantly. But he agrees with Aquinas's claim that Christ's soul and blood are present with the body only concomitantly. Even though Christ's soul and blood are not the proper end term of the conversion from bread to body, nevertheless they are automatically present wherever Christ's living body is. Their presence is thus concomitant upon the presence of the body.[72]

The Eucharistic Sacrifice

The Reformers were greatly exercised by the medieval doctrine of the Eucharistic sacrifice, believing that it derogated from the sufficiency of Christ's "one oblation of himself once offered" on Calvary. The Council of Trent, however, usefully clarified the Catholic view. In the Eucharist, Christ offers himself by means of the ministry of his priests, making the sacrifice of Calvary present again.[73] Central to both Tridentine and Reformed views is the notion of *anamnesis*: the Eucharist *recalls* Christ's offering on Calvary, either—on the Catholic view—by making that sacrifice somehow present, or—on the Protestant view—by reminding the assembled congregation of Christ's salvific work.

Scotus accepts the Catholic view that the Eucharistic offering makes Christ's offering on Calvary present—it "represents" it.[74] The merits of the Eucharist are given "through the passion."[75] And Scotus claims that Christ somehow offers himself in the Eucharist.[76] Scotus does not spell out this last claim. But there are clear indications that he would want to reject the obvious possible sense: that Christ offers himself in the Eucharist using the priest as his instrument. Scotus is quite clear that the priest—or at any rate the Church—does not have any sort of *instrumental* role in sacrifice of Christ's body in the Mass: the Church is rather the *principal agent* offering the Eucharistic sacrifice.[77] And Scotus argues on scriptural grounds that there is no obvious sense in which Christ sacrifices himself in the Eucharist.[78]

In fact, Scotus is clear that there is a real sacrifice in the Mass which is *distinct* from the sacrifice of Calvary. So his view seems dangerously close to the view of the Eucharistic sacrifice later rejected by both Protestants and Catholics alike. He argues that, in the Eucharist, the Church offers Christ's body and blood to God.[79] By making this offering, the Church gains merit for its members.[80] On Scotus's view, then, not only is the Eucharistic sacrifice distinct from Christ's sacrifice on Calvary, it is offered not by Christ but by the Church. Presumably, the sorts of causal powers involved in offering Christ's body and blood to God are not supernatural, since, as we have seen, none of the causal powers of a creature can be supernatural. Scotus must be assuming that the Church has some sort of natural active causal power in virtue of which its priests can offer Christ's body and blood, and that this power can be delegated to the priest. (Scotus claims that the priest is the "organ" of the Church.)[81] Doubtless, Scotus would want to see that power as related in some way to the priest's power for being an occasion of divine sacramental activity, but he does not discuss this and I do not know what further speculation to offer about it.

Conclusion

In Scotus's view, sacraments do not cause God's grace; rather, God has decided that whenever a sacrament is received, he will give the appropriate supernatural gift. This divine decision has been formalized in a covenant (*pactio Divina*) with the Church. God's pact guarantees sacramental reliability. The Old Testament "sacraments" owe their efficacy to Christ's foreseen merits, whereas the New Testament sacraments owe their efficacy to the actual merits of Christ. Scotus is clear that the effect of sacraments is the gift of grace.

NOTES
1. For Scotus's life and works, see, e.g., my *Duns Scotus*, Great Medieval Thinkers (New York: Oxford University Press, 1999), 3–6.
2. Scotus, *Ordinatio* book IV, distinction 1, part 2, question 2, number 226, ed. C. Balić and others, 21 vols. (Vatican City: Vatican Press, 1950–2013), 11:79.
3. Ibid., IV, d. 2, q. 1, nn. 13–17 (Vatican, 11:145–46)

4. Ibid., IV, d. 2, q. 1, nn. 18–26 (Vatican, 11:146–48).
5. Ibid., IV, d. 2, q. 1, nn. 18–26 (Vatican, 11:148–50). Contrary to Scotus's claim, of course, the number and identity of the sacraments did not become fixed until the middle of the twelfth century. Peter Lombard is perhaps one of the best-known early defenders of the seven sacraments as we now have them: see Lombard, *Sententiae* IV, c. 2, 1.1, 3rd ed., 2 vols., Spicilegium Bonaventurianum (Grottaferrata: Collegium Sancti Bonaventurae, 1971–81), 2:239.
6. Scotus, *Ordinatio* IV, d. 1, p. 2, q. 1, n. 207 (Vatican, 11:73).
7. See Bonaventure, *Commentaria in quatuor libros Sententiarum* IV, d. 1, p. 1, a. un, q. 1 (*Opera omnia*, 10 vols. [Quaracchi: Collegium Sancti Bonaventurae, 1882–1902], 4:12b).
8. Aquinas, *Summa Theologiae* III, q. 62, a. 1 c., www.corpusthomisticum.org (accessed 20 January 2017).
9. Ibid., III, q. 62, a. 4 c.
10. Ibid., III, q. 62, a. 4 ad 1.
11. I deal in greater detail with some of the issues that arise in the rest of this section in my "On the Polity of God: The Ecclesiology of Duns Scotus," *International Journal for the Study of the Christian Church* 7 (2007): 29–45, 32–35.
12. Scotus, *Ordinatio* IV, d. 1, p. 1, q. un., nn. 119–27, 152, 167–73 (Vatican, 11:43–47, 54–55, 59–60).
13. Ibid., IV, d. 1, p. 3, qq. 1–2, n. 296 (Vatican, 11:105).
14. Ibid., IV, d. 1, p. 3, qq. 1–2, nn. 297–98 (Vatican, 11:105–6).
15. Ibid., IV, d. 1, p. 3, qq. 1–2, nn. 285–86 (Vatican, 11:98–99). I discuss Scotus's argument in *The Physics of Duns Scotus: The Scientific Context of a Theological Vision* (Oxford: Clarendon, 1998), 256–63.
16. Scotus, *Ordinatio* IV, d. 1, p. 3, qq. 1–2, nn. 287–90 (Vatican, 11:99–101).
17. Ibid., IV, d. 1, p. 3, qq. 1–2, nn. 310–13 (Vatican, 11:110–12); ibid., IV, d. 2, q. 1, nn. 27–31 (Vatican, 11:150–51).
18. Ibid., IV, d. 1, p. 3, qq. 1–2, n. 309 (Vatican, 11:110). Scotus is happy to call this sort of occasion an instrumental cause. But he is careful to distinguish this use of instrumental cause from Aquinas's: see ibid., IV, d. 1, p. 3, qq. 1–2, nn. 311, 317–22 (Vatican, 11:110, 113–14). For Scotus on the varieties of instrumental causality, see my "Some Varieties of Semantic Externalism in Duns Scotus's Cognitive Psychology," *Vivarium* 46 (2008): 275–301, 286–92.
19. Scotus, *Ordinatio* IV, d. 1, p. 3, qq. 1–2, n. 323 (Vatican, 11:115).
20. God's truthfulness means that he cannot lie: see ibid., III, d. 39, q. un., n. 11 (Vatican, 10:325). So I take it he cannot break a promise either.
21. Ibid., IV, d. 13, q. 1, n. 149 (Vatican, 12:481). This does not compromise the *ex opere operato* aspect of the sacraments. In the case of the Eucharist the content of God's covenant, as revealed by Jesus, reported in 1 Cor. 11:26, includes a promise to convert the bread and wine into the body and blood of Christ: see Scotus's discussion of this passage at ibid., IV, d. 13, q. 2, n. 175 (Vatican, 12:486).
22. Ibid., IV, d. 2, q. 1, nn. 36–37 (Vatican, 11:153–54).

23. Ibid., IV, d. 7, qq. 1, 2, 3, 4, n. 58 (Vatican, 11:429).
24. Ibid., IV, d. 1, p. 4, q. 1, n. 384 (Vatican, 11:137).
25. For original sin, ibid., IV, d. 4, p. 1, q. 1, nn. 14–16 (Vatican, 11:226–27); ibid., IV, d. 4, p. 1, q. 2, n. 27 (Vatican, 11:230–31). For actual sin, ibid., IV, d. 4, p. 2, q. 2, n. 119 (Vatican, 11:260).
26. Ibid., IV, d. 7, qq. 1, 2, 3, 4, n. 55 (Vatican, 11:429).
27. Ibid., IV, d. 4, p. 2, q, 2, n. 97 (Vatican, 11:253); ibid., IV, d. 6, p. 4, a. 1, q. 1, n. 165 (Vatican, 11:346).
28. Ibid., IV, d. 2, q. 1, n. 17 (Vatican, 11:148).
29. Ibid., IV, d. 4, p. 2, q. 1, n. 83 (Vatican, 11:248).
30. Ibid., IV, d. 6, p. 1, q. 1, n. 20 (Vatican, 11:305).
31. Ibid., IV, d. 14, q. 4, n. 195 (Vatican, 13:50); ibid., IV, d. 14, q. 2, n. 132 (Vatican, 13:34).
32. Ibid., IV, d. 8, q. 3, n. 163 (Vatican, 12:40–41). For a more detailed treatment of Scotus on sacramental character, see my "On the Polity of God," 35–39.
33. Scotus, *Ordinatio* IV, d. 6, p. 4, a. 2, q. 2, n. 334 (Vatican, 11:398); ibid., IV, d. 6, p. 4, a. 2, q. 1, n. 199 (Vatican, 11:355).
34. Ibid., IV, d. 6, p. 4, a. 2, q. 1, n. 199 (Vatican, 11:355).
35. Ibid., IV, d. 6, p. 4, a. 2, q. 1, n. 199 (Vatican, 11:355). At ibid., IV, d. 6, p. 4, a. 2, q. 2, n. 344 (Vatican, 11:398) and IV, d. 6, p. 4, a. 2, a. 1, n. 262 (Vatican, 11:374), Scotus refers to character as a "configurative sign" insofar as it places those who have it under an obligation to Christ. The idea, I think, is that we receive the sacraments through the merits of Christ; so our receiving them places us under some sort of obligation to him.
36. Ibid., IV, d. 6, p. 4, a. 2, q. 1, n. 199 (Vatican, 11:355); ibid., IV, d. 6, p. 4, q. 2, a. 2, nn. 290, 344 (Vatican, 11:384, 398).
37. Aquinas, *Scriptum super libros Sententiarum* IV, d. 4, q. 1, a. 1, ed. P. Mandonnet and M. F. Moos, 4 vols. (Paris: Lethielleux, 1929–47), 4:147–52, discussed by Scotus at *Ordinatio* IV, d. 6, p. 4. q, 2, a. 2, nn. 285–89 (Vatican, 11:381–83).
38. Ibid., IV, d. 4, q. 1, a. 3 (4:156, 159), discussed by Scotus at *Ordinatio* IV, d. 6, p. 4, a. 2, q. 3, nn. 362–63 (Vatican, 11:407).
39. Aquinas, *Scriptum super libros Sententiarum* IV, d. 4, q. 1, a. 1 ad 4 (4:152).
40. Scotus, *Ordinatio* IV, d. 6, p. 4, q. 2, a. 2, nn. 294–96 (Vatican, 11:385).
41. Ibid., IV, d. 6, p. 4, a. 2, q. 3, n. 371 (Vatican, 11:410).
42. Ibid., IV, d. 6, p. 4, a. 2, q. 3, n. 371 (Vatican, 11:409–10).
43. Ibid., IV, d. 6, p. 4, q. 2, a. 2, n. 331 (Vatican, 11:397). This priestly character seems to be distinct from priestly power. According to Scotus, God gives a priest certain (presumably natural) powers in virtue of which he can be an appropriate occasion for a divine activity (see ibid., IV, d. 6, p. 4, a. 2, q. 2, n. 313 [Vatican, 11:391]). Scotus likens priestly power to judicial power. A judge's legal powers are relative to the real powers of some authority. Priestly power is like this: relative to some authority—in this case, God—capable of actually bringing about the relevant effect (see ibid., IV, d. 6, p. 4, a. 2, q, 2, nn. 309–12 [Vatican, 11:390–91]; ibid., IV, d. 13, q. 1, nn. 149–51 [Vatican, 11:481]). (It is not clear to me why Scotus should think

of this priestly function in terms of a power at all.) Again, on this, see my "On the Polity of God," 34–36. As we shall see below, the priest also has some active powers delegated to him by the Church. Such powers cannot, of course, be *supernatural* powers, for reasons examined above.

44. Scotus, *Ordinatio* IV, d. 25, q. 2, n. 76 (Vatican, 13:333).
45. Ibid., IV, d. 25, q. 2, n. 79 (Vatican, 13:334).
46. Lateran IV, const. 1 (Norman P. Tanner, ed., *Decrees of the Ecumenical Councils*, 2 vols. [Washington, DC: Georgetown University Press, 1990], 1:230).
47. Aristotle, *Categoriae*, c. 4 (1b25–27), *Opera omnia*, ed. I. Bekker, 5 vols. (Berlin: Reimer, 1831).
48. For a thorough account of Scotus on transubstantiation, see Marilyn McCord Adams, *Some Later Medieval Theories of the Eucharist: Thomas Aquinas, Giles of Rome, Duns Scotus, and William of Ockham* (Oxford: Oxford University Press, 2010), 111–51, 197–210.
49. Aquinas, *Summa Theologiae* III, q. 75, a 4 c; see Scotus, *Quodlibetum*, q. 10, n. 3 (Wadding, *Opera omnia*, ed. L. Wadding, 12 vols. [Lyons, 1639], 12:241; trans. Alluntis and Wolter, Duns Scotus, *God and Creatures: The Quodlibetal Questions*, ed. and trans. Felix Alluntis and Allan B. Wolter [Princeton, NJ: Princeton University Press, 1975], 237 [n. 10.4]); *Ordinatio* IV, d. 11, p. 1, a. 1, q. 1, n. 14 (Vatican, 12:188).
50. Aquinas, *Summa Theologiae* III, q. 75, q. 2 c.
51. Scotus, *Quodlibetum*, q. 10, n. 20 (Wadding, 12:255; trans. Alluntis and Wolter, 251 [n. 10.54]); *Ordinatio* IV, d. 10, p. 1, q. 1, n. 36 (Vatican, 12:65).
52. Scotus, *Quodlibetum*, q. 10, n. 11 (Wadding, 12:249; trans. Alluntis and Wolter, 243 [n. 10.32]); *Ordinatio* IV, d. 10, p. 1, q. 1, nn. 42–50 (Vatican, 12:66–68).
53. Aristotle, *Physica* IV, Bekker, *Opera omnia*, c. 2 (209a31–b1); see Scotus, *Ordinatio* II, d. 2, p. 2, qq. 1–2, nn. 219–20 (Vatican, 7:254–55).
54. Scotus, *Ordinatio* IV, d. 10, p. 1, q. 1, nn. 46, 48 (Vatican, 12:67).
55. Ibid., IV, d. 11, p. 1, a. 2, q. 1, nn. 100–102, 138 (Vatican, 12:209, 220).
56. Ibid., IV, d. 11, p. 1, a. 2, q. 1, nn. 103–4, 139 (Vatican, 12:209–10, 220–21).
57. Ibid., IV, d. 11, p. 1, a. 2, q. 1, nn. 105–6 (Vatican, 12:210–11).
58. Ibid., IV, d. 11, p. 1, a. 2, q. 1, nn. 135, 140 (Vatican, 12:219, 221). On Scotus's de facto acceptance of a two-source theory of revelation, see my *Duns Scotus*, c. 1.
59. Scotus, *Ordinatio* IV, d. 12, p. 1, q. 1, nn. 39–41 (Vatican, 12:310–11). Scotus refers to Aristotle, *Metaphysica* V, Bekker, *Opera omnia*, c. 30 (1025a19–21); and *Metaphysica* VII, Bekker, *Opera omnia*, c. 5 (1030b20–21).
60. The whole discussion is Scotus, *Ordinatio* IV, d. 12, p. 1, q. 1, nn. 39–41 (Vatican, 12:310–11). I give a detailed account of Scotus's argument in my *Physics of Duns Scotus*, 100–104.
61. For the arguments, see Scotus, *Ordinatio* II, d. 3, p. 1, q. 4, nn. 89–92 (Vatican, 434–36), discussed in my *Physics of Duns Scotus*, 97–100. Scotus's account might seem to blur the distinction between substances and accidents. For his attempt to give an account of this distinction, see *Ordinatio* IV, d. 11, p. 1, a. 2, q. 1, nn. 243–47 (Vatican, 12:251–54), and my discussion in *Physics of Duns Scotus*, 103–7.

62. Aquinas, *Summa Theologiae* III, q. 77, a. 1 ad 3.
63. Scotus, *Ordinatio* IV, d. 12, p. 1, q. 2, n. 151 (Vatican, 12:342–43); see my discussion in *Physics of Duns Scotus*, 105n28. Scotus refers to Aristotle, *Categoriae*, c. 5 (5b2-3): "A white object is often called large because the surface it covers is large."
64. Aquinas, *Summa Theologiae* III, q. 76, a. 4 ad 1.
65. Aquinas uses concomitance to explain how two bodies could exist in the same place: see ibid., III, q. 76, a. 4 ad 2.
66. Ibid., III, q. 76, a. 1 ad 1.
67. Ibid., III, q. 76, a. 2 c.
68. Scotus, *Ordinatio* IV, d. 10, p. 1, q. 1, n. 60 (Vatican, 12:72).
69. Ibid., IV, d. 10, p. 1, q. 1, nn. 57–80 (Vatican, 12:71).
70. I discuss what this sort of presence would be like in *Physics of Duns Scotus*, 196–202. Scotus has an (unsound) philosophical argument in favor of the possibility of such presence: see *Ordinatio* IV, d. 10, p. 1, q. 1, nn. 64–66 (Vatican, 12:73–74).
71. Scotus, *Quodlibetum*, q. 11, n. 15 (Wadding, 12:271; trans. Alluntis and Wolter, 268 [n. 11.44]). I discuss the arguments in chap. 11 of *Physics of Duns Scotus*.
72. Scotus, *Ordinatio* IV, d. 10, p. 2, q. 1, nn. 253–56 (Vatican, 12:129–31); ibid., IV, d. 11. p. 1, a. 2, q. 1, nn. 189–90, 196 (Vatican, 12:235–36, 237–38). Scotus suggests that the claim that the soul is present only concomitantly means that its presence with the body is not absolutely necessary (see ibid., IV, d. 10, q. 4, nn. 217, 222 (Vatican, 12:121–22). As far as I can tell, Scotus never suggests that Christ's divinity is present in any special way at all in the Eucharist.
73. Session 22, c. 1 (Tanner, 2:733).
74. Scotus, *Quodlibetum*, q. 20, n. 22 (Wadding, 12:529, trans. Alluntis and Wolter, 460 [n. 20.48]); ibid., q. 20, n. 34 (Wadding, 12:535; trans. Alluntis and Wolter, 468 [n. 20.71]).
75. Ibid., q. 20, n. 22 (Wadding, 12:529; trans. Alluntis and Wolter, 460 [n. 20.48]).
76. Ibid., q. 20, nn. 1–2 (Wadding, 12:514–15; trans. Alluntis and Wolter, 443 [nn. 20.2–20.3]).
77. Ibid., q. 20, n. 22 (Wadding, 12:529; trans. Alluntis and Wolter, 460 [n. 20.48]).
78. Ibid., q. 20, n. 22 (Wadding, 12:529; trans. Alluntis and Wolter, 460 [n. 20.48]), citing Heb. 9.25, "Not that Christ might offer himself there again and again."
79. Ibid., q. 20, n. 22 (Wadding, 12:529; trans. Alluntis and Wolter, 460 [n. 20.48]).
80. Ibid., q. 20, n. 2 (Wadding, 12:515; trans. Alluntis and Wolter, 443–44 [n. 20.3]); ibid., q. 20, n. 21 (Wadding, 12:529; trans. Alluntis and Wolter, 459 [n. 20.47]).
81. Ibid., q. 20, n. 14 (Wadding, 12:525; trans. Alluntis and Wolter, 454 [n. 20.33]).

PART II

Reformation and Catholic Counter-Reformation

7

Theologies of Sacraments in the Reformation and Catholic Counter-Reformation

MICHAEL S. HORTON

Living in a secular age, it may be difficult to understand the importance of debates over the sacraments in the West during the sixteenth century. At least in terms of the importance attached to the sacraments, the disputants shared more in common with each other than with many of their spiritual descendants.

Theologies of Sacraments

As the movement's name suggests, the Reformation was not a revolution; no attempt was made to start from scratch, with simple negations of medieval teaching. Differences were due chiefly to the implications drawn from other key tenets.

At the head of these evangelical tenets was the belief that sinners are justified by grace alone, through faith alone, in Christ alone. In the medieval understanding, "created" grace is a substance infused into the sinner to bring spiritual and moral healing.[1] A sacrament "makes people holy."[2] Thus, "only those are called sacraments which signify the perfection of holiness in man."[3] According to the Council of Trent (1545–63), the first justification in baptism eradicates original sin, and through cooperation with God's grace, the believer merits an increase in grace in the hope of final justification.[4] If one does not put an obstacle in its path, the sacraments confer grace *ex opere operato* ("by doing it, it is done").[5] Trent's canons and decrees (seventh and thirteenth sessions) affirmed seven sacraments, the Eucharist as a true propitiatory sacrifice offered by the church, transubstantiation, and withholding the cup from the laity.

The label "Anabaptist" covers a variety of individuals and groups owing more to late medieval lay movements (viz., Brethren of the Common Life), the influence of mystics such as Meister Eckhart, and the humanism of Erasmus than to the magisterial Reformation. The distinction between grace and nature was mapped onto a metaphysical opposition of immaterial and material substances.[6] Noting this point, contemporary Anabaptist theologian Thomas N. Finger explains that grace is "a divine substance that elevates the soul," destroying "all creaturely desires."[7] "This grace divinized people so fully that they passed beyond 'the creaturely.'"[8] Further, Anabaptists expressed either disinterest or outright rejection of the magisterial Reformation's understanding of justification, stressing instead ethical separation and perfection.[9] For Anabaptists, "the purity of the group is a paramount principle."[10] Consequently, baptism and the Supper were conceived more as means of discipline than as means of grace.

Luther, Calvin, and other magisterial Reformers argued that grace is God's *favor et donum*. Instead of a created substance, grace is the *favor* of the uncreated Godhead: the Father, in the Son, through the Holy Spirit; the *gift* is union with Christ that brings fellowship with the Father and the indwelling presence of the Holy Spirit. Thus, divine favor solely through the imputation of Christ's merits (justification) is the legal basis of the inseparable divine gifts of renewal (sanctification) and final beatitude (glorification).[11]

The Nature of the Sacraments

Given the centrality of the doctrine of grace in the sixteenth-century debate, it is not surprising that they contributed to divergent views of the means of grace. Lutheran and Reformed confessions agree that the sacraments receive their efficacy from the external Word.[12] In fact, the proclamation of the gospel is the *verbum sacramentale*—"sacramental word."[13] "The preached Word is the Word of God" (*Second Helvetic Confession*).[14] The opposition between the Word and the sacraments that critics allege, though often exhibited in Protestantism, is far from the Reformers' conception. "Christ communicates his riches and blessings to us by his word," writes Calvin, "so he distributes them to us by his sacraments."[15] The Spirit creates faith through the Word, says Calvin. "But the sacraments bring the clearest promises."[16] According to the *Heidelberg Catechism*, "The Spirit creates faith in our hearts by the preaching of the holy gospel and confirms it by the use of the holy sacraments."[17]

With the covenant of grace as the context, preaching and sacrament become integrally related. It is the sphere of promise making—God's own performative speech with living and life-giving power—rather than metaphysical changes in the properties of creaturely elements. Lutheran and Reformed churches consequently regard the sacraments as God's visible pledge—or signs and seals of the covenant of grace (*Apology of the Augsburg Confession*, 13.5 and 24.7; *Belgic Confession*, art. 33; *Heidelberg Catechism*, question 66; *Westminster Confession*, chap. 27). Because God does not pledge in vain, there is a sacramental union of sign and reality: God gives what he represents in the sacraments (*Apology*, 24.70; Luther's *Large Catechism*, 5.30; *Belgic Confession*, art. 33; *Heidelberg Catechism*, questions 65–67; *Thirty-Nine Articles*, art. 25; *Westminster Confession*, chap. 27). In contrast, the leading Counter-Reformation theologian Robert Bellarmine said that the Word does not give efficacy to the sacraments, but vice versa, and rejected explicitly the definition of sacraments as covenantal seals. "The sacrament, therefore, should not be called the seal of the Word, but the Word the seal of the sacrament."[18]

Like the Lutheran position, the Reformed stresses the objective force of the sacraments as God's means of grace. "Nor does he feed our eyes with only a bare show but leads us to the reality (*rem praesentem*), and what he depicts (*figurat*) he effectively accomplishes at the same time.... God works through external means."[19] According to Calvin, Rome binds God to earthly means, while the Anabaptists and Zwingli disallow that God can freely bind himself to them.[20]

Lutheran and Reformed confessions are quite similar in defining sacraments in general, especially in assigning their efficacy to the work of God rather than to human activity—whether of priests and the corporate church or individual believers. The Word and the sacraments are "the outward and ordinary means whereby Christ communicates to us the benefits of redemption" (*Westminster Shorter Catechism*).[21]

Nevertheless, there are important differences. At Marburg in 1529, Luther and Zwingli reached agreement on fourteen points, but could not agree on the last: namely, the real presence of Christ in the Supper. Like his friend Erasmus, Zwingli assumed a spirit-matter dualism that led some of his students to the logical conclusion of the Anabaptist position.[22] Zwingli thought of the sacraments almost exclusively as the believer's pledge to God and fellow believers, like a soldier's oath or badge.[23] "For if your faith is not so perfect as not to need a ceremonial sign to confirm it," he adds, "it is not faith."[24]

Like Bucer and other Reformed leaders, Calvin sharply rejected Zwingli's dualistic thinking. He challenged the view that baptism is "nothing but a token and mark by which we confess our religion before men" and insisted that the sacraments are necessary for strengthening the weak faith of believers.[25] All of the Reformed confessions, even the one written by Zwingli's successor, Heinrich Bullinger, explicitly reject the view that sacraments are "mere badges of our Christian profession" (*Second Helvetic Confession*, art. 14).

A similar tendency was discerned in both Roman Catholic and Anabaptist views (including Zwingli's) to assimilate the sacraments to the matrix of human cooperation with divine initiative. Like Luther, Calvin insisted, "In Sacraments God alone properly acts; men bring nothing of their own."[26] They are God's testimonies to us and only secondarily "serve our confession before men."[27] What Calvin calls here the secondary benefit Anabaptists made the primary benefit—indeed, the entire essence—of the sacraments. The following section focuses specifically on the two rites that all parties recognized as sacraments.

Holy Baptism

According to the Augsburg Confession, "the grace of God is offered through Baptism, and . . . children should be baptized, for being offered to God through Baptism they are received into his grace."[28] Baptism is "the seal of the covenant of grace."[29] The Word and the water make baptism valid, according to Luther's *Large Catechism*, "even though faith be lacking." "For my faith does not constitute Baptism but receives it."[30] The sign is compared to a "precious jeweled clasp" that fastens the reality to it.[31] While "ordinary water could not have such an effect," as God's Word is joined to it, baptism "receives the power to become the 'washing of regeneration,' as St. Paul calls it in Titus 3:5."[32]

On one hand, the Reformed shared the Lutheran antipathy to the "enthusiasts" who *separated* the external Word and sacraments from their internal reality. There is a real sacramental union of sign and reality;

thus, they could speak of baptism as a bath of rebirth.[33] "Baptism, viewed in regard to us, is a passive work," Calvin wrote, "and all that belongs to it is laid up in Christ."[34] "Through baptism," he added, "believers are assured that this condemnation has been removed and withdrawn from them . . . by imputation only, since the Lord of his own mercy considers them righteous and innocent."[35] On the other hand, precisely as God's work, the sign must be *distinguished* from the reality. The Spirit is free to regenerate whom he will, where and when he will. And yet, he ordinarily uses baptism as his means of grace. Holding together both of those points is a recurring pattern in Reformed confessions. For example, according to the *Westminster Confession*, "The efficacy of baptism is not tied to that moment wherein it is administered; yet, notwithstanding, by the right use of this ordinance, the grace promised is not only offered, but really exhibited and conferred, by the Holy Ghost, to such (whether of age or infants) as that grace belongeth unto, according to the counsel of God's own will in His appointed time."[36]

Since baptism is God's testimony, according to the Reformers, there is no reason to exclude under the new covenant the children of believers who were included in the old covenant. Parents "see with their very eyes the covenant of the Lord engraved upon the bodies of their children."[37] "Furthermore," according to the *Belgic Confession*, "baptism does for our children what circumcision did for the Jewish people. That is why Paul calls baptism the 'circumcision of Christ' [Col. 2:11]."[38]

As the sign and seal of the gospel itself, baptism is effective not merely for the past but for the present and future, Luther states.[39] It is an anchor to our weak faith. Only a weak view of baptism could account for the addition of sacraments like penance, Calvin argues. "But we must realize that at whatever time we are baptized, we are once for all washed and purged for our whole life. Therefore, as often as we fall away, we ought to recall the memory of our baptism and fortify our mind with it, that we may always be sure and confident of the forgiveness of sins."[40] Its efficacy is "not destroyed by subsequent sins," but on the contrary, gives us a place to stand in lifelong faith and repentance.[41]

The Eucharist

Reflecting to some extent earlier debates, the controversy over the Eucharist provoked enduring divisions even among the Reformers.

According to Trent, after priestly consecration the bread and wine are converted into the substance of Christ's body and blood, although the accidents (appearances) remain. "This change the holy Catholic Church properly and appropriately calls transubstantiation,"[42] a dogma necessary to believe for salvation.[43] The sacrifice of the Mass is "truly propitiatory." "For, appeased by this sacrifice, the Lord grants the grace and gift of penitence and pardons even the gravest crimes and sins" and is offered also "for those departed in Christ but not yet fully purified."[44] "There is, therefore, no room to doubt that all the faithful of Christ may . . . give to this most holy sacrament in veneration the worship of *latria*, which is due to the true God."[45]

Lutheran View

An "abominable error" was introduced, according to the Augsburg Confession, when the Mass was transformed "into a sacrifice for the living and the dead, a sacrifice by means of which sin was taken away and God was reconciled."[46] Rejecting transubstantiation, Luther and his heirs nevertheless affirm that Christ's body and blood are present "*under* the bread, *with* the bread, *in* the bread."[47] The sign and the signified become "coupled," according to the *Large Catechism*.[48] The Word brings forgiveness through the sacrament.[49] As such, the bread and wine are only secondarily "signs by which people might be identified outwardly as Christians"; they are primarily "signs and testimonies of God's will toward us."[50] The Lutheran view emphasizes that the words of institution, "This is my body," "This is my blood," are not figurative,[51] and also stresses the importance of the words, "given *for you*," "shed *for you*."[52]

Over against the Anabaptists and Zwingli, Lutherans insisted that Christ's *true and natural body and blood* are *received orally*, and *by every participant*. In short, "all who eat and drink the blessed bread and wine in the Lord's Supper receive and partake of the true, essential body and blood of Christ orally. Believers receive it as a certain pledge and assurance that their sins are truly forgiven, that Christ dwells and is efficacious in them; unbelievers receive it orally, too, but to their judgment and damnation."[53]

If Christ ascended bodily and now sits in heaven until his return, how can he be said to be present bodily at every altar? To say with Zwingli that he is merely present according to his omnipresent deity is to separate Christ's two natures (the Nestorian heresy). Believers have life in Christ not merely according to his divinity or spirituality but in his flesh.[54] Christ's exaltation to the right hand of the Father refers not to a place but to a position.[55] Because the attributes of Christ's divinity have so penetrated those of his humanity, Christ may by his omnipotence be bodily present "wherever he desires and especially where he has promised his presence in his Word, as in the Holy Communion."[56] However, in opposing Nestorianism, how does one avoid the opposite error of Eutychianism (viz., confusing Christ's two natures)? At this point, arguments broke out among Lutherans themselves and were not fully resolved even in the Formula of Concord.[57] The Council of Trent condemned this view that Christ is substantially present with the bread and wine and its Christological implications.[58]

Reformed View

If Bucer, Calvin, Vermigli, and other Reformed theologians bristled at Luther's odd solution of Christ's omnipresent (or at least multi-present) humanity as opening the door to Eutychian errors, they were just as dissatisfied with Zwingli's dualistic ontology and implicit Nestorianism. "We must note in passing," Zwingli wrote, "that Christ is our salvation by virtue of that part of his nature by which he came down from heaven, not of that by which he was born of an immaculate Virgin, though he had to suffer and die by this part."[59] If Christ's divinity saves us, why would we need to be united to Christ's *humanity*, even if it were capable of omnipresence? Rather, concluded Zwingli, in the Supper we remember the work of Jesus Christ, long for his return, and testify to the world that we belong to him.

This downplaying of the saving significance of Christ's humanity and the necessity of our participation in the whole Christ struck at the heart of the Reformed doctrine of union with Christ, as Calvin especially emphasized. In his *Short Treatise on the Holy Supper*, which Luther reportedly approved, Calvin wrote, "All the benefit which we would seek in the Supper is annihilated if Jesus Christ be not given to us as the substance and foundation of all."[60] Zwingli does not understand why we must be united to Christ's flesh. Yet, especially drawing on the Eastern fathers, Calvin writes, "The flesh of Christ is like a rich and inexhaustible fountain that pours into us the life springing forth from the Godhead into itself. Now who does not see that communion of Christ's flesh and blood is necessary for all who aspire to heavenly life?"[61]

"It would be extreme madness to recognize no communion of believers with the flesh and blood of the Lord," he asserted in the *Institutes*.[62] To be saved is to share in the whole Christ, not just his deity, and in his person, not just his benefits.

Affirming with Luther the maxim *distinctio sed non separatio*, Calvin refused to separate the sign (bread and wine) from the signified (body and blood of Christ). Where Zwingli can only force a choice between God's action and creaturely action, Calvin says, "Whatever implements God employs, they detract nothing from his primary operation."[63] Yet Calvin recognized also that the question about *where* Christ is was decisive for determining *who* Christ is in his post-resurrection existence. If his humanity can be rendered infinite (omnipresent) by his deity, then is he truly human—and what continuity may we expect with him in the resurrection?[64] So where Rome, Luther, and Zwingli concentrated on how Christ was or was not present *in the bread and the wine*, Calvin directed his attention to how Christ is present *in action* in the sacrament even though he is absent from earth in the flesh until his return.

This required a robustly pneumatological understanding of the sacrament. If Luther quoted Christ's promise to be present among us (Matt. 18:20), "even to the end of the age" (Matt. 28:20), Zwingli quoted Christ's references to his ascension (John 14–17; Acts 1:11), leaving the earth until he returns in the flesh. Where Zwingli seemed to stop at Jesus's words in John 16:7, "It is to your advantage that I go away," because his divinity would finally be unobscured by his humanity, Calvin focused on Jesus's answer: "for if I do not go away, the Helper will not come to you. But if I go, I will send him to you." Thus, "The Spirit makes things which are widely separated by space to be united with each other, and accordingly causes life from the flesh of Christ to reach us from heaven."[65] So the question for Calvin is not how to relate spirit and matter, but how Christ, being glorified in heaven, can be related to us in our present condition.[66] The *Belgic Confession* states that while the mode "cannot be comprehended by us, as the operations of the Holy Spirit are hidden and incomprehensible, . . . we nevertheless do not err when we say that what is eaten and drunk by us is the proper and natural body and the proper blood of Christ."[67]

Even Zwingli's successor, Heinrich Bullinger, distanced himself from the view of the sacraments as "bare and naked signs," both in the *Second Helvetic Confession* and in his consensus statement with Calvin.[68] "Nor do we approve of those who despise the visible aspect of the sacraments because of the invisible," as if the signs were superfluous for those who already enjoyed the inner reality.[69] Calvin could assert regarding their consensus, "Although we distinguish, as is proper, between the signs and the things signified, yet we do not sever the reality from the signs."[70]

B. A. Gerrish observes that throughout his many treatments of the topic (see *Institutes* 4.17.6), Calvin underscores four points: First, "the Supper is a gift; it does not merely remind us of a gift." As with the Word and baptism, in the Eucharist we are receivers: it is "an *actio mere passiva* (a 'purely passive action')."[71] The human response to a gift is thanksgiving, says Calvin, which is why it is called the Eucharist. "The sacrifice [of the Mass] differs from the Sacrament of the Supper as widely as giving differs from receiving."[72] "And we ought carefully to observe, that the chief, and almost the whole energy of the sacrament, consists in these words, 'It is broken *for you*: it is shed *for you*.'"[73] Second, "The gift is given with the signs. Once again a criticism of both Zwingli and Rome is implied."[74] Third, "The gift is given by the Holy Spirit," which Calvin goes on to detail in 4.14.9 and 12.[75] Fourth, "The gift is given to all who communicate, pious and impious, believers and unbelievers."[76] One may refuse the gift, but this does not negate the sacrament any more than the preaching of the gospel is invalidated by unbelief. "The integrity of the Sacrament, which the whole world cannot violate," says Calvin, "lies in this: that the flesh and blood of Christ are no less truly given to the unworthy than to God's elect believers."[77] Yet only in faith do we receive the reality, which is, according to the *Belgic Confession*, nothing less than "the proper and natural body and the proper blood of Christ."[78]

Thomas Cranmer's sacramental thinking went through three phases: Roman Catholic, Zwinglian, and Reformed ("Calvinian"),[79] the last finding clear expression in the *Thirty-Nine Articles* (arts. 28–31).[80]

NOTES

1. Thomas Aquinas, *Summa Theologiae*, part III, question 69, article 9, trans. Fathers of the English Dominican Province (repr., Westminster, MD: Christian Classics, 1948), 4:2409.
2. Ibid., III, q. 60, a. 2, 4: 2340; cf. III, q 69, a. 9, 4:2409.
3. Ibid., III, q. 60, a. 2, 4: 2340.
4. *The Canons and Decrees of the Council of Trent*, Sixth Session, trans. H. J. Schroeder, O.P. (Rockford, IL: TAN Books, 1978), 29–46.
5. Ibid., Seventh Session, canons 6–8, 52.
6. A typical example is Caspar Schwenckfeld (1489–1561), who expressed this dualism in terms of Spirit versus letter and external elements (Eucharistic bread and wine) versus heavenly (which meant inner) reality. See, for example, R. Emmet McLaughlin, *Caspar Schwenckfeld: Reluctant Radical* (New Haven, CT: Yale University Press, 1986), 73–74.
7. Thomas N. Finger, *A Contemporary Anabaptist Theology: Biblical, Historical, Constructive* (Downers Grove, IL: InterVarsity, 2004), 563, 474.
8. Ibid., 474.
9. Robert Friedmann, *The Theology of Anabaptism* (Scottsdale, PA: Herald Press, 1973), 36, 91. See the same argument, with a number of examples, in Finger, *Contemporary Anabaptist Theology*, 109.
10. Friedmann, *Theology of Anabaptism*, 127.
11. Many sources could be cited from the magisterial Reformers, as in John Calvin's *Institutes of the Christian Religion*, ed. J. T. McNeill, trans. Ford Lewis Battles (Philadelphia: Westminster, 1960), 3.1.1–5.
12. See, for example, Jeffrey G. Silcock, "Luther on the Holy Spirit and His Use of God's Word," in *The Oxford Handbook of Martin Luther's Theology*, ed. Robert Kolb, Irene Dingel, and L'ubomir Batka (Oxford: Oxford University Press, 2014), 294–309. Cf. Calvin, *Institutes* 4.14.4 and, for a summary of Lutheran and Reformed treatment of this topic, see Michael Horton, *People and Place: A Covenant Ecclesiology* (Louisville: Westminster John Knox, 2008), 35–71.
13. B. A. Gerrish, *Grace and Gratitude: The Eucharistic Theology of John Calvin* (Minneapolis: Augsburg Fortress, 1993), 84–85. Gerrish refers here especially to Calvin's *Petit tracté de la sancta Cene* (1541), OS 1:504–5 and the *Institutes* 4.14.4; cf. 3.2.6–7, 3.2.28–30.
14. *Second Helvetic Confession*, chap. 1, in *The Book of Confessions* (Louisville: PCUSA, General Assembly, 1991).
15. Calvin, "Form for Administration of the Sacraments," in *Selected Works of John Calvin*, ed. Henry Beveridge and Jules Bonnet, 7 vols. (Grand Rapids, MI: Baker, 1983), 2:115.
16. Calvin, *Institutes* 4.14.5.
17. *Heidelberg Catechism*, Lord's Day 25, question 65, in *Ecumenical Creeds and Reformed Confessions* (Grand Rapids, MI: CRC Publications, 1988), 41.

18. Robert Bellarmine, preface to vol. 3 of *De Sacrament*, quoted in James Henry Thornwell, *Collected Writings of James Henry Thornwell: Theological and Controversial*, ed. John B. Adger and John L. Girardeau (Richmond: Presbyterian Committee of Publication, 1873), 321.
19. Calvin, *Institutes* 4.15.14–15.
20. Calvin, *Institutes* 4.1.5.
21. *Westminster Shorter Catechism*, question 88, in *Trinity Hymnal* (Atlanta: Great Commission Publications, 1990), 867.
22. Huldrych Zwingli, *Commentary on the True and False Religion*, ed. Samuel Macauley Jackson and Clarence Nevin Heller, trans. Sammuel Macauley Jackson (Durham, NC: Labyrinth Press, 1981), 214.
23. Ibid., 181.
24. Ibid., 184.
25. Ibid., 184.
26. Calvin, "Antidote to the Council of Trent," in *Selected Works of John Calvin*, 3:176.
27. Calvin, *Institutes* 4.15.1.
28. Augsburg Confession, in *The Book of Concord: The Confessions of the Evangelical Lutheran Church*, trans. and ed. Theodore G. Tappert (Philadelphia: Fortress, 1959), 33.
29. Martin Chemnitz, *Ministry, Word and Sacraments: An Enchiridion* (St. Louis: Concordia, 1981), 119.
30. Large Catechism, in *Book of Concord*, 443.
31. Ibid., 438.
32. Ibid., 440.
33. Martin Bucer, "A Brief Summary of Christian Doctrine" (1548), in *Commonplaces of Martin Bucer*, trans. and ed. David F. Wright (Appleford, England: Sutton Press, 1972), 85: "We confess and teach that holy baptism . . . is in the case of adults and of young children truly a baptism of regeneration and renewal in the Holy Spirit, whereby those who are baptised have all their sins washed away, are buried into the death of our Lord Jesus Christ, are incorporated into him and put on him for the death of their sins, for a new and godly life and the blessed resurrection, and through him become children and heirs of God."
34. Calvin, Galatians, in *Calvin's Commentaries*, vol. 21, trans. William Pringle (Grand Rapids, MI: Baker, 1996), 150.
35. Calvin, *Institutes* 4.15.10.
36. *Westminster Confession of Faith*, chap. 28.7, in *The Book of Confessions* (Louisville: PCUSA General Assembly, 1991).
37. Calvin, *Institutes* 4.16.9.
38. *Belgic Confession*, art. 34, in *Ecumenical Creeds and Reformed Confessions*.
39. *Book of Concord*, 444–46.
40. Calvin, *Institutes* 4.15.3.
41. Ibid.
42. *Canons and Decrees of the Council of Trent*, Thirteenth Session, chap. 4, 75.

43. Ibid., Thirteenth Session, Decree Concerning the Most Holy Sacrament of the Eucharist, chap. 1, 73.
44. Ibid., Twenty-Second Session, chap. 2, 146.
45. Ibid., Thirteenth Session, chap. 5, 76.
46. Augsburg Confession 24.21–22, in *Book of Concord*, 58.
47. Solid Declaration, art. 7, in *Book of Concord*, 575.
48. Large Catechism 5.18, in *Book of Concord*, 448.
49. Large Catechism 5.32–33, 35, in *Book of Concord*, 450.
50. *Book of Concord*, 35 (Augsburg Confession 13.1), 589 (Solid Declaration 7.115).
51. Solid Declaration, art. 7, in *Book of Concord*, 580.
52. Small Catechism 6.6, in *Book of Concord*, 352 and Large Catechism 5.64–65, in *Book of Concord*, 454.
53. Solid Declaration 7.63, in *Book of Concord*, 581.
54. *Apology of the Augsburg Confession* 10.3 in *Book of Concord*, 179.
55. Solid Declaration 8.28 in *Book of Concord*, 596.
56. Solid Declaration 8.4 in *Book of Concord*, 609. Not surprisingly, this article on the person of Christ follows the one on the Supper and focuses on the Christological center of the Eucharistic controversy—namely, the communication of attributes (*communicatio idiomatum*) (591–610).
57. Edmund Schlink, *Theology of the Lutheran Confessions* (Minneapolis: Fortress, 1961), 189–93.
58. *Canons and Decrees of the Council of Trent*, Thirteenth Session, chap. 8, 79.
59. Zwingli, *Commentary on the True and False Religion*, 204. Besides Gerrish's work, a growing number of helpful studies have appeared, including Ronald S. Wallace, *Calvin's Doctrine of Word and Sacrament* (Grand Rapids, MI: Baker, 1988); Jill Rait, *The Eucharistic Theology of Theodore Beza: Development of the Reformed Doctrine*, AAR Studies in Religion (Chambersburg, PA: American Academy of Religion, 1972); Keith Matheson, *Given for You: Reclaiming Calvin's Doctrine of the Lord's Supper* (Phillipsburg, NJ: Presbyterian and Reformed, 2002).
60. Calvin, "Short Treatise on the Holy Supper," in *Selected Works of John Calvin*, 2:170.
61. Calvin, *Institutes* 4.17.9.
62. Ibid.
63. Ibid., 4.14.17.
64. If Zwingli downplays Christ's humanity in favor of his deity, the Lutheran concept of ubiquity "transfigure[s] Christ, stripped of his own flesh, into a phantasm" (*Institutes* 4.17.7). Douglas Farrow, *Ascension and Ecclesia* (Edinburgh: T&T Clark, 1999), 204, sees Calvin as unique among the disputants in focusing on the reality of Christ's bodily ascension and absence from the earth while affirming Christ's true presence in the sacrament.
65. Calvin, "The Best Method of Obtaining Concord," in *Selected Works of John Calvin*, 2:578.

66. See also Louis Berkhof's superb summary of the Reformed critique of Zwingli's position in his *Systematic Theology*, 2nd rev. enlarged ed. (Grand Rapids, MI: Eerdmans, 1996), 653. After contrasting this position with Calvin's, he adds, "This view of Calvin is that found in our confessional standards" (654, citing *Belgic Confession*, art. 35; *Heidelberg Catechism*, questions 75–76, and the Communion Form).
67. *Belgic Confession of Faith*, in *Psalter Hymnal, Doctrinal Standards and Liturgy of the Christian Reformed Church* (Grand Rapids, MI: Board of Publications of the CRC, 1976), 87–88.
68. The *Consensus Tigurinus* can be found in *CO* 35:733, and in English translation in John Calvin, *Tracts and Treatises*, vol. 2, trans. Henry Beveridge (Grand Rapids, MI: Eerdmans, 1958), 212–20. See Timothy George, "John Calvin and the Agreement of Zurich (1549)," in *John Calvin and the Church: A Prism of Reform*, ed. Timothy George (Louisville: Westminster John Knox, 1990), 42–58.
69. *Second Helvetic Confession*, chap. 19, 5:180–81.
70. *Consensus Tigurinus*, in Ioannis Calvini, *Opera Selecta*, 5 vols., ed. P. Barth and G. Niesel (Munich: Kaiser, 1926–36), 2:249.
71. Gerrish, *Grace and Gratitude*, 150, from 4.14.26.
72. Calvin, *Institutes* 4.18.7.
73. This summary by Gerrish is taken especially from the *Institutes* 4.17.1–34.
74. Gerrish, *Grace and Gratitude*, 137.
75. Ibid., 137.
76. Ibid., 138.
77. Calvin, *Institutes* 4.17.33. Greater focus is given to this question in 4.17.34, drawing on Augustine.
78. *Belgic Confession of Faith*, art. 35, 87–88. The same article adds, "Christ communicates himself to us with all his benefits. At that table he makes us enjoy himself as much as the merits of his suffering and death, as he nourishes, strengthens, and comforts our poor, desolate souls by the eating of his flesh, and relieves and renews them by the drinking of his blood."
79. See esp. Peter Newman Brooks, *Cranmer in Context* (Philadelphia: Fortress, 1989).
80. "The Thirty-Nine Articles," in *The Anglican Tradition: A Handbook of Sources*, ed. G. R. Evans and J. Robert Wright (London: SPCK/Fortress, 1991), arts. 28–31, 238–40.

8

Martin Luther

ROBERT KOLB

Born in Eisleben, Germany, Martin Luther (1483–1546) was baptized on the feast day of St. Martin of Tours, for whom he was named. From 1501 to 1505, Luther attended the University of Erfurt, where he earned bachelor's and master's of arts degrees. At his father's urging, he embarked on the study of law, but soon left and joined the mendicant order of Augustinian Hermits. He took final vows shortly afterward, and in 1507 was ordained a priest. Luther was intellectually gifted, but a keen awareness of his own sinfulness left him frequently melancholy and fearful of God's wrath. His superior, Johannes von Staupitz, a significant theologian in his own right, ordered Luther to undertake advanced study in theology, in part to take his mind off his spiritual struggles. In 1512, Luther received the doctorate in theology and assumed the chair in Bible at the University of Wittenberg. Lecturing intensively on Scripture, he soon developed a deeply Augustinian but in some ways radically new understanding of sin, grace, and faith. In 1517, he protested the plenary indulgence that was being proffered for the building of a new St. Peter's Basilica in Rome. The ensuing controversy—the so-called Luther affair—soon embroiled much of Christendom in heated dispute. Luther was brought before the Diet of Worms (an Imperial Congress under the leadership of the new Holy Roman Emperor, Charles V) and condemned in 1521. Afterward, however, the princes of Electoral Saxony protected him from extradition, and Luther lived out his life preaching and teaching in Wittenberg, even serving as dean of the faculty there. In 1525, he married Katharina von Bora, and their happy home, into which six children were born, instantly epitomized the emerging Protestant parsonage. Luther personally taught much of the first generation of Lutheran ministers, shaping their outlook decisively on such matters as biblical authority, the right of clerical marriage, the real presence of Christ in the sacrament of Holy Communion, and much more. His *Small Catechism* and *Large Catechism* have been used to teach the Christian faith among Lutherans down to the present. In 1534, the "Luther Bible" brought the Scriptures into middle-high German; it remains a classic. Luther also commented or preached on most of the Bible. The still incomplete critical edition of his works comprises well over one hundred massive volumes, including letters and "table talks," and it continues to fuel the endeavors of a small army of scholars.

Introduction

In explaining the Third Commandment (according to the medieval numbering that he used), Martin Luther commented on observing the Sabbath or "sanctifying the holy day":

> Non-Christians can spend a day in rest and idleness, too, and so can the whole swarm of clerics in our time who stand day after day in the church, singing and ringing bells, but without keeping a single day holy because they neither preach nor practice God's Word but rather teach and live contrary to it.[1]

Much more than a snide remark about fellow priests and monks, this comment reflects a fundamental redefinition of what it means to be Christian, one that laid the foundation of the Protestant Reformation and guided Luther's implementation of this new definition in the church's life.

Growing up in a small mining town in central Germany, Luther experienced Christianity first as a system in which human beings approached God with their own performance, particularly of works of a sacred nature. The most important of these works took place in the mass, the key ritual in the believer's establishment of a relationship with God and the procurement of temporal and eternal benefits. The more religious their works were, the more confident they could be that God would dispense such blessings. The outward performance of ritual brought its benefits to the one performing the sacred activity. Theologians spoke of this as the *ex opere operato* (accomplished by/in performing the work) transmission of the benefits. Originally designed to safeguard the effectiveness of

God's Word, it had become, all sixteenth-century reformers concluded, a denial of the necessity of faith in the believer's reception of grace.

Luther's encounter with Scripture as a monk led him into thinking in the rhythms of the Psalms, reinforced by reading the rest of the Bible, especially John's account of the gospel and Paul's epistles. There he found that God takes the initiative in establishing and maintaining the relationship he treasures with his human creatures, a relationship in which they trust him completely. Luther also realized that God reveals himself as a God of conversation and community. In Genesis 1, God brought all reality into being by speaking. He created human creatures for trusting and faithful fellowship and dialogue with him. When Adam and Eve did not come to chat in the cool of the day, he called to them, inviting them back into conversation with himself. Luther began to define being Christian, first of all, as abandoning Adam and Eve's doubt of what God had said and instead listening to God's Word and trusting him, responding in prayer and praise of God and love and service for neighbor.

Luther's engagement with Scripture led him to believe that God's Word functions in his creation as an instrument of his power; from Paul he gained the insight that the gospel of Jesus Christ is the re-creative power to refashion rebellious sinners into children of God (Rom. 1:16), and the gospel actually delivers that power and accomplishes the task. Luther applied Scripture presuming what modern linguists call the "performative" nature of some human language.[2] Indeed, the Wittenberg professor believed that God's Word is creative and re-creative.

The Sacraments as Forms of God's Re-creative Word

Luther believed that God's Word comes in three different forms. Originally, the Creator spoke directly with Adam and Eve and later spoke through the prophets with his chosen Israel. But the oral forms of the Word needed support in writing, particularly in the written form that the Holy Spirit originated in the biblical writers, in which he continues to dwell, and through whom he does his re-creative work. Furthermore, in Luther's view God is a multimedia communicator and combines his oral Word of promise with external signs in the sacraments. (In his non-literate culture, Luther did not ignore the written Word but focused on delivering the biblical message through means that reached ordinary people.) The use of these three forms of God's Word stood at the heart of the Wittenberg call for reform. For Luther, the promise that God gives in baptism and the Lord's Supper provides yet another way in which God communicates with his people. In the reformer's instructions composed in 1529 for conducting private confession and absolution, the layperson, who has just received absolution from the pastor, asks when he may receive the Lord's Supper. "Why do you desire the Supper when you just received forgiveness in the absolution?" The layperson responds, "So what! I want to add the sign of God to his Word. To receive God's Word in many ways is so much better."[3]

In 1520, Luther issued several treatises outlining various aspects of his program for reform. Fundamental was his treatment of the justification of sinners in *The Freedom of a Christian*. Defining that justification as liberation from sin, guilt, death, Satan, and God's wrath, which makes believers "perfectly free lord(s) of all, subject to none [of the powers that corrupt humanity]," Luther bound this freedom tightly to the resulting freedom to live truly human lives in relationship to God's creation. This freedom in life's horizontal realm he summarized as being "a perfectly dutiful servant of all [God's creatures], subject to all."[4] At the beginning of this treatise, he made it clear that "all kinds of works," even "the sacred, religious activities of the soul," have no saving worth in God's sight. "One thing, and only one thing is necessary for Christian life, righteousness, and freedom": "the most holy Word of God, the gospel of Christ." "The soul can do without anything except God's Word; where God's Word is missing, there is no help at all for the soul." Luther defined the gospel's heart in terms of Christ's resurrection (John 11:25), his liberating power (John 8:36), and living from and in God's Word (Matt. 4:4).[5] This gospel creates trust in God's promise in his chosen people.

The "Ockhamist" school of medieval thought had provided the framework for the thinking of the young monk. Although he rejected much of that heritage, certain "Ockhamist" ideas (scholars today are uncertain how accurate the twentieth-century uses of "Ockhamist" and "nominalist" have been) remained with Luther. One that appears to have continued to guide his thinking was the belief that God is truly sovereign and almighty and that his will created rather than simply coincided with the rules for the functioning of his universe. Thus, Luther never was tempted to bind his reading of Scripture by the medieval principle that the finite is not capable of conveying the infinite (*finitum non est capax infiniti*), which makes sense in some Greek philosophical systems that operate without a strong sense of a Creator. These systems clearly divide the "spiritual" and the "material," viewing the material order as not capable of serving the Creator as an instrument through which he accomplishes his purposes. Luther believed that God has selected certain elements of the material, created order, including the flesh and blood of Jesus and human language, as well as the physical elements joined to the promise in the sacraments, as truly his instruments through which he accomplishes the re-creation of those dead in sin to life as his children. All three forms of his Word restore conversation and community with them.[6]

In response to Anabaptist remarks about "mere water," Luther taught children learning from his *Small Catechism* to answer the question, "how can water do such great things [give forgiveness of sins, redemption from death and the devil, and eternal salvation]?": "clearly, the water does not do it, but God's Word which is with and alongside the water, and faith, which trusts this Word of God in the water. For without God's Word the water is plain water and not a baptism, but with the Word of God it is a baptism, that is, a grace-filled water of life and a 'bath of the new birth in the Holy Spirit'" (Titus 3:5–8).[7] His treatment of the Lord's Supper echoes this: "how can bodily eating and drinking do such a great thing?": "eating and drinking certainly do not do it, but rather the words that are recorded, 'given for you' and 'shed for you for the forgiveness of sins.'"[8] These promises elicit faith that clings to the Promiser.

This reflects the reformer's redefinition of the term "sacrament," which had only slowly developed over the course of the church's history. Since the Council of Florence (1439), the medieval church had designated those rites that conveyed special grace in connection with material elements as seven: baptism, penance, confirmation, the Lord's Supper, marriage, ordination, and extreme unction. Luther restricted that number by defining "sacrament" as a form of the Word that (1) conveys forgiveness of sins, (2) was instituted by Christ, and (3) is connected with an external sign.[9] Thus, he regarded only baptism and the Lord's Supper as sacraments, occasionally adding confession and absolution to this list but most often regarding them as an extension of baptism into the daily lives of believers.[10] Luther's aversion toward any attempt at theodicy led him to avoid trying to explain the mystery of the continued existence of sin and evil in the lives of God's faithful people,[11] but he made contending with this mystery the center of his ministry. He did so by insisting on daily repentance as a rejection of and flight from sin and on daily reception through faith of Christ's promise of forgiveness and new life, which expresses itself in trust in God and love for him and all his creatures.

In 1538, as he expanded an agenda he had prepared for his followers to use at the papally called council, his *Smalcald Articles*, for publication, Luther reiterated his insistence that the comfort of the gospel comes precisely because the Holy Spirit uses external means, such as human language and also the sacramental elements that accompany it, to effect his saving will. In this regard, he saw no difference between spiritualist opponents such as Thomas Müntzer and papal theologians: both tried to find the Holy Spirit apart from Scripture. "In these matters, which concern the spoken, external Word, it must be firmly maintained that God gives no one his Spirit or grace apart from the external Word which initiates [his saving action]." These "spirits" (a reference to both those spiritualizing theologians like Müntzer and the papal theologians) "boast that they have the Spirit apart from and before contact with the Word. On this basis, they judge, interpret and twist the Scripture or the oral Word according to their pleasure."[12]

Baptism

Jonathan Trigg suggests that the Wittenberg professor's understanding of justification is "intimately related to—indeed even predicated upon—Luther's understanding of the abiding covenant of Baptism."[13] Indeed, from at least 1520 on, he viewed baptism as a matter of death and life,[14] the Holy Spirit's instrument for burying sinners in Christ's tomb and raising them up to walk in newness of life (Rom. 6:3-4; cf. Col. 2:11-15). He applied Paul's words in Romans 6 to the extension of the Spirit's baptismal action through daily repentant drowning of the sinner and daily resurrection to new life through the gospel's promise of the benefits of Christ. God's promise of new life in Christ that baptism delivers is an active, re-creative Word from God, and God is faithful to his promises. But Luther experienced his own flirtations with sin and those of others.

His "solution" to the problem was not an explanation but instead, first, the application of the demands of God's law for human performance, also the "performance" of trusting in the Creator and Re-creator, to those who need to be called to repentance, and, second, the bestowal of Christ's gospel assurance on the broken, repenting believer. Thus, he held that God's promise remains for the prodigal, but he recognized that prodigals die on the streets of foreign cities, far from their Father's banquet table. In this daily eschatological struggle against the murderer and liar who stands behind all human sin, the devil (John 8:44), Luther used the three forms of God's Word as swords of the Spirit (Eph. 6:17). Baptism, for example, makes the devil and the child into enemies, he "warned" parents.[15]

Pastoral concern for the broken, terrified conscience initiated Luther's engagement with the biblical teaching on baptism and its use. In 1520, he expressed his deep regret that medieval theologians had viewed baptism as only an entry portal to Christian living and then forgotten it as a part of the daily cultivation of repentance and faith. Although they could not "quench the power of baptism" for children, they had quenched its ongoing impact for adults, who were led to disregard its continuing mark on their daily lives. Luther taught that the sacrament should continue to awaken and nourish faith through the continual remembrance of God's promise. It leads the repentant to call to mind their forsaking of the divine promise, to "acknowledge that promise before the Lord, and rejoice that they are still within the fortress of salvation" because of God's baptismal promise.[16] Baptism became an integral part of the way in which he spoke of the Holy Spirit's continuing activity in the lives of believers, in devotional treatises, lectures, and the sermons that continued his practice begun in the monastery of preaching on the catechism as a form of basic instruction in biblical teaching for the people.[17]

By the late 1520s, polemical concerns from another direction were threatening this pastoral use of baptism. These concerns also shaped what Luther preached and wrote about this sacrament. His older colleague Andreas Bodenstein von Karlstadt caught Luther's enthusiasm for reform in the mid-1510s, but placed that enthusiasm within a familiar framework: the medieval reform mind-set that had arisen at least a half millennium earlier in reaction to the ritualistic religion of the time.

Groups, never organized over longer periods, repeatedly arose; they shared a certain approach to improving church life: they were biblicistic, relying on Scripture rather than ecclesiastical traditions; they were moralistic, stressing imitating Christ rather than performing sacred ritual; they opposed the clerical establishment openly showing contempt for and defying parish priests, and their anti-clericalism led to a rejection of the clergy's instrument of power, the sacramental system. Often they were millennial as well, expecting that God would initiate his thousand-year reign of peace and justice on earth.[18]

Karlstadt fell into much this same pattern,[19] and in 1525 Luther composed *Against the Heavenly Prophets*, a strong criticism of his colleague's rejection of God's use of external elements as instruments for working his saving will.[20] Luther's sense of betrayal bellows from its first lines: "Doctor Andreas Karlstadt has abandoned us, and above and beyond that has become our worst enemy."[21] Far more serious than his sense of personal betrayal, however, was the younger professor's conviction that Karlstadt's mystical-spiritualistic approach robbed believers of the comfort of the assurance God gives through his use of selected elements of his material creation.

> When God sends forth his holy gospel, he deals with us in a twofold manner, first outwardly, then inwardly. Outwardly he deals with us through the oral word of the gospel and through material signs, that is, baptism and the sacrament of the altar. Inwardly, he deals with us through the Holy Spirit, faith, and other gifts. But whatever their measure or order, the outward factors should and must precede. The inward experience follows and is effected by the outward. God has determined to give the inward to no one except through the outward.[22]

As the basis for this viewpoint, Luther offered Jesus's reference to dependence on and the sufficiency of "Moses and the prophets" (Luke 16:29), Paul's calling baptism a "washing of regeneration" in which God grants his Holy Spirit (Titus 3:5), and Paul's reference to the gospel as "the power of God for salvation to everyone who believes" (Rom. 1:16). Karlstadt not only ignored God's ordained means of exercising his re-creating power among sinners but also placed dependence on the individual's own emotions and spiritual actions.

> With all [the devil's] mouthing of the words "Spirit, Spirit, Spirit," he tears down the bridge, path, way, ladder and all the means by which the Spirit might come to you. Instead of the outward order of God in the material sign of baptism and the oral proclamation of God's Word, he wants to teach you not how the Spirit comes to you but how you come to the Spirit.[23]

Like defenders of medieval sacred performance, Karlstadt in practice had the directions wrong: for Luther, God initiates and governs the relationship with his people; his Word, not human feelings, is the only reliable source of his comfort.[24]

Anabaptists, encouraged by leaders including Hans Hut and Melchior Rink, spread from southern Germany and Switzerland into Luther's Saxony by 1526/1527.[25] They shared Karlstadt's convictions regarding God's way of working in the inner person. Luther had almost no personal contact with them, and because they published little, his information regarding their message often remained imprecise. Luther formed his impressions of the Anabaptist movement from a variety of preachers with various approaches to what they regarded as critical questions. This made his rebuttals of them often less than precise and clear when applied to the larger group called Anabaptists. However, common ideas coming from the medieval program of reform mentioned above did give him the basis for his critique, which merged with his pastoral concern for the assurance that the Holy Spirit offers in the external forms of God's Word. Anabaptist rejection of the power of baptism to bring forgiveness and life on the basis of its being "a mere sign" may have led to his largely abandoning the term "sign" for the sacramental elements after about 1530. God had always used physical signs, Luther insisted. His Word is able to place re-creative power into their use if God has ordained it.[26]

His *Large Catechism*, adapted from catechetical sermons he held over several months, laid out his program for Christian living on the basis of God's baptismal promise:

> In Baptism, therefore, every Christian has enough to study and practice an entire lifetime. Christians always have enough to do to believe firmly what Baptism promises and brings—victory over death and the devil, forgiveness of sin, God's grace, the entire Christ, and the Holy Spirit with

his gifts.... In Baptism there is brought, free of charge, to every person's door ... a treasure and medicine that swallows up death and keeps all people alive. Thus, we must regard Baptism and put it to use in such a way that we may draw strength and comfort from it when our sins or conscience oppress us and say: "But I am baptized! And if I have been baptized, I have the promise that I shall be saved and have eternal life, both in soul and body."[27]

That is possible because God is the actor in baptism. The pastor who baptizes "is an instrument which carries out the baptism. He lends God his hands and tongue, but the words are God's, not the pastor's. 'I baptize you' is not said by the one who is performing the baptism but by the Trinity. The Trinity is baptizing through this tool."[28] "God's omnipotence itself is in baptism. He does not give a simple bath but rather a bath for the soul, through which he cleanses us from all sins and sludge."[29] Assurance of salvation is thus grounded on the Word that is heard and grasped in faith as it comes from outside the self.

Luther's defense of baptism of infants rested on several grounds. He understood the rite to carry in its words God's promise and thus the forgiveness of sins. God acts in the sacrament, he insisted. Furthermore, he had transformed the medieval term "original sin" by defining it as the abiding doubt of God's Word, the lack of faith, that emerges again and again in all Christians, and so he regarded all mortals as showing the marks of sin. He held out the possibility of faith in infants, but in all cases, the validity of God's promise does not rest for him upon its reception in faith: God's baptismal Word established his relationship with every baptized person on the basis of the baptismal Word of God. Its promise eventually cultivates the psychological aspects of the relationship in the human hearer of the Word.[30]

Operating with an element of his "theology of the cross," one facet of which posits that God reveals himself by "hiding" where human reason would not expect him, also in the weakness and foolishness of the Word of the cross (1 Cor. 1:16–2:16), Luther acknowledged that God's Word in baptismal form did not impress "the world" because God's "Word must be the slightest of things."[31] Luther insisted that the way in which God works with his Word is a mystery beyond human comprehension, but nonetheless, he attempted a glimpse at the coordination of Word and elements with analogies: like a rod placed in fire, Word and water permeate each other; like water mixed with tasty spices and sugar for a sick person, baptismal water carries the Word's life-restoring forgiveness.[32] The promissory nature of God's baptismal Word led Luther to set aside his usual reluctance to use the term "covenant." The Ockhamist use of "covenant" defined it as a mutually obliging agreements reached by two partners, both of whom contributed something. But it was clear that infants could not say of their baptisms, "I did this myself." Therefore, Luther thought of the baptismal covenant in much the same fashion as modern Old Testament scholars see God's covenants with his chosen people as "suzerainty covenants." Such covenants mandate that the suzerain retains complete control while requiring an appropriate response, in this case, trust in the promise.[33] God causes this rhythm of repentance and trust in the promise that takes form in confession and absolution, whether personal, private with another Christian, or general in the congregation's liturgy. This rhythm actualizes Luther's distinction of law and gospel.[34]

Baptism not only establishes the believer's relationship with God. It also creates the community of Christ's people and serves as a "sign" that they are one in him.[35] However, most important for Luther was that baptism "delivers forgiveness of sins, redeems from death and the devil, and gives eternal salvation to all who believe, as the Word and promises of God declare."[36]

The Lord's Supper

Pastoral and polemical concerns also shaped Luther's public presentation of the Lord's Supper. The latter sometimes overshadowed the former, although the pastoral application of comfort in the body and blood of Christ given and shed "for you" determined the intensity and seriousness with which he addressed differing viewpoints. Because the mass stood at the center of the religious belief and practice of his youth, Luther first focused on its abuses because he saw in its use *ex opere operato* a denial of the key role of faith and thus a rejection of God's established way of relating to his human creatures through his Word and their response of trust. Secondary in his initial critique of medieval sacramental thinking was his objection to the attempt to explain

Christ's presence in the Lord's Supper through the resort to rational elucidation in the terms of Aristotelian physics, transubstantiation, or consubstantiation.

Luther's teaching on the Lord's Supper evolved quickly. In 1519, he composed his *Sermon on the Blessed Sacrament of the Holy, True Body of Christ*. It diverged from much medieval dogmatic and devotional writing on the subject by highlighting the communal aspects of the sacrament: it joins Christians together with one another and with the Lord, whose body and blood they receive, a theme that never completely disappeared from the reformer's sacramental writings but that diminished in prominence as other topics commanded his attention. Without accenting the nature of the Supper as a promise that delivers forgiveness and life, he praised it as a "ford, bridge, door, ship, or stretcher, by and in which we pass from this world into eternal life," through faith.[37] Emphasis on the promise clearly emerged in his *Sermon on the New Testament*, which appeared in the mid-1520s. The essential elements of his mature understanding of the Holy Spirit's use of Word and elements in the sacrament had fallen into place. Apart from the promise and trust in the promise of the benefits of Christ's death and resurrection "for you," the sacraments are nothing. To make this clear, polemical critique of what Luther regarded as magical sacramental practice and dogmatic disregard for the necessity of faith was required.[38]

This work laid out ideas that Luther's *Babylonian Captivity* developed in detail three months later. It set forth three objections to medieval sacramental practice, each of which grew out of pastoral concern and found expression in polemical criticism. First, he found the refusal of the chalice to the laity a tyrannous defiance of Christ's command and an unjustified assertion of the power and position of the priest over the laity.[39] Second, less seriously, he recounted his doubts about the theory of transubstantiation, grounded in the fifteenth-century theologian Pierre d'Ailly's venturing to say that, had the church not decreed otherwise, consubstantiation would be a plausible explanation of Christ's presence in the Lord's Supper. Luther found both theories unjustified assertions of human reason into God's mystery of Christ's true presence in body and blood in the sacrament.[40]

Third, most seriously, he rejected the interpretation of the Lord's Supper as the repetition of Christ's sacrifice for sin through the priest's actions, as he understood the church's teaching. Always granting that worship is a human thanksgiving directed toward God, Luther could not tolerate the idea that what priests do in celebrating the mass contributed to the removal of sin from participants and replicated in any way what Christ had accomplished on the cross. In addition, he rejected the ritualism and commercialization of the liturgy of the Lord's Supper, the mass, as well as its diversion of trust from Christ's promise in the words of institution to the actions of the priest and the participation of the laity in the sacramental liturgy.[41] Instead, he insisted that the Lord's Supper is a testament, "a promise made by one about to die, in which he designates his bequest and appoints his heirs.... What we call the mass is a promise of the forgiveness of sins made to us by God and ... confirmed by the death of the Son of God."[42] God's action and gift elicit faith: "where there is the Word of the promising God, there must necessarily be the faith of the accepting human being," from which love proceeds in fulfilling God's law.[43] Luther demanded abolition of a series of abuses, including private masses and masses for the dead. In the following five years, Luther cultivated faith in God's saving gift and action in the Lord's Supper through a series of pointed appraisals of medieval practice: *The Misuse of the Mass* (1521),[44] *Receiving Both Kinds in the Sacrament* (1522),[45] *The Adoration of the Sacrament* (1523),[46] and *The Abomination of the Secret Mass* (1525).[47]

By 1525, however, a new challenge to Luther's understanding of the Lord's Supper arose. He believed that Christ's body and blood are truly present and received in and with the consecrated bread and wine of the Lord's Supper. He saw no reason not to interpret Christ's words literally, even though his literary sensitivities recognized the vital role of metaphor in Scripture. His Ockhamist understanding of God's power to order the world and thus create the ways in which his universe functions enabled him to set aside the presuppositions about the relationship of material and spiritual realities that in different ways arose out of Platonic and Aristotelian systems of defining the possible. The fifteenth-century revival of Plato's thought influenced the biblical humanism that played a role in the thinking of all reformers; Aristotle had dominated the European intellectual scene since the thirteenth century. Humanists such as Zurich's reformer Ulrich Zwingli, a product of both Scotist Aristotelianism and biblical humanism, reiterated Karlstadt's rejection of Luther's view in 1524.⁴⁸ Basel's reformer, Johannes Oecolampadius, supported him, sharing Zwingli's fear that Luther remained stuck in a superstitious, magical use of the sacraments' physical elements. Their emphasis on the symbolic or representative nature of the bread and wine of the sacrament seemed to Luther to threaten the way in which the Holy Spirit delivers the gospel's comfort through the Supper. He reacted in a series of treatises from 1526 to 1528.

The Sacrament of the Body and Blood of Christ contained the Wittenberg professor's assertion of God's use of material elements, including the flesh of Jesus Christ, human language, and the sacramental elements, to convey the benefits of Christ's death and resurrection to his people. He argued that God's way of accomplishing his will consistently defies human reason. Objections that it is neither necessary nor appropriate for Christ's body and blood to be in the bread and wine ignore what Christ says in the words instituting the Supper.⁴⁹ His "theology of the cross" led Luther to conclude that his opponents were

> mak[ing] God's glory an altogether earthly and carnal thing, just as it would be inglorious for a worldly king to be hanged or crucified. But the glory of our God is precisely that for our sakes he comes down to the very depths, into human flesh, into bread, into our mouth, our heart, our bosom; moreover, for our sakes he allows himself to be treated ingloriously both on the cross and on the altar.⁵⁰

His opponents replied with stinging criticism,⁵¹ eliciting longer rejoinders from Luther, in which he examined their arguments in detail and reinforced his own position on Christ's presence in the Lord's Supper: *That These Words of Christ, "This Is my Body," etc., Still Stand Firm against the Ravers* (1527),⁵² and *Confession Concerning Christ's Supper* (1528).⁵³ The sides squared off in two camps even if they both found contradictions among adherents of the other side: the Lutherans could not agree, the Swiss observed, on whether Christ's body was in or under the bread, "a clear contradiction," while Luther noted that Zwingli held that the bread represented the body, Oecolampadius that the bread is a sign of the body, and Karlstadt that Jesus said "this" in the words of institution while pointing to his own body at the table.⁵⁴ Detailed analysis of the rules of grammar and syntax accompanied meticulous examination of the relevant Scripture texts from both sides in the exchange.[55] Not only did biblical exegesis play a critical role in these debates, but citations from the Church Fathers also filled the argument of both sides, as they would in subsequent Reformed-Lutheran debates on the Supper.[56]

His opponents not only diminished God's omnipotence by contending that the bestowal of Christ's body and blood in the Supper was impossible and inappropriate for the divine, Luther believed, but also threatened a proper understanding of the hypostatic union of Christ's two natures. All Reformation-era theologians held to the doctrine of the communication of attributes (*communicatio idiomatum*) promulgated at the Council of Chalcedon in 451. It taught that the human and divine natures of Christ are so united that they share characteristics although the natures do not as such possess the characteristics of the other. They retain their own distinct integrity and identity. Zwingli argued that Jesus's ascension to the "right hand of the Father" meant that his human nature could be located only in heaven at the Father's right hand. Luther replied, "The Scriptures teach us that God's right hand is not a specific place in which a body must or may be . . . but is God's almighty power, which at one and the same time can be nowhere and yet must be everywhere. It cannot be [restricted to] any one place."[57] Because the human nature could share the divine nature's characteristic of being present wherever God wills to be present in whatever form, Christ's body and blood could be present in the Lord's Supper.

The Christological context for understanding Christ's presence in the Lord's Supper became an ever more important part of the exchange. Luther argued that the biblical concept of God's presence, specifically that of the God-man, Jesus Christ, has several aspects. He is present in the "circumscribed corporeal mode of his Incarnation." He exhibited his "incomprehensible, spiritual mode" of presence as he passed through the locked door on Easter evening (John 10:19). Without presuming to describe or explain his presence in the Lord's Supper, Luther held out on the basis of these various modes of presence that his body and blood could be present in the Supper and that, not on the basis of this theorizing, but on the basis of his words of institution, they truly are present.[58]

Zwingli also argued that Christ's body cannot be present in the Supper because "the flesh is of no avail" (John 6:63). Luther followed one medieval tradition of interpreting this chapter and held that it did not discuss the Lord's Supper, but he also argued that Jesus indeed claimed that his flesh brings a saving benefit to the faithful (John 6:53, 55–56).[59] He defined "flesh" on the basis of Paul's contrast with "spirit": "flesh" here refers to all that opposes the Holy Spirit.

The desire to reach accord among the forces opposing the papacy within the German lands brought Luther and his Wittenberg colleagues together with Zwingli, Oecolampadius, and several of their supporters in a colloquy at Marburg in October 1529. They agreed on fourteen articles of doctrine but could not agree on the nature of Christ's presence in the sacrament.[60] The conversation cooled the public polemic, however, which remained true for a while after Zwingli's death on the battlefield, 11 October 1531.

Martin Bucer, reformer in Strasbourg, had held a position closer to Luther's than to Zwingli's while sharing much of the philosophical underpinnings of Zwingli's teaching. Bucer had aroused animosity in Wittenberg with translations of passages by Luther's colleague Johannes Bugenhagen on the Lord's Supper, which misrepresented their teaching, giving it a Zwinglian shade. However, Philip Melanchthon negotiated with Bucer and formulated the "Wittenberg Concord" of 1536. Both sides agreed that "with the bread and wine the body and blood of Christ are truly and essentially present, distributed, and received . . . and the body and blood of Christ are truly distributed even to the unworthy; the unworthy truly receive the body and blood when the sacrament is conducted according to Christ's command."[61] Three points of compromise mark this wording. Bucer affirmed that Christ's body and blood are received "with" but not "in" or "under" the elements; Luther held the three prepositions to be synonymous, no more than attempts to confess the mystery of the presence. Luther's definition of "reception of the body and blood through the mouth" (*manducatio oralis*) was missing. Instead of Luther's "reception by the impious" (*manducatio impiorum*), an affirmation that God's Word alone effects Christ's presence, an almost synonymous expression, "partaking by the unworthy" (*manducatio indignorum*), allowed Bucer to hold that Christ is present only for those who receive the sacrament in faith, albeit in this case weak faith. Both sides went away teaching their own interpretations of the agreement.[62] A year later, in his *Smalcald Articles*, Luther defined Christ's presence simply: "the bread and the wine in the Supper are the true body and blood of Christ and they are not only offered to and received by upright Christians but also by evil people."[63]

The question of the presence of Christ was important for Luther because it was the basis of the comfort given to anxious repentant sinners through the Lord's Supper. He expressed this pastoral concern in the midst of his polemic in sermons, lectures on Scripture, and devotional treatises. His *Large Catechism* taught that the Lord's Supper "is appropriately called food of the soul, for it nourishes and strengthens the new creature. . . . [It] is given as a daily food and sustenance so that our faith may be refreshed and strengthened and that it may not succumb in the struggle but become stronger and stronger."[64] Indeed,

> because he offers and promises forgiveness of sins, it can be received in no other way than by faith. This faith he himself demands in the Word when he says, "given FOR YOU" and "shed FOR YOU." . . . The treasure is opened and placed at everyone's door, yes upon the table, but it also falls to you to take it and confidently believe that it is just as the words tell you.[65]

Ockhamist presuppositions permitted Luther to be comfortable with the possibility of God's using the material elements of his creation in executing his saving will.

Conclusion

Pastoral concerns focused Luther's attention on finding the comfort of the gospel of Christ's death and resurrection in God's address in Scripture and the various forms of communication that arise out of it. His doctrine of creation and his understanding of human nature pointed him to God's desire to engage his people with all the senses. Thus, Luther processed the medieval heritage of sacramental practice with a sharp critique of what he regarded as a magical use of sacramental words and as a disregard for the necessity of faith. But he also rejected those opinions that spiritualized God's sacramental approach to his chosen people. He found in baptism and the Lord's Supper, as in the oral and written Word of God, the created, material means by which God gives the forgiveness of sins, life, and salvation. God used the sacramental elements as settings for the Word of promise that created and sustained new life in these sacramental forms of his Word.

NOTES

1. *Die Bekenntnisschriften der Evangelisch-lutherischen Kirche*, ed. Irene Dingel (Göttingen: Vandenhoeck & Ruprecht, 2014), 583 (hereafter cited as BSELK); *The Book of Concord*, ed. Robert Kolb and Timothy J. Wengert (Minneapolis: Fortress, 2000), 398 (hereafter cited as BC).
2. J. L. Austin, *How to Do Things with Words* (Oxford: Oxford University Press, 1961); John R. Searle, *Speech Acts: An Essay in the Philosophy of Language* (Cambridge: Cambridge University Press, 1969).
3. *D. Martin Luthers Werke* (Weimar: Böhlau, 1883–1993), vol. 30, p. 1:345, lines 1–12 (hereafter cited as WA); *Luther's Works* (St. Louis: Concordia/Fortress, 1958–1986), 53:118 (hereafter cited as LW).
4. WA 7:49, 22–25; LW 31:344.
5. LW 7:50, 32–51, 3; LW 31:345.
6. As he noted in a sermon on baptism, 1528, WA 27:53, 5–17.
7. BSELK 884/885; BC 359.
8. BSELK 890/891; BC 362–63.
9. *Babylonian Captivity of the Church*, WA 6:571, 35–572, 34; LW 36:123–25.
10. WA 7:543, 4–549, 19; 572, 15–17; LW 36:81–91, 124.
11. Robert Kolb, *Bound Choice, Election, and Wittenberg Theological Method: From Martin Luther to the Formula of Concord* (Grand Rapids, MI: Eerdmans, 2005), 21–23, 62–65.
12. BSELK 770/771–72/773; BC 322–23.
13. Jonathan D. Trigg, *Baptism in the Theology of Martin Luther* (Leiden: Brill, 1992), 2.
14. As Gerhard O. Forde defined justification, understood in the context of Luther's thought, in *Justification by Faith: A Matter of Death and Life* (1982; repr., Mifflintown, PA: Sigler, 1991); see Luther's affirmation of this in his *Babylonian Captivity*, WA 6:534, 3–20; LW 36:67–68. References to baptism as new birth or new creation abound in his preaching, e.g., WA 37:645, 15, 46:167, 13–17, 29–31; 174, 17–22; 175, 1–2; WA 47:650, 18–562, 21; 47:654, 17–20.
15. In his 1523 order for baptism, WA 12:47, 11–20; LW 53:102; cf. a sermon of 1538, WA 46:179–83.
16. WA 6:527, 33–528, 35; LW 36:58–60.
17. E.g., his *Sermon on the Holy, Blessed Sacrament of Baptism*, 1519, WA 2:727–37; LW 35:29–43; on Luther's later baptismal, see Robert Kolb, "'What Benefit Does the Soul Receive from a Handful of Water?' Luther's Preaching on Baptism, 1528–1539," *Concordia Journal* 25 (1999): 346–63.
18. Norman Cohn, *The Pursuit of the Millennium*, 3rd ed. (Oxford: Oxford University Press, 1970).

19. Amy Nelson Burnett, *Karlstadt and the Origins of the Eucharistic Controversy: A Study in the Circulation of Ideas* (Oxford: Oxford University Press, 2011).
20. Issued in two parts in early 1525: *Against the Heavenly Prophets in the Matter of Images and Sacraments*, WA 18:62–125 and 134–214; LW 40:79–143 and 144–223.
21. WA 18:62, 6–7; LW 40:79.
22. WA 18:136, 9–17; LW 40:146.
23. WA 18:137, 12–16; LW 40:147.
24. WA 18:136, 24–137, 19; LW 40:146–47.
25. John S. Oyer, *Lutheran Reformers against Anabaptists: Luther, Melanchthon and Menius and the Anabaptists of Central Germany* (The Hague: Nijhoff, 1964), esp. 46–74.
26. Cf. a sermon from 1528, WA 27:53, 5–17; 55, 24–56, 10; 57, 6–29; 60, 2–21.
27. WA 699–700; LC 41–44.
28. WA 46:148, 36–149, 27. Luther repeated the point in another sermon in 1539, WA 47:648, 2–3, 23–25.
29. WA 46:169, 10–170, 31.
30. BSELK 1122/1123–32/1133; BC 462–67.
31. WA 37:258, 12–15.
32. WA 37:258, 15–25. This is a paraphrase of what follows, WA 37:258, 12–15.
33. E.g., Luther's sermon of 1528, WA 27:50, 16–52, 35; or sermons of 1538, WA 46:172, 12–35, 195–99. On ancient Near Eastern suzerainty covenants, see George E. Mendenhall and Gary A. Herion, "Covenant," in *The Anchor Bible Dictionary*, ed. David Noel Freedman (New York: Doubleday, 1992), 1:1180–82.
34. Robert Kolb, *Martin Luther, Confessor of the Faith* (Oxford: Oxford University Press, 2009), 68–71, 167–70.
35. WA 27:57, 30–58, 1.
36. Small Catechism, BSELK 882/883; BC 359.
37. WA 2:742, 5–747, 3; LW 35:49–56.
38. WA 2:751, 18–752, 24; LW 35:63–65; WA 6:364, 14–373, 8; LW 35:93–106. Luther repeated this critique often; cf. *The Misuse of the Mass*, 1521, WA 8:506–37; LW 36:162–98; and *The Adoration of the Sacrament*, 1523, WA 11:431–56; LW 36:275–305.
39. WA 6:502, 1–507, 34; LW 36:19–28.
40. WA 6:508, 1–512, 6; LW 36:28–35.
41. WA 6:512, 7–536, 33; LW 36:35–57.
42. WA 6:513, 24–36; LW 36:38.
43. WA 6:514, 13–25; LW 36:39.
44. WA 8:482–563; LW 36:133–230.
45. WA 10, 2:11–41; LW 36:237–67.
46. WA 11:431–56; LW 36:275–305.
47. WA 18:22–36; LW 36:311–28.
48. On the Scotist influence on Zwingli, see Daniel Bolliger, *Infiniti contemplatio: Grundzüge der Scotus- und Scotismusrezeption im Werk Huldrych Zwinglis* (Leiden: Brill, 2003).

49. WA 19:492–523; LW 36:335–61.
50. WA 23:156, 28–34; LW 37:72.
51. Walter Köhler, *Zwingli und Luther*, 2 vols. (Leipzig: Heinsius, 1924; Gütersloh: Bertelsmann, 1953), 1:619–729; cf. Huldrych Zwingli Werke, *Amica Exegesis* (Berlin: Schwetschke; Leipzig: Heinsius, 1905–63), 1527, *Corpus Reformatorum*, vols. 88–101 (hereafter cited as CR) 92:548–758; *Klare Unterricht*, 1526, CR 91:773–862; *Das diese Worte*, 1527, CR 92:795–977.
52. WA 23:64–283; LW 37:13–159. Luther coined the term "Schwärmer," here translated "Raver," often translated "Enthusiast," from the cognate of the English "swarm" referring to those who, he believed, ignored Scripture and used reason to spin their own ideas. He applied it to Anabaptists and spiritualists first but then also to those who differed from him regarding Christ's presence in the Lord's Supper.
53. WA 26:261–509; LW 37:161–372.
54. WA 23:88, 33–124, 25; LW 37:30–51.
55. In Luther's writings, see, e.g., WA 26:437, 30–445, 17; LW 37:294–303 for detailed analysis. In Luther's writings, see, e.g., WA 26:445, 18–498, 30; LW 37:303–60 for meticulous examination.
56. Esther Chung-Kim, *Inventing Authority: The Use of the Church Fathers in Reformation Debates over the Eucharist* (Waco, TX: Baylor University Press, 2011).
57. WA 23:133, 19–134, 11; LW 37:57.
58. WA 26:326, 12–338, 17; LW 37:214–26.
59. WA 23:167, 28–208, 27; LW 37:78–104; WA 26:360, 26–377, 31; LW 37:241–51.
60. See reports on the colloquy in WA 30, 3:160–71; LW 38:15–89.
61. *Martin Bucers Deutsche Schriften, Band 6,1. Wittenberger Konkordie (1536)*, ed. Robert Stuperich et al. (Gütersloh: Mohn, 1988), 120–25. The passage is found on these pages because there are parallels in the Latin and German texts and lots of notes.
62. Gordon A. Jensen, "Luther and Bucer on the Lord's Supper," *Lutheran Quarterly* 27 (2013): 167–87.
63. BSELK 766/767; BC 320.
64. BSELK 1138/1139; BC 469.
65. BSELK 1142/1143; BC 470.

9

Huldrych Zwingli

BRUCE GORDON

Huldrych Zwingli (1484–1531) was born in the Swiss valley of Toggenburg and began his studies with his uncle, who taught him Latin. After further study in Bern, Vienna, and Basel, Zwingli earned his baccalaureate and master's of liberal arts in 1504 and 1506. At the age of twenty-two he was ordained a priest and served in the mountainous canton of Glarus, a center of the mercenary service. During the time in Glarus he began his humanist studies, inspired by the great Erasmus. Zwingli came to know the Dutchman well and by 1516 was fully persuaded of the place of humanist studies in Christian life. One of the formative moments of Zwingli's life was his experience as chaplain to the Swiss mercenaries in Italy, where the senseless slaughter of young men for the profit of others shocked the young priest. The same year Zwingli went to serve as priest at the great Benedictine Abbey at Einsiedeln, where he preached regularly to pilgrims and studied the works of the Church Fathers in the monastery's wonderful library. In 1519 Zwingli moved to serve as priest in the Grossmünster church in Zurich, where he remained till his death in 1531. Something of a conversion experience followed in 1519 when Zwingli nearly died of the plague. He began to articulate a new vision of the Christian life in which a loving, omnipotent God demanded a faithfulness of the people fulfilled in lives of communal holiness. From the pulpit, Zwingli took aim at the mercenary service and its corrupting force in the community. He persuaded the city magistrates not to renew the military alliance with France, a highly controversial move. By 1522 Zwingli was preaching against the mass and other aspects of Catholic theology. Without doubt he was highly influenced by the writings of Martin Luther. In 1523 after a series of debates Zwingli succeeded in having the evangelical faith gain the upper hand. Preaching from the Bible was declared the standard to be expected. The Reformation in

Zurich was not introduced until two years later, in 1525, when the first Reformed Lord's Supper was performed in the Grossmünster at Easter. By that point Zwingli was already locked in a vicious struggle with Martin Luther over the sacraments. The debate divided the Reformation world, and the attempt by Philipp of Hesse to have the matter settled by a meeting of the reformers at Marburg in 1529 failed. During the last years of his life Zwingli pursued an aggressive policy of attempting to have the Swiss Catholic Cantons coerced into accepting the Reformation. He failed miserably. In 1531, in a nocturnal skirmish he was killed by Catholic opponents and his body was ritually desecrated. During his career as a reformer Zwingli was a prolific author, most of his writings printed by his friend Christoph Froschauer. Zwingli was a talented preacher and a gifted writer, and his major theological works, such as *On True and False Religion*, *On Providence*, and *Fidei Ratio*, have remained admired texts of Reformation thought. His influence on the development of the Reformed theological tradition was enormous.

Introduction

It was a tragic moment of the Reformation in 1529 when Martin Luther and Huldrych Zwingli parted from their colloquy at Marburg without acknowledgment as brothers.[1] There was to be no unified Protestant view of the sacraments other than that they numbered two, and the centers of the Reformation, Wittenberg and Zurich, remained fully estranged.[2] The encounter had not been a farce, a mere war of words. On many points there was a degree of consensus. Yet, their parting handshake confirmed that the two reformers held fundamentally different theological understandings of the nature of the Son of God and of his presence in the sacrament of the Lord's Supper. They were never to meet again, and in two years Zwingli was dead. To the end, Luther and Zwingli believed that at Marburg they had defended the essential teaching of the Gospel. And both were convinced that the other held an erroneous view of Christ.

From the earliest years of the Reformation Luther and Zwingli led the revolt against the Catholic Church and its doctrine of transubstantiation. Differences in their positions, however, were soon exposed. By the time of the meeting at Marburg in 1529, the rancorous debate between the Wittenberg and Zurich churches had lasted almost six years. The toll taken by the endless polemical exchange, in which a bundle of issues were subsumed into the quarrel over the nature of the sacraments, was incalculable. The curtain of the Reformation was torn, never to be mended, defeating the efforts of John Calvin and others who later sought to reconcile the Lutheran and Reformed churches.[3]

Certainly, although Luther and Zwingli bore no fondness for one another, there was a degree of grudging respect. Zwingli acknowledged Luther's prophetic role as the first reformer, and the Wittenberg professor recognized the Swiss churchman as a man of formidable learning. The battle over the sacraments in the 1520s, however, cannot be reduced to a clash of personalities or egos, whatever personal acrimony existed. The theological differences in the sacramental debates of the 1520s were profound, revealing conflicting theologies based on divergent readings of Scripture. This chapter deals with Zwingli and the distinctiveness of the Swiss reformer's understanding of the relationship between the divine and human, and how his interpretation shaped his teaching on the sacraments. Although a broadly chronological order is followed, the argument focuses on the significant theological issues rather than the history of the exchanges.[4]

To speak of Zwingli's "theology" of the sacraments is misleading. Between 1524 and 1531 he wrote prodigiously on both Baptism and the Lord's Supper, and his thought evolved over the years, particularly on the Lord's Supper. Rather than systematic works, we encounter the combative manner in which Zwingli wrote and argued about the sacraments. Some key texts, such as his *On True and False Religion* and the later *Fidei Ratio*, were comprehensive in character; however, for the most part he penned his writing on the sacraments almost entirely in the polemical cut and thrust of the 1520s. Zwingli engaged in theological battle over the sacraments on three fronts: on Baptism, he faced the Anabaptists in his own city, while on the Lord's Supper he was at war with two opponents: Catholics and Lutherans. Much of the time the Zurich reformer stood on the back foot, responding to accusations of heresy furiously hurled against him.

Famously, at the Colloquy of Marburg in 1529, Luther chalked the words *Hoc est corpus meum* ("This is my body") onto the table.[5] Whatever his hosts may have thought of the damage done to their furniture, these words of Christ divided the Reformation. What did Jesus intend? What Luther aimed was to argue that "is" meant "is," a bodily, real presence. Zwingli, in reply, looked to Scripture to argue that "is" meant "signifies," as in pointing to the reality of the ascended body of Christ. The matter was not mere semantics, but revelatory of two entirely contrasting understandings of the presence of the Son of God in the world—two positions that necessarily led to divergent teachings on the sacraments. Luther and Zwingli held to radically opposing Christologies, while they both looked to the ancient church and its councils for support. The two reformers spoke of the "real presence" of Christ, but their language left unanswered questions. The principal conundrum was how or whether Christ could be present in both his divine and human natures. Zwingli argued that in the Lord's Supper Christ was present in his divine nature alone. His human body was ascended to heaven. Luther countered that Christ's humanity was for eternity and that a radical separation of the two was untenable. This debate, which focused on different aspects of Christ's salvific work, lay at the core of the sacramental quarrel that irreparably divided Protestantism.

For Zwingli, and his followers, there was an absolute gulf between the divine and the human.[6] God was Spirit and pure, while humanity, in sharp contrast, was flesh and corrupted. Zwingli did not adhere to the Augustinian idea of original sin. The Zurich reformer preferred to speak of a disease that is not in itself bad until manifested in the works of humans.[7] What Zwingli further claimed, however, made him a distinctive voice in the early Reformation. Objects of the material world can never be conduits or instruments by which the Spirit is conveyed. In other words, Zwingli was adamant that the divine could by no means be limited by the fleshly or earthly creations through which it acted. Materials such as bread, wine, or water, and human rituals such as Baptism or the Lord's Supper cannot make any claim on the divine. Priests cannot conjure God by performing the liturgy, and God cannot be confined to the space and form of bread. Zwingli's emphasis on the sovereignty and freedom of God left him with an understanding of sacrament and ritual that precluded both as means of grace. Both sacrament and ritual were symbolic, outward manifestations of what God had already done in Christ.

The Nature of Sacraments

At the heart of his liturgical efforts was Zwingli's understanding of sacrament. In his *Fidei Ratio* to Charles V, written in the summer of 1530, the reformer argued,

> I believe, therefore, O Emperor, that a sacrament is a sign of a sacred thing, i.e., of grace that has been given. I believe that it is a visible figure or form of the invisible grace, provided and bestowed by God's bounty; i.e., a visible example that presents an analogy to something done by the Spirit. I believe that it is a public testimony.[8]

It would take Zwingli some time to arrive at this formulation at the end of his life, but the essential point was clear. His crucial conviction was an absolute refusal to countenance that sacrament and sacrifice could be the same thing. Otherwise, how could the last rites be a sacrament, for it is not found in the Bible? A sacrament can only be something mandated by God. It was the sign (*signum*) of a holy thing, such as the body and blood of Christ. Zwingli did not much care for the term "sacrament," using the word only because it was commonly employed in the church. The designation of sacrament did not interest him theologically.[9] What mattered far more was the distinction between what came from the Word of God and what did not, between that which is divine command and the human response. For Zwingli the only real sacrament is the work of God in the death and resurrection of Jesus Christ. This was the true unity of Word and action.[10]

In November 1523, Zwingli wrote his *Brief Christian Introduction*, in which he summarized his early thinking on the sacraments.[11] He made it clear that central to his teaching was the rejection of the sacrificial nature of the priesthood and the mass. The language of sacrifice, he held, was wholly misplaced, and to hold to any propitiatory quality to the sacraments was to diminish Christ's saving work. According to Romans 12:1 ("I plead with you to give your bodies to God because of all he has done for you. Let them be a living and holy sacrifice—the kind he will find acceptable. This is truly the way to worship him"), Zwingli wrote, the highest sacrifice a person can make is of himself or herself.

The only proper rituals of the church were the water of font and the meal given by Christ, who taught the church to celebrate a "testament" and "commemoration." Through his blood believers were reconciled with the Father and a new covenant founded, the testament of Christ. The bread and wine were for the reformer visible symbols of Christ's flesh and blood left for the benefit of the faithful after he had ascended. It was this message of hope, Zwingli argued, that was to be preached throughout the year.

In 1525, Froschauer printed Zwingli's *On True and False Religion*, which was dedicated to Francis I of France, though it most likely was never received.[12] We find in this lengthy work, which appeared the year Zurich adopted the Reformation, an extensive treatment of the sacraments. After exploring several versions of the "sacrament," including meanings that it denoted a pledge (Varro), an oath, and a military sacrament by which soldiers swear obedience, Zwingli rejected any suggestion that the word meant a sacred or secret thing.[13] Instead, he argued that the sacrament was an initiatory rite whereby those who enter into a covenantal relationship give of themselves, as Romans 12:1 described. "A sacrament," Zwingli continued, "since it cannot be anything more than an initiation or public inauguration, cannot have any power to free the conscience."[14]

Zwingli opened *On True and False Religion* by refuting positions he attributed to unnamed opponents before arriving at his own key definition. There are two sacraments, Baptism and the Lord's Supper. Although he dropped his early belief in the sacramental nature of penance, he continued to believe that confession and repentance were essential parts of Christian spirituality.[15] The Zurich reformer offers his classic definition in his *Fidei Ratio* of 1530.

Baptism

In his *On True and False Religion* of 1525 Zwingli set out the relationship between Baptism and the Lord's Supper. The former begins a life of godliness that is to be sustained by the latter. "We receive," Zwingli writes,

> a token that we are to fashion our lives according to the rule of Christ; by the Lord's Supper we give proof that we trust in the death of Christ, glad

and thankful to be in that company which gives thanks to the Lord for the blessing of redemption that he freely gave us by dying for us.[16]

For Zwingli, the sacrament of Baptism signified the entrance of the child into the body of the church, where he or she should learn to live, following the example of the faithful parents, a life of rectitude. Central to his conception of the Christian life was the concept of purity, which Zwingli understood as holiness. The faithful should live in imitation of the perfection of God as expressed in 1 Peter 1:16 ("Be holy as I am holy"). Purity is a recurring theme in the reformer's writings, a distinctive yearning for moral betterment that expressed Zwingli's profound sense of the distance between God and humanity. As God was pure Spirit, Zwingli preached against the moral turpitude he saw plaguing society, separating it from the divine image. Baptism was entrance into a covenantal relationship in which the church was committed to holiness.

Augustine's doctrine of the sacraments, to which Zwingli repeatedly appealed, possessed a language of signification that the reformer found helpful. Yet, Zwingli and the church father differed on significant points. In particular, Zwingli's approach to the relationship between grace in baptism and the ritual of the sacrament was expressed in language of analogy.[17] He fiercely repudiated any sense of the sacrament being the conduit through which grace was transmitted by God to his faithful. Such an understanding, which Zwingli attributed to the Roman church, shifted the emphasis away from God to the human performance and the working of the rite. It limited the unlimited grace of God to the deeds and actions of a priest, so Zwingli argued.

In contrast, the reformer taught that when the child is baptized in the church, the ritual of the sacrament is an analogy of what God has done in the Spirit. The water does not convey the Spirit, which alone conveys grace and brings about true repentance. Zwingli saw Catholic and Lutheran teaching on the sacraments as an assault on God's freedom. "It divides his singular will, that is, to be how, where, and what he wants."[18] God acts upon the inner person, leaving no salvific role for external elements such as water in baptism and bread and wine in the Lord's Supper.

A major statement on baptism came in 1525 with *Baptism, Rebaptism, and Infant Baptism*, in which his emerging positions were clearly set out.[19] For Zwingli, it was crucial to establish that the baptism of John and that of Christ were the same thing. This argument was directed against the Anabaptists, demonstrating that Christ submitted to John's baptism, as we should.[20] Zwingli proceeded to his two major arguments for infant baptism. First, that children are no less a part of the family of God than their parents and, second, that God would not refuse them baptism, as he did not reject them in the Old Testament and Christ welcomed them. Zwingli drew on a tradition of equating baptism with the covenantal act of circumcision by which the Israelites entered into relationship with God. "For there is one Church, one Faith, and God," Zwingli writes,

> is not more angry with us and our children than he was with the Jews, whose children were just as much in the covenant and in the Church as their fathers were. Here also there is an analogy: circumcision was given to the children of the Hebrews. Therefore baptism ought not to be refused the children of Christians.[21]

In *On True and False Religion*, Zwingli spoke of two forms of Baptism. The first was the inflowing of the Holy Spirit without which no one can be saved, "for no one can be saved without faith, and faith is not born save at the instance of the Holy Spirit"[22] Second, there is outward rite of baptism, which does not bring salvation but does edify others, who by the baptism of water feel faith within themselves and "enlightenment of soul"[23].

Zwingli returned to the baptism administered by John and concluded that it was no different from baptism in Christ, otherwise the Son of God would have baptized his followers again. Christ allowed himself to be baptized by John in order to commend the sacrament to his followers.

> Since, therefore, John taught that life must be changed and modeled after the pattern of Christ, to whom he sent men, and since he proclaimed that Christ himself is our hope, and since Christ taught the same thing (for what does all the teaching of Christ demand but a new life formed according to the will of God and having unwavering trust in Christ?).[24]

Turning to Matthew 28:19, Zwingli considered what it meant to be baptized in the name of the Father, Son, and Holy Ghost, and declared that "name" meant power, majesty, and grace. He turned to the relationship between the words in the outward rite of Baptism and the inner working of the Spirit, arguing that in Baptism those who put on Christ are "thus dedicated to the Father, Son, and Holy Spirit, that is, joined and bound to them."[25] The ritual of the sacrament, the dipping in water, is a sign signifying the real thing.

As his 1525 liturgy represented, Zwingli emphasized the role of the faithful parents in presenting their child to be baptized. Only those who were believing members could do so. The purpose of baptism was greater for those present than for the child, although it bore witness to the faith of the child and God's love. The baptism was a symbol to the people of God's salvific work in Jesus Christ. It was an outward sign of the Christian community.[26]

The Lord's Supper

From the fall of 1524, Zwingli was fully engaged in an attack on the sacrificial nature of the Mass, emphasizing the uniqueness and sufficiency of Christ's death and resurrection. His first response was to move toward the Lord's Supper as a visible symbol of what Christ had achieved in his sacrifice, which believers had access to through God's mercy. The Lord's Supper, he argued, was the faithful response of the community in obedience to God's saving act. Zwingli's assault on the Mass was focused on his unequivocal repudiation of transubstantiation, for which he found no ground in the New Testament.

Zwingli's interest in these years was focused on the real presence of Christ in the Supper, which he vigorously affirmed and emphasized. A profound influence was the letter written by the Dutchman Cornelius Hoen (1440–1524), which circulated in 1524 and was printed a year later. Hoen robustly denied the doctrine of transubstantiation and argued for a symbolic understanding of both the Lord's Supper and the meal as commemoration.[27] Zwingli likely read the letter in 1523, and many of its arguments became foundations of his theology.

Yet, Zwingli's understanding of Christ's real presence did not find clear expression in his early writings. It was in *On True and False Religion* (1525) that the reader finds the reformer's most important treatments of the Lord's Supper. Zwingli argued that the food of which Christ spoke was faith. "It is faith, therefore," he wrote, "that allays all hunger and thirst. But what hunger, and what thirst? Those of the soul, of course."[28] It is faith alone that feeds the soul. Referring to John 6:51, Zwingli states his view succinctly. "Christ," he continued,

> is not speaking here of sacramental eating; for he is only so far salvation unto us as He was slain for us; but he could be slain only according to the flesh and could be salvation bringing only according to his divinity. In this way, then, is Christ the food of the soul, because the soul, seeing that God spared not his only begotten son but delivered him to an ignominious death in order to restore us to life, becomes sure of the grace of God and of salvation.[29]

The crux of the matter was Christ's words "this is my body," which Zwingli famously interpreted to mean "this signifies my body," which he adopted from Hoen. Zwingli's purpose was to establish how Christ commanded the faithful to eat the bread and drink the wine in remembrance of him. He named the Lord's Supper a commemoration of Christ's death that did not, as a ritual, expiate sins. That expiation belonged to Christ's death alone. The people were to give thanks and proclaim the good news of Jesus Christ. When Luke 22:20 speaks of the "testament in my blood," Zwingli interpreted the passage thus: "for in this we commemorate the blessing that Christ's death and the shedding of his blood have brought us, and enjoying these blessings we are grateful unto the Lord God for the testament that he has freely bestowed upon us."[30]

Zwingli's Eucharistic thought was the most distinctive aspect of his theology, offering us a path to his understanding of the relationship between the divine and human, as well as to his teaching on Christian community. The beginning point was the glory of God as expressed in Exodus 20:2: "I am the Lord, your God, who brought you out of the land of Egypt, out of the house of slavery." The import of the first words of the Ten Commandments formed the heart of Zwingli's theology. All that happened in the church and community was through hearing the Word of God under the power of the Spirit. Nothing, no human words, could ever rival God's Word.

Zwingli insisted that God alone was the active agent in the divine/human relationship and that men and women were the passive recipients of his grace. The two sides must never be confused, for the basis for this relationship was not legal and it was grounded not in human merit but in God's election.[31] God alone chooses his own because it pleased him to enter into relationship with humanity through the incarnation, an act entirely from his freedom. Zwingli was loath to speak of God as limited in any way in his actions, and the reformer referred not to God's relationship to the individual or church alone, but to the whole of humanity. It is this conception of God as free, wholly supreme, and gracious that forms the foundation of Zwingli's teaching on the sacraments.

The Zurich reformer did not think in terms of a "sacramental theology." It is more helpful to consider the manner in which he saw the sacraments performed. They were for Zwingli the proper response of God's faithful to their election. They were possible only once one fully acknowledged the nature of the divine, at which point the sacraments assumed the character of a required response shaped by the full realization that God alone speaks. The sacraments exist only insofar as they form part of the relationship between God and humanity and have no independent value.

What was truly for Zwingli holy was that which stood in contrast to fallen humanity, which remained mired in sinfulness and materiality. In other words, Zwingli rejoiced in the possibility of individuals, the church, and human communities being transformed from their fetid state into God's people. Such a glorious change cannot come from the people alone, which is why Zwingli rejected the Lord's Supper as a sacrifice; God in Jesus Christ had once sacrificed himself on the cross, and that propitiatory death sufficed for all humanity. To think otherwise is to deceive oneself that somehow God left open the possibility for his redemptive action to be fulfilled or completed by a human act of sacrifice.

This brings us back to Zwingli's understanding of God. For the reformer, it was unthinkable that an omnipotent God could be restricted to a particular form of action. That proposal would put his sovereignty in question. Rather, God freely chose to act in the manner he did because of his decision to enter into relationship with men and women, who for their part have access to salvation only through Jesus Christ. God both reaches out to humanity and gives the gift of faith to whom he will. No human mind can comprehend that decision. Zwingli emphatically argued that the sole object of God's gracious actions is humanity, with whom God has chosen to enter into a covenantal relationship.

Zwingli's God was an omniscient and all-powerful deity guiding all that happens within his providential care. Such an emphasis on God's power, central to Zwingli's theology, raised questions about human sin and culpability. For Zwingli God's providence and election was an extension of his grace, meaning the elect of God were possibly large communities, including the virtuous pagans. He saw the churches as full of true believers, not some small rump. The church is both the universal body of Christ that holds together believers of all ages and the particular community. The local church is linked to the universal through the faith of believers; when faith is lacking they are not united.

The celebration of the Lord's Supper was the response of the community to God's actions, a response under the guidance of the Holy Spirit to Christ's words, "This is my body given for you, do this in remembrance of me" (Luke 22:19). The foundation of the communal response is God's action in Jesus Christ, and it is in this respect that Zwingli speaks of the Lord's Supper as *commemoratio*.[32] Memory takes the people back to the crucifixion with the words of institution. These words are linked to the symbols of bread and the cup, which serve the weakness of faith of the people. The Lord's Supper is a bringing to mind or revisualizing of Christ's death on the cross.

Crucial to this understanding of the sacrament was memory and remembering. Zwingli, particularly in his later writings, spoke of a *fidei contemplatio*, which was a faithful meditation that moves from the external symbols of Christ to an inward sense of "our Christ." The *fidei contemplatio* was key to understanding Zwingli's view of remembrance and how Christ is present in the bread and wine in both his natures.[33] For Zwingli, Christ is present at the celebration of the Lord's Supper. Zwingli was hesitant to speak in terms of presence, because of the associations with the Mass, but he was clear that with reference to real presence, Christ was present in his divinity. In what manner, precisely, the Holy Spirit works in the Lord's Supper was not a subject on which Zwingli wished to speculate. He preferred to argue that the Spirit could not be limited to or restrained by the institutional church. It could move and act as it wished without in any way damaging God's covenant with humanity.

The relationship between symbol and what is signified in Zwingli was delicately balanced. The bread and wine did not become the body of

Christ; those qualities remained with the Son. Everything that happened did so through the Holy Spirit, through whom the bread and wine, as symbols or images, revealed the similarity to the body and blood. At the same time, however, God was not in any respect bound to that relationship between symbol and reality. Zwingli wanted to preserve the reality of the symbolic relationship while maintaining the absolute freedom of God. The combination of outward form and inner reality of faith confirmed by the Holy Spirit encourages men and women of God's promises. The Lord's Supper is a celebration of God's saving action and of his continuing love toward his chosen.

The Disputations in Zurich in 1523 brought Zwingli's position to light. Drawing attention to Hebrews 10:12–14, Zwingli considered the nature of Christ's sacrifice, rejecting any suggestion that the Mass could claim that there could be a priestly reenactment of that sacrifice on the altar. The eighteenth article of the *Exposition of the 67 Articles*, written following the January Disputation, reads,

> Christ, who sacrificed himself once on the cross, is eternally the effective and ransoming sacrifice for the sins of all the faithful. One that the mass is no sacrifice but rather a repetition of the sacrifice and an assurance of the salvation that Christ has won for us.[34]

The language of sacrifice, so much part of Christian tradition, was difficult to understand in the debates of the 1520s. For those beyond an inner circle of elites, the differences between Luther and Zwingli were not readily clear. One of the issues about the sacramental controversy not widely recognized in Reformation textbooks was the easy confusion of terms, which made it difficult for people to follow the confrontation. Both Luther and Zwingli continued to use the term *sacramentum*, which made the Zurich reformer uneasy, but the German *Opfer* yielded no greater clarity because of its multiple meanings.[35] Many people began to adopt theological positions on the sacraments that drew from both sides.

During 1524, the Lord's Supper dominated Zwingli's writing, and at the end of the year he wrote to the brethren in Strasbourg. Significant at this point was Zwingli's first mention of the place of Christ at the right hand of the Father in heaven. Shortly thereafter, in the early months of 1525 Zwingli realized his long-standing desire to prepare a new liturgy for the Lord's Supper, which was named the *Aktion oder Brauch des Nachtmals*, which was introduced with the abolition of the Mass on 12 April 1525.[36]

In 1526, Zwingli made his first intervention in the Eucharistic Discussion in German, with his *Clear Instruction on Christ's Supper*, where he made clear use of Hussite material.[37] Although not many new arguments are found in the text, Zwingli did provide an account of the Apostles' Creed that focused on Christ's divine and human natures. The distinction made between the Son of God's humanity and divinity became important to Zwingli's treatment of the separation of the two in the Lord's Supper.[38] In particular, Zwingli emphasized that as Christ had ascended to the right hand of the Father he could not be physically present in the sacrament. Further, one of the distinctive elements of Zwingli's Eucharist thought to emerge during the middle years of the 1520s was the analogy between the Lord's Supper and the Jewish Passover meal. The connection was of signal importance in developing Zwingli's idea of the meal as an act of remembrance of Israel's deliverance out of Egypt.

Confrontation with Luther

Zwingli was intensely aware of the dangers posed by the growing split between Zurich and Wittenberg over the Lord's Supper.[39] Luther had written against the Swiss and the Strasbourgers, and Zwingli's friend, Martin Bucer, had urged a personal appeal from Zwingli to the German reformer in German. At stake, naturally, was the common Protestant front on the sacrament. Zwingli chose to write his *Amica Exegesis* (1527) in Latin, so as to not draw too much attention to the debate, and in the text declared both his debt and his gratitude to Luther.

In the *Amica*, the core issue, according to Zwingli, was the bodily presence of Christ in the sacrament.[40] However, the debate was spurious, for the question of real presence in the Lord's Supper was resolved in Scripture. Therefore, to hold to some form of physical eating, as Luther did, was to hew to an unbiblical error of the past. At the same time, Zwingli rejected those "sacramentarians" or "fanatics" who denied any form of real presence whatsoever. The key was the proper understanding of John 6:69, the text to which Zwingli continually returned in explicating his Eucharistic theology. In *On True and False Religion* he interpreted the passage to reveal the true nature of Christ as the Son of God.[41]

It was clear that the theological core of the dispute between Zwingli and Luther was their Christologies.[42] Zwingli held that Luther made an unfortunate mixture of the divine and human natures in Christ. The Zurich reformer argued that Luther attributed to one nature what properly belonged to the other in the error of the *communicatio idiomatum*.[43] It was the revival of old church debates over the relationship of the two natures of Christ and the possibility of a *communicatio idiomatum*. For Zwingli, it was crucial to uphold the Chalcedonian formula by which the two natures of Christ are not mixed, a position that lay at the heart of his rejection of any notion of bodily presence in the Lord's Supper.

Distinctive to Zwingli's theology was his assertion that the human nature of Christ is limited, while his divine is not. This had the consequence that when he spoke of Christ, he referred primarily to his divinity, and then to his humanity. The former is to be found everywhere, but the latter not, allowing Zwingli to say that wherever the body of Christ is, the Godhead is, but where the Godhead is, the body is not. This was the root of his Eucharistic thinking and was drawn largely from his reading of the Johannine literature.[44]

By 1527, Zwingli had developed his ideas about the relationship of Scripture and faith, which was to trust wholly in God, for God alone gives the gift of believing. Faith is not in any manner dependent on created things, even Scripture. God alone enables men and women to read the Bible with the eyes of faith and discern the truth of the Word. Only that revealed by God can be true, and faith holds to Jesus Christ, declaring that his death is our life. Zwingli was adamant that in no place does God teach that there is a bodily eating of the Eucharist and in no place was it commissioned. Instead, "we believe that he is bodily resurrected, so that he cannot be among us, and that after the resurrection his body can no longer be in one place."[45] Addressing Luther, Zwingli continued to accuse the Wittenberg reformer of not having moved sufficiently away from the Catholic mass. As we have said, for Zwingli, two biblical texts were decisive, Matthew 16:19 and John 6:63, in revealing the nature of the Lord's Supper.[46] In particular, Zwingli made extensive reference to Christ's words in John that "the Spirit gives life; the flesh counts for nothing. The words I have spoken to you are spirit and they give life."

The 1529 meeting at Marburg, which had been brought about by the mediation of Martin Bucer and the Landgraf Philipp of Hesse, was extraordinary for many reasons. The two great leaders of the Reformation, who had carved out such different positions on the Lord's Supper, had come together in one room.[47] It has long been noted that in terms of agreement there was the appearance of success. Of the fifteen articles drawn up, the reformers concurred on fourteen, and on the fifteenth (concerning the Eucharist), five of the six points were agreed. The operative word, however, is "appearance," for much of the language was so vague that both sides could take it home without significantly altering their positions. In truth, on crucial issues, the theological differences were of such weight that agreement would have required significant concessions.

Zwingli's Final Years

In late June 1531, Zwingli prepared an "Exposition of the Christian Faith" for Francis I. Once more, the Zurich reformer rejected Luther's position on ubiquity, and did so through a robust defense of his own understanding of the two natures of Christ. "I have made it plain enough before," he wrote,

> that whatever is said in the sacred scriptures of Christ is said in such a way of the whole and entire Christ that even if it may be easily detected to which of His natures the thing applies, yet Christ is not divided into two persons, however much each nature possesses its own peculiarity. For having two natures does not sever unity of person, as is clear in the case of man. And again, even if the things that belonged to Christ's divinity are attributed to His humanity, and, on the other hand, the things that belong to His humanity to His divinity, yet the natures are not confused, as if the divinity had denigrated and been weakened to humanity, or the humanity changed into divinity. This will be made more transparently clear by the testimonies of Scripture.[48]

In article 6, on the presence of Christ's body in the Lord's Supper, Zwingli returned to his familiar position, arguing that "that natural, material body of Christ's in which He suffered here and now sits in heaven at the right hand of the Father, is not eaten literally and in its essence, but only spiritually, in the Lord's Supper."[49]

Sacraments Visualized

For Zwingli the sacraments were primarily an act of the church, signs that reminded men and women of the gift of faith through the Holy Spirit. That gift was neither in the bread and wine nor in the water but was in the transforming presence of the Spirit, who speaks through the Word and lifts up the faithful through the Lord's Supper. Zwingli was an elegant liturgist (together with Leo Jud), and his vision found expression in corporate worship. The liturgical changes in Zurich were gradual; Jud and Zwingli's initial revision of Baptism and Lord's Supper in 1523 largely retained the older forms and was deemed insufficient by 1525, when the new order was introduced at Easter.

In the preface to his 1559 *De ritibus et institutis ecclesiae Tigurinae*, a remarkable account of the institutions, liturgy, and prayers of the Zurich church, Ludwig Lavater, Heinrich Bullinger's successor as head of the Zurich church, commented that the Zurich church was everywhere traduced for its teaching on the sacraments.[50] Four years later, Bullinger's son-in-law published a history of the quarrel between Zurich and Wittenberg over the Lord's Supper. His purpose in *De ritibus*, however, was to provide a description of the liturgy and practices of the Zurich church in order to prove its historical and doctrinal orthodoxy.

Lavater's account is useful, because although written later after the liturgical changes under Bullinger, *De ritibus* provides the fullest account of the Zwinglian order of Baptism. Lavater, drawing on the authority of Zwingli for his own time, claimed that the service in Zurich remained faithful to his liturgy.

The communal nature of the sacrament was stressed. The women of the community brought the child to the church for baptism shortly after birth.[51] Although baptism of newborns was crucial to Zwingli's understanding of the church as the covenanted people of God, the reformer took the view that the unbaptized infants of faithful parents were guaranteed salvation.[52] He rejected the medieval practice of burying the unbaptized in a liminal location. The pastor began the service with a prayer that included the statement "when it is your will that the child should be baptized with the baptism of our Lord Jesus Christ, answer 'yes.'" Then the child was named. It was crucial that the names be known in order that they were recorded. Zwingli insisted that the names of baptized children be recorded in a book. The act of record keeping enabled the church to identify those, mostly Anabaptists, who were not having their children baptized. It was God's will, the pastor continued, that all people should come to the knowledge of truth through the only mediator, Jesus Christ. "Let us then pray to the Lord that he might bring this infant to faith and that the outer baptism will through the Holy Spirit be an inward salvation bringing water."[53]

The service continued with prayers recalling God's destruction of the sinful world in the great flood, the parting of the Red Sea, and water in the desert as harbingers of baptism. The pastor named the child and prayed with the people that the "light of faith" might be upon him or her. With every intercession, the emphasis was upon God as the sole bestower of truth and faith. Then, Jesus's blessing of the children in Matthew 10 was read. Finally, the godparents were asked if it was their will that the child should be baptized. When a positive reply was received, the pastor sprinkled the child three times with water. Lavater was emphatic that there was no immersion, nor was there oil, salt, spittle, or exorcism of the devil. The pastor wished the child God's blessing that he or she might grow in faith. Finally, the names of the child, parents, and godparents were entered in the parish baptismal book.[54]

For the Lord's Supper, during the sermon, unleavened bread and wine were placed on a plain table in front of the people. The elements were to be presented on simple wooden dishes in order not to distract the eye from the bread and wine as symbols of faith. After the Words of Institution were clearly recited, the elements were distributed among the people, most of whom would have been standing. At the completion of the service the people came together in a prayer of thanksgiving. Such practice, according to Zwingli, was to take place four times a year.

The structure of the 1525 liturgy was relatively simple. After opening prayers and a reading of 1 Corinthians 11, the people were admonished against the unworthy reception of the bread and wine, at which point the men and women recited the Gloria antiphonally, saying the Amen together. At the conclusion of the Gloria the faithful were read passages from John 6, principally verses 47 ("In truth, he who believes has everlasting life") and 63 ("the spirit gives life; the flesh counts for nothing. The words I have spoken to you are spirit, and they are life"). The pastor then kissed the Bible and proclaimed, "Praise and thanks be to God. He willeth to forgive all our sins according to his holy Word."

Following the confession of sin, the men and women sang the Apostolicum antiphonally, after which was pronounced the invitation and admonition to the Supper, which warned against "anyone [who might] pretend to be a believer who is not, and so be guilty of the Lord's death." The people knelt for the Lord's Prayer and a prayer said by the pastor beseeching God that the people might live "purely as becomes the body."

The Words of Institution were read at the table over unleavened bread and wine. The pastors served themselves first before the servers took the elements to the people, who knelt to receive. The bread and wine were passed among the people in silence, which was their response to the gift of God. Following reception, Psalm 113 was recited, once more antiphonally. At the conclusion of this Psalm, the benediction was pronounced and the people departed.

The reading of Psalm 113 at the end was significant because of its association with the Passover, where it formed part of the Halal. It was to be recited on joyous occasions, such as the first night of Passover, and its inclusion in the worship of the 1525 and 1529 liturgies was an intentional link between the Lord's Supper and the Passover meal, one that placed the people of Zurich in the salvation history of the Israelites.

The 1525 liturgy, and its slightly revised 1529 form, focused the people on their obligation to live holy lives within the community while constantly reminding them that salvation is a gracious gift of God, thus linking together ethical obligations of the earthly and heavenly cities.[55] For Zwingli the community is the body of Christ, not so because of any liturgical action, but because of the divine promises. Liturgy for Zwingli, therefore, has an ambivalent aspect, as do the elements. It is nothing in itself and serves only to point people to higher realities. Yet it is indispensable as a means by which memory and thanksgiving are stirred. Liturgy shapes the emotions and senses, while reflecting social, political, and gender distinctions.

What takes place in worship is entirely directed by the Holy Spirit. The memory of the people, that is, those whom God has elected, is recalled by the Holy Spirit to the divine promises; that God's election and mercy are their salvation; that they alone must confess their sins; that God is gracious to them in the death and resurrection of Christ; and that they must trust that they are his people.

Both liturgies of the sacraments had a carefully defined aesthetic.[56] The churches had been stripped of all images and their walls whitewashed. Music had been removed from worship, leaving a service of word and visual image. In both of the liturgies, there was an interplay of words, the Word, and ritual act in which memory was central. Every part of the liturgy was accompanied by prayer or readings in which the people were reminded of the salvation history in which they stood: the exodus from Egypt or the upper-room Passover meal. In this interweaving of words to stimulate memory and faith, the eyes of people were directed to the font and table. The words spoken were directly connected to the material images of Christ's saving action in Baptism and the Lord's Supper. The white walls and absence of music were meant to ensure undivided contemplation of what God has done for his people.

Conclusion

Zwingli never intended to spend most of the 1520s writing about the nature of the sacraments, but the results were quite extraordinary. He saw Baptism and the Lord's Supper as acts of the church, of the covenantal community between God and humanity in which believers through commemoration and recollection found unity with Christ and the Church Universal. He made a radical separation of the material and spiritual that left the water, bread, and wine to be symbols of spiritual realities. They pointed the people to the work of the Holy Spirit in imparting faith. Without that faith the ceremony was empty and of no value whatsoever. Zwingli's God was gracious, loving, and generous in imparting saving grace, but the response of the people in godly lives, rejoicing, and thanksgiving was essential. Zwingli divested Christianity of its overly material attachments and restored the freedom of the Spirit. His dichotomous theology, however influential on the Reformed tradition, awaited further refinement.

NOTES

1. On Zwingli, Luther, and Marburg, see G. R. Potter, *Zwingli* (Cambridge: Cambridge University Press, 1976), 287–342. On Zwingli, see Bruce Gordon, "Huldrych Zwingli," *Expository Times* 126 (2015): 157–68.
2. August Pieper, "What Makes Up the 'Different Spirit' of Which Luther Accused the Zwinglians?," *Wisconsin Lutheran Quarterly* 107 (2010): 166–90.
3. On Calvin's attempts to reconcile the Swiss and Lutheran churches, see Bruce Gordon, *Calvin* (New Haven, CT: Yale University Press, 2009), 161–80.
4. For a narrative of events, see Bruce Gordon, *The Swiss Reformation* (Manchester: Manchester University Press, 2002), 71–72.
5. Potter, *Zwingli*, 325.
6. The most comprehensive survey in English of Zwingli's theology remains, Peter Stephens, *The Theology of Huldrych Zwingli* (Oxford: Clarendon, 1986). See also Gottfried W. Locher, "Zwingli's Theology Compared with Luther and Calvin," in his *Zwingli's Thought: New Perspectives* (Leiden: Brill, 1981), 142–234.
7. Timothy George, *The Theology of the Reformers* (Nashville: Broadman & Holman, 2013), 142.
8. *Fidei Ratio* Z VI.2 805, 48. I use the translation of the *Fidei Ratio* found in Huldrych Zwingli, *On Providence and Other Essays*, ed. Samuel Macauley Jackson (1922; repr., Durham, NC: Labyrinth Press, 1983); Z = *Huldreich Zwinglis sämtliche Werke*, ed. Emil Egli et al. (Berlin, 1905–). The volumes are also found in Bretschneider, *Corpus Reformatorum*, vol. 1 (Halis Saxonem, 1834), 88–101.
9. Johannes Voigländer, *Ein Fest der Befreiung. Huldrych Zwinglis Abendmahlslehre* (Neukirchen-Vluyn: Neukirchener Theologie, 2013), 40.
10. Ibid., 41.
11. *Eine kurze christliche Einleitung*, November 1523, Z II 628–63.
12. *De vera et falsa religione commentaries*, Z III 628–912. I use the translation (amended according to the Latin) found in Huldrych Zwingli, *Commentary on True and False Religion*, ed. Samuel Macauley Jackson and Clarence Nevin Heller (ca. 1929; repr., Durham, NC: Labyrinth, 1981), 180.
13. Z III 758; Zwingli, *Commentary*, 180.
14. Z III 759; Zwingli, *Commentary*, 181.
15. Scott H. Hendrix, *Early Protestant Spirituality* (Mahwah, NJ: Paulist Press, 2009), 242–43.
16. Z III 761; Zwingli, *Commentary*, 184.
17. On analogy, see *Zwingli and Bullinger*, ed. G. W. Bromiley (Louisville: Westminster John Knox, 1953), 263.
18. Quotation from Joar Haga, *Was There a Lutheran Metaphysics? The Interpretation of communicatio idiomatum in Early Modern Lutheranism* (Göttingen: Vandenhoeck & Ruprecht, 2012), 36.
19. *Von der Taufe, von der Wiedertaufe und von der Kindertaufe*, Z IV 206–337.
20. Stephens, *Theology of Huldrych Zwingli*, 202.

21. Quoted in J. V. Fesko, *Word, Water, and Spirit: A Reformed Perspective on Baptism* (Grand Rapids, MI: Reformation Heritage Books, 2013).
22. Z III 764; Zwingli, *Commentary*, 187.
23. Ibid.
24. Z III 769; Zwingli, *Commentary*, 193.
25. Z III 772; Zwingli, *Commentary*, 197.
26. George, *Theology of the Reformers*, 147.
27. See Jan Spruypt Bart, *Cornelius Henrici Hoen (Honius) and His Epistle on the Eucharist: Medieval Heresy, Erasmian Humanist, and Reform in the Early Sixteenth Century Low Countries* (Leiden: Brill, 2006).
28. Z III 777; Zwingli, *Commentary*, 202.
29. Z III 779; Zwingli, *Commentary*, 205.
30. Z III 800; Zwingli, *Commentary*, 229.
31. See Peter Stephens, "The Place of Predestination in Zwingli and Bucer," *Zwingliana* 19 (1992): 393–410.
32. Z III 785; Zwingli, *Commentary*, 213.
33. The expression *fidei contemplatio* is used in the *Fidei Ratio* of 1530; see Z VI.2 806.
34. *Exposition of the Sixty-Seven Articles*, art. 18, Z II 117.
35. Amy Nelson Burnett, *Karlstadt and the Origins of the Eucharistic Controversy: A Study in the Circulation of Ideas* (Oxford: Oxford University Press, 2011), 49.
36. *Aktion oder Brauch des Nachtmahls*, March or early April 1525, Z IV 13–24.
37. Nelson Burnett, *Karlstadt*, 88.
38. See the discussion in Carrie Eular, "Huldrych Zwingli and Heinrich Bullinger," in *A Companion to the Eucharist in the Reformation*, ed. Lee Palmer Wandel (Leiden: Brill, 2013), 59–61.
39. Gordon, *Swiss Reformation*, 72–73.
40. Fritz Blanke, "Zu Zwinglis Vorrede an Luther in der Schrift 'Amica Exegesis' 1527," *Zwingliana* 5 (1930): 185–92.
41. *True and False Religion*, 155, Z III 722.
42. Voigländer, *Ein Fest*, 110.
43. On Zwingli on the *communicatio idiomatum*, see Joar Haga, *Was There a Lutheran Metaphysics? The Interpretation of the Communicatio Idiomatum in Early Modern Lutheranism* (Göttingen: Vandenhoek and Ruprecht, 2012), 43–49.
44. Voigländer, *Ein Fest*, 113.
45. Ibid., 117.
46. Ibid., 119.
47. Lee Palmer Wandel, "The Body of Christ at Marburg," in *Image and Imagination of the Self in Late Medieval and Early Modern Europe*, ed. Reindert L. Falkenburg, Walter S. Melion, and Todd M. Richardson (Turnhout: Brepols, 2007), 195–213.
48. Z VI.5 143; "Exposition of the Faith," in Zwingli, *On Providence and Other Essays*, 250.
49. Z VI.5 140; "Exposition of the Faith," 248.

50. Ludwig Lavater, *De ritibus et institutis ecclesiae Tigurinae* (Zurich, 1565), sig. a2r.
51. Ibid., sig. b5r.
52. George, *Theology of the Reformers*, 143.
53. Lavater, *De ritibus et institutis*, sig. b5v.
54. Ibid., sig. b7r.
55. Voigtländer, *Ein Fest*, 205–6.
56. Lee Palmer Wandel, "Envisioning God: Image and Liturgy in Reformation Zurich," *Sixteenth Century Journal* 24 (1993): 21–40. Also see Bruce Gordon, with Luca Baserca and Christian Moser, "Emulating the Past and Creating the Present: Reformation and the Use of Historical and Theological Models in Zurich in the Sixteenth century," in *Following Zwingli: Applying the Past in Reformation Zurich*, ed. Luca Bascera, Bruce Gordon, and Christian Moser (Farnham: Ashgate, 2014), 1–39.

10

Menno Simons

SCOT MCKNIGHT

Menno Simons (1496–1561) was the so-called founder of an Anabaptist wing now called the "Mennonites," though it is more accurate to say Anabaptism was founded in Switzerland in 1525, that Obbe Philips founded the Mennonite way of Anabaptism, and that "Mennonite" speaks to the impact of Menno himself upon his many followers. Ordained in 1524 as a largely uncommitted Roman Catholic priest in Friesland (today's Netherlands), Menno began to read Luther in the wake of the impulses of both the Lutheran and Swiss Reformers as well as some early Anabaptists, but even more he devoted himself to reading the New Testament. By 1528 his own readings were leading him out of the Catholic Church, and by 1531 he was leading a kind of double life—Anabaptist in theology and faith but Catholic in vocation. He was opposed to the extreme wing of the Anabaptists—that led by Jan Matthys and Jan of Leiden—but was soon in the circle of Philips, renounced his Catholicism officially on 30 January 1536 (in his hometown Witmarsum), and was then finally ordained into the Anabaptist ministry under Philips early in 1537. He married Gertrude during 1536 or 1537. Following this conversion he became a vigilant, devout, and courageous proponent of the distinctives of Anabaptism: the baptism of professing believers, the importance and centrality of the fellowship of local believers, the necessity of growth into discipleship, and a radical posture of separation between church and state. His apologetics for the radical Reformation, over against the magisterial Reformations of both Luther and Calvin, as well as his opposition to Roman Catholicism led to his pursuit, Menno's constant travel and hiding and teaching and writing in secrecy, and a thick book full of occasional pieces. His writings reflect his theological method: eschew the sophistications and contentiousness of the debates among professional systematicians and ground theology in the exposition of Scripture itself.

Introduction

Sacraments for the earliest Anabaptists were a matter of life and death. To participate in a clandestine Eucharist gathering apart from the state church imperiled the life of the communicant, while undergoing a re-baptism (sometimes called "katabaptism" or "anabaptism") could lead to a third baptism, drowning, or other forms of execution. The authorities put to death thousands of Anabaptists for their praxis of the sacraments. Yet, the threat of death created opportunities for the Anabaptists to see through death into the graces of new creation life at work in the redemption of Christ. Prior to and during the ministry of the courageous and holy man Menno Simons,[1] the sacraments were not simply a symbolic or memorial (Zwinglian influence) form of worship, but communicated a palpable knock-on-the-door reality of a cruciform life. Indeed, Menno lived much of his life with the state and religious empires breathing down his neck. In the Netherlands, not long after Menno's conversion, Charles V put a price of a hundred gold guilders on Menno's head.

The Anabaptist sacraments take on special existential significance because they were public acts done under the threat of martyrdom. During Menno's ministry, which began almost two decades after Luther's famous nailing of the Ninety-Five Theses, he clarified, sometimes in confessional writings and at other times in letters of refutation, a theology of the sacraments that was already under way among other Anabaptists, like Balthasar Hubmaier, Pilgram Marpeck, and Dirk Philips. Beyond clarifying, Menno established categories that would become fixed in Anabaptist theology.[2] It is a pity that late in his life Menno and other Anabaptist leaders engaged so much of their time in debates about excommunication and the ban, including Menno's harsh view that family members were to be shunned.[3] Contemporary Anabaptist sacramental thinking, a topic quite often more ignored than studied,[4] is not the same as the sixteenth-century beliefs, nor should the more dominant voices (John Howard Yoder) or textual concentrations (like the Sermon on the Mount) in today's Anabaptism be seen as mirrors of sixteenth-century Anabaptism.[5] The Anabaptism of Menno was fundamentally Protestant in soteriology, pietistic in spirituality, and more populist-shaped, polemically-driven, and praxis-oriented in theology than that found among Catholics, Lutherans, and the Swiss Reformed. Its first unifying articulation of theology, the *Schleitheim Confession* (1527),[6] addresses baptism, ban, the Lord's Supper, separation, shepherds in congregations, the sword, and the oath. Their focus is the cutting edge of authority and the local church, driven as well by the courage to live out what was believed to be clearly taught in Scripture.

What then is Anabaptism? Menno answers that question in a 1539 book, *Christian Baptism*, in these words: "we teach the new life, baptism on the confession of faith, and the Supper in both elements in an unblamable church, according to the holy Gospel of Jesus Christ" (232). Anabaptism, then, is marked by the following: personal regeneration and conversion, believer's baptism over against infant baptism, the view that each believer can partake in both bread and wine, a church made of up believers, and all this according to the teachings of the New Testament. This is the core of the Anabaptist vision as these items are also the cutting edge of difference between the Anabaptists and Catholicism and Lutheranism. The core was also the source of relentless persecution against them. Anabaptism then is a decentralizing process of rooting out traditions not found explicitly in Scripture, rooting down into what is explicitly taught, and forming local church communities committed to both. Those churches were "an assembly of the righteous, and a community of the saints" (234). Anabaptism then radicalizes the reforms in Germany under Luther and in Switzerland under Calvin and therefore both disestablished the church and pleaded for toleration for the private conscience.[7]

This chapter probes sacraments in their concrete reality as expounded in Menno's teachings about baptism and the Lord's Supper, the only two sacraments of the Anabaptists.[8] One could argue quite forcefully, and this is demonstrated in the absence of theoretical discussions of the Anabaptist theory of sacraments in standard texts about Anabaptist history, that Anabaptism is anti-sacramental because it is sacramentarian. That is, those who rejected sacramental, infant baptism, and transubstantiation and mass as a sacrifice, sometimes called "sacramentalism," and instead believed the Lord's Supper was symbolic and spiritual and baptism required personal faith were called "sacramentarians."[9] As such, one can expand the so-called sacramental theology of the Anabaptists into the communal practices to include church discipline and economic sharing, as Thomas Finger does.[10] We focus here on Anabaptism's classic two forms of sacraments, baptism and the Lord's Supper.

Menno's Anabaptist Heritage

To set the full stage for Menno's theology of baptism (or of the Lord's Supper) would require examination of late medieval Catholicism, the Swiss Reformation in Geneva under Calvin, and then Ulrich Zwingli's reforms in Zurich, beginning from 1517 and becoming Anabaptist only on 21 January 1525, when a dozen or so were baptized at the home of Felix Manz, including Conrad Grebel and Georg Blaurock. Then, we would have to move to the *Schleitheim Confession*, onto Balthasar Hubmaier, dip into the works of Anabaptists in southern Germany and Austria—such as Hans Hut and Pilgram Marpeck. Subsequently, we would have to ponder sacramental thinking in the Netherlands, the home of Menno and location of his early ministry, before he stayed in Germany where he was "safer." For the purposes of this chapter, the scope is limited to brief descriptions of Balthasar Hubmaier,[11] even though a full background for Menno's theology of sacraments would require an examination of these various thinkers.[12]

Hubmaier's Anabaptist ministry lasted about six years, before he was burned at the stake. Three days later his wife was thrown into the Danube with a heavy stone tied around her neck. In Hubmaier's *Summa of the Entire Christian Life* is a sketch that focuses on an *ordo* of conversion: repentance, surrender to Christ and commitment to him, confession, baptism, and submission to Christ and obedience and to the discipline of the local congregation of baptized, obedient believers who celebrate a memorial vision of the Lord's Supper (84–89). Hubmaier, too, first articulated in written form the Anabaptist theory of baptism in his 1525 *On the Christian Baptism of Believers* (95–149) and debated Zwingli's own teachings in *Dialogue with Zwingli's Baptism Book*, in 1525 (166–233, esp. 227–28).[13] Hubmaier, the first great Anabaptist theologian, was theoretical enough to form alongside his baptism teachings movement-shaping theories about both the freedom of the will and regeneration.[14] Indeed, at the core of the Anabaptist vision is the will's capacity and necessity to respond to the offer of grace and the consequent new birth that comes to the one with faith.[15] As for the Eucharist, Balthasar taught a rigorous memorialist version of the Lord's Supper in his 1526 *A Simple Instruction* (314–38). As with all Anabaptists, a relentless methodology shapes the whole: all teachings are based on Scripture and Scripture alone (*nuda scriptura*), and this is highlighted in Balthasar's refrain "truth is immortal" or, as Yoder prefers, "truth is unkillable."[16] Life and death then are the major themes from the very beginning.

Menno on Baptism

Baptism among the Anabaptists showed some variety, and Thomas Finger's masterful examination of the sources reveals two major emphases: that baptism was a conscious act of faith and obedience, a *covenant* commitment to focus on the term often used,[17] and that it had a singularly important corporate commitment aspect.[18] The Swiss, German, and Austrian Anabaptists focused on a threefold emphasis on baptism: Spirit, water, and blood.[19] The Spirit made baptism the act of the regenerate alone, the water was the outer action in public confession and commitment to the church, and the blood was participation in suffering. The Dutch, however, shifted the "blood" to the blood of Christ and, as Finger puts it, did not see the Christian life "under the baptismal motif"[20] as much.

I will concentrate on Menno's 1539–40 *Foundation of Christian Doctrine*, not only because it became his most influential theological essay, but because it was revised just a few years before his death in 1561 and therefore gives expression to his theology of the sacraments in the last years of his life.[21]

The living realities of Menno's teachings about baptism are all found in this:

> Christ does not command that infants should be baptized but believers; but the world commands that we should baptize children and not believers. Yes, more than that, if anyone is baptized upon his faith because the Lord has so commanded, and if for conscience's sake he dares not have his children baptized because God does not command it, such a man must bear a hateful name, and torture, misery, and death besides.[22]

The motive (Christ's command), the object (adults not infants), the requirement (faith, not birth), the context of opposition (the world of institutional Catholicism, Lutheranism, and the Swiss Reformed), the context's theology (infant baptism), the integrity of faith (one's conscience), and the consequences (persecution) sum up Menno's baptismal theology. What is not mentioned here, though implied, is the *mode* of baptism, and the Anabaptists of the sixteenth century seemingly baptized by "affusion," that is, in the words of Menno himself, the person baptized was a "recipient of a handful of water" (139). Baptism, then, *accomplished nothing in sacramental terms*. Menno repudiates any sense of an *ex opere operato* or that baptism was sacramental in that by administering it the person was redeemed or purified. Baptism for Menno was an act of obedience to the Lord's command (Matt. 28:16–20) and the Lord's example (3:13–17). To think baptism itself accomplished salvation was, for Menno, superstition. The proper order is preaching, hearing, faith through hearing, new birth by faith, new birth compelling baptism, and then the promise of redemption (265).

The opening, even alarming theme for Menno is that baptism is for adults and not for infants. The New Testament's kind of baptism for Menno was to be administered to believers, genuine obedient believers. The singular theology at work is simple: redemption is on the basis of the merits of the blood of Christ and it is appropriate solely through faith, not the external rite of baptism. This theology of the necessity of conscious faith is the line in the sand drawn by all early Anabaptists, it earned them their name, and it was the source of their persecution, hiding, and separation. Infant baptism, the practice of the whole church, was wrong. Why? Baptism for Jesus and the apostles required faith. "For where there is no renewing, regenerating faith, leading to obedience, there is no baptism" (139). No other baptism counts, and that means infant baptism is not genuine baptism for Menno, in part because it was performed by heretics (140–41). Infant baptism for him is the "baptism of Antichrist" (141) and, according to the *Schleitheim Confession* "the greatest and first abomination of the pope."[23] Menno's anchor for his belief in adult baptism is "in the Scriptures no command is given to baptize" infants (131). Infant baptism, then, is a construct of false teaching at work in the church of his day. He takes aim at the practice in these words: "maintained by tyranny, is nothing but a ceremony of Antichrist, open blasphemy, a bewitching sin, a molten calf; yes, abomination and idolatry" (133).

In addition, for Menno baptism is the act of surrender and obedience, like Christ's baptism, and therefore an act of dying with Christ and rising with Christ. If believer baptism stands out as the distinctive element of Menno's baptismal theology, surely it is because baptism is the principal act expressing that one's faith is accompanied by works, that the inner spiritual rebirth finds its way to the outer action of baptism, and that what is demonstrated in baptism is that one has died to self and is now alive unto God. Christ, he says, "as a willing obedient child resigned Himself to the will of His almighty Father" (121). So, too, with believers who "profess their faith and declare that they will henceforth live not according to their own will, but according to the will of God" (121) so they are "prepared to forsake their homes, possessions, lands, and lives and to suffer hunger, affliction, oppression, persecution, the cross and death for the same" (121–22). That is, baptism means they "die unto sin so as to be no longer subjects to their impure lusts" (122). One more time: Those who are baptized "leave self and human wisdom behind, and submit to the Word and ordinances of the Lord without reluctance or opposition" (123). In summary, "For where there is not faith through love working obedience . . . there is no promise" (123). Menno's perception of baptism is that it is the external act of baptism visibly witnessing to the regenerate person's surrender in faith and obedience to Christ and his church. In this, the Anabaptists faulted Catholics, Lutherans, and the Reformed for compromising in full obedience to the Lord's demands.

Menno knows the entire church and its tradition is against him, but there can be no wavering for him. His own conversion, which began just two years into his Catholic priestly duties, revolved around perceiving that both the Catholic mass and its teaching about infant baptism were contrary to Scripture. His troubled conscience led him to ponder Scriptures, and only over time, too long in some historians' views, was he able to root himself entirely into Scripture and let Scripture shape his theology. Eventually he did and that meant he would face the stiff winds of opposition. He was unafraid to offer to his opponents the fruit of his study of Scripture—including opposing Martin Luther, whom he says teaches that infant baptism is right because it expresses the dormant faith of the child, to which Menno says, "If Luther writes this as his sincere opinion, then he proves that he has written in vain a great deal concerning faith and its power. But if he writes this to please men, may God have mercy on him" (126). What he means by pleasing men is a regular feature of Menno's diatribes against his opponents: he is calling into question both the church's tradition that finds no root in Scripture and the lack of courage on the part of leaders to hold firm to a Scripture-based theology in the face of the authorities.

The authorities opposed Menno, and he responded to their defenses of infant baptism (130–38). The present problem, a problem Luther faced his entire ministry, was the lack of genuine obedience and conversion in so many of the baptized. As Menno describes them, "those who receive it [infant baptism]—even though their whole life is so completely pagan, undisciplined, reckless, and nothing but dissipation, drinking, fornication, cursings, swearings, etc.—are called Christians nevertheless" (128; also 252). Those who opposed Menno appealed to texts like Acts 2:38 (repent and be baptized for the forgiveness of sins) or Colossians 2:11–12 but are rebutted in standard Anabaptist moves: the former text assumes the priority of faith, therefore baptism itself does not save; the latter text makes an analogy with inward, not exterior, circumcision (133; also 260–61). One prop after another is knocked down by Menno: the institution of godfathers (253–55), the corruption of priests (255), and the belief that original sin is removed by baptism (130–32) and circumcision as the remedy for the sins for ancient Israelites (131, 132–34). Abraham, like everyone else, was saved "through the fatherly election of grace through Jesus Christ" (132). What becomes of females who, if circumcision was the primary means, could not have been saved (132)? The argument that baptism regenerates cannot be true because faith precedes regeneration (134), and any suggestion that original sin's curse is not counted against a child, though present, because of infant baptism runs aground yet again on the necessity of faith (134–35). Over and over for Menno, infant baptism is subjected to two deeper criteria: salvation is procured by the merits of Christ's death and conscious faith is required. This means baptism cannot procure redemption until accompanied by personal faith, and this means infants ought not to be baptized.[24]

Other arguments are also examined: Did the apostles baptize whole families when they baptized households? Menno's response is that no children are mentioned, infant baptism is not otherwise taught in the New Testament, faith is the requirement, and infants do not have it, so suggesting so is "conjecture" (136). No doubt in regular debates Menno has heard the claim that both Origen and Augustine believed in pedobaptism. His response: what were their scriptural grounds? There are none. To top it off, Cyprian leaves this matter as open, and then Menno knows a number of theologians, including Tertullian, Rhenanus, Rufinus's translation of Eusebius's *Church History*, Erasmus, and Zwingli, who support the view that the apostles did not baptize infants (137–38; also 695–96). All in all, to Gellius Faber he responds to twenty-two separate defenses of infant baptism (681–717). The murkiness of the teachings of theologians leads Menno to a classic Protestant and Anabaptist move: return to Scripture, the Word of God, for constructing our theology. That source, Menno reminds us often, teaches baptism for believers not for infants.

But, this generates another question, one all the Anabaptists faced though with differing answers: What of infants or, as Menno says it, "particularly those of Christian parentage" (280)? Will they be saved or damned? Does original sin condemn the infant who has not yet exercised faith? Menno is overwhelmingly confident in his answers: "To innocent and minor children sin is for Jesus' sake not imputed. Life is promised, not through any ceremony, but of pure grace, though the blood of the Lord, as He Himself says: 'Suffer the little children to come unto me . . .'" (131). This grace of God for the child, and here he means the child prior to an age of accountability and of exercising faith, is also connected to election: "through the election, so also are our children in the covenant of God, even though unbaptized." And then "to children the kingdom of heaven belongs, and they are under the promise of the grace of God through Christ, . . . and therefore we truly believe that they are saved, holy and pure, and pleasing to God, under the covenant and in His church, but by no means through an external sign" (133; also 135). Menno's confidence in the salvation of infants is rooted in that promise of Christ about children: "Yes, on account of this promise [Mark 10:14] all sincere Christian believers may assuredly rejoice and comfort themselves in the salvation of their children" (135; also 245).

Baptism, we need to remember, was a matter of life and death for Menno. Swiss, southern German and Austrian, as well as Dutch Anabaptists were dying simply because they acted out their belief that baptism was for believers and that infant baptism was not what the Bible taught. This act of obedience and surrender, then, was simultaneously the assumption of a cruciform life. For this reason alone, the warnings of Menno take on ultimate tones: "The fruits [of the opponents] show who is their father," and here he is referring to John 8:44 and therefore assigning them the ultimate punishment. He continues, "men who with their false doctrine, vicious counsel, and hard hearts have drunk the blood of the righteous, have executed and killed.... For as the sun shines before all and is seen by everyone, so manifest is the inhuman raving tyranny of the learned ones against the Lamb and His elect" (132). We live in a day when rhetorical accusations like this strike us as excessively judgmental.[25] Menno's language is closer to the cool rational logic with occasional outbursts of accusation found in Calvin than it is to the bombast of Luther, but I make no excuse for Menno's at times unseasoned rhetoric. He does make routine pastoral appeals to turn from their ways to the ways of Scripture-founded theology. Not unlike what he says next in the passage: "God grant the eyes of these blind, perverted, bloodthirsty teachers with their tyrants may be opened; that they may tire and weary of their false doctrine and bloodshed. Amen" (132).

That appeal reveals as much about Menno's context of suffering as it does about his desire for others to respond to the gospel message and the teachings of the New Testament as he and other Anabaptists understood them. What for him were words of life were for others words deserving of death.

Menno on the Lord's Supper

The Anabaptist understanding of the Lord's Supper, in some ways just as glaringly at odds with the magisterial Reformers and the Catholic Church as was its understanding of baptism, owes its genesis to Ulrich Zwingli's memorialist, symbolic view. Yet, as Thomas Finger ably shows, the memorialist theme is not uppermost in Anabaptist writers about the Lord's Supper.[26] Instead, the communal and participationist themes precede memorialism thinking. It is clear that for the Anabaptist an ecclesiology shaped by separation from the state-shaped churches, rigorous commitment to live together under the Word alone, including economic sharing, and a fellowship rigorously shaped by church discipline had its impact on how to understand the Lord's Supper.

A distinctive feature of the Anabaptist understanding of the Lord's Supper is its other-orientation, highlighting Finger's conclusion that the memorial themes are not as central as some have suggested. The Anabaptists were fond of telling the parable of unity through the many kernels that become one loaf and the many grapes that become one wine.[27] In Balthasar's 1526–27 *A Christian Catechism* we read in dialogue format about the unity formed at the Table:

> LEONHART: What is the Lord's Supper?
> HANS: It is a public sign and testimonial of the love in which one brother obligates himself to another before the congregation that just as they now break and eat the bread with each other and share and drink the cup, likewise they wish now to sacrifice and shed their body and blood for one another; this they will do in the strength of our Lord Jesus Christ, whose suffering they are now commemorating . . . and proclaiming his death.[28]

Again, the life-and-death ecclesial realities come to the surface in the earliest Anabaptist understandings of the sacraments, not the least in some sophisticated ways in Balthasar's own appropriations of the theology and metaphysics of the Fourth Gospel.[29]

To catch the import of Menno's diatribes against Catholicism on the Lord's Supper, it is worth our while to hear Menno himself describe what happens in the Eucharist celebrations of Roman Catholicism. Whether Menno is accurate or not is not important; it is to these representations that he and other Anabaptists are responding. Three noteworthy features of his descriptions are worthy of notice here: first, the priest breaks the bread into three pieces—one to reconcile God, one to intercede for the world, and one to pray for souls in purgatory.[30] Second, the liturgical accompaniments include "carrying the bread in procession, raising it aloft for adoration, praying to it, offering incense to it, requesting it at a given place, and paying divine honor and service to it" (155–56). Third, "the cup is withheld from the people among Catholics" (156). In contrast to the ceremony found so prevalent among the Roman Catholics—not to mention the Eastern Orthodox as well as the Lutherans and less simply among the Reformed, the Anabaptist approach to the Eucharist, usually called the "Lord's Supper" but also called a "sacrament," though no effective sacramental theology is affirmed—the Anabaptist form of the Lord's Supper was simple and democratic. Each ate and each drank, an eating and drinking that were both life and death and the establishment of another kind of ecclesiology.

At the core of the Anabaptist critique of Catholic sacramental Eucharist worship is the belief that the Catholic theology affirms an ongoing, daily re-sacrifice of the sacrifice of Christ. Menno calls this a "holy, divine negotiation" and a "bewitching sacrifice" (152). The Anabaptist counter to the Catholic mass is that there is "one sacrifice" (152) made by Christ when he died for sins. Relentless is Menno's affirmation of this single point: "we have no other sacrifice for sin than the body and blood of the Lord" (151). This one sacrifice of Christ "appeases the Father's wrath, makes atonement for the race of men, opened heaven, closed hell, made with Him who inhabits heaven and earth, and sits henceforth at the right hand of the Father till His enemies be made His footstool" (152).

The second critique concerns transubstantiation and the real presence of Christ in the actual bread and wine (153–56). Menno's words: "they have made the bread in the Holy Supper into the actual flesh, and the wine into the actual blood, of Christ, and that by virtue of Christ's Word taken literally: Take, eat; this is my body" (153). As so many critics of the real presence theory of the Eucharist have done since, appeal is made to John 6, where he infers it is not literal but spiritual. Christ is ascended and therefore "cannot be masticated nor confined in an alimentary tract nor be consumed by time, by fire and worms, as is the case with the visible bread and wine as one can see" (153). Menno's logic becomes epigrammatic: "the outward perishable man eats and drinks perishable bread and wine, and the inner imperishable man of the heart eats in a spiritual sense the imperishable body and blood of Christ" (153).

Third, Catholicism teaches that the bread and wine are "dispensed for the remission of sins" (156), and here we touch on sacramentalism, or the effectiveness of the bread and wine themselves. There is, Menno argues, "no other remedy for your sins that is satisfactory to God than the one we have pointed out to you, which is Christ Jesus" (157). It was not just the Anabaptists but Luther and Calvin who led the way for the Anabaptists in seeing less than the real presence in the Lord's Supper. Among the Anabaptists there is much less discussion of the ontology of being and accidents so formative from Aquinas on in Catholic thinking about the bread and wine, and it was that ontology to which the magisterial Reformers responded.

Catholic thinkers, like Gellius Faber, had responses, but Menno countered each one.[31] In essence, Gellius does not go far enough: warning his audiences and teaching the Catholic laity the importance of repentance and faith and obedience do no good if the Eucharist is offered without meeting the appropriate conditions. Menno turns to his own readers with these words: "External preaching, hearing, baptism, and Supper (which are done in appearance) do not count before God. But before Him teaching and believing count, believing and doing, outward baptism and Supper according to the letter, and inwardly according to the Spirit and truth" (719).

At work in all of this is Menno's ecclesiology of a regenerated Body of Christ who alone is worthy of presence at the table, made worthy not by sainthood but made saints by the merits of Christ, and hence he appeals routinely to the importance of the Lord's Supper as designed for the regenerate. He uses classic formulas to respond: "For outside of the church of Christ, which is a gathering of the penitent, there is neither baptism nor Holy supper" (719). The Reformation saw a tightening of the circle of participation: Catholics admit all to the table; the Lutherans and the Reformed the baptized; the Anabaptists the regenerate who are obedient, who have broken from Catholicism, and who have been baptized.[32] Out of this ecclesiology, grounded in Scripture, emerges Menno's succinct formulae for an ontology of the Lord's Supper:

> It is so that it may become to you a living and impressive sign, that it might represent and signify the Lord's great and abundant kindness, the heartfelt peace, the love and union of His church, the communion of his flesh and blood; so that you may die to wickedness and pursue righteousness and godliness, fly from the devil's table and sit down at the Lord's table in the church of Christ, with true faith, a pious, penitent, and regenerated life, and with unfeigned, brotherly love. (142)

That is, the bread and the wine are signs, representations of the reality—that reality being the spiritual redemption in the spiritual work of Christ (717). Balthasar had said the elements of the Lord's Supper were "nothing but memorial symbols of Christ's suffering and death for the forgiveness of our sins."[33] Furthermore, the Lord's Supper is an expression of the love of God for God's people, the church of Jesus Christ. And a distinctive emphasis in the Anabaptist tradition is that the Lord's Supper expresses, as Menno puts it, "Christian unity, love, and peace" (145, 717).

They, too, are "signified" in the meal (145). Finally, the Lord's Supper is a communion with Christ, a participation in Christ (146). This theme of communion, while not spelled out in Menno's work as it is in other Anabaptists' works, evokes a number of themes, not the least of which is the mode of how Christ communes and how the believer communes and this modal theory connects to ontology. This ontology at times is understood in an almost real presence manner and at other times in an eschatological new creation reality.[34]

The reality of Menno's theory of the Lord's Supper is that it was "closed" or, to say it the other way, open only to genuine believers who are living obediently. Which leads deeper into his ecclesiology: since the priests are deceivers and idolaters and heretics (149) and so create the "table of the devil" (142), the only worthy dispensers of the bread and wine are the regenerate, which means the adult-baptized believer. In Menno's words, summarizing decades of pondering Scripture, engaging with others, and debating Catholics, "the sum of the whole matter: he who would with the disciples and guests of Christ sit at the Lord's table, be he rich or poor, high or low, must be sound in the faith and unblameable in conduct and life" (150).

Conclusion

The Anabaptist understanding of the sacraments is non-sacramental; it is shaped by what Scripture says over against whatever the traditions teach; it is formed in the rugged realities of persecution and martyrdom; and it was a life-giving act of fellowship with God and with one another as these radical Christians sought to follow their Lord by severing ties with ecclesiastical powers. For Anabaptists like Menno Simons the kingdom breaks into this world in Jesus Christ and in his Body, the congregation of the faithful, and that ecclesial embodiment of the kingdom takes precedence over the empire. Death for them was a sacrament of life.

NOTES

1. On Menno's life, see Harold S. Bender's admirable sketch in Menno Simons, *The Complete Writings of Menno Simons*, ed. J. C. Wenger, trans. Leonard Verduin (Scottdale, PA: Herald Press, 1984), 3–29. All of Menno's writings and incidents

referred to in this chapter can be found in Wenger's volume; page numbers cited parenthetically in the text refer to this book. There is no critical biography of Menno.
2. The best sketch of Anabaptist theology, showing nuance in both historical sources and ecumenical theological discussion, is Thomas N. Finger, *A Contemporary Anabaptist Theology: Biblical, Historical, Constructive* (Downers Grove, IL: InterVarsity, 2004). For the history, see William R. Estep, *The Anabaptist Story: An Introduction to Sixteenth-Century Anabaptism*, 3rd ed. (Grand Rapids, MI: Eerdmans, 1996); J. Denny Weaver, *Becoming Anabaptist: The Origin and Significance of Sixteenth-Century Anabaptism*, 2nd ed. (Scottdale, PA: Herald Press, 2005). For theology, see also Robert Friedmann, *The Theology of Anabaptism: An Interpretation* (Scottdale, PA: Herald Press, 1973).
3. See "Instruction on Excommunication" (1558), in Simons, *Complete Writings*, 959–98.
4. John Howard Yoder, *Body Politics: Five Practices of the Christian Community before the Watching World* (Scottdale, PA: Herald Press, 2001). On Yoder, see Finger, *Contemporary Anabaptist Theology*, 60–63.
5. See, e.g., the recent study of Anabaptism and evangelicalism in Jared S. Burkholder and David C. Cramer, eds., *The Activist Impulse: Essays on the Intersection of Evangelicalism and Anabaptism* (Eugene, OR: Pickwick, 2012).
6. John Howard Yoder, trans., *The Schleitheim Confession* (Scottdale, PA: Herald Press, 1977).
7. There is some dispute on how best to define Anabaptism, but a good start can be found in Friedmann, *Theology of Anabaptism*, 17–26; Harold S. Bender, *The Anabaptist Vision* (Scottdale, PA: Herald Press, 1944); Weaver, *Becoming Anabaptist*, 161–222, 223–31; Finger, *Contemporary Anabaptist Theology*, 9–104.
8. So in the *Schleitheim Confession*, art. 1 (on baptism), 3 (on the breaking of bread). See Yoder, *Schleitheim Confession*, 10, 11.
9. Weaver, *Becoming Anabaptist*, 112–13.
10. Finger, *Contemporary Anabaptist Theology*, 157–254.
11. H. Wayne Pipkin and John Howard Yoder, trans., *Balthasar Hubmaier: Theologian of Anabaptism* (Scottdale, PA: Herald Press, 1989). All page numbers cited parenthetically in the text refer to this book.
12. Finger, *Contemporary Anabaptist Theology*, 160–70, 184–97.
13. Rollin Stely Armour, *Anabaptist Baptism: A Representative Study*, Studies in Anabaptist and Mennonite History 11 (Scottdale, PA: Herald Press, 1966), 19–57.
14. Pipkin and Yoder, *Balthasar Hubmaier*, 426–91.
15. Armour, *Anabaptist Baptism*, 135–39.
16. Pipkin and Yoder, *Balthasar Hubmaier*, 42 n. 12.
17. On this see esp. Armour, *Anabaptist Baptism*. Also see Friedmann, *Theology of Anabaptism*, 134–38.
18. Finger, *Contemporary Anabaptist Theology*, 169–70.

19. Pipkin and Yoder, *Balthasar Hubmaier*, 349. On which see Finger, *Contemporary Anabaptist Theology*, 163.
20. Finger, *Contemporary Anabaptist Theology*, 170.
21. For his major discussions, see three selections from books in Simons, *Complete Writings*, 120–42, 227–87, 681–717. The second book is *Christian Baptism* (1539), published at the time of his first edition of *Foundation of Christian Doctrine* (1539–40), and the third selection is from his *Reply to Gellius Faber* (1554), which rebuts Gellius's own defense of infant baptism. The second and third, then, are prior to the final editing of the first book, *Foundation of Christian Doctrine*, published in 1539–40 and then edited finally in 1558.
22. *Foundation of Christian Doctrine*, in Simons, *Complete Writings*, 132. Subsequent page citations to this important text are included parenthetically in the text.
23. Yoder, *Schleitheim Confession*, 10.
24. In some ways the Anabaptists anticipate the moves of the later Lutheran Pietist movement led by Philip Jakob Spener. For a comparison of Anabaptism and Pietism, see Scot McKnight, "Pietism, Anabaptism, and Conversion: Paradigms for the Contemporary Church," *Covenant Quarterly* 70, nos. 3–4 (2012): 4–20.
25. For Menno's graphic description of corruption among priests, see Simons, *Complete Writings*, 250–51.
26. Finger, *Contemporary Anabaptist Theology*, 184–97.
27. Friedmann, *Theology of Anabaptism*, 140–43.
28. Pipkin and Yoder, *Balthasar Hubmaier*, 354.
29. John D. Rempel, *The Lord's Supper in Anabaptism: A Study in the Christology of Balthasar Hubmaier, Pilgram Marpeck, and Dirk Philips*, Studies in Anabaptist and Mennonite History 33 (Scottdale, PA: Herald Press, 1993), 41–90.
30. Simons, *Complete Writings*, 151–52. Again, all subsequent page citations to this most important work of Menno's, *The Foundation of Christian Doctrine*, are included parenthetically in the text.
31. The replies by Gellius Faber and Menno's counters can be found at 717–23.
32. Yoder, *Schleitheim Confession*, 11 (art. 3).
33. Pipkin and Yoder, *Balthasar Hubmaier*, 354–55.
34. Finger, *Contemporary Anabaptist Theology*, 194–97. This theme is examined by Rempel, *Lord's Supper in Anabaptism*.

11

John Calvin

RANDALL C. ZACHMAN

John Calvin (1509–64) was born in Noyon, France, and was trained in the study of law at Orleans and Bourges. During his legal studies, Calvin also developed a love of Latin and Greek classical literature. After his sudden conversion to the evangelical movement started by Martin Luther, Calvin used his skill in languages to teach doctrine and interpret Scripture for the evangelicals in France. Calvin was called to be a reader of Scripture and a pastor in Geneva in 1536. He and his colleague Guiaumme Farel were expelled from Geneva in 1538, and Calvin spent the next three years in Strasbourg, where he taught in the new Academy and was the pastor of the French congregation in that city. Calvin was called back to Geneva in 1541, and spent the rest of his life in that city as its head pastor and teacher. Calvin produced many editions of his primary teaching manual, the *Institutes of the Christian Religion*, culminating in the final edition of 1559. He also published commentaries on the whole of the New Testament (except 2 and 3 John and Revelation), and lectures and commentaries on the books of Moses, the Psalms, and the Prophets. Calvin also preached hundreds of sermons on many of the books of the Old and New Testament, including Genesis, Deuteronomy, Job, and Galatians. Calvin was one of the major teachers of evangelical theology of his time, and has exercised a profound influence on the subsequent Western Christian tradition, especially in the English-speaking world.

Introduction

John Calvin endorsed Augustine's description of the sacraments as "visible words," thereby revealing the dynamic interplay Calvin creates between the word or promise that we hear, and the image or representation that we see.[1] Indeed, for Calvin, the word itself can be understood as a kind of image or painting, even as the image can be understood as a kind of writing or proclamation. One sees this dynamic interplay between word and image throughout Calvin's theology, beginning with his understanding of the knowledge of God the Creator, and continuing through the knowledge of God the Redeemer. Both the universe and Jesus Christ are images in which God represents and manifests Godself to us, even though we can rightly discern these images only if we cling to the Word of God that is inseparable from the visible self-manifestation of God. Moreover, Christ manifests and offers himself to humanity first in the Law given to Israel, and then in the Gospel proclaimed throughout the world. The Law and the Gospel reveal Christ by the message or teaching that is proclaimed in concert with the sacraments that represent and portray this message visually, thereby confirming the truth of the teaching.

However, Calvin consistently distinguishes between the representation of Christ in the sacraments and the reality of Christ himself, so that we do not confine Christ to the sacraments on the one hand, or divorce Christ from the sacraments on the other. This concern leads Calvin to describe the efficacy of the sacraments in two distinct ways. On the one hand, the sacraments both represent and offer the reality they portray, out of accommodation to our creaturely capacities. On the other hand, the reality portrayed in the sacraments is given only to those who use the signs as ladders or vehicles to ascend from earth to heaven, so that their faith may attain the reality being represented in the earthly signs. Calvin combines these two ways of understanding the efficacy of the sacraments without attempting to resolve the tension that these two views create.

We will look first at the way the invisible God becomes somewhat visible in the images of creation and Christ. We will then examine the self-representation of Christ to us in Word and sacrament. Finally, we will explore the way the self-representation of Christ takes place in two distinct ways: in the sacraments of the Law before his death and resurrection, and the sacraments of the Gospel after his resurrection.

The Self-Manifestation of God in Creation and Christ

Calvin's understanding of the sacraments is best understood in light of the sacramental character of his understanding of the self-revelation of God.

In order that the invisible and infinite God might be known by embodied and finite creatures, such as we are, God must become somewhat visible in the temporal and finite world, in order to raise embodied and finite creatures to God. God does this by manifesting God's nature or divinity in God's works in the universe. God's nature is manifested by God's powers or perfections, such as goodness, wisdom, power, mercy, truth, and justice: "For the Lord manifests himself by his powers, the force of which we feel within ourselves and the benefits of which we enjoy."[2] These powers become somewhat visible to us in God's works, which vividly represent these powers to us as in an image or painting. "We must therefore admit in God's individual works—but especially in them as a whole—that God's powers are actually represented as in a painting."[3] We come to the true knowledge of God when we rightly perceive these powers in God's works to the point that we both feel and enjoy these powers in ourselves. Our experience and enjoyment of these powers take root in the inmost affection of our hearts, in order to draw us from the depths of our hearts to the source of these powers in God alone. "For, quite clearly, the mighty gifts with which we are endowed are hardly from ourselves; indeed, our very being is nothing but subsistence in the one God. Then, by these benefits shed like dew from heaven upon us, we are led as by rivulets to the spring itself."[4] Thus, the self-manifestation of God involves the radical descent of God into our minds and hearts, so that we might feel and enjoy the powers of God deeply within ourselves, which should lead us to ascend to God out of the acknowledgment that God alone is the fountain and source of all these powers. "For nothing is more preposterous than to enjoy the very remarkable gifts that attest the divine nature within us, yet to overlook the Author who gives them to us at our asking."[5]

However, given human ingratitude and blindness, the self-representation of God in the universe does not lead to the true knowledge of God without the simultaneous proclamation of the Word of God, revealing God the Creator to us by accurately describing God from God's works. Without the Word of God, we tend either to collapse God into God's works, thereby confining God to creation, or to bypass creation altogether, thereby inventing a god out of our imaginations.

> For with regard to the most beautiful structure and order of the universe, how many of us are there who, when we lift up our eyes to heaven or cast

them about through the various regions of earth, recall our minds to a remembrance of the Creator, and do not rather, disregarding their Author, sit idly in contemplation of his works?[6]

The knowledge of God the Creator is therefore made possible by means of the dynamic interaction between the visible image that we see in the works of God, with the verbal proclamation that we hear, which rightly directs our hearts and minds to the true God manifested in God's works. The Word of God does not replace the living image of God set forth in God's works, but rather allows us to see the powers of God more clearly in those works, so that we might feel and enjoy those powers in our hearts, and be drawn upward to God as the source and author of those powers. "Hence we must strive onward by this straight path if we seriously aspire to the pure contemplation of God. We must come, I say, to the Word, where God is truly and vividly described to us from his works, while these very works are appraised not by our depraved judgment but by the rule of eternal truth."[7]

The knowledge of God the Creator is sufficient to reveal to us the source of the blessings of this life, but it of itself cannot undo the loss inflicted on humanity by the sin of Adam. According to Calvin, God had placed in Adam all of the powers of God by which both Adam and we would be united to God in eternal life. When Adam fell into sin, he lost those gifts not only for himself, but also for us. "With this we ought to be content: that the Lord entrusted to Adam those gifts which he willed to be conferred upon human nature. Hence Adam, when he lost the gifts received, lost them not only for himself but for us all."[8] If human beings are to be reunited to God in eternal life, God must restore to us the good things that were lost in Adam, and must remove from us the evil things that replaced them. And God must do this not in an image outside of us, as in the universe, but in a human being like Adam, making that human being himself the self-manifestation of the one true God, the Author and fountain of every good thing we need for eternal life. "For God would have remained hidden afar off if Christ's splendor had not beamed upon us. For this purpose the Father laid up with his only-begotten Son all that he had to reveal himself in Christ so that Christ, by communicating his Father's benefits, might express the true image of his glory [cf. Heb. 1:3]."[9]

The image of God in Christ shares in the dynamic of descent and ascent that we saw in the self-manifestation of the Creator, only in an even more pronounced manner. The descent of the Son of God begins with his birth and culminates in his death on the cross, during which time Christ increasingly takes upon himself all the evil that afflicts us and alienates us from God. At the nadir of this descent, we can see nothing of the divinity of Christ, as it is completely concealed beneath the appearance of the horrible death of a condemned and God-forsaken sinner. "We see that Christ was so cast down as to be compelled to cry out in deep anguish: 'My God, my God, why hast thou forsaken me?' [Ps. 22:1; Matt. 27:46]."[10] The descent of Christ to the condition of God-forsaken sinners is followed by the ascent of Christ back to God, which restores to sinners all the good things they lost in Adam that can unite them to God in eternal life. Christ's ascent begins with his resurrection, which begins to reveal the divine powers manifested in him, but it culminates in his ascension into heaven, where he is enthroned as King. "Now having laid aside the mean and lowly state of mortal life and the shame of the cross, Christ by rising again began to show forth his glory and power more fully. Yet he truly inaugurated his Kingdom only at his ascension into heaven."[11]

Once Christ ascends into heaven, he fully receives from the Father all that God wishes to bestow on us, and communicates these blessings to us from heaven by the power of the Holy Spirit.

> Especially with regard to heavenly life, there is no drop of vigor in us save what the Holy Spirit instills. For the Spirit has chosen Christ as his seat, that from him might abundantly flow the heavenly riches of which we are in such need. The believers stand unconquered through the strength of their king, and his spiritual riches abound in them. Hence they are justly called Christians.[12]

God has not only made the ascended Christ the source of every good thing that we need, but also revealed that access to eternal life is pledged to us by the presence of Christ in heaven. "Since he entered heaven in our flesh, as if in our name, it follows, as the apostle says, that in a sense we already 'sit with God in the heavenly places in him' [Eph. 2:6], so that we do not await heaven with a bare hope, but in our Head already possess it."[13] Believers must mirror this dynamic of descent and ascent in their knowledge of Christ. They must see their own sin, guilt, curse, death, and eternal damnation in the suffering and death of Christ; and they must seek righteousness, innocence, blessing, eternal life, and eternal happiness in the resurrection and ascension of Christ.

The Self-Revelation of Christ in Word and Sacrament

Even as the Father endows Christ with the blessings that God wishes to bestow on us, making Christ the image of the invisible God, so Christ must offer himself and his benefits to needy sinners, so that they can feel and enjoy his powers in themselves.[14]

> This, then, is the true knowledge of Christ, if we receive him as he is offered by the Father: namely, clothed with his gospel. For just as he has been appointed as the goal of our faith, so we cannot take the right road to him unless the gospel goes before us. And there, surely, the treasures of grace are opened to us; for if they had been closed, Christ would have benefitted us little.[15]

The Gospel is the proclamation in which Christ offers himself and his benefits to those who hear the message with faith. Hence, Calvin agrees with Luther that faith comes from what is heard, and what is heard comes from the preaching of the Gospel. However, even as God descends to our level as creatures by manifesting God's powers in the image of God's works in the universe, so also God descends to our level by revealing and offering Christ not only in the proclamation that we hear, but also in the sacraments that we see.

> The sacraments, therefore, are exercises which make us more certain of the trustworthiness of God's Word. And because we are of flesh, they are shown to us under things of flesh, to instruct us according to our dull capacity, and to lead us by the hand as tutors lead children. Augustine calls a sacrament "a visible word" for the reason that it represents God's promises as painted in a picture and sets them before our sight, portrayed graphically and in the manner of images.[16]

The sacraments confirm our faith in the promise of the Gospel by portraying that promise to us vividly in a living image. "For the clearer anything is, the fitter it is to support faith. But the sacraments bring the clearest promises; and they have this characteristic over and above the word because they represent them for us as painted in a picture from life."[17]

Since the sacraments give a visual representation of the promise of the Gospel, there can be no sacrament where there is no prior promise of God. This promise must be present in order for the visual representation to be a sacrament, and it must be proclaimed to the congregation, and not muttered inaudibly over the sacramental elements like a magical incantation. "For we ought to understand the word not as one whispered without meaning and without faith, mere noise, like a magic incantation, which has the force to consecrate the element. Rather, it should, when preached, make us understand what the visible sign means."[18] Calvin often claims that the promise or word is the soul of the sacraments, meaning that they are lifeless ceremonies without the proclamation of the Word. The promise also directs the attention of the congregation from the sacrament to Christ in heaven, who is the source of the blessings represented in the sacrament, so that they do not turn their attention only to the sign, and so remain on earth. "Accordingly, when we hear the sacramental word mentioned, let us understand the promise, proclaimed in a clear voice by the minister, to lead the people by the hand wherever the sign tends and directs us."[19]

By calling the sacraments iconic representations of Christ and his benefits, Calvin draws an explicit distinction between the sacraments and Christ. If the sacraments represent Christ, then they must be distinguished from Christ, and can never be identified with him, just as I should be distinguished from a portrait painted of me. On the other hand, the whole purpose of the sacraments is to direct our minds and hearts to Christ by portraying his promise to give himself and all his blessings to us. Hence, they direct us from themselves to Christ both by the analogy between the sacramental representation and the truth it represents, and also by the anagogical elevation that must also take place between the earthly sign and the spiritual reality it represents. The analogy is destroyed if Christ is identified with the sign, and the anagogical elevation from sign to reality is undermined if Christ is seen to be contained or enclosed in the sign. "By this error the simple and unskilled are dangerously deceived, while they are both taught to seek God's gifts where they cannot be found, and are gradually drawn away from God to embrace mere vanity rather than his truth."[20] If this happens, the sacrament becomes an idol, and not a living representation of Christ.

The key question remains whether the sacraments only *represent* Christ, and thus serve an epistemological function, or whether they also *offer* Christ. In his first writings, Calvin seems to have held that the sacraments only represent Christ, and strengthen faith by the clarity of their visual representation of God's promises. However, by 1543, Calvin increasingly teaches that the sacraments both represent and present Christ and his benefits. Just as it would be an error to identify Christ with the sacraments, thereby making the sacraments into idols, so it would also be an error to separate Christ from the sacraments, thereby making the sacraments into empty signs. Calvin came to describe the sacraments as instruments God uses to portray and convey God's blessings to us. However, he was very concerned that the reality offered in the sacrament not be bound to the sacrament, as though it offered Christ of itself. Calvin thought that this is what the Roman Church taught when it said that grace is given by the performance of the sacrament (*ex opera operato*), and is always received unless obstructed by mortal sin in the recipient. "That is to think that a hidden power is joined and fastened to the sacraments by which they of themselves confer the graces of the Holy Spirit upon us, as wine is given in a cup."[21] Calvin thought that God must always be seen as the one who gives the reality that the sacrament represents, by means of the freely given Holy Spirit. "We must also note this: that God accomplishes within what the minister represents and attests by outward action, lest what God claims for himself alone should be turned over to a mortal man."[22]

Calvin describes two ways in which reality can be divorced from the sacrament, so that it fails to offer what it represents. The first is the lack of repentance and faith on the part of the recipient, which blocks the reception of Christ, even though he is truly offered with the sacraments. "Therefore, let it be regarded as a settled principle that the sacraments have the same office as the Word of God: to offer and set forth Christ to us, and in him the treasures of heavenly grace. But they avail and profit nothing unless received in faith."[23] The second is divine election, in which God decides to give the reality only to the elect, whom God has chosen to receive the Holy Spirit. "The Holy Spirit (whom the sacraments do not bring indiscriminately to all men but whom the Lord exclusively bestows on his own people) is he who brings the graces of God with him, gives a place for the sacraments among us, and makes them bear fruit."[24] In this model, the reality represented in the sacraments is offered only to the elect: the reprobate are simply shown an empty sign that does not offer the reality it represents. In either model, recipients must examine themselves to see if they have repentance and faith, for without these they do not receive the reality offered in the sacrament, because their lack of faith blocks Christ from reaching them, and shows that they have not (yet) been elected by God to receive the Holy Spirit. However, in the former model, the sacrament truly offers Christ, but Christ is not received due to the lack of faith in the recipient, whereas in the latter, the sacrament only represents Christ, but does not offer him to the recipient.

Similarly, the Holy Spirit cannot be bound to the sacrament in such a way as to be unable to convey the reality of the sacrament without participation in the sacrament. As we shall see, this issue was especially pressing for Calvin with regard to the sacrament of baptism. The Holy Spirit uses sacraments as instruments, but it is not bound or tied to these instruments, and so can offer Christ and his benefits to those who do not receive the sacraments. "From this something else follows: assurance of salvation does not depend upon participation in the sacrament, as if justification consisted in it."[25] Hence, Calvin does not teach that baptism is necessary for salvation, contrary to both the Roman Church and the Augsburg Confession, and he insists that God can save the infants of believers even if they lack baptism. Similarly, a person who is unable to participate in the Holy Supper of the Lord is not deprived of feeding on the spiritual food of his body and blood, for this can be given by the Spirit apart from the Supper.

The Self-Manifestation of Christ in the Sacraments of the Law

According to Calvin, Christ reveals and offers himself not only in the Gospel that is proclaimed to the whole world, but also in the Law that was revealed only to Israel. We only truly know Christ when we see him as the one who is revealed to us in both the Law and the Gospel.

Calvin understands the Law to include the entire covenant of adoption made with Abraham and his descendants, renewed in the Law revealed by God to Moses. "And Moses was not made a lawgiver to wipe out the blessing promised to the race of Abraham. Rather, we see him repeatedly reminding the Jews of the freely given covenant made with their fathers of which they were the heirs. It was as if he were sent to renew it."[26] Calvin understands the Law to comprise the whole order of worship established by God for Israel, especially the sacrifices and rites of purification that God required of the Israelites. All of these rites and ceremonies portrayed and offered Christ and his benefits to Israel with the same efficacy as the rites and ceremonies of the Gospel.

> Further, when Paul says that the fathers ate the same spiritual meat, he first of all gives a hint of what the power and efficacy of the sacrament is; and secondly he shows that the old sacraments of the law had the same power as ours have today. For if manna was spiritual food, it follows that bare forms are not exhibited to us in the sacraments, but the reality figured is truly given at the same time.[27]

Even though the sacraments of the Law have the same efficacy as the sacraments of the Gospel, Calvin carefully distinguishes between the way Christ is represented in the Law and the way he is portrayed in the Gospel. The Law portrays Christ in a way to make it clear to Israel that he is absent and is coming in the future, whereas the Gospel reveals that Christ has come and is now present. Thus, Calvin speaks of the sacraments of the Law as shadows cast by the coming reality of Christ, which truly offer the one whom they shadow, even though their solidity entirely depends on the one to come. "For the substance of those things which the ceremonies once figured is now presented before our eyes in Christ, in that he contains in himself everything that they pointed to as future."[28] Calvin also speaks of Christ as the archetype seen by Moses on Mount Sinai, after which all of the types of the Law were patterned. He uses these models to show that the sacraments of the Law have no intrinsic meaning or solidity except as portraying and offering Christ to Israel. "In short, the whole cultus of the law, taken literally and not as shadows and figures corresponding to the truth, will be utterly ridiculous."[29]

However, the representations of Christ in the Law are accommodated to the capacities of the people of Israel, which develop over time as Israel matures from infancy to adolescence throughout its history. Thus, Calvin describes the Law as a shadow sketch that initially represents Christ in an outline, but then fills out this representation over time until the living portrait of Christ is revealed in the Gospel. "For as painters do not in the first draft bring out a likeness in lifelike colors and as in an image, but first sketch rude and obscure lines with charcoal, so the representation of Christ under the law was unpolished, and was, as it were, a first sketch, but in our sacraments a true likeness is seen."[30] Calvin combines the increasing clarity and fullness of the representation of Christ in the Law with the increasing light of manifestation that reveals the one who is being portrayed in this shadowy manner. "The Lord held to this orderly plan in administering the covenant of his mercy: as the day of full revelation approached with the passing of time, the more he increased each day the brightness of its manifestation."[31]

Calvin also notes the way the representations of Christ in the Law make more use of temporal realities such as the land of Canaan or the kingship of David to represent the spiritual realities set forth in Christ. This does not mean that the Law set forth only temporal blessings, but rather that the Israelites had to move by analogy from the temporal signs to Christ, and also had to elevate themselves by analogy from the temporal sign to the spiritual reality represented therein.

> The better to commend God's goodness, the prophets represented it for the people under the lineaments, so to speak, of temporal benefits. But they painted a portrait such as to lift up the minds of the people above the earth, above the elements of this world and the perishing age, and that would of necessity arouse them to ponder the happiness of the spiritual life to come.[32]

Since the sacraments of the Law set forth Christ with the same efficacy as do those of the Gospel, Calvin uses the sacraments of the Law to develop a greater understanding of the sacraments of the Gospel. For instance, since both circumcision and baptism refer to Christ, Calvin defends infant baptism on the basis of Israel's practice of circumcision, in which the children of believers were circumcised in their infancy. On the other hand, since the sacraments of the Law represent one who is yet to come, those who employ the sacraments of the Law during the time of the Gospel actually proclaim that Christ has yet to come. Thus, when the Roman Church ordains priests to offer the sacrifice of the Mass every day on their altars, they declare by this sacramental practice that Christ has not yet offered himself on the cross as the once for all sacrifice for sin, and thereby return the Church to the sacrificial system of the Law. The truth of the sacraments of the Law rests entirely in Christ, according to Calvin, and this truth can be maintained only if the sacraments of the Law come to an end with the coming of Christ, since he is the one to whom all of the Law bears witness.

The Self-Representation of Christ in the Sacraments of the Gospel

In order to reveal that he is the one who is offered to Israel in the Law, Christ participates in all of the sacraments of the Law, beginning with his circumcision, and culminating in his burial. However, once Christ is raised from the dead and ascends into heaven, the sacraments of the Law must come to an end, and be replaced by the sacraments of the Gospel. The sacraments of the Gospel are noteworthy for their simplicity, over against the complex ceremonies of the Law; and for their clarity, over against the shadowy nature of the sacraments of the Law. Calvin distinguishes between three kinds of sacraments of the Gospel: those common to all believers (baptism and the Holy Supper of the Lord), those unique to a group of believers (the laying on of hands for ordination), and those that were given to the Church only for a short period of time (the laying on of hands to bestow the visible gifts of the Spirit, and anointing for healing). Calvin denies that confirmation, penance, and marriage were ever sacraments, and he argues that the temporary sacraments should not be observed in his day, since God no longer offers the reality they represent to the Church.

The development of Calvin's understanding of baptism reveals most clearly the way in which he wrestled with the idea that the sacraments of themselves convey grace, which he claimed was the teaching of the Roman Church. At the beginning of his career, Calvin emphasizes the representational character of baptism, but is silent about the offer of the reality through baptism. Baptism represents three things to the believer: the forgiveness of sins, renewal of life, and participation in Christ himself, from whom both forgiveness and renewal flow. Baptism confirms faith when the believer follows the analogy of the sign to the reality signified, so that we know that God forgives and renews us as surely as we see our bodies being outwardly cleansed by the water of baptism. However, at the beginning of his career, Calvin explicitly denies that baptism is an "organ or instrument" by which the gifts of God are bestowed upon us.[33]

The first major development in Calvin's understanding of baptism takes place in 1539, when he defends the practice of infant baptism by means of an analogical appeal to circumcision. Since both circumcision and baptism represent the same reality—namely, the forgiveness and regeneration brought by Christ—Calvin appeals to the practice of circumcision to provide the warrant for the legitimacy of infant baptism. God assured Israelite parents that their children were included in the covenant of adoption by having them inscribe the symbol of circumcision on their male children in their infancy. How much more would God wish to assure the parents of believers about the adoption of their children once Christ has come to fulfill the Law? "Otherwise, if the testimony by which the Jews were assured of the salvation of their posterity is taken away from us, Christ's coming would have the effect of making grace more obscure and less attested than it had previously been for the Jews."[34] However, baptism does not of itself make them children of God, but rather attests and seals to the parents that their children have already been adopted. Hence, the death of an infant without baptism should not cause believing parents to despair, as the adoption of their child is not tied to the reception of baptism.

The next major development in Calvin's teaching on baptism occurs in his *Catechism* of 1545, when he finally acknowledges that baptism both represents and offers forgiveness of sin and renewal of life in Christ. "Minister: But do you attribute nothing more to the water than to be a mere symbol of ablution? Child: I think it to be such a symbol that reality is attached to it. For God does not disappoint us when he promises us his gifts. Hence both pardon and newness of life are certainly offered to us and received by us in Baptism."[35] From this point onward, Calvin will insist that the reality represented in baptism is actually given by Christ through the Holy Spirit, using the sign as an instrument or means. "And he does not feed our eyes with a mere appearance only, but leads us to the present reality and effectively performs what it symbolizes."[36] However, to keep baptism from becoming an idol again, as he thought had happened in the Roman Church, Calvin insists that we ought to "leave to Christ and also to the Holy Spirit each his own honor, so that no part of our salvation should be transferred to the sign."[37]

We see a similar development with regard to Calvin's understanding of the Holy Supper of the Lord. In the first edition of the *Institutes*, Calvin claims that this sacrament vividly attests and portrays our unity with Christ, and the abundance of blessings that flow to us from him. "Great indeed is the fruit of sweetness and comfort our souls can gather from this sacrament: because we recognize Christ to have been so engrafted in us that we, in turn, have been engrafted in him, so that whatever is his we are permitted to call ours, whatever is ours to reckon as his."[38] Christ sets forth the bread and wine as symbols of his body and blood as our spiritual food, so that we may know that we are spiritually fed and strengthened by him in the same way our bodies are fed and strengthened by the bread and wine.[39] However, at this point Calvin claims that the Supper reminds us only of the unity we have with Christ by faith, and does not offer the reality of Christ's body and blood represented in the symbols of bread and wine.

The first major development in Calvin's teaching on the Supper takes place in the 1539 edition of the *Institutes*. Calvin insists that God is not a deceiver, and thus does not set forth an empty symbol before us in the Supper. Thus, even though "the breaking of the bread is a symbol; it is not the thing itself," Calvin nevertheless insists that "by showing the symbol the thing itself is shown."[40] Even as the godly ought to distinguish the symbol from the reality symbolized, so they ought always to join the reality to the symbol, for it is truly presented by the symbol. "And the godly ought by all means to keep this rule: whenever they see symbols appointed by the Lord, to think and be persuaded that the truth of the thing signified is surely present there."[41] From this point on, Calvin insists that the Supper truly offers the reality it represents, so that when the godly feed on the bread and wine, they should be assured that they are thereby feeding on the body and blood of Christ. "But if it is true that a visible sign is given us to seal the gift of a thing invisible, when we have received the symbol of the body, let us no less surely trust that the body itself is also given to us."[42]

However, Calvin also insists that the body and blood of Christ are in heaven, and must not be sought under the signs of bread and wine. To do so would confine the minds and hearts of believers to the earth, and thereby turn the Supper into an idol, as he claims happened in the Roman Church. "While the sacrament ought to have been a means of elevating pious minds to heaven, the sacred symbols of the Supper were abused for an entirely different purpose, and men, content with gazing upon them and worshipping them, never once raised their mind to Christ."[43] We must therefore seek communion with Christ's body and blood in heaven, and not in the earthly signs of bread and wine per se. The Holy Spirit will unite us with the body and blood of Christ in heaven so long as we do not enclose, confine, or seek the body and blood of Christ in the bread and wine. "Rather, I think that in order to enjoy the reality of the signs we must be raised to heaven where Christ is and whence we expect him to come as judge and redeemer. But in these earthly elements it is improper to seek him."[44]

Calvin's concern to seek the body and blood of Christ in heaven leads to the second major development in his teaching on the Supper. Beginning in 1549, Calvin begins to describe the Supper as a ladder or vehicle by which we climb from earth to heaven, in order to seek communion with Christ's flesh and blood there, and not in the earthly signs of bread and wine. "Christ invites us to himself. As we cannot climb so high, he himself lends us his hand, and assists us with the helps which he knows to be suited to us, and even lifts us to heaven, as it is very appropriately expressed by those who compare the sacraments to ladders."[45] Unless we use the Supper as a ladder to climb to heaven, the reality represented in the Supper will not be given to us. "For to what end does Christ hold forth a pledge of his flesh and blood under earthly elements unless it be to raise us upward? If they are helps to our weakness, no man will ever attain to the reality, but he who thus assisted shall climb, as it were, step by step from earth to heaven."[46]

Calvin thereby creates a significant tension in his teaching on the Supper that he never successfully resolves. On the one hand, he clearly teaches that Christ not only represents his body and blood to us, but also offers them to us with the bread and the wine. "For Christ is neither a painter, nor an actor, nor a kind of Archimedes who presents an empty image to amuse the eye; but he truly and in reality performs what by external symbol he promises. Hence I conclude that the bread which we break is truly the communion of the body of Christ."[47] On the other hand, he clearly teaches that the reality of Christ's body and blood is given only to those who ascend to heaven by the ladder of the Supper in order to acquire grace for themselves there. "But if faith must intervene, no man of sense will deny that the same God who helps our infirmity by these aids, also gives faith, which, elevated by proper ladders, may climb to Christ and obtain his grace."[48] One way by which this tension might be resolved would be to see the ascent to heaven as being facilitated by the prior descent of Christ, which would echo the way God is revealed both in creation and in Christ himself. "For they think they only communicate with [the body of Christ] if it descends into the bread; but they do not understand the true manner of descent by which he lifts us up to himself."[49]

Conclusion

The tension we see in Calvin's doctrine of the Supper reveals a theme one finds throughout his theology. On the one hand, God descends to us by both the works we see and the Word we hear so that the invisible God might become somewhat visible, and might communicate God's blessing to us. On the other hand, we must ascend from these visible and verbal self-representations of God to the God being represented therein, lest we confine God to the works that manifest and offer God's gifts to us.

NOTES

1. See Randall C. Zachman, *Image and Word in the Theology of John Calvin* (Notre Dame, IN: University of Notre Dame Press, 2007).
2. John Calvin, *The Institutes of the Christian Religion*, vol. I, 9 (hereafter cited as Inst.), in *Ioannis Calvini opera selecta*, ed. Peter Barth, Wilhelm Niesel, and Dora Scheuner (Munich: Chr. Kaiser, 1926–52), vol. III, 53, lines 14–16 (hereafter cited as OS III.53.14–16); *Calvin: Institutes of the Christian Religion*, ed. John T. McNeill, trans. Ford Lewis Battles (Philadelphia: Westminster, 1960), vol. 1, 62 (hereafter cited as LCC 62).
3. Inst. I.v.10, OS III.54.14–21; LCC 63.
4. Inst. I.i.1, OS III.31.12–16; LCC 35.

5. Inst. I.v.6, OS III.51.1–3; LCC 58–59.
6. Inst. I.v.11, OS III.55.6–11; LCC 63.
7. Inst. I.vi.3, OS III.63.24–28; LCC 72–73.
8. Inst. II.i.7, OS III.236.1–4; LCC 249.
9. Inst. III.ii.1, OS IV.8.11–15; LCC 544.
10. Inst. II.xvi.11, OS III.496.10–13; LCC 516–17.
11. Inst. II.xvi.14, OS III.501.22–25; LCC 522.
12. Inst. II.xv.5, OS III.478.2–5; LCC 500.
13. Inst. II.xvi.16, OS III.503–4; LCC 524.
14. See B. A. Gerrish, *Grace and Gratitude: Calvin's Eucharistic Theology* (Minneapolis, MN: Fortress, 1993); Thomas Davis, *The Clearest Promises of God: The Development of Calvin's Eucharistic Teaching* (New York: AMS Press, 1995).
15. Inst. III.ii.6, OS IV.13.15–18; LCC 548.
16. Inst. IV.xiv.6, OS V.263.9–17; LCC 1281.
17. Inst. IV.xiv.5, OS V.262.20–24; LCC 1280.
18. Inst. IV.xiv.4, OS V.261.5–8; LCC 1279.
19. Inst. IV.xiv.4, OS V.261–62; LCC 1279–80.
20. Inst. IV.xiv.14, OS V.271.12–15; LCC 1289.
21. Inst. IV.xiv.17, OS V.275.23–25; LCC 1292.
22. Inst. IV.xiv.17, OS V.275.26–29; LCC 1293.
23. Inst. IV.xiv.17, OS V.274.18–21; LCC 1292.
24. Inst. IV.xiv.17, OS V.275.4–7; LCC 1293.
25. Inst. IV.xiv.14, OS V.272.1–2; LCC 1290.
26. Inst. II.vii.1, OS III.326.30–34; LCC 348.
27. Comm. 1 Cor. 10:3, in *Ioannis Calvini opera quae supersunt omnia*, ed. Wilhelm Baum, Edward Cunitz, and Eduard Reuss (Brunswick: A. Schwetschke and Son (M. Bruhn), 1863–1900), vol. 49, 453 (hereafter cited as CO 49:453); *Calvin's New Testament Commentaries*, ed. David W. Torrance and Thomas F. Torrance (Grand Rapids, MI: Eerdmans, 1959–72), vol. 9, 203 (hereafter cited as CNTC 9:203).
28. John Calvin, Commentary on Colossians 2:17, in *Ioannis Calvini Opera Omnia, Series II, Opera Exegetica Veteris et Novi Testamenti* (Geneva: Librairie Droz, 1992–), vol. 16, 434, lines 9–15 (hereafter cited as OE 16.434.9–15); CNTC 11:338.
29. Inst. II.vii.1, OS III.327.13–15; LCC 349.
30. Commentary on Colossians 2:17, OE 16.434.25–34; CNTC 11:338.
31. *Institutio 1539* VII.20, CO 1:815B; LCC 446.
32. *Institutio 1539* VII.20, CO 1:815–16; LCC 447.
33. *Institutio 1536* IV.21, CO 1:115A; *Institutes of the Christian Religion, 1536*, trans. Ford Lewis Battles (Grand Rapids, MI: Eerdmans, 1986), 99 (hereafter cited as *Inst. 1536*:99).
34. *Institutio 1539* XI.24, CO 1:972A; LCC 1329.
35. *Catechismus Ecclesiae Genevensis*, OS II.134.16–20; *Calvin: Theological Treatises*, ed. J. K. S. Reid (Philadelphia: Westminster Press, 1954), 133.
36. Inst. IV.xv.14, OS V.295.26–28; LCC 1314.

37. John Calvin, *Commentary on 1 Peter*, 3:21, CO 55:269A; CNTC 12:296–97.
38. *Institutio 1536* IV.24, CO 1:118–19; *Inst.* 1536:102.
39. *Institutio 1536* IV.26, CO 1:119C; *Inst.* 1536:103.
40. *Institutio 1539* XII.18, CO 1:1002C; LCC 1371.
41. *Institutio 1539* XII.18, CO 1:1002–3; LCC 1371.
42. Ibid.
43. Supplex exhortatio ad Caesarem, in Reid, *Calvin: Theological Treatises*, 205.
44. Catechismus Ecclesiae Genevensis, OS II.140–41; Reid, *Calvin: Theological Treatises*, 137.
45. *Vera Ecclesiae Reformandae Ratio*, CO 7:623A; John Calvin, *Tracts and Treatises*, vol. 3, trans. Henry Beveridge (Grand Rapids, MI: Eerdmans, 1958), 279–80.
46. Secunda defensio contra Ioachimi Westphali calumnias, CO 9:48–49; *Tracts and Treatises* 2:250.
47. Dilucida Explicatio Sanae Doctrinae de Vera Participatione Carnis et Sanguinis Christi in Sacra Coena, CO 9:470–71; Reid, *Calvin: Theological Treatises*, 268.
48. Defensio sanae et orthodoxae doctrinae de sacramentis, CO 9:25C; *Tracts and Treatises* 2:232.
49. *Inst.* IV.xvii.16, OS V.362.33–34; LCC 1379.

12

Thomas Cranmer

ASHLEY NULL

Thomas Cranmer (1489–1556) was baptized into the medieval Catholic Church. He studied at Cambridge, receiving a doctorate of divinity in 1526, and served there as a don. As a theologian, Cranmer was very much influenced by Erasmus's emphasis on going back to the original sources for the Christian faith, in particular, of course, the Bible.

In the late 1520s, the authority of Scripture was at the center of the most pressing English political issue of the day—Henry VIII's divorce case. The king and his scholars argued that the pope did not have the authority to set aside a clear Scriptural commandment against a moral sin. Since Leviticus 20:21 specifically forbids taking the wife of one's brother, Henry's marriage to Catherine of Aragon was invalid, despite having received papal approval. True to his own theological convictions on Scripture, Cranmer agreed.

Once Henry learned of Cranmer's views on the subject, he invited the Cambridge don to join his team of scholars. In 1532, as part of that effort, Henry sent Cranmer to Germany as his ambassador to the emperor.

While in Germany, Cranmer came under the influence of Protestantism. Not only did he acquire a new wife—who was the niece of the wife of the German reformer Andreas Osiander—but he also acquired a clearly Protestant understanding of justification.

His commitment to Scripture and to the early Church Fathers, like Augustine, helped Cranmer to grasp the Protestants' emphasis on salvation by grace alone. His Erasmian studies, therefore, laid the bridge for him to cross over from being a Catholic to a Protestant.

Then, quite unexpectedly, Henry VIII called Cranmer back to be the next Archbishop of Canterbury. Naturally, he was quite reluctant. No doubt, though, he accepted the position because he saw it as his task to use such a powerful position to restore the English Church to its scriptural roots. And, of course, that's what Cranmer did for the rest of his life as the Archbishop of Canterbury—seeking to bring the Church of England back to a sound, biblical faith.

Under Henry's successor, the boy-king Edward VI, he was primarily responsible for the three key formularies of the Church of England: the *Book of Homilies*, the *Book of Common Prayer*, and the *Articles of Religion*. Therefore, understanding Cranmer's theology is essential for understanding the theological origins of the Anglican Communion.

* * *

According to medieval Scholasticism, Jesus had established the church as the intermediary between God and his people. The bishops served as the administrators of saving apostolic spiritual power, and the sacraments, *ex opere operato*, were the effective means of dispensing that heavenly grace to the people. However, during the 1530s Thomas Cranmer chose to embrace justification by faith, which completely rejected that narrative.[1] Now he believed that Jesus had come to preach a saving message, which had supernatural power to create a community linking God to his elect by inspiring trust in his divine promises. The question that would occupy Cranmer for the remainder of his life was how exactly the sacraments of the church fit into this new narrative.

As the Archbishop of Canterbury of an independent Church of England from 1534 onward, Cranmer initially sought to redefine the English teaching on sacraments in a Lutheran direction. Henry's diplomatic essays to join the German Protestant military alliance gave Cranmer an opportunity to do so, since an adherence to the Augsburg Confession was a requirement for membership in the Schmalkaldic League. Influenced by these negotiations, in July 1536 the Church of England adopted the Ten Articles as a doctrinal compromise. Like the Augsburg Confession, the Ten Articles restricted the number of sacraments to baptism, Eucharist, and penance. Moreover, the description of baptism noted the importance of having "firm credence and trust in the promise of God adjoined to the said sacrament," while the article on penance went even further in an explicitly Lutheran direction.[2] Whereas medieval Scholasticism had defined contrition as regret for sin out of love for God, the Ten Articles followed the classic Lutheran narrative of an initial heartfelt struggle with fear of damnation (medieval attrition), which then gave way to certain hope of eternal salvation through faith in Christ:

> The penitent and contrite man must first knowledge the filthiness and abomination of his own sin, (unto which knowledge he is brought by hearing and considering of the will of God declared in his laws,) and feeling and perceiving in his own conscience that God is angry and displeased with him for the same; he must also conceive not only great sorrow and inward shame that he hath so grievously offended God, but also great fear of God's displeasure towards him, considering he hath no works or merits of his own which he may worthily lay before God, as sufficient satisfaction for his sins; which done, then afterward with this fear, shame and sorrow must needs succeed and be conjoined . . . a certain faith, trust, and confidence of the mercy and goodness of God, whereby the penitent must conceive certain hope and faith that God will forgive him his sins, and repute him justified, and of the number of his elect children, not for the worthiness of any merit or work done by the penitent, but for the only merits of the blood and passion of our Saviour Jesus Christ.[3]

Evidently, conservatives could live with this rejection of medieval contrition, since the article also insisted that auricular confession was necessary for salvation, as was the performance of good works.[4]

A year later the article was wholly incorporated into the Bishops' Book.[5] Equally a mixture of evangelical and conservative teaching, this much more fulsome doctrinal statement covered the Apostles' Creed, the Ten Commandments, the sacraments, the Lord's Prayer, the Hail Mary, justification, and purgatory. Although all seven medieval sacraments were now included, a crucial final paragraph continued to distinguish between the "dignity and necessity" of baptism, Eucharist, and penance and the other four, for only the first three were instituted by Christ for the forgiveness of sins and, thus, were necessary for salvation.[6]

In his response to a questionnaire associated with these doctrinal debates, Cranmer made clear he considered as a sacrament only something that the New Testament recorded as being commanded by Christ for the forgiveness of sins. While Henry's conservative bishops appealed to apostolic oral tradition concerning the dominical institution of Confirmation, Cranmer rejected that as insufficient. As a result, its efficacy was simply that of any "prayer of the bishop made in the name of the church."[7] Similarly, when commenting on Henry VIII's 1538 corrections to the Bishops' Book, Cranmer denied that the apostolic command for presbyters to anoint the sick constituted a sacrament. Rather, he insisted that the efficacy of extreme unction was also simply as a prayer said in faith.[8] Although the Bishops' Book taught that marriage was instituted by God in Eden to bring about a spiritual union between a man and woman "for mutual aid and comfort,"[9] we have seen that the ceremony still did not qualify as a sacrament. When Henry VIII sought to have the text amended so as to move matrimony into the "higher" category, Cranmer objected, simply reiterating what the Bishops' Book had already stated, that wedlock was not "by the manifest institution of Christ: or, that it is of necessity to salvation: or, that thereby we should have the forgiveness of sins, renovation of life, and justification, etc."[10]

As to the nature of the Eucharistic presence, the description of the "Sacrament of the Altar" found in both the Ten Articles and Bishops' Book asserted that "under the form and figure of bread and wine" was "verily, substantially and really contained and comprehended the very self same body and blood of our saviour Jesus Christ," which was universally distributed to all who received the sacrament, although those who partook unworthily did so to their damnation.[11] As for Cranmer's personal opinion, his 1537 letter to Joachim von Watt (Vadianus) suggests that he held a Lutheran position at this time. Rejecting both "papistical and sophistical errors" on the sacrament, that is, transubstantiation, as well as the Oecolampadius and Zwingli's symbolic understanding of the elements, Cranmer appealed to biblical and early patristic support for a real presence position:

> I have seen almost every thing that has been written and published either by Oecolampadius or Zwingli, and I have come to the conclusion that the writings of every man must be read with discrimination. . . . As far indeed as they have endeavoured to point out, confute, and correct papistical and sophistical errors and abuses, I commend and approve them. And I wish that they had confined themselves within those limits, and . . . had not at the same time done violence to the authority of the ancient doctors and chief writers in the church of Christ. . . . And this error, most certainly, if er-

ror it be, has been handed down to us by the fathers themselves, and men of apostolic character, from the very beginning of the church. And what godly man could endure to hear this, much less to believe it? Not to mention in the mean time, that our gracious Lord would never have left his beloved spouse in such lamentable blindness for so long a period. Wherefore, since this catholic faith which we hold respecting the real presence has been declared to the church from the beginning by such evident and manifest passages of scripture, and the same has also been subsequently commended to the ears of the faithful with so much clearness and diligence by the first ecclesiastical writers, do not I pray, persist in wishing any longer to carp at or subvert a doctrine so well grounded and supported.... I beg ... you ... to agree and unite in a Christian concord ... so that we may ... extend as widely as possible one sound, pure, evangelical doctrine, conformable to the discipline of the primitive church.[12]

In short, Cranmer insisted that he would have to see "stronger evidence brought forward" than that which Vadianus had provided before he would agree "to be the patron" or "the approver" of Reformed sacramental theology.[13]

Finally, Cranmer also used his comments to the king's corrections as an opportunity to describe his understanding of how justification by faith provided the chief motivation for the Christian life. Because assurance of salvation came with solifidianism, Cranmer believed that Luther's chief tenet was the true source for the indwelling, transforming love so emphasized by the medieval English affective tradition and Erasmus's humanism, which had shaped his education:[14]

But, if the profession of our faith of the remission of our own sins enter within us into the deepness of our hearts, then it must needs kindle a warm fire of love in our hearts towards God, and towards all other for the love of God,—a fervent mind to seek and procure God's honour, will, and pleasure in all things,—a good will and mind to help every man and to do good unto them, so far as our might, wisdom, learning, counsel, health, strength, and all other gifts which we have received of God, will extend,—and, *in summa*, a firm intent and purpose to do all that is good, and leave all that is evil.[15]

Despite such efforts by Cranmer to promote the Reformation theology of grace and gratitude, Henry never accepted solifidianism.

The king, however, was much more receptive to Cranmer's arguments that equated sacerdotal claims to unique authority for applying the benefits of Christ's death to sinners with papal pretensions to universal spiritual authority. We can see this argument already in a letter to Thomas Cromwell dated 28 January 1537. Cranmer considered it seditious that Hugh Payne had preached the common medieval teaching that a penance assigned by a priest was a thousand times more effective than a good work done at the sinner's own initiative.[16] About this time, Cranmer specifically attacked the fundamental basis for such claims in his answers on Confirmation. In his view, the apostles' special anointing to pass on the Holy Spirit through the laying on of hands was to confirm the Word of God only at that time and was not passed down to the bishops who followed them.[17] Although Cranmer at this point did not draw out the consequences for either penance or ordination, the implication was clear. If bishops did not have apostolic power themselves, they could not pass it on to priests in ordination for the exercising of an *ex opere operato* functioning of the sacraments.

During the second round of English theological negotiations with the Schmalkaldic League in 1538, Cranmer did his best to seize the opportunity to revisit the necessity of auricular confession for the forgiveness of sins, for here was the root of all pretensions to special sacerdotal control over forgiveness. Where the proposed Thirteen Articles said that sacramental penance was "necessary," Cranmer wrote in his copy "beneficial." When these failed discussions led to the conservative Act of Six Articles, Cranmer made the same Erasmian argument about the article on penance. Henry agreed with Cranmer and even joined the public debate in the House of Lords himself in the archbishop's defense. As a result, the description of auricular confession in the Six Articles was changed from "necessary" for salvation to only "beneficial" for good pastoral care.[18]

When in late 1540 another questionnaire on the sacraments was sent out in preparation for what eventually became the *King's Book* (1543), Cranmer recognized only two clear biblical sacraments: (1) baptism "in which we be regenerated and pardoned of our sins by the blood of Christ"; (2) Eucharist "in which we be concorporated unto Christ, and made lively members of his body, nourished and fed to the everlasting life, if we receive it as we ought to do." He then noted that both penance and matrimony were mentioned in Scripture, but he declined to name them explicitly as sacraments. Penance, according to Scripture, was "a pure conversion of a sinner in heart and mind from his sins unto God" rather than confessing to a priest and being assigned works of satisfaction. As for marriage, Cranmer found it described in the Bible as "a means whereby God doth use the infirmity of our concupiscence to the setting forth of his glory, and increase of the world, thereby sanctifying the act of carnal commixtion between the man and the wife to that use." He flatly denied that Scripture had anything to say about Confirmation, order, or extreme unction as sacraments.[19]

Cranmer now made explicit the consequences of his rejection of apostolic succession in his previous discussion of Confirmation. Concerning penance, he denied that the power of binding and loosing Jesus promised to his followers made confession to a priest necessary for salvation. Concerning ordination, he denied that laying on of hands by a bishop was necessary to make a priest. Rather, Cranmer noted that God had given the monarch "the whole cure of all their subjects, as well concerning the administration of God's word for the cure of souls, as concerning the ministration of things political and civil governance"; consequently, there was "no more promise of God, that grace is given in the committing of the ecclesiastical office, than it is in the committing of the civil office." Even if ecclesiastical offices were given without the customary "comely ceremonies and solemnities," they were "nevertheless truly committed." For "he that is appointed to be a bishop or a priest, needeth no consecration by the scripture; for election or appointing thereto is sufficient." Since mere appointment made someone a priest, a bishop could make priests, but so could princes and even the people before there were Christian princes, whoever had the right to choose the person for the office.[20]

Thus, as the 1540s began, Cranmer was moving toward a more reformed understanding of the sacraments. Departing from the Augsburg Confession, he had completely dropped penance from the list. Equally significant, his definition of *eucharistia* made no mention of biblical support for the real presence, but rather emphasized the sacrament as a means of union with Christ. Cranmer later admitted that he had held a real presence view of the sacrament well into the 1540s, so this statement should not be taken as a fundamental change of Cranmer on this point.[21] However, it does indicate that the aim of the Eucharist, rather than its means, had come to the fore in his thinking, and remained his overriding consideration. Cranmer's final view would still be consistent with this aim, even if the mechanics by how this was achieved did change.

Cranmer's Mature Understanding of the Sacraments

During the 1530s justification by faith became the foundation of Cranmer's soteriology. The work of salvation was Christ's, both in providing its grounds in his sinless life and self-offering propitiatory sacrifice on the cross as well as in providing its means, the revelation of saving truth to the apostles written down in the Scriptures. Through the church's proclamation of the efficacious Word, the Holy Spirit would inspire faith in Christ's redeeming work in the heart of the elect, imputing to them his saving righteousness and kindling a purifying love to serve him as well as others so binding them to Christ and one another. In short, ever-increasing appropriation of the new life made possible by union with Christ was the goal of Christian discipleship, and its means was ruminating on Scripture.

Cranmer enshrined these soteriological principles in his first formulary for the Church of England under the boy-king Edward VI. Popularly known as the *Book of Homilies* (1547), these twelve sermons were required to be read in order in every parish church every Sunday. On the one hand, its first homily on Scripture clearly taught the supernatural power of the Bible to turn people's hearts to God and the doing of his will: "[The words of Holy Scripture] have power to convert through God's promise, and they be effectual through God's assistance." Those who devoted themselves to "continual reading and meditation of God's Word" would discover that "the great affection to the transitory things of this world shall be diminished in him, and the great desire of heavenly things that be therein promised of God shall increase in him." Hence, "the hearing and keeping of [Scripture] maketh us blessed, sanctifieth us and maketh us holy."[22] On the other hand, the third homily on salvation described how Scripture's transforming power imparted two key gifts to believers, saving faith and loving obedience, with the latter being the fruit of the former. A "sure trust and confidence in God's merciful promises, to be saved from everlasting damnation by Christ" justified sinners. Gratitude for this assurance of salvation then led to "a loving heart to obey his commandments," drawing believers closer to God and to one another.[23]

Since ruminating on the efficacious Word was the key to ever-increasing new life in Christ, Cranmer publicly embraced an understanding of the sacraments based on the notion of believing as spiritually "feeding on Christ." He explained this fundamental concept in his *A Defence of the True and Catholike Doctrine of the Sacrament of the Body and Blood of Our Saviour Christ* (1550):[24]

> Faithful Christian people, such as be Christ's true disciples, continually from time to time record in their minds the beneficial death of our Saviour Christ, chewing it by faith in the cud of their spirit, and digesting it in their hearts, feeding and comforting themselves with that heavenly meat, although they daily receive not the sacrament thereof; and so they eat Christ's body spiritually, although not the sacrament thereof. But when such men for their more comfort and confirmation of eternal life, given unto them by Christ's death, come unto the Lord's holy table; then, as before they fed spiritually upon Christ, so now they feed corporally also upon the sacramental bread: by which sacramental feeding in Christ's promises, their former spiritual feeding is increased, and they grow and wax continually more strong in Christ, until at the last they shall come to the full measure and perfection in Christ.[25]

By relying on the transforming power of Scripture in the English affective tradition rather than an *ex opere operato* understanding of the sacraments, Cranmer used one aspect of medieval theology as the basis for rejecting another. Those who ruminated on the promises of God's Word written strengthened their supernatural union with God's Word Incarnate, whether through prayer and Bible reading or by receiving the sacraments. Cranmer institutionalized these two ways of feeding in his new English-language liturgies for the Church of England: spiritual feeding through morning and evening prayer as well as sacramental feeding through Holy Communion.

The *Book of Common Prayer* (1549 and 1552) condensed the seven daily monastic offices into just two for the parish. In keeping with the English affective tradition, the stated goal for these Word-based services was that "the people (by daily hearing of holy scripture read in the Church) should continually profit more and more in the knowledge of God, and be the more inflamed with the love of his true religion."[26] To that end, he devised a new lectionary for morning and evening prayer that read through most of the Bible in one year. The Psalter was read through monthly. As the first lesson, the remainder of the Old Testament was read over ten months, "except for books and chapters, which be least edifying." For the other two months readings came from the Apocrypha. As the second lesson, the New Testament was read three times a year, except for Revelation, which was used sparingly for certain proper feasts.[27] Hence, Cranmer could write that the "minister of the church speaketh unto us God's own words, which we must take as spoken from God's own mouth, because that from his mouth it came, and his word it is, and not the minister's."[28] By fitting his Word-based services around the average person's work day, Cranmer was consciously trying to restructure the rhythms of normal daily English life to follow the heartbeat of rumination spirituality. Instead of parishioners seeking to see their "Maker once a-day" by "gazing" at an elevated consecrated host, they could now spiritually feed on Christ by hearing his Word daily.[29]

Cranmer's liturgies for sacramental feeding must be seen as intensified means of feeding on Christ through believing in his promises. We have already seen Cranmer's deep concern for the renovation of human affections as integral to the Christian life. According to medieval anthropology, sense impressions deeply influenced the affections.[30] When sheep smell a wolf, they experience fear and flee. When sheep see grass, they experience desire and draw near. Much of medieval pastoral theology was directed at controlling the sense experiences of the faithful by substituting positive sensory influences for negative ones.[31] Hence, medieval liturgical practices called for the use of lights, bells, incense, images, painted interiors, holy water, blessed salt, prayer beads, processions, and dramas. As a Protestant theologian, Cranmer wanted the Word of God to inspire Christian affections, rather than traditional rituals. However, he saw in the sacramental elements commanded by Scripture a divinely appointed means to proclaim biblical truth with much greater impact on the human senses. If preaching the Word appealed only to the sense of hearing, baptism and Holy Communion used all five.

And although our carnal generation and our carnal nourishment be known to all men by daily experience, and by our common senses; yet this our spiritual generation and our spiritual nutrition be so obscure and hid unto us, that we cannot attain to the true and perfect knowledge and feeling of them, but only by faith, which must be grounded upon God's most holy word and sacraments. And for this consideration our Saviour Christ hath not only set forth these things most plainly in his holy word, that we may hear them with our ears, but he hath also ordained one visible sacrament of spiritual regeneration in water, and another visible sacrament of spiritual nourishment in bread and wine, to the intent, that as much as is possible for man, we may see Christ with our eyes, smell him at our nose, taste him with our mouths, grope him with our hands, and perceive him with all our senses. For as the word of God preached putteth Christ into our ears, so likewise these elements of water, bread, and wine, joined to God's word, do after a sacramental manner put Christ into our eyes, mouths, hands, and all our senses.[32]

In short, according to Cranmer, the sacraments were a more efficacious means for ruminating on Scripture than private Bible reading, not because they had greater spiritual power, but because God designed them to be more effective in proclaiming biblical truth to the human means of perception. For by having all of their senses encountering the Word of God, believers would grow not only in "knowledge" but also in "feeling" of the Holy Spirit's work in their lives. In the end, both their hearts and minds would be moved more thoroughly.

And what was the work of the Holy Spirit? An ever-increasing new life through union with Christ, "whole body and soul, manhood and Godhead, unto everlasting life."[33] Baptism began the process with spiritual rebirth. Yet, this inner renovation should not be confused with the scholastic understanding of an infusion of perfect saving personal righteousness. True to justification by faith, Cranmer's preferred language for baptism was a washing away of sin and being clothed with Christ.[34] For Christ's externally imputed righteousness hid the ongoing sinfulness of the believer's inherent concupiscence from God's sight so that a union could be established. However, because of the continuing presence of the "infirmity of the flesh," as Cranmer liked to call it, this "being grafted in the stock of Christ's own body" needed to be deepened daily by crucifying the old man and choosing to walk in loving new obedience to God.[35] Holy Communion assisted in this process by giving believers supernatural nourishment. By spiritually eating Christ's flesh and drinking his blood by faith, communicants grew toward "spiritual perfection in God."[36] Citing John 6:56, Cranmer like to described the communion between believers and Christ as mutual indwelling: "He that eateth my flesh, and drinketh my blood, *dwelleth in me and I in him*."[37]

This spiritual union with Christ did not happen automatically to all participants. In baptism, only the elect were regenerated, and their regeneration did not necessarily have to coincide with the administration of the sacrament. The sacrament was a sign of the justification and renovation that God would assuredly bring about in their lives.[38] In Communion, only true believers, that is, the elect who had now come to saving faith, would come into contact with Christ.[39] The wicked partook of only the sacramental elements. They did not feed on Christ himself.[40] For the sacraments did not make union with Christ possible, the earthly ministry of the Incarnate Word did that, and only faith inspired by the Holy Spirit through Scripture made its benefits available to humankind.[41] Therefore, the role of the sacraments was to proclaim most effectively the biblical narrative of what the Incarnate Word had done so that the Spirit would give believers a deeper personal faith in God's promised salvation:

> So that the washing in water of baptism is, as it were, shewing of Christ before our eyes, and a sensible touching, feeling, and groping of him, to the confirmation of the inward faith, which we have in him. . . . And for this cause Christ ordained this sacrament in bread and wine (which we eat and drink, and be chief nutriments of our body), to the intent that as surely as we see the bread and wine with our eyes, smell them with our noses, touch them with our hands, and taste them with our mouths, so assuredly ought we to believe that Christ is a spiritual life and sustenance of our souls, like as the said bread and wine is the food and sustenance of our bodies. . . . Thus our Saviour Christ . . . hath ordained sensible signs and tokens whereby to allure and to draw us to more strength and more constant faith in him.[42]

Yet it would be a grave misunderstanding to think that Cranmer conceived of a believer's connection to Christ as only a matter of a renewed will to believe and its fruit of love. He insisted that godly recipients in fact became fundamentally one with the divine:

> we be united together and with Christ, not only in will, but also in nature, and be made one, not only in consent of godly religion, but also that Christ, taking our corporal nature upon him, hath made us partakers of his godly nature, knitting us together with him unto his Father and to his Holy Spirit.[43]

As we have seen, Cranmer summarized this oneness in nature as mutual indwelling, but what did he actually mean? To answer this question, we will need to take a careful look at Cyril of Alexandria's Christology.

Cranmer and Cyril of Alexandria

First, Cyril had no wish to fall into Apollinarianism, the heresy that Christ had a divine mind in a human body. Nor would he accept the teaching of Nestorius, which was eventually condemned at the urging of Cyril for maintaining a strict separation between Christ's humanity and divinity when describing his activities, such as the man Jesus wept, but God the Logos raised Lazarus from the dead. Cyril's Christology insisted that Jesus Christ had two natures, one fully human, one fully divine, which came together as an inseparable union in the Incarnation to form a singular entity.[44] The two natures were distinct, not mingled: "the Word's nature has not transferred to the nature of the flesh or that of the flesh to that of the Word."[45] Second, Cyril taught the doctrine of *communicatio idiomatum* (communication of properties). While not violating the basic nature of either his divinity or humanity, the Incarnate Word's union of the Divine Logos with human flesh resulted in human flesh being not only restored, but enhanced. Having been joined to divine life, Christ's flesh now had the power to give life to the fallen flesh of other human beings. As the antidote to human corruption, Christ's flesh worked to heal "the infirmity of the flesh" in the bodies of Christians during this present age and, despite their physical decay, would bring them to immortality in the age to come. The bodies of Christians received these benefits through being united, in fact, being "commingled with," the true, life-giving flesh of Christ in the

Eucharist.[46] Finally, because the Incarnate Word could not be divided, as a single entity, when Jesus's humanity walked the earth, his divinity still filled the heavens. Likewise, as a single entity, when Jesus's humanity ascended to Heaven to be seated at the right hand of God, his divinity still filled the whole earth. Cranmer would appropriate all three points in his explanation of what he meant by the mutual indwelling of Christ and Christians.

At its most basic, he understood mutual indwelling as theological shorthand for deification, namely, that God became human so that humanity could become immortal like God. He interpreted Hilary's usage of the language accordingly:

> For although [Hilary] saith Christ is naturally in us, yet he saith also that we be naturally in him. And nevertheless, in so saying he meant not of the natural and corporal presence of the substance of Christ's body and of ours, (for as our bodies be not after that sort within his body, so is not his body after that sort within our bodies;) but he meant, that Christ in his incarnation received of us a mortal nature, and united the same unto his divinity, and so be we naturally in him.[47]

> And as [Christ] may be said to dwell in us by receiving of our mortal nature, so may we be said to dwell in him by receiving the nature of his immortality.[48]

> For as Christ being in his Father, and his Father in him, hath life of his Father, so he being in us, and we in him, giveth unto us the nature of his eternity, which he received of his Father; that is to say, immortality and life everlasting, which is the nature of his Godhead.[49]

Clearly, Cranmer rejected any suggestion that the concept involved Christ dwelling bodily in individual believers and them dwelling bodily in Christ. Mutual indwelling was a matter of the Spirit of Life coming upon humanity in the Incarnation and, through saving faith, the passing on of that Spirit of Life to believers so that they might be united to the Trinity. Here was the message the sacraments proclaimed.

However, since the faithful participated in the divine nature, Cranmer could also speak of Christ spiritually dwelling in individual believers, and not just in human nature in general through the Incarnation. He usually did so as a way of explaining Christ's presence in the sacraments.

> And although we do affirm (according to God's word), that Christ is in all persons that truly believe in him, in such sort, that with his flesh and blood he doth spiritually nourish and feed them, and giveth them everlasting life, and doth assure them thereof, as well by the promise of his word, as by the sacramental bread and wine in his holy supper, which he did institute for the same purpose; yet we do not a little vary from the heinous errors of the papists. For they teach, that Christ is in the bread and wine; but we say (according to the truth), that he is in them that worthily eat and drink the bread and wine.[50]

> And the sacraments of baptism and of his holy supper, (if we rightly use the same,) do most assuredly certify us, that we be partakers of his godly nature, having given unto us by him immortality and life everlasting; and so is Christ naturally in us. And so be we one with Christ, and Christ with us, not only in will and mind, but also in very natural properties.[51]

Cranmer found Cyril's *Commentary on John* a useful resource for understanding the nature of Christ's presence in the Christian life. He had recorded in his research notes for the *Defence* seventeen folios from Cyril's writings.[52] Four entries from the *Commentary on John* are especially illuminating for how Cranmer could think Cyril supported a spiritual presence of Christ in the faithful who received Holy Communion:

> He showed his own whole body to be filled with the quickening power of the Spirit. *For he called this very same flesh Spirit, not because it lost its nature as flesh and was changed into Spirit, but since it had been perfectly united to him, his flesh was now endued with his entire life-giving power.*[53]

> Christ quickens all things . . . *he himself, through the Holy Spirit, quickens our spirit, and frees our very body from corruption.*[54]

> *When Christ remains in us, he pacifies the law raging in our members, strengthening godliness and quenching our passions. He does not look at the sins in which we find ourselves, but heals us as sick.*[55]

According to these entries from Cyril, those who partook of the sacrament of Communion received spiritual power that fought concupiscence, transformed the affections, and brought the believer to ever-lasting life.

Yet, one significant aspect of Cyril's Eucharistic theology proved a challenge to Cranmer, for Cyril explicitly taught that Christ dwelled in Christians corporally as well as spiritually through receiving his life-giving flesh in the Eucharist. Indeed, Henry Chadwick has argued that Cyril developed his Christology specifically to defend his understanding of Christ's corporal presence in the sacrament.[56] Cranmer acknowledged the issue, rightly saying that Cyril never explicitly defined how Christ's flesh was present.[57] Arguing from Cyril's own principles, Cranmer provided his own answer, namely, that a "corporal" presence was the presence of the natural properties of Christ's body in those who received Communion. Because of its union with the Divine Logos, the most important property of Christ's body was its supernatural power to give everlasting life.

> But [Cyril] saith as well, that we dwell in him, as that he dwelleth in us. Which dwelling is neither corporal nor local, but an heavenly, spiritual, and supernatural dwelling, whereby so long as we dwell in him and he in us, we have by him everlasting life.[58]

> St. Cyril declareth the dignity of Christ's flesh being inseparably annexed unto divinity, saying, that it is of such force and power, that it giveth everlasting life.[59]

> And therefore Cyril saith in the same place, that Christ is the vine, and we the branches, because that by him we have life. For as the branches receive life and nourishment of the body of the vine, so receive we by him the natural property of his body, which is life and immortality, and by that means we, being his members, do live and are spiritually nourished.[60]

> So St. Cyril, when he said that Christ is in us "corporally," he meant that we have him in us, not lightly and to small effect and purpose, but that we have him in us substantially, pithily, and effectually, in such wise that we have by him redemption and everlasting life.[61]

And this I suck not out of mine own fingers, but have it of Cyril's own express words, where he saith: "A little benediction draweth the whole man to God, and filleth him with his grace, and after this manner Christ dwelleth in us and we in Christ."[62]

Therefore, as Cranmer noted when discussing Hilary's use of mutual indwelling: "the union between Christ and us in baptism is spiritual, and requireth no real and corporal presence; so likewise our union with Christ in his holy supper is spiritual, and therefore requireth no real and corporal presence."[63]

How could Cranmer be so sure that Cyril did not, in fact, really mean "corporally" as a bodily indwelling? Because by the reign of Edward VI Cranmer had concluded such a concept violated Cyril's teaching on the *communicatio idiomatum*. The Incarnation may have enhanced the properties of Christ's human flesh, but it had not changed its essential nature as a created thing that could not be in more than one place at a time. Cyril himself had written that the divine nature of the Incarnate Word was omnipresent, but his human nature was now absent from the earth. Cranmer quoted the passage in the *Defence*: "Christian people must believe, that although Christ be absent from us as concerning his body, yet by his power he governeth us and all things, and is present with all them that love him."[64] In Cyril's writings Cranmer had at last found the strong patristic argument he needed to embrace Reformed sacramental thought.

Yet, it would again be a mistake to infer from Cranmer's strong insistence that Christ dwelled in believers only spiritually, that he thought that a believer's union with Christ was only spiritual. In fact, he stressed the opposite:

> [In baptism] we receive not only the spirit of Christ, but also Christ himself, whole body and soul, manhood and Godhead, unto everlasting life, as well as in the holy communion.[65]

How did Cranmer think it was possible to have only a spiritual presence of Christ in the faithful, yet for it still to be right to teach that a believer was united to the whole Christ? Once again the answer lies in Cranmer's appropriation of Cyril's Christology. Since Cyril stressed that the two natures of the Incarnate Word were undivided, Cranmer argued that being united to Christ by his spiritual power at work within the faithful was to be united to the whole, undivided Christ in some mystical fashion:

> If the word were made very flesh, and we verily receive the word being flesh, in our Lord's meat, how shall not Christ be thought to dwell naturally in us? who being born man, hath taken unto him the nature of our flesh, that cannot be severed, and hath put together the nature of his flesh to the nature of his eternity under the sacrament of the communion of his flesh unto us. For so we be all one, because the Father is in Christ, and Christ in us.[66]

In Holy Communion the nature of Christ's eternity was inseparably joined to his flesh, so that to have the nature of his eternity dwelling within believers by faith was also to link them to Christ's human nature now present with God the Father in Heaven. Therefore, believers were fully united, body and soul, with the whole Christ, God and man, as Cranmer quoted Cyril to that effect:

> But as two waxes, that be molten and put together, they close so in one, that every part of the one is joined to every part of the other, even so," saith Cyril, "he that receiveth the flesh and blood of the Lord, must needs be so joined with Christ, that Christ must be in him, and he in Christ.[67]

During his disputation on the Eucharist at Oxford while under arrest by Mary (1554), Cranmer gave a description of how this mystical connection worked:

> lifting up our minds, we should look up to the blood of Christ with our faith, should touch him with our mind, and receive him with our inward man; and that, being like eagles in this life, we should fly up into heaven in our hearts, where that Lamb is resident at the right hand of his Father, which taketh away the sins of the world; by whose stripes we are made whole; by whose passion we are filled at his table, and whose blood we receiving out of his holy side, do live for ever; being made the guests of Christ, having him dwelling in us through the grace of his true nature,

and through the virtue and efficacy of his whole passion; being no less assured and certified that we are fed spiritually unto eternal life by Christ's flesh crucified, and by his blood shed, the true food of our minds, than that our bodies be fed with meat and drink in this life.[68]

In sum, on Holy Communion Cranmer was, to use Brian Gerrish's highly influential terminology for the various strains of Reformed sacramental thought, a symbolic parallelist.[69] Cranmer's focus was not a change in, or even instrumental use of, the bread and wine, but rather the transformation of the recipients, who by the power of the Spirit were linked afresh to the saving efficacy of Christ's Incarnation and Passion. As an expression of his solifidianism, Cranmer believed that as the faithful ruminated on the Gospel message of the Last Supper, at the same time they ate the unchanged bread and wine, the Holy Spirit went afresh straight into their hearts, fighting concupiscence in their flesh, deepening their faith, strengthening their love, giving them ever-increasing new life as a member of Christ's mystical body now, and leading them closer to immortal life with Christ and the other members of his eternal body forever.

Conclusion

Cranmer penned two progressively more Protestant versions of Holy Communion in his prayers books for the Church of England.[70] The 1549 *Book of Common Prayer* removed all references to personal merit and emphasized a Eucharistic sacrifice of praise and thanksgiving only. The 1552 prayer book, however, broke up the traditional order of the prayers in the Canon of the Mass so that the thanksgiving of the people was now their response to the grace received with the elements, not its grounds. In addition, the prayers themselves were revised to clarify that Christ's Eucharistic presence was spiritual in nature, a holy communion in the heart of the believer through personal faith. Cranmer's second service for Holy Communion was clearly reformed, but how reformed?

Recently, a 1549 *Book of Common Prayer* amended by the 1552 prayer book revision committee has been identified in the Bibliothèque nationale de France.[71] Significantly, the members initially twice deleted the phrase "to dwell in him and he in us" from the Communion service. In each case, the phrase was appositional to define the nature of the Eucharistic presence: (1) "and made one body with thy son Jesus Christ, that he may dwell in them, and they in him"; (2) "in these holy mysteries that we may continually dwell in him and he in us."[72] In the second instance, the text is also underlined, as if flagged as an issue that was then resolved by its deletion.

We know that the key dispute on the Lord's Supper among leading Reformed theologians in Edwardian England was whether reception was passive (i.e., memorialist) or active (conveying an increase in participation in Christ, resulting in more crucifixion of the old nature and more life-giving to the new nature). Jan Laski was the leading proponent of the former, Bucer of the latter. In fact, Bucer's favorite language for active reception was mutual indwelling, and his desire that these phrases be retained was duly noted in the margins. Cranmer held a position in between the two. Like Laski, but against Bucer, Cranmer insisted that Christ's human body remained exclusively in heaven. However, like Bucer, but against Laski, Cranmer believed that the sacraments increased the recipients' participation in Christ. Since Bucer's favorite language for active reception was mutual indwelling, the striking of all such references in the Eucharistic prayers suggests that Laski's position, at least initially, had the upper hand.[73] Despite his own use of the language, Cranmer may have agreed to the deletions so as to avoid anything suggestive of Bucer's commitment to both a spiritual and corporal presence in the sacrament.

So it would seem remarkable that an annotation made by a new hand restored the controversial mutual indwelling language in a new place, at the very end of the Prayer of Humble Access. This addition made its way into the 1552 prayer book at exactly this point.[74] Its new location greatly increased the importance of the phrase, for now "that we may evermore dwell in him and he in us" immediately preceded the prayer that recited the Institution Narrative, thus establishing supernatural growth in sanctification through faithful participation as its purpose. In the end, it would seem Cranmer deemed emphasizing the role of Holy Communion as an effectual means of ever-increasing new life in Christ outweighed avoiding any language possibly supportive of a corporal presence. As a result, the influence of St. Cyril's Christology and soteriology now lies at the very heart of the Anglican liturgical heritage, a legacy that Richard Hooker would incorporate in his own highly influential description of the sacrament almost fifty years later.[75]

NOTES

1. For a description of the process that led to Cranmer's adoption of solifidianism, see Ashley Null, *Thomas Cranmer's Doctrine of Repentance: Renewing the Power of Love* (Oxford: Oxford University Press, 2000), 98–115.
2. Charles Lloyd, ed., *Formularies of Faith Put Forth by Authority during the Reign of Henry VIII* (Oxford: Clarendon, 1825), xx.
3. Ibid., xxi–xxii.
4. Ibid., xx, xxiv.
5. *The Institution of a Christian Man* (London: Thomas Berthelet, 1537), fol. 37. Spelling has been modernized for all quotations from this source.
6. Ibid., 54.
7. J. E. Cox, ed., *Miscellaneous Writings of Thomas Cranmer* (Cambridge: Parker Society, 1846), 80. For the comments of the other bishops, see Diarmaid MacCulloch, *Thomas Cranmer: A Life* (New Haven, CT: Yale University Press, 1996), 189.
8. Cox, *Miscellaneous Writings of Thomas Cranmer*, 99. Cf. James 5:14–15, where James both commands the practices and specifically states that the "prayer of faith" will bring healing.
9. *Institution of a Christian Man*, 29r.
10. Cox, *Miscellaneous Writings of Thomas Cranmer*, 99–100.
11. Lloyd, *Formularies of Faith*, xxv–xxvi, 100–101.
12. Cox, *Miscellaneous Writings of Thomas Cranmer*, 344 (spelling modernized).
13. Ibid., 343. For further discussion, see MacCulloch, *Thomas Cranmer*, 179–81; Peter Newman Brooks, *Thomas Cranmer's Doctrine of the Eucharist*, 2nd ed. (London: Macmillan, 1992), 3–37.
14. For the influence of the medieval English mystical tradition and Erasmus's humanism on Cranmer's own affective theology, see Ashley Null, "Divine Allurement: Thomas Cranmer and Tudor Church Growth," in *Towards a Theology of Church Growth*, ed. David Goodhew (Aldershot: Ashgate, 2015), 197–215.
15. Cox, *Miscellaneous Writings of Thomas Cranmer*, 86.
16. Null, *Thomas Cranmer's Doctrine of Repentance*, 120–21.
17. "There is no place in scripture that declareth [confirmation] to be instituted of Christ. First, for the places alleged for the same be no institutions, but acts and deeds of the apostles. Second, these acts were done by a special gift given to the apostles for the confirmation of God's word at that time. Thirdly, the said special gift doth not now remain with the successors of the apostles." Cox, *Miscellaneous Writings of Thomas Cranmer*, 80. Cf. *Institution of a Christian Man*, 36r.
18. Null, *Thomas Cranmer's Doctrine of Repentance*, 153–55.
19. Cox, *Miscellaneous Writings of Thomas Cranmer*, 116–17.
20. Ibid., 116–17.

21. J. E. Cox, *Writings and Disputations of Thomas Cranmer Relative to the Lord's Supper* (Cambridge: Parker Society, 1844), 374.
22. Ronald B. Bond, ed., *Certain Sermons or Homilies (1547) and A Homily against Disobedience and Wilful Rebellion (1570): A Critical Edition* (Toronto: University of Toronto Press, 1987), 62–63 (spelling modernized).
23. Cox, *Miscellaneous Writings of Thomas Cranmer*, 133.
24. Thomas Cranmer, *A Defence of the True and Catholike Doctrine of the Sacrament of the Body and Blood of Our Saviour Christ* (London: Reyner Wolfe, 1550).
25. Cox, *Writings and Disputations*, 70–71.
26. Joseph Ketley, ed., *The Two Liturgies, A.D. 1549, and A.D. 1552* (Cambridge: Parker Society, 1844), 2, 193.
27. Ibid., 20–28, 200–212.
28. Cox, *Writings and Disputations*, 366.
29. Ibid., 229.
30. See Matthew Milner, *The Senses and the English Reformation* (Farnham: Ashgate, 2011), 13–51.
31. Ibid., 67–78.
32. Cox, *Writings and Disputations*, 41.
33. Ibid., 25.
34. Ibid., 17, 41, 71, 342, 366.
35. Ibid., 41; Null, *Thomas Cranmer's Doctrine of Repentance*, 180–84.
36. Cox, *Writings and Disputations*, 89.
37. Ibid., 24. Cf. 26–27.
38. See Null, *Thomas Cranmer's Doctrine of Repentance*, 225–29; Gordon Jeanes, *Signs of God's Promise: Thomas Cranmer's Sacramental Theology and the Book of Common Prayer* (London: T&T Clark, 2008), 175.
39. For Cranmer's understanding of the relationship between the elect and those justified by faith, see Null, *Thomas Cranmer's Doctrine of Repentance*, 128–29, 195–204.
40. Cox, *Writings and Disputations*, 68, 203–5.
41. "[T]his unity of faithful people unto God is by faith taught by the sacrament of baptism and of the Lord's table, but wrought by Christ by the sacrament and mystery of his incarnation and redemption, whereby he humbled himself unto the lowliness of our feeble nature, that he might exalt us to the dignity of his godly nature, and join us unto his Father in the nature of his eternity." Ibid., 164.
42. Ibid., 41–42.
43. Ibid., 169.
44. See John McGuckin, *Saint Cyril of Alexandria and the Christological Controversy* (Crestwood, NY: Saint Valdimir's Seminary Press, 2004), esp. 175–226; Hans van Loon, *The Dyophysite Christology of Cyril of Alexandria* (Leiden: Brill, 2009).
45. Norman Russell, *Cyril of Alexandria* (London: Routledge, 2000), 42.
46. Cyril of Alexandria, *Commentary on the Gospel according to S. John*, translated by P. E. Pusey (Oxford: James Parker, 1874), 1:376.

47. Cox, *Writings and Disputations*, 161.
48. Ibid., 165.
49. Ibid., 164.
50. Ibid., 52.
51. Ibid., 161.
52. See Ashley Null, "Bucer's Writings in Cranmer's Edwardian Eucharistic Papers," in *England and North-Eastern France: Religious Interactions from the Reformation to the Enlightenment*, ed. Anne Bandry and Jean-Jacques Chardin (Strasbourg: Presses universitaires de Strasbourg, forthcoming).
53. Bibliothèque nationale de France (BnF) Latin Manuscript 3396, "Loci communes ex Patribus de sacramento eucharistiae, nec non controversiae theologicae," fol. 71r. All quotations from this manuscript are English translations from the original Latin text. All emphasis is original.
54. Ibid., 65v–66r.
55. Ibid., 70r.
56. Henry Chadwick, "Eucharist and Christology in the Nestorian Controversy," *Journal of Theological Studies*, NS, 2 (1951): 145–64, esp. 153–56.
57. When challenged on the issue by Bishop Stephen Gardiner, his chief theological opponent, Cranmer retorted that the best Gardiner could do was point to where Cyril said man was united corporally to God "by the mystical benediction, but he telleth not the meaning thereof." Cox, *Writings and Disputations*, 170.
58. Ibid., 166.
59. Ibid., 213.
60. Ibid., 166.
61. Ibid.
62. Ibid., 166–67.
63. Ibid., 161.
64. Ibid., 96.
65. Ibid., 25.
66. Ibid., 160. Failing to appreciate that Cranmer grounded his Eucharistic teaching on Cyril of Alexandria's Christology, Cyril Richardson argued that Cranmer's insistence of Christ's body being confined to heaven (because of his very broad nominalism) conflicted with his realist language of believers' union with Christ both spiritual and corporally. See Cyril Richardson, "Cranmer and the Analysis of Eucharistic Doctrine," *Journal of Theological Studies*, NS, 16 (1965): 421–37; cf. Jeanes, *Signs of God's Promise*, 6–10; Brian Douglas, *A Companion to Anglican Eucharistic Theology: Volume One. The Reformation to the 19th Century* (Leiden: Brill, 2012), 87–90.
67. Cox, *Writings and Disputations*, 167.
68. Ibid., 398.
69. Brian Gerrish, "Sign and Reality: The Lord's Supper in the Reformed Confessions," in *The Old Protestantism and the New: Essays on the Reformation Heritage* (London: T&T Clark, 1982), 118–30.

70. Ketley, *Two Liturgies*, 76–99, 265–83.
71. BnF Rés. B-278. See Null, "Bucer's Writings."
72. BnF Rés. B-278, fols. 117r, 118r (spelling modernized).
73. For a more detailed discussion, see Null, "Bucer's Writings."
74. Ketley, *Two Liturgies*, 279.
75. Concerning the *communicatio idiomatum*: "Supernatural endowments are an advancement, they are no extinguishment of that nature whereto they are given"; hence, Christ's body is limited to only one place (Richard Hooker, *Ecclesiastical Laws* V.55.6, in *The Works of Richard Hooker*, 7th ed., ed. John Keble [Oxford: Clarendon, 1888], II, 241). "His human substance in itself is naturally absent from the earth, his soul and body not on earth but in heaven only. Yet because the substance is inseparably joined to that personal Word which by his very divine essence is present with all things, the nature which cannot have in itself universal presence has it *after a sort* by being *nowhere severed* from that which every where is present" (V.55.7, Keble edition, II, 243). Concerning new life in Christ: "That which quickeneth us is the Spirit of the second Adam, and his flesh that wherewith he quickeneth" (V.56.8, Keble edition, II, 251); "These things St. Cyril duly considering, reproveth their speeches which taught that only the deity of Christ is the vine whereupon we by faith do depend as branches. . . . For doth any man doubt but that even from the flesh of Christ our very bodies do receive that life which shall make them glorious at the later day" (V.56.9, Keble edition, II, 251); "So that Christ imparteth plainly himself by degrees" (V.56.10, Keble edition, II, 253); "Thus we participate Christ partly by imputation, as when those things which he did and suffered for us are imputed unto us for righteousness; partly by habitual and real infusion, as when grace is inwardly bestowed while we are on earth, and afterwards more fully both our souls and bodies made like unto his in glory" (V.56.11, Keble edition, II, 254). Concerning Christ's presence in Holy Communion: "The real presence of Christ's most blessed body and blood is not therefore to be sought for in the sacrament, but in the worthy receiver of the sacrament . . . only in the very heart and soul of him which receiveth" (*Laws*, V.67.6, Keble edition, II, 352).

13

The Catholic Reform

DONALD S. PRUDLO

The Counter-Reformation is a period in the history of the Roman Catholic Church that dealt with issues arising from the rise of Protestantism. Though Catholic reform predated the coming of Luther, nonetheless the challenge of the reformers led the Church to make serious and sustained changes. The focus of the Counter-Reformation was the Council of Trent (1545–63). This Council left few areas of Catholic life untouched. It issued far-reaching dogmatic decrees on the sacraments, the scriptures, justification, and Church government, in addition to passing very many ordinances on internal Church reform. So thoroughly did Trent do its work that the loss of Catholics in Europe was largely stanched, catechesis and priestly formation became more systematic, and doctrine was well clarified in opposition to Protestant ideas. Indeed, the whole period from Trent until at least the nineteenth century can really be called the Counter-Reformation in the Catholic Church.

Various things were associated with the Catholic Counter-Reformation. The first was the foundation of the Jesuit order, an elite group of intellectual priests that grew quickly and became commonplace both in the highest echelons of European society and on the front line of missionary territories. There was an explosion of Catholic education with the foundation of seminaries and schools. The vulgate Latin edition of the scriptures was updated to agree more fully with ancient texts, and the Catholic liturgy was simplified and systematized throughout the Catholic world. A proliferation of missionary efforts in Africa, Asia, Latin America, and Canada more than made up for numerical losses sustained in Northern Europe, and made Roman Catholicism a worldwide religion. The Church also continued its patronage of the arts, especially in relation to the Baroque style and to polyphonic music. While portrayed by many as a reactionary period in the Church's history, it was at the same time a healthy and innovative age for Roman Catholicism.

Introduction

The Council of Trent (1545–63) responded to the Protestant Reformation and brought together various corrective strands in Catholic history, thus giving powerful impetus to the period known as the "Catholic Reform."[1] Far more than a simple response to the challenges of the Protestant Reformation, Trent undertook a wholesale purification of the Roman Catholic Church, from top to bottom. It was a council equally occupied with reform and renewal on the one hand, and the definition of dogma on the other. At Trent's core was the reaffirmation of the practice of the faith as it had developed in the Christian Church over the previous fifteen hundred years, against what it considered to be the novelties of the rising tide of Reformers. Its activities extended to the refutation of Protestant claims, the adjustment and monitoring of Church devotions and liturgy, the moral and academic quality of church officeholders, and a wholesale recommitment to the sacramental, incarnational, and mystical Christianity that had so characterized the Middle Ages. In a certain sense, Trent was a narrowing of Catholicism, in that it pared away some of the accretions of centuries, censuring and prohibiting practices that it saw as inimical to reformed Catholicism, but it was also a purification and renewal that established the Church so strongly that it was able to retake massive areas that had been Protestantized, stabilize the Church for its massive worldwide expansion, and regulate Catholic life so smoothly that no ecumenical council was to be called for over three hundred years.[2]

Sacraments in Catholicism

At the heart of Catholic life is the practice of the sacraments; therefore it was a topic of major and systematic attention at the Council.[3] Church life had revolved around the celebration of the Christian mysteries since the time of the Apostles. The rich, varied, participatory liturgical and para-liturgical life of the Middle Ages extended into the period of the Reformation, and Trent was keen to preserve it, while trimming away some of the excesses and establishing closer curial oversight. In the end, the Catholic doctrine of the sacraments flowed from two related sources. The first was from the fundamental Christian doctrine of the Incarnation; God had become man, and in so doing, had sanctified matter itself, making it into a means of salvation. We are saved through the humanity of Christ. Christ instituted channels of grace that came to the believer through the medium of material things. Salvation came through water, through bread, through wine, through oil, even through the procreation of the species itself. Such was an extension of the Incarnational reality. Christ had redeemed human nature by his coming, but now individual human persons had to access and participate in that salvation, through the mediation of these instruments of salvation. They became affiliated to Christ by water, they participated in the life of Christ through the application of sacred oil, they became incorporated into Christ through the eating of his body and blood.

The second issue that drove the development of Catholic sacramental practice was the challenge of heresies throughout the centuries. From the earliest days, the Church—even discernable in the later books of the New Testament—struggled against spiritualizing Docetism and Gnosticism, spurning the Incarnation, and denying of the goodness of bodies and material things.[4] For this reason, the sacraments became the chief badges of the early Church, along with the veneration of saints and their relics—two of the most fundamentally Incarnational beliefs and practices of orthodox Christianity. The Church later struggled against the Manicheans and Donatists, puritans who demanded a sanitized church of the perfect. The Church defeated them too, holding tightly to the Incarnational center. Later in the Middle Ages another spiritualizing dualist group, the Albigensians, and proponents of a latter-day Donatism, the Waldensians, assailed the Church. Here too the Church held its ground. Now in the 1500s the Church was faced with a new threat, not dualism, nor even mere Donatism, but rather a wholesale, substantial, scriptural, and subtle critique of the whole edifice of medieval Catholicism: the Protestant Reformation.

As had happened many times in Catholic history, the Church reacted from the perspective of its experiences with the past. It detected in the Reformers a wholesale attack on the Catholic view of the economy of salvation. The Protestants had assailed the sacraments, throwing at least five of them out with no ceremony. (These were Sacramental Marriage, Holy Orders, Confirmation, Extreme Unction, and Confession; Luther's position on Confession is complicated, but the other great Reformers had no such compunction.) Of the two left—Baptism and the Eucharist—the Reformers changed them beyond recognition from traditional Catholic theology. Particularly the sacrament of the Eucharist, with its attendant doctrine of the sacrifice of the Mass—the beating heart of Catholic life—was a central concern of defenders of the faith; therefore, it became a centerpiece of the Council of Trent.[5] In light of the avowed traditionalism of Trent's approach to the sacraments, one is right to ask whether there was any innovation. While it is true that the Counter-Reform of this period was essentially defensive in posture, nonetheless the Fathers of Trent did ally themselves with certain trends in Catholic theology, which allowed them to innovate in continuity with tradition. They affirmed some aspects of debated Catholic theology, particularly relying on the Aristotelian-Thomist tradition, while downplaying others, such as late medieval nominalism. Further, the Council was also informed by a growing tendency to move from controversialism and polemics, toward the employment of texts from the Bible and the Fathers, marking a move from speculative to positive theology that would endure in the post-Tridentine Church.[6] Amid these broad tendencies, the Council began its work.

The Council of Trent

Trent began with the topic of justification, whose correct understanding was critical for the Catholic doctrine of the sacraments. The theories of justification propounded by the Reformers were inimical to a sacramental soteriology, therefore Trent had to work to clarify the Catholic idea of justification and salvation before it could make a comprehensive declaration regarding the sacraments themselves.[7] In terms of the sacraments, two aspects of the Council's decree on justification (promulgated in 1547) are essential. The Council was insistent that there was a real cooperation of the human will with grace. The human will make a graced assent to God, and in so doing, begins the process of justification. One should notice the word "process." Catholics had always seen justification as a process of "working out their salvation in fear and trembling," rather than an instantaneous imputation of righteousness.[8] This process, combined with the cooperation of the human will with grace (in genuine metaphysical freedom guaranteed only by the omnipotence of God), led to the second key issue: that humans received sanctifying grace that enabled them to grow in holiness.[9] The primary means for the conferral of this sanctifying grace was the seven sacraments of the Church.

After the doctrine of justification was more clearly defined, the Fathers could then proceed more readily to the sacraments. First, they had to draft a statement about the sacraments in general, before proceeding to each one individually. The Fathers speak of this document as the "completion" of what was begun in their decree on justification, clearly demonstrating the close tie between the two in Roman Catholic thought and in the work of the Council. These decrees regarding the sacraments were rooted in the living tradition and practice of the Church. As guardians of the deposit of faith, the Fathers felt it necessary to defend and explain the reasons why the Church had practiced as it did all those long centuries.[10] What they were defending was not simply papal or conciliar theology, but the lived, orthopractic reality of the Church of Christ practiced for over a millennium. For Catholics, this orthopraxis was symbiotically linked to orthodoxy. To attack the received practices of the Church was to lose the theological truth behind them. Both theology and practice had to be defended.[11] In truth, the defenders of Catholic practices were puzzled by the Reformers' claims of *sola scriptura*. For Catholics, the Church and its practices had preceded formal theology and, in a sense, preceded Scripture, since the biblical canon was not settled upon until the turn of the fifth century. That very canon had been discerned through the liturgy of the Church. For Catholics, the Church was rooted in oral preaching and practice, only later was some of that content written down and recognized as authoritative.[12] How could one then remove Scripture from its lived context in the liturgy of the Christian faith? The Council Fathers then embedded their declarations not simply in theological terms, but in this lived orthopraxis of the Christian Faith.

In their general declaration about the sacraments, the Council was insistent that all seven (Baptism, Eucharist, Confirmation, Marriage, Confession, Orders, and Extreme Unction) of them had been instituted by Christ himself.[13] While there was unanimity on Christ's institution of the sacraments, a debate arose regarding the manner of this establishment. The question was whether he established each formally, or only in substance, later to be developed by the Apostles. Because of this, the Council Fathers left undefined the exact manner of Christ's institution. As long as one admitted that the sacraments were substantially derived from Christ, one was within the bounds of Catholic orthodoxy. Many Fathers knew that they could not prove each sacrament explicitly from Scripture, so this reticence shows they were sensitive to the claims of the Reformers.[14] Nonetheless, because they had existed in the early Church, and immemorially, the Bishops defined their origin from him who was the source of all sacramental graces. In the same canon, the Fathers also again solemnly defined the number of sacraments to be seven.[15] The remainder of the general sacramental canons reaffirmed established Catholic belief, such as that not all were ministers of each sacrament, that the sacrament confers the grace that it signifies, and that a minister in mortal sin can validly perform a sacrament. All of these served to confirm already established Catholic belief and practice. Having done this, the Council moved on to each sacrament in particular.

Sacraments of Initiation

Immediately after the general conciliar declarations on the sacraments, the Fathers moved on to Baptism and Confirmation (1547), the two rituals focused on Christian initiation.[16] In order to situate the debate about these better, one must turn back to one of the first declarations of the Council, that on Original Sin (1546).[17] Further underlining the bishops' concern to answer the Reformers fairly, this decree began with a condemnation of Pelagianism. It then went on to confirm regular ecclesiastical practices then in use, most notably infant baptism (then accepted by Luther and Calvin, but just beginning to be challenged by groups such as the Anabaptists). The Council then took aim at Luther in the final canon, and asserted strongly that Baptism truly and actually remits sin so that the subject becomes a new creation in and of himself—a position arising from the Catholic doctrine of sanctification—and not by the imputation of the righteousness of another. Catholic theology recognized that while Baptism washed away the guilt of original sin, Concupiscence yet remained (understood by Catholics as a tendency to sin). It was not considered original sin itself, as some Reformers understood it. To put it another way, human nature, for the Tridentine Fathers, was not shattered by original sin, merely damaged, awaiting the sovereign remedy of the grace of Christ for its repristination.

The formal declarations on Baptism and Confirmation were more specific. First of all, the Fathers were insistent in defending the material necessity of water for baptism against spiritualizing tendencies. Further, the Council was eager to protect a doctrine that traced itself to the third century: that the baptisms performed by heretics with correct matter and form were valid. In light of the Reformation, this was a significant affirmation. First, Protestants and other Reformed Christians were true Christians by virtue of their reception of baptism. Their baptisms were valid and fruitful. This could form the basis for dialogue and common Christian cooperation, but only long after the tensions of the Age of Reform had died down. Second, it ensured that Protestants were affiliated with the Church, for in Catholic Canon Law all who were baptized were subsequently subject to Church Law, unless they separated themselves from it and formally professed heresy. In this, the Council safeguarded the possibility for salvation for millions outside the visible confines of the Roman Catholic Church. The Council went still further in one of the most significant developments in Baptismal theology. Tucked away in chapter 4 of the decree on justification is a paragraph that describes how one can be saved.

> The Justification of the impious is indicated as being a translation from that state in which man is born a child of the first Adam, to the state of grace, and of the adoption of the sons of God, through the second Adam, Jesus Christ, our Saviour. This translation, since the promulgation of the Gospel, cannot be effected except through the laver of regeneration, *or the desire thereof*, as it is written; unless a man be born again of water and the Holy Ghost, he cannot enter into the Kingdom of God.[18]

The Baptism of desire (*Baptisma Flaminis*) opened the door for the possibility of salvation without formal water baptism (*Baptisma Fluminis*). Though such a Baptism of desire was a common teaching as far back as Saint Ambrose, this was the first time that a Council had formally and dogmatically recognized its existence. Deftly the Council again broadened the possibility for salvation, outside the visible bonds of—but still in relationship to—the Roman Catholic Church. This position had further implications. Trent also refused to condemn a speculative position taken by the creative Thomas de Vio, Cardinal Cajetan (1469–1534; one of the most original thinkers of the Catholic Reform). He had proposed that babies who died before birth could be considered baptized in virtue of the desire of their parents to perform the sacrament when they were born.[19] Such a solution was proposed because of the intractable problem of the final destination of unbaptized infants. That Trent permitted such speculations to continue would lead to one of the most productive areas of post-Tridentine theological speculation.

As for Confirmation, not much theological development occurred at Trent, nor for a long time after it. Indeed some have alleged that Confirmation is "a sacrament in search of a theology." Trent spent only three canons on this topic. What the Council was interested in defending was the religious reality and dignity of the ceremony, to be numbered among the seven extraordinary means of grace. The Council was also keen to assert its reservation to the bishop as the ordinary minister, but this was merely a shot in the Roman Church's desultory confrontation with Eastern Christianity, which contended that the ordinary minister was a simple priest. Lack of solid theological underpinnings hampered the Counter-Reformation's efforts to answer Protestant objections, but eventually Confirmation became tied to the increasing deployment of solid catechesis in Catholic countries, leading to later considerations of Confirmation as the fulfillment or completion of the baptismal rite.[20]

The Eucharist and the Mass

Of far more concern for the Council Fathers was the comprehensive defense of the Catholic position on the Eucharist and the Holy Sacrifice of the Mass. From the very beginning, the Reformers, for a variety of reasons, had particularly targeted their wrath at this central Catholic ritual. Attacks had been leveled at the propitiatory character of the Mass, Mass offerings, elaborate unbiblical liturgy, the scholastic language describing the Eucharist, and even Christ's substantial and real presence. Though Reformers agreed on most of these, the last began to produce permanent schisms among them. From Luther's consubstantiation to

Calvin's "spiritual presence" and Zwingli's utter symbolism, the Sacrament of Unity came to be one of the gravest causes of dissension among Christians of the sixteenth century. In spite of that, the Eucharist and Eucharistic devotion were at the epicenter of Catholic life. The Fathers of Trent knew that this would be the most substantial case that they had to make. Due to their efforts, they laid the foundation for the entirety of the post-Tridentine Church.

In one of the longest decrees of the whole of the Council (1551), the Fathers took up the problem.[21] In the first place, they were crystal clear that Transubstantiation, as defined at the Fourth Lateran Council of 1215, was absolutely nonnegotiable. The body, blood, soul, and divinity of Jesus Christ were "contained truly, really, and substantially" in the Holy Eucharist. The bread and wine were wholly changed in their substance into Christ. Only the accidents (the outward appearances) remained those of material food. On this the Council Fathers were relying on the unanimous testimony of Church Tradition (confirmed by similar beliefs among the Eastern Orthodox), not to mention a highly literal rendering of the Scriptures, particularly John 6 and the institution narratives of the Synoptics (Matt. 26:20–29; Luke 22:14–20; Mark 14:17–25) and St. Paul (1 Cor. 11:23–25). Following that, the Council condemned Luther's doctrine of consubstantiation and Calvin's doctrine of "spiritual eating." Whether or not the Council managed correctly to relay Calvin's subtle position is a matter for debate. Trent is also careful to confirm existing experiences of lived, devotional Catholicism, where devotion to the Most Holy Eucharist ran very deep. The reservation and exposition of the sacrament for worship were affirmed. Building upon their explanation of sanctification in previous documents, the Council Fathers were clear that the reception of the Eucharist—of him who is Holiness itself—was the primary means of attaining holiness in this world. These decrees found widespread approval among the Fathers, expressing as they did an immemorial understanding of the Sacrament of the Altar. While these were confirmed with near unanimity, more difficult issues existed to contend with, namely the reception of the Eucharist and the character of the Mass. So complex were these topics that no decree was issued on them until eleven years later, near the close of the Council in 1562.[22]

The reason that the manner of reception of the Eucharist occasioned so much debate was because the question had been in the air for a long time. During the Late Middle Ages, both Jan Hus (1369–1415) and John Wycliffe (1320–84) had condemned the denial of the chalice to the laity. Since the Early Middle Ages, it had been standard liturgical practice that the laity, when they communicated, would do so under the form of bread alone. This was for several reasons, the most salient being the danger of spilling the Precious Blood coupled with a developed theology known as "concomitance" or that Christ was not separated in the bread and wine.[23] The whole Christ—body, blood, soul, and divinity—was present in each of the elements. To receive one was to receive the whole Christ. The laity seemed to have accepted this change with little fuss, but later theologians such as Wycliffe and Hus saw it as a clerical hegemony over the fullness of the central sacrament of Christianity. Because of serious disturbances provoked by their followers, there had been some talk of conceding the cup to the laity in the fifteenth century, and in a few cases, it was. The concession of the chalice was one of Luther's earliest demands. This had two effects: (1) to make him suspect of Hussitism and (2) to call attention to a matter of Church discipline rather than dogma. Because many in the Catholic Church considered that this might be legitimately extended to some Protestant countries (along with a dispensation from clerical celibacy, another discipline rather than a dogma), the Council wanted to take its time. The decision for communion under both kinds was reserved to the papacy: if the Pope saw that the salvation of souls would be advanced by such the concession of the chalice to the laity, he was free to give it. By the 1560s, though, most areas were far too committed to Protestantism for the mere concession of the chalice to effect much change. The Council contented itself with defining the reality of concomitance, and with declaring that the reception of communion under both kinds was in no way necessary to salvation.

Far more problematic was a reaffirmation and explanation of the Catholic doctrine on the Mass. This was similarly addressed in 1562 near the conclusion of the Council. Directly responding to Luther's criticisms, the Fathers maintained that the Mass was a real sacrifice, identical to the sacrifice of Christ on the Cross. This was the critical idea: that the Sacrifice of the Mass was a bloodless re-presentation of the bloody sacrifice of Calvary. The hyphen is important, for the Mass is no symbolic *representation*; it is the same identical sacrifice. Catholics did not kill Christ over and over, as some alleged, but rather, across time and space, the crucifixion was made present with all of its fruits to overflow on the Christian people. Not only was the Mass the same sacrifice of the same victim, but it also had the same priest, for the Catholic priest at Mass acted *in persona Christi*, in the person of Christ Himself. Mass did not detract from the crucifixion of Christ because it was *identical* with it.[24] A number of things followed from this determination. Because it was really a sacrifice, it was really propitiatory, and its fruits and merits could be applied to the living and the dead. Similarly, when the Church celebrated the masses of the saints, it was sacrificing not to them, but in honor of them. In this schema, the dignity of the Mass is great, indeed the highest activity in which man can participate. In light of that, it is proper to offer the best of art, music, and human effort in its celebration and elaboration. Trent made a ringing endorsement of liturgical Christianity here and gave birth to the aptly named "Counter Reformation of the Senses."[25] At the same time the Council cautioned that abuses were to be curbed, and that Mass should be celebrated with all due reverence. As a result of Trent, there was a thoroughgoing reform of the Latin rite, streamlining and standardizing the Roman liturgy, a reform that was done so thoroughly that no further substantive reforms were proposed for over four hundred years; indeed what became known as the Tridentine Rite survives today in the Catholic Church as the Extraordinary Form of the Roman Rite.[26]

The Sacrament of Confession

Another sacrament that received significant attention at Trent was that of Penance, or Confession (1551).[27] Pursuant to Catholic doctrine on justification as a process, Confession was advocated as one of the singular occasions for that ongoing transition. By it, one who was spiritually dead by mortal sin could again be restored to the life of grace and holiness, or those who had committed only minor (venial) sins could be sped along the road to sanctification. Confession came to be seen by the Counter-Reformation Church as an occasion for personal enrichment, self-knowledge, and spiritual guidance. It was a time at which the sinner could personally experience the forgiveness of God, and through the ministry of the Church, improve his life so as to become a saint. The Bishops rooted their defense of the sacrament in John 20:22–23: "Receive the Holy Spirit, Whose sins you shall forgive, they are forgiven them."

Their understanding of the sacrament was predicated on the Western understanding of passages such as Matthew 3:2 and Acts 2:38, where Jerome had translated "Poenitentiam agite" for Μετανοεῖτε, a defensible translation certainly, and one hallowed by tradition, but which certainly laid emphasis on the doing of works. The Council Fathers reinforced this understanding in their decrees.

They articulated the classical scholastic distinction of this sacrament into three essential parts: contrition, private confession to a priest, and sacramental absolution. The penitent, first of all, had to have sincere contrition for his sins. For a long time the scholastics had debated among themselves about the nature of such contrition. Some more rigorous theologians, like Thomas Aquinas, demanded *Perfect Contrition*.[28] This was a horror and detestation of the sin itself, because it had offended God. If made perfect through grace and charity, this type of contrition forgave sins and reconciled one with God, even without sacramental Confession (though the bishops were careful to note that such perfect contrition necessarily implied desire for Confession). On the other hand, many theologians knew that some did not approach Confession with this perfected contrition, but rather because they feared the pains of hell. This was called imperfect contrition or, sometimes, *attrition*. The Fathers of Trent sided with those who advocated this attrition. Imperfect contrition was sufficient to approach the sacrament, and become perfected by the infusion of the grace of absolution. By avoiding the more rigorous path, the bishops' declaration was a sincere desire for mercy and increased reception of the sacrament. Attrition then was to be a beginning, with the hope that it might become perfected through grace.[29] Note that the bishops, throughout the entirety of the Council, were absolutely insistent in their agreement with the Protestants: all justification comes about through grace. Without grace, we cannot become justified or become holy. Unlike the Reformers' contention though, we must prepare ourselves to receive that grace, and through that grace we can become new creations, holy not because of an Alien Righteousness, but our own, genuine righteousness made possible only through the sacrifice of Christ. In any case, it was through the absolution of the Church whereby imperfect contrition could be raised to perfect contrition, and sins could be really forgiven, by a face-to-face encounter of the penitent with Christ himself, acting in the person of his priest.

Trent also innovated in the practice of the sacrament of Penance. Since 1215 it had been an obligation to confess one's sins at least once a year. Trent specified that it was all mortal sins that had to be confessed by divine law, whereas there were numerous ways to expiate venial sins. That said, the Council highly recommended the confession of venial sins, for it discerned that the sacrament was not simply to be a sort of last resort or spiritual defibrillator, but rather the regular practice of Confession could be used to guide souls to better self-knowledge and greater perfection. In that sense, Confession became something of a "key sacrament" of Catholic Reform, and of the Catholic doctrines about perfectibility and progress in justification.[30] To that end, the Council mandated as one of its reforming decrees that confessors receive much better training, so that they could dispense useful spiritual and practical advice to sinners. This became a touchstone for a thoroughly reformed and much better educated clergy, which was a hallmark of the Tridentine age.

Something of a footnote to the sacrament of Confession, the decrees on Extreme Unction (or the Anointing of the Sick) were appended to those on Penance. Forming the core of the "Last Rites" of Catholics, it accompanied the dying along with Viaticum (or the last Eucharist) and Confession. The Fathers contented themselves with reaffirming the sacramentality of the anointing, citing the usual proof text of James 5:14–15. For them the sacrament is a genuine occasion of grace and the forgiveness of sins, and can bring real comfort and genuine healing to the sick. There was also an oblique condemnation of nascent Presbyterianism, as the Fathers defined that James truly meant "priests" when he says πρεσβυτέρους, and not merely "elders." In the end, Trent merely confirmed existing Catholic doctrine, and did not innovate with regard to this sacrament.

Sacraments of Vocation

More intractable were issues dealing with the sacraments related to states in life: Marriage and Holy Orders. These were deferred until the very end of the Council in 1563.[31] Orders was closely bound up with the Catholic hierarchical conception of the Church, not to mention the previous emphasis on the Eucharist as sacrifice and the necessity for Orders to confer absolution. The decree followed the outlines of the previous discussions. For the Fathers of Trent the Catholic priesthood was the priesthood of the new covenant, whose power and authority descended from Christ himself. It was a genuine sacrament, as established by 2 Timothy 1:6, and granted the recipient a spiritual character that was indelible (like Baptism and Confirmation). Orders gave a man power to act *in persona Christi* and to administer the sacraments, not indeed through his own power, but by the power of Christ acting through him. Orders was then bound up, in the Catholic mind, with the power to administer the sacraments and rule the Church of God, and not simply to preach the word. In reinforcing this traditional Catholic vision, the Council left several questions unresolved. The first was the sacramentality of Episcopal consecration. Was the ordination of deacons, priests, and bishops essentially distinct, or were they all one singular sacrament received in different degrees? This question would remain open until the Second Vatican Council. The sacramentality of the minor orders, specifically the subdiaconate, was also left untouched in favor of the common theological opinion that they were not. Another difficult issue, contemporary with the Council, was the question about the validity of Anglican orders. While it was common opinion that the changes in the ordinal under Archbishop Parker (r. 1559–74) rendered the rite invalid, no definitive decision was rendered until Pope Leo XIII declared Anglican orders null in 1896.[32] Such a decision was in line with Trent's affirmation of the sacrificial nature of the Catholic priesthood, and its opposition to a more Protestant idea of orders as simply a non-sacramental office of preaching and leadership.[33]

The status of marriage as a sacrament had also been hotly contested during the Reformation; indeed one branch of the Church had wholly broken with Rome over issues surrounding it: the Church of England. Because of the legal intricacies and theological speculations surrounding marriage, the Bishops made it the last of the sacraments that they addressed in the Council. Once again, the status of marriage as a genuine, grace-conferring sacrament of the New Law was affirmed. Christian marriage was also seen not as detracting from natural marriage, but rather as bringing it to its perfection. Once again the Church reaffirmed its ancient teaching: there was no power on earth that could dissolve a ratified and consummated marriage, alluding to Matthew 19:6. Divorce was not to be tolerated among Catholics.[34] The Council knew it also had to address abuses, and marriage was no exception. In the Middle Ages a dispute had arisen as to what made a sacramental marriage, the exchange of vows or sexual consummation. Eventually there was something of a consensus that the vows made a real marriage, called a "ratified" marriage, but it was consummation that made the marriage indissoluble. Because of this, the view developed that the ministers of the sacrament were the couples themselves. This resulted in huge numbers of "secret marriages" or two people who made private vows and then had intercourse, causing no end of legal difficulties. This led to the famous decree, known by its Latin name *Tametsi*. While the Church defended the validity of previous clandestine marriages, by this decree it declared them invalid in the future, continuing the example of the Church's supervisory role over marriage exercised since the early years of Christianity. After *Tametsi*, marriages had to be contracted in the presence of the parish priest, or at the bare minimum in front of two or three witnesses. As we will see later, this decree would prove problematic when the Church confronted the issue of Protestant or mixed Protestant and Catholic marriages in the future.

The Council of Trent formally closed in 1563. While it defined more dogma solemnly than all other Councils put together, on balance Trent was a body dedicated to preserving and reaffirming the immemorial practices and beliefs of the Catholic faith. It is true that the Council reached some significant decisions about Catholic doctrine, for instance with the wholesale affirmation of a Thomistic-leaning scholastic understanding of theology. It also was revolutionary in its reform decrees, producing a purified Counter-Reformation that echoes in the Catholic Church to this day. As far as the sacraments themselves are concerned the Council offered only slight innovations. What it did do was to pave the way for a comprehensive review of, and purified recommitment to, the central rituals of Catholic life. In its calls for catechesis and the reformation of clergy, it established the necessary preconditions for not only answering the Protestant movements, but also launching a counteroffensive, and undertaking missionary endeavors that would take the Church to the four corners of the earth.

Putting Trent into Practice

The results of the Council were not long in coming. The breach with Protestantism was too great to be overcome, so the Church focused on internal reform and missionary enterprises. The first mighty effort was the consolidation of the Roman liturgy, which was the normative liturgy for the Latin rite. Most Western liturgies and rituals had spread from Rome during the early Church, and had experienced substantial standardization in the wake of the Carolingian reforms during the 800s.[35] After that the organic development of the liturgy allowed differing practices in the celebration of the Mass and sacraments in various places and among various groups. This led to "usages" (not really separate rites), such as the usage of Braga in Portugal, or that of Sarum in England. In addition various religious orders had established common usages for themselves, such as the Cistercian, Norbertine, and Dominican rites. It was Pope Pius V (r. 1565–72) who began the mighty task of reconciling and purifying the various rituals of Christendom. While he allowed varying usages that had continuous history of over two hundred years to endure, everyone else had to conform to the purified practices of his liturgical commission. In some cases Pius was heavy-handed, eliminating many medieval accretions that had organically developed in the liturgy (such as troped Kyries and a multiplication of sequences), but ultimately he produced a missal that was elevated, refined, and purified. So well did this revision work that it remained intact until the liturgical reforms of Vatican II, and continues to be used in the Catholic Church today.[36] This liturgical reform had one serious effect on the sacramental life of the Church. Increasingly the Mass came to dominate as the public ritual of the Catholic faith, while the other sacraments tended to become privatized in both ritual and practice.

This led to two distinct trajectories in post-Tridentine Catholicism. The first was the architectural and musical elaboration called the Baroque movement. At its heart was the design of churches and the embellishment of the Catholic Mass. The liturgical contributions of such artists as Palestrina, Byrd, and Victoria not only set the stage for the ornamentation of the Mass, but indeed laid the groundwork for all further developments in music.[37] Similarly the ebullient and exuberant Baroque style of churches was a "sermon in stone" against the puritanizing tendencies of Protestantism.[38] Both of these were virile affirmations of the Incarnational and sacramental vision of the Council of Trent. The Church was a visible society that found its height in the celebration of the Mass—the Sacrifice of Calvary re-presented, with the elements transubstantiated into the real body and blood of Jesus. Such was the vision of the Tridentine reform, and it has delineated Catholicism nearly to the present day.

Bolstered by these musical and architectural settings, the Mass remained the epicenter of Catholic life, and the Tridentine reforms provided impetus for the deepening of this perennial Catholic devotion to the Eucharist. The Jesuit order, as part of its mission, emphasized the Holy Eucharist as the heart of Catholic life. To that end its members developed special ceremonies marking First Communion, setting it apart as a singular moment in the lives of the faithful.[39] Even today, First Communion is a significant celebration in Roman Catholicism. Further, they were also in the vanguard of orchestrating an outpouring of devotion to the Holy Eucharist in extra-liturgical settings. These included the exposition of the Blessed Sacrament, whereby the consecrated host was placed in a monstrance (usually, but not always, a sunburst executed in precious metals), for the silent and paraliturgical devotion of the faithful. This eventually morphed into Perpetual Adoration (whereby the host was made continually visible to the faithful) and practices such as the "Forty Hours Devotion" were developed, usually in the context of a parish mission).[40] They also were instrumental in the extension of the celebration of the feast of Corpus Christi. The post-Tridentine Church seized on this feast, already popular in the Middle Ages, along with its innumerable civic ceremonies and magnificent processions, not only to arouse the devotion of the faithful, but because it was a public rejection of Protestant doctrine about the sacrament. Public Catholicism was polemical as well as devotional.[41]

On the other hand one could trace the increasing privatization of the sacraments. Baptism had ceased to be the irrepressible celebration of the Middle Ages when, on Holy Saturday, the infants of a town would be marshaled and sent in, assembly-line style, to the baptistery for immersion by the bishop. Now it became a ceremony conducted privately, usually within days (sometimes hours) of a child's birth. This was due to the increasing clarity with which the doctrine of original sin had been outlined by the Council of Trent. This privatization however was most apparent in the sacrament of Confession. With the emphasis on training of priests and catechesis of the laity, Confession came to be seen as a privileged nexus not only for forgiveness of sins, but for the search for perfection in the context of spiritual direction. One notable development in its ongoing privatization was the evolution of purpose-built confessionals, where the priest sat on one side, separated from the kneeling penitent by a screen. This not only protected the privacy of the penitent, but curtailed abuses by means of enforcing separation between him or her and the priest.[42] This was an innovation of the great reformer, St. Charles Borromeo, Archbishop of Milan (r. 1564–84). He was a model of the Tridentine reform, and his Ambrosian diocese set the pattern for the Catholic world.[43]

Trends in Sacramental Thought

One truly astonishing development had taken place in the context of the Tridentine decrees, led by another reforming bishop in the mold of Borromeo. In the face of the purification and elevation of the clergy, and the emphasis on ongoing sanctification, a Swiss bishop named Francis de Sales (1567–1622) made a revolutionary breakthrough. His work *Introduction to the Devout Life* suggested that holiness was attainable for anyone, in any state in life, through prayer, discipline, and conformity to God's will.[44] In previous generations, going back to the earliest days of the Church, holiness was viewed as something of a specialty, a particular gift of God saved for a few chosen souls. De Sales's position would become exceptionally popular, and eventually lead to the declaration of the doctrine called the Universal Call to Holiness at the Second Vatican Council. At the heart of de Sales's program was the practice of Confession and spiritual direction. In this case the sacrament of Confession would not be merely, as Tertullian called it, a "second plank."[45] It rather became the springboard to self-knowledge and mastery, undergirding the practice of the virtues, and preparatory to a life of sainthood.

In the optimistic vision of St. Francis de Sales one can detect hints of Trent's affirmation of sanctification and free will, with further evocations of the Renaissance humanists. Not all Catholics embraced this sort of optimism. The confrontation with Protestantism had not left the internal theology of the Church unaffected. As we saw above, the first condemnations the Council of Trent issued were of Pelagianism, Luther's bugbear. The Council had also defined the absolute necessity of grace for salvation, and the unmerited nature of the first grace. In the seventeenth century many were meditating on the teachings of Augustine, and of his brilliant but rigoristic interpreter John Calvin. Two friends, Cornelius Jansen and Jean du Vergier (better known as Saint-Cyran, after the abbey that provided his income), corresponded for years, coming ever more deeply to the conclusion that St. Augustine was entirely in favor of a type of limited atonement and irresistible grace. Jansen, by the 1630s a bishop in the Netherlands, had written a massive work defending his theses called *Augustinus*.[46] It was not published until after his death, but proved to be the founding theological document of a movement known after his name as Jansenism.

The partisans of Jansenism professed to be practicing an austere, rigorous, and purified Christianity. Indeed, in light of the easygoing Gallicanism of many of the French bishops and their hesitancy to implement the reforms of Trent, this was a believable stance. Theirs was a sort of Catholic Calvinism (ironically articulated at the same time that Arminius was beginning his declension from orthodox Calvinism), though recent scholarship has demonstrated that it was far from a monolithic movement.[47] For our present purposes, this rigoristic Augustinianism had a marked effect on the sacramental practices of the group. In particular, the Jansenists were horrified at the ease with which people were absolved and approached communion. Given their rigorous theology of the elect, they excoriated the vanguard of the Tridentine Church—the Jesuit order—for what they saw as excessive laxity in the administration of the sacraments. They also deplored the pious devotionalism that continued to exist among the Catholic laity, and they would be the major opponents of the developing cult of the Sacred Heart of Jesus. In 1643 their intellectual leader, Antoine Arnauld, wrote a provocative work on frequent communion, which was rapidly being developed as a spiritual complement to frequent Confession for the cultivation of holiness. Under the guise of devotion to the Eucharist, he reversed the contemporary trend of viewing communion as a means of grace, and focused on it as a terminal reward for exceptional virtue, achieved only after much penance. For him, refusing to communicate was a sign of personal humility and holiness. In addition, the Jansenists had reworked the practice of Confession as well. Unlike the rather easygoing Jesuits, their confessors imposed rigorous penances, and sometimes withheld absolution until they were completed. Because the Jansenists were seen as the spiritually superior group in France (as opposed to the "lax" Gallican bishops and the Jesuits) many devout Catholics began to hew ever closer to their way of thinking. Even after Jansenism's theological condemnation by the Church, its effects on church practices were chilling. In some French parishes no one communicated at all, with one Jansenist pastor bragging that because of that, he guaranteed there were no sacrilegious communions.[48] Of course there was opposition to them from the Jesuits, from Rome, from the Gallicanist hierarchy, but most of all from Catholic saints including Vincent de Paul (1581–1660) and Alphonsus Ligouri (1696–1787). Slowly the Church worked to exorcise this specter of rigorism, but it was not until the pontificate of St. Pius X (r. 1903–14) that the time for First Communion was lowered to the age of reason (around seven years old) and frequent communion was recommended to the faithful. It is likely that, without the Jansenists, it would have happened centuries sooner, following the pastoral tenor of the Council of Trent.

In terms of the doctrine of the sacraments, Trent had righted the foundering ship, and had fixed the teachings about them in perpetuity for Catholics. Little development occurred in formal theology about them. One could say that the post-Tridentine Church was heavily involved in debates *around* the sacraments, rather than about them. For instance there was a long debate on the sacrificial nature of the Last Supper, which itself was the continuation of a bitter dispute at the Council itself.[49] Further problems appeared after the conclusion of military hostilities between the Catholics and Protestants after the Thirty Years' War (1618–48): how was the Catholic Church to approach the validity of the Protestant sacraments? Trent was able to provide some easy answers. Their Baptisms were valid, but their Eucharists were not (since they had either broken Apostolic Succession or denied the sacrificial character of the Mass). Given the former, canon law recognized them as subjects of the Church and bound by her law. Of course the Catholic Church could not enforce these claims, and it was unclear what happened in case of a legal conflict. This most frequently happened in the celebration of marriage. If Protestants were validly baptized, and thus subject to the Church's law on marriage, then were their marriages, contracted without a church witness (as required by *Tametsi*), valid? Further, what of mixed marriages between Protestants and Catholics; how were these to be understood from the point of view of Church law? Such questions hung in the air for generations, with Catholic bishops in Protestant areas being generally lenient, and with Rome mostly choosing to look the other way. The brilliant Pope Benedict XIV (r. 1740–58) was the one who came up with a solution.[50] Benedict prevailed over the theologians who demanded that the presence of the priest was necessary for sacramental marriage, and affirmed the classic Catholic doctrine that the man and woman were themselves the ministers of this sacrament. This meant that Protestant marriages were sacramental, because both the man and the woman had valid baptisms and were capable of ministering the sacrament to one another. Further, Benedict permitted mixed marriages with two conditions: (1) the children had to be raised Catholic and (2) no ecclesiastical solemnity was to be celebrated. All in all it was an equitable solution to an intractable problem.

Conclusion

In terms of sacramental practice, the reforms of Trent solidified their theologies and rituals, and very little changed during the period of the Counter-Reformation. The real achievement of Trent was to distill and solidify fifteen hundred years of Catholic teaching and practice on the sacraments, to establish strongly Catholic doctrine on the matter, and to entrust successfully the reform of the Church's liturgical life to competent men. This allowed the stabilization (though some would say the ossification) of the Catholic sacraments. Because of this, and because of Trent's emphasis on sanctification and Incarnational Christianity, the arts flourished, the devotional life of Catholics was enriched immeasurably over the subsequent centuries, and the Roman Church not only was able to stabilize itself, but was equipped to launch missionary journeys that made it the first worldwide organization in history. Its evangelists carried with them the Tridentine dogmas and practices, standardized and exported to the four corners of the earth, establishing a Church that was genuinely catholic—universal.

NOTES

1. This period in Church history has variously been called the Counter-Reformation, the Catholic Reformation, the Catholic Restoration, and many

others. Each name betokens certain characteristics of the Catholic response to the Protestant Reformation, but each term also lacks certain nuances, particularly concerning the reform efforts under way long before the religious split. This controversy opens most every contemporary book on early modern Catholicism. For a good summary, see John W. O'Malley, *Trent and All That: Renaming Catholicism in the Early Modern Era* (Cambridge, MA: Harvard University Press, 2000). Other studies include Robert Bireley SJ, *The Refashioning of Catholicism: 1450–1700* (Washington, DC: Catholic University of America Press, 1999), 1–24; R. Po-Chia Hsia, *The World of Catholic Renewal 1540–1770* (Cambridge: Cambridge University Press, 1998), 1–9. The classic work of A. G. Dickens, *The Counter Reformation* (New York: Harcourt, 1969), has been superseded by those above, as well as by the studies of Michael A. Mullett, *The Catholic Reformation* (New York: Routledge, 2002); and Carter Lindberg, "Catholic Renewal in the Counter-Reformation," in his *The European Reformations* (Oxford, Blackwell, 1996). Also useful are some Catholic perspectives such as Henri-Daniel Rops, *The Catholic Reformation* (London: Dent, 1962) and Msgr. Philip Hughes, *A Popular History of the Reformation* (Garden City, NY: Hanover House, 1957). Eamon Duffy's works are all excellent for the Catholic Reform in England.
2. The standard history of the Council of Trent is Hubert Jedin, *Geschichte des Konzils von Trient*, 4 vols. (Freiburg: Herder, 1951–75); the first two volumes are translated in Hubert Jedin, *A History of the Council of Trent*, trans. Dom Ernest Graf OSB, 2 vols. (St. Louis: Herder, 1957–61). See also Jedin, *Papal Legate at the Council of Trent: Cardinal Seripando*, trans. Frederick C. Eckhoff (St. Louis: Herder, 1947).
3. Significant resources for beginning such a study can be found in *Catholicism in Early Modern History: A Guide to Research*, ed. John. O'Malley SJ (St. Louis, MO: Center for Reformation Research, 1988), esp. the chapters on liturgy, popular piety, and Catholic theology. One should also consult *The Ashgate Research Companion to the Counter-Reformation*, ed. Alexandra Bamji, Geert Janssen, and Mary Laven (Aldershot: Ashgate, 2013), especially part II, "Catholic Lives and Devotional Identities." By far the most pertinent and useful study for this topic is A. Duval, *Des sacraments au Concile de Trente* (Paris: Cerf 1985).
4. For an excellent account of the Church's defense of materiality, which informed the Church of the middle ages, no less than that of Trent, see Robert Wilken, *The Spirit of Early Christian Thought* (New Haven, CT: Yale University Press, 2005), esp. 232–311. The works of Caroline Walker Bynum and Peter Brown also give testimony to the Christian meanings of the body and the material world.
5. The corpus of work done at and around the Council is edited in *Concilium Tridentinum actorum*, ed. Sebastien Merkle et al., 13 vols. (Fribourg: Herder, 1901–67).
6. "Tridentine" is a common adjective for this period. It comes from the Latin name for Trent, "Tridentinum," and the Council, "Concilium Tridentinum." For this theological move, see Jared Wicks SJ, "Dogma and Theology," in O'Malley, *Catholicism in Early Modern History*, 229.

7. For an excellent overview of the Catholic-Lutheran debate on this point, see Christopher Malloy, *Engrafted into Christ* (New York: Peter Lang, 2005).
8. Phil. 2:12.
9. The Council was careful to take into account the very true contentions of the early Reformers, that our salvation is from grace alone. In the first two canons of the declaration, the Council Fathers assert that man can in no way merit the first grace of conversion and salvation. Man cannot save himself. The Fathers recognized that Luther had correctly identified latent semi-Pelagianism in late medieval scholasticism. The first grace could not be merited by man, only God could save, through Jesus Christ. The Council of Trent, in true Augustinian-Thomist fashion, always gave the primacy to grace. "Canon 1.—If anyone says that man may be justified before God by his own works, whether done through the teaching of human nature, or that of the law, without the grace of God through Jesus Christ; let him be anathema. Canon 2.—If any one says that the grace of God, through Jesus Christ, is given only for this, that man may be able more easily to live justly, and to merit eternal life, as if, by free will without grace, he were able to do both, though hardly indeed and with difficulty; let him be anathema." Let it not be said that Trent did not take the Reformers' theology seriously. Note that this also did not settle the vexed question of human freedom and Predestination, both of which were held as dogma by Roman Catholics. *Canons and Decrees of the Council of Trent*, ed. H. J. Schroeder OP (St. Louis, MO: Herder, 1941), 42.
10. Joseph Martos calls this the restoration of the "experiential" basis of Catholic sacramental theology. See Martos, *Doors to the Sacred: A Historical Introduction to Sacraments in the Catholic Church* (Garden City, NY: Doubleday, 1982), 118.
11. This was rooted in the classic expression "legem credendi lex statuat supplicandi," first used by Augustine's disciple Prosper of Aquitaine. It indicates the grave duty to theological and liturgical continuity borne by the historical Christian Churches, whether Orthodox or Catholic.
12. For a discussion of this, see my chapter, "Scripture and Theology in the Counter-Reformation," in *Christian Theologies of Scripture: A Comparative Introduction*, ed. Justin Holcomb (New York: New York University Press, 2006), 134–57, esp. 138–39, 144–45.
13. *Canons and Decrees*, 51–52.
14. Nevertheless, all Catholic apologists knew that the sacraments could all be found in seed in the New Testament, more or less explicitly, but that their provenance from Christ himself was not as clear as Baptism, the Eucharist, and the power to remit sins.
15. This was in accord with previous conciliar definition, and the consensus of the early medieval theologians. The formal declarations of Lyon I (1245) and Florence (1439) were both worked out in consultation with the Greeks, in order to pave the way to full communion. One of the strongest arguments of the Council of Trent was that its sacramental theology was in accord on nearly all points with the

divided Churches of the East, pointing to the immemorial practice of the sacraments throughout the Church.
16. *Canons and Decrees*, 53–54. See Duval, *Des sacraments*, 11–20.
17. *Canons and Decrees*, 21–24.
18. Decree on Justification, chapter 4, *Canons and Decrees*, 31, italics added. For the implications of this decree, see Riccardo Lombardi SJ, *The Salvation of the Unbeliever*, trans. Dorothy M. White (Westminster, MD: Newman Press, 1956), esp. 27–61.
19. For this, see J. B. Umberg, "Cajetans Lehre von der Kinderersatztaufe auf dem Trienter Konzil," *Zeitschrift für katholische Theologie* 34 (1915): 452–64.
20. The literature on Catholic catechesis is extensive. The outpouring of Catholic catechesis can be traced to the masterful *Catechismus Romanus*, directed toward parish priests. It proved instrumental for the Catholic Counter Reform. *Catechism of the Council of Trent for Parish Priests*, ed. Charles Callan and John McHugh (London: Herder, 1934); see the recent critical edition, based on the original manuscript of the Catechism, in *Catechismus Romanus, seu Catechismus ex decreto Concilii Tridentini ad parochos Pii Quinti Pont. Max. iussu editis*, ed. Pedro Rodriguez (Vatican City: Libreria Editrice Vaticana, 1989). See the bibliography on Catechesis: Paul Grendler, "Schools, Seminaries, and Catechetical Instruction," in O'Malley, *Catholicism in Early Modern History*, 323–26. See also Bireley, *Refashioning of Catholicism*, 101–4.
21. *Canons and Decrees*, 72–81; Duval, *Des sacraments*, 21–60.
22. *Canons and Decrees*, 144–52; Duval, *Des sacraments*, 61–150.
23. On this question, see James Megivern CM, *Concomitance and Communion: A Study in Eucharistic Doctrine and Practice* (New York: Herder, 1963), esp. 183–84.
24. This solution had been worked out as early as 1531 by Girolamo Seripando, later legate at the Council; see Jedin, *Papal Legate*, 642.
25. For this, see Wietse de Boer's contribution to *The Ashgate Research Companion*.
26. For a thoroughgoing introduction to liturgical reform in this period, see Joseph Jungmann's magisterial *The Mass of the Roman Rite*, 2 vols. (New York: Benzinger, 1951–55), esp. 1:127–59.
27. *Canons and Decrees*, 88–105; Duval, *Des sacraments*, 151–222.
28. For this debate, see P. de Letter SJ, "Two Concepts of Attrition and Contrition," *Theological Studies* 11 (1950): 3–33.
29. Martos, *Doors to the Sacred*, 351–52.
30. For this, see Bireley, *Refashioning of Catholicism*, 105.
31. *Canons and Decrees*, 160–90; Duval, *Des sacraments*, 281–313, 327–60.
32. Leo XIII, *Apostolicae curae* [on the nullity of Anglican Orders], 18 September 1896.
33. Unlike Baptism, whose validity the Council affirmed when accomplished by heretics, Anglican priests were unconditionally reordained when they converted to Catholicism.
34. This is not to say the Church was inhuman on this topic, but was merely trying to be faithful to the teaching of Christ. The Council affirmed that there were reasons

whereby a couple might separate, but not remarry while the separated spouse still lived. In addition, there was a long canonical tradition of impediments to marriage (such as blood relation, force, error concerning the person, etc.). If such an impediment was later found, the marriage could be *annulled*, that is, the Church would issue a declaration that a sacramental marriage had never taken place. What the Church could not do was to sanction divorce, or effect the dissolution of a valid sacramental marriage.

35. Again, see Jungmann's *Mass of the Roman Rite*, 1:60–102.
36. For this period, see the bibliographical effort of Niels Krogh Rasmussen OP, "Liturgy and Liturgical Arts," in O'Malley, *Catholicism in Early Modern History*, particularly his section on Trent and the "Tridentine Books," 278–80.
37. See E. Weber, *Le Concile de Trente et la musique* (Paris: 1982).
38. An exceptionally interesting contemporary view of this can be found in E. C. Voelker, "Charles Borromeo's *Instructiones fabricae et suppellectilis ecclesiasticae 1577*: A Translation and Commentary with Analysis" (PhD diss., Syracuse University, 1977).
39. Bireley, *Refashioning of Catholicism*, 104.
40. Some liturgical scholars have bemoaned that the cult of the Eucharist came to displace liturgy, but they have not been sufficiently attentive to how the liturgy itself came to undergird this cult. It was in essence a development of orthopraxis fully understandable from the Catholic liturgy itself. See Theodor Klauser, *A Short History of the Western Liturgy: An Account and Some Reflections* (New York: Oxford University Press, 1969), esp. 139.
41. Ibid., 107–9.
42. Bireley, *Refashioning of Catholicism*, 105. Martos, *Doors to the Sacred*, 353. Screens became mandatory in the new edition of the *Rituale Romanum* published in 1614.
43. For Borromeo, see John M. Headlet and John B. Tormaro, *San Carlo Borromeo: Catholic Reform and Ecclesiastical Politics in the Second Half of the Sixteenth Century* (Washington, DC: Folger Shakespeare Library, 1988); and Franco Buzzi and Danilo Zardin, *Carlo Borromeo e l'opera della "grande reforma": Cultura, religione e arti del governo nella Milano del pieno Cinquecento* (Milan: Silvana, 1997); an older, Catholic perspective may be found in Margaret Yeo, *Reformer: St. Charles Borromeo* (Milwaukee: Bruce, 1938).
44. Francis de Sales, *Introduction to the Devout Life* (New York: Vintage, 2002).
45. Tertullian, *De Penitentia*, chaps. 6–12, in *Patrologia Latina 1* (Paris: Migne, 1844), 1224–48; translated in Tertullian, *Treatises on Penance: On Penitence and Purity*, trans. William le Saint (Westminster, MD: Newman Press, 1959).
46. For Jansen, see Jean Orcibal, *Jansénius d'Ypres (1585–1638)* (Paris: Études augustiniennes, 1989). The *Augustinus* was reprinted by Minerva Verlag in 1964.
47. For a good overview, see William Doyle, *Jansenism: Catholic Resistance to Authority from the Reformation to the French Revolution* (Basingstoke: Macmillan, 2000).
48. Rops, *Catholic Reformation*, 432.
49. See Jedin, *Papal Legate*, 645–48.

50. Benedict was also the great pope of reunion, with hundreds of thousands of Eastern Christians resuming communion with the See of Rome during his pontificate. These acts of union bolstered the Roman Church's claim to historical continuity, and commonality of practice and belief with Eastern Christianity. While there were some unfortunate periodic "Latinizations" of their liturgies, by and large the Roman Church permitted the Eastern Catholics to retain their laws and traditions. See Sacred Congregation for the Oriental Churches, *Oriente Cattolico, Cenni storice e statistiche* (Vatican City, 1974).

PART III

Eighteenth to Twenty-First Centuries

14

Theologies of Sacraments in the Eighteenth to Twenty-First Centuries

JAMES R. GORDON

The Context of Modernity

If the Middle Ages observed the maturation and refinement of the church's theology of the sacraments, and if the Reformation saw the theological disagreements implicit in the sacraments boil over into other theological disputes, then the period from the eighteenth century to the twenty-first witnessed the church's attempt to engage with Modernity and to situate the sacraments within the social, cultural, and theological shifts taking place at the time.

In order to understand this engagement, it is important first to grasp just what we mean by "Modernity." While one might focus on any number of scientific, philosophical, social, political, or other features of the modern era to define the concept of "Modernity,"[1] here we are choosing to use the term as a theological concept that signifies a shifting attitude of numerous theologians situated within the late modern era. Theologian Bruce McCormack argues that so-called "modern" theology was born when

> church-based theologians ceased trying to defend and protect the received orthodoxies of the past against erosion and took up the more fundamental challenge of asking how the theological values resident in those orthodoxies might be given an altogether new expression, dressed out in new categories for reflection.[2]

The transition, in other words, was from a posture of, as he puts it, "accommodation"—wherein traditional church doctrines were taken for granted and the scientific knowledge of the day was "fit," so to speak, within these doctrines. Instead, "Modern" theologians tended to embrace "mediation," in which scientific and philosophical advancements in knowledge were not bracketed off but rather embraced, such that theology was seen as a mediating party between the church and the body of knowledge advanced by the sciences and humanities.[3]

In this modern shift, the sacraments—especially the Eucharist—were especially vulnerable since they had long been viewed as mysterious instances of God's grace breaking into the created order. Aside from the Zwinglian memorial view of the Eucharist after the Reformation, all other branches of the church (Orthodox, Catholic, and Protestant) saw Christ's body and blood as present in some real and mysterious way in the bread and wine on the altar. But, with the rise of scientific materialism and the critique of supernatural occurrences such as miracles, theologians had several choices of how to treat the sacraments. On the one hand, they could retreat to a "memorial" or "symbolic" view of the sacraments, in which the act of baptism and the ceremony of the Eucharist were strictly acts of remembrance that did not communicate any mysterious supernatural grace.[4] Or, on the other hand, they could return to the premodern church teaching and embrace the concept of mystery and swim against the stream of culture.[5]

Given the intense debates during the Middle Ages and the Reformation concerning the nature of the sacraments, it might seem that the relative lack of polemical discussion of the sacraments during the modern period signals their decline. However, one must not view the minimization of the sacraments during this period as mere historical contingency arising from either changing notions of piety or the waning power of the church as a social institution; rather, the distinct views of the sacraments during this period must be viewed through a *theological* lens.

If one neglects to view discussion of the sacraments from the eighteenth century to the twenty-first in light of the challenges of Modernity, one will inevitably miss the theological contributions made during this time period.

Eighteenth Century

Perhaps the most significant issue related to the sacraments in the eighteenth century is their relation to the Christian doctrine called "regeneration" (or "conversion"). The question is this: do the Christian sacraments play a causative role in an individual's salvation, or is an individual's salvation a prerequisite for participating in the sacramental life of the church? While these issues were discussed in great detail during and after the Reformation, they became particularly pronounced as Modernity's "turn to the subject" caused individuals to focus less on the ecclesial community's role in their religious lives and more on their own personal salvation. This inward focus can be seen in particular in the rise of revivalism over and against historical confessional Christianity in Europe and America during the First and Second Great Awakenings.

The First Great Awakening began in the 1730s, and the New England Calvinist pastor Jonathan Edwards played a significant role in the movement and, for our purposes, in what he saw as sacramental reform in his Northampton church. In particular, Edwards objected to the teaching of his grandfather and predecessor, Solomon Stoddard, who had instituted what came to be known as the "Half-Way Covenant." According to this standard for church membership, no proof of conversion (i.e., regeneration) was required of aspiring congregants to allow them to participate in the church's sacramental life—that is, in receiving the Eucharist and in having their children baptized. Edwards worried that such a practice obscured the true nature of baptism and the Lord's Supper; the former was an admission into the *visible* (rather than invisible) church and not a means of conversion, while the latter was reserved for those believing Christians as a nourishment, seal, and confirmation of Christ's covenantal promises when received by faith. The efficacy of the sacraments, in other words, consisted in the response they evoked in an individual's life rather than anything intrinsic to the acts themselves. As a result of his position, Jonathan Edwards was dismissed from his Northampton congregation in 1750 because of his attempt to reform its sacramental practices.

Similar ideas can be found in the teachings of John Wesley, Charles Wesley, and George Whitefield, all of whom played a significant role in watering the seeds of the First Great Awakening in Europe during the first half of the eighteenth century. While the Awakening is often seen as contributing to the collapse of the confessional church and its attendant sacramentalism, those involved were motivated by a desire to see the sacraments regain their value as contributing to the practical piety of churchgoers—a similar ideal shared by the Catholic Church's Liturgical Movement, whose commitments are seen in the First and Second Vatican Councils (discussed below).

Nineteenth Century

Vatican I

In one sense, the Catholic Church's response to Modernity is illustrated in the First Vatican Council (1868). Concerned that "even the holy Bible itself, which they at one time claimed to be the sole source and judge of the Christian faith, is no longer held to be divine, but they begin to assimilate it to the inventions of myth,"[6] the Catholic Church rejected the prevalent naturalism/materialism of the day such that "every assertion contrary to the truth of enlightened faith is totally false."[7] In rejecting materialism, Vatican I asserted the mysteries of faith as essential to the church's teaching. In addition, Vatican I went further in declaring the infallibility of the papal office as a way to restore the fidelity of the church in the face of its declining cultural authority.

Though the only mention of the sacraments in Vatican I—aside from Pius IX's affirmation of the seven sacraments in his confession of faith[8]—is an admonition to their frequent practice in order to foster the "renewal of the moral life of the Christian people,"[9] it is easy to see how the Council as a whole is fighting for ground in what the Catholic Church saw as important doctrines "upstream" of the ecclesial practices of the sacraments. If one, for instance, professes a belief in nothing other than that which is material in the world, it is hard to see how the Catholic teaching of the Eucharist, namely, transubstantiation, established at the Fourth Lateran Council (1215) and the Council of Trent (1551) wherein the substances of the bread and wine are changed into the substances of Christ's body and blood, respectively, could possibly be held.

Friedrich Schleiermacher

Yet, at the same time, some within the Protestant tradition were not willing to engage in a tug-of-war contest with the social, political, scientific, and philosophical challenges of Modernity but were instead interested in meeting those challenges head-on so as to express the Christian faith in an ever-changing culture. One such theologian, Friedrich Schleiermacher, frequently referred to as the Father of Modern Liberal Theology, worried about so-called "magical" elements of the faith such as the Catholic Eucharistic theology, for such infringements upon the ordered system of nature and the integrity of the natural sciences would undermine God's one, creative act.[10] Schleiermacher claims that "creation is supernatural, but it afterwards becomes the natural order."[11] Even still, he allows for "one great miracle" in the coming of Christ.[12]

Given this naturalization of the supernatural and, in particular, the way that Schleiermacher accounts for the work of the Holy Spirit as carrying on the ministry of Christ in the church's natural, intersubjective practices, one might expect Schleiermacher to give a wholly naturalized account of the sacraments; instead, however, he merely outlines the boundaries within which Protestant accounts of baptism and the Eucharist must fall.[13]

For both baptism and the Eucharist, Schleiermacher desires to tie the acts directly to the work of Christ and of the Spirit that carries on that work. In his discussion of the sacrament of baptism, Schleiermacher considers the relationship between it, the giving of the Spirit, and regeneration, and he relates these concepts as relevant to the issue of infant baptism.[14] In the Lord's Supper, Schleiermacher wants to locate Protestant accounts between the antitheses of the Catholic account on the one hand, which attaches "magical spiritual effects to an effect that is bodily,"[15] and the "Sacramentarian" account on the other hand, which rejects any connection between the physical act of eating the bread and drinking the wine and the spiritual reality of participating in union with Christ.[16]

More generally, regarding the very idea of a "sacrament," Schleiermacher acknowledges the historical development of the seven sacraments of the Catholic Church, but wishes "even more unreservedly than Zwingli did that Church terminology never adopted the word, and also that it might be found possible to dispense with it."[17] His main concern here is to avoid the idea that it is *by virtue of the fact that they are sacraments* that baptism and the Lord's Supper receive their importance; rather, their significance lies "solely on a common relation to one of the essential activities of Christ's vocation."[18] He sees the conflict within the Catholic Church concerning what counts as a sacrament as "empty," since there is a much more obvious connection between Christ's ministry and baptism and the Lord's Supper than there is between Christ's ministry and the other so-called sacraments.[19]

The Oxford Movement

Not all Protestants, however, were of the same mediating mind of Friedrich Schleiermacher, and, in fact, other Protestant movements during the nineteenth century simultaneously called the church to its ancient origins and away from the state's influence on religious life. The Oxford Movement, for example, was a movement within the Church of England to push the church toward its liturgical, Catholic roots. Those who pushed the church to renewal were known as the Tractarians because of the tracts they wrote that were directed at clergy in an effort to embolden robust priestly ministry. The pushback from the other side came not from those who wished instead to downplay the sacramental life of the church, but from those who worried that liturgical renewal was the sign of the "papists" and the slippery path back to Rome.

These Protestant renewal movements wanted to recover the purity of the apostolic church not only by emphasizing the importance of the sacraments but also by promoting the preaching of the gospel. In this way, these movements exemplify continuity with Luther's original protest—and the subsequent Protestant ethos—that the true church of Christ is marked by the proclamation of the Word and the faithful administration of the sacraments.

The Twentieth Century

Perhaps the most significant development in the sacraments in the twentieth century is the Second Vatican Council of the Roman Catholic Church. While Vatican I may be viewed as a defensive move against the shifting cultural tides, Vatican II lays out a robust vision for the sacramental life of the church as encompassing much more than mere participation in institutional activities. According to the Council, "the Church is in Christ like a sacrament or as a sign and instrument both of a very closely knit union with God and of the unity of the whole human race."[20] The Eucharist is a vehicle for expressing and enacting the reality of the church's unity in Christ.[21]

One of the greatest motivations of Vatican II was to incorporate members of the laity into the liturgical life of the church. The people of God—not merely the ordained clergy—as "the common priesthood of the faithful" participate in the sacraments as "a participation in the one priesthood of Christ."[22] These sacraments are Baptism, Confirmation, Eucharist, Confession/Penance, Sacred Anointing, Holy Orders, and Marriage.

Another significant figure whose voice is often ignored in discussions of the sacraments is the Reformed Protestant theologian Karl Barth. This is not without due cause, owing in large part to the fact that in the scope of his massive *Church Dogmatics*, Barth never got around to giving the sacraments as full and proper a treatment as one might have expected.[23] Barth claims, for instance, as a self-identified "Neo-Zwinglian,"[24] that Baptism is not itself a sacrament but only a response to "the sacrament of the history of Jesus Christ, of His resurrection, of the outpouring of the Holy Spirit."[25] Further, Barth thought that there was "no provision in the New Testament" for the sacrament of Confirmation and critically worried that infant baptism was "only half a baptism."[26] Despite these misgivings, Barth's earlier theology—and, in particular, his account of the doctrines of revelation, of God, and of Jesus Christ—contains the seeds for developing a full Protestant account of the sacraments in ways that some scholars are beginning to realize.

Two other significant movements in the twentieth century have sought to "ontologize" the concept of the sacraments by expanding the concept from the two or seven recognized sacraments to an entire picture of the reality of the God/world relationship. Some have seen the way forward for the church in a backward movement to the greater tradition that already existed. Such a *ressourcement* or *nouvelle théologie* was led by prominent Catholic theologians such as Henri de Lubac and Hans Urs von Balthasar (among others) and sought to reconnect the relationship between nature and grace, to recapture the concept of mystery as essential to the church's identity, and to recast the sacraments as intensifying moments of the cosmic presence of Christ.

Others, such as Alexander Schmemann in the Orthodox tradition, have pursued similar paths. Schmemann notes that "in Christ, life—life in all its totality—was returned to man, given again as sacrament and communion, made Eucharist."[27] He worries that Christian mission has become associated with the proclamation of the Word; the sacraments are viewed as an "act *of* the Church and *within* the Church, but not of the Church as being itself the sacrament of Christ's presence and action."[28] As such, Schmemann casts a vision for the church as a sacramental presence of God in, with, and for the sake of the world.

Finally, one other twentieth-century development in the sacraments that should not be overlooked is the 1982 document *Baptism, Eucharist, and Ministry* from the World Council of Churches.[29] This important ecumenical document called for the unity in the Sacraments of Baptism and the Eucharist across all branches of the church.

The Twenty-First Century

While it is challenging to state the development of the sacraments in the twenty-first century less than two full decades into it, there is at least one trend that can be seen beginning in the work of Schmemann. Above we saw how the questions of doctrine concerning God, Christ, creation, revelation, and the Holy Spirit were "upstream," so to speak, from the ecclesial doctrines of the sacraments. The decisions made about who God is, in other words, flow downstream and shape how we view baptism and the Eucharist, among other things. Schmemann's work, however, lays the ground for a reversal of the direction the stream flows. That is, the things the church does in the liturgy, including the sacraments, *already implicitly contain* the things we believe about God and therefore should be a foundational starting point for thinking about who God is. To put it slightly differently, if Barth's revolution was to show that all talk of God must begin and end with Jesus Christ, so-called liturgical theology calls the church to attend to its pneumatic roots and to talk of God on the basis of the Spirit's mission-giving work in the church's liturgy.

NOTES

1. Generally, the modern era is broken into two periods: early and late—the former spanning the time between the beginning of the sixteenth century with the Renaissance and the French Revolution, which began in 1789, and the latter beginning with the French Revolution and ending sometime during the mid-twentieth century (typically after World War II, at which point "postmodernism" begins).

2. Bruce L. McCormack, "Introduction: On 'Modernity' as a Theological Concept," in *Mapping Modern Theology: A Thematic and Historical Introduction*, ed. Kelly M. Kapic and Bruce L. McCormack (Grand Rapids, MI: Baker Academic, 2012), 3.
3. Ibid., 4–11, 16.
4. I am not claiming that Zwingli's position on the sacraments (or his followers' positions) was motivated by the scientific and philosophical advancements of the modern period; however, it would be difficult to avoid the conclusion that the rise of the merely symbolic view of the sacraments during the modern period was at least in some way made possible by the harsh critiques of the immaterial during the modern period.
5. There could, of course, be a third option more along the lines of something of a "Schleiermacherian" account of the sacraments, such as the account of baptism given by Kevin W. Hector, in which the human act of baptism is appropriated. Hector, "The Recognition of Baptism: An Ecumenical Proposal," *Koinonia* 29 (2007): 13–38.
6. Norman P. Tanner, ed., *Decrees of the Ecumenical Councils*, vol. 2 (Washington, DC: Georgetown University Press, 1990), 804.
7. Ibid., 809.
8. Ibid., 803.
9. Ibid., 804.
10. Cf. Friedrich Schleiermacher, *The Christian Faith*, ed. H. R. Mackintosh and J. S. Stewart (Edinburgh: T&T Clark, 1989), §140.4 and §47.
11. Friedrich Schleiermacher, *On the* Glaubenslehre: *Two Letters to Dr. Lücke*, trans. James Due and Francis Fiorenza (Atlanta: Scholars Press, 1981), 89.
12. Friedrich Schleiermacher, *The Christian Faith*, §47.1.
13. Thus the oft-repeated and mistaken claim that Schleiermacher reduces theology to anthropology. For an account of Schleiermacher's pneumatology, see Kevin W. Hector, "The Mediation of Christ's Normative Spirit: A Constructive Reading of Schleiermacher's Pneumatology," *Modern Theology* 24 (January 2008): 1–22.
14. Cf. Schleiermacher, *The Christian Faith*, §§136–38.
15. Ibid., §140.2.
16. Ibid., §140.3.
17. Ibid., §143.1. Indeed, Schleiermacher looks somewhat approvingly upon the Eastern Church which, he says, avoids use of the term "sacraments" and instead employs the concept of "mysteries."
18. Ibid., §143.1.
19. Ibid., §143.2.
20. Pope John Paul VI, "Dogmatic Constitution of the Church: *Lumen Gentium*" (21 November 1964), www.vatican.va (accessed 17 January 2017), 1.1; cf. 2.9 .
21. Ibid., 1.3, 1.7.
22. Ibid., 2.10.
23. As James J. Buckley notes in "Christian Community, Baptism, and the Lord's Supper," in *The Cambridge Companion to Karl Barth*, ed. John Webster (Cambridge: Cambridge University Press, 2000), 196.

24. Karl Barth, *Church Dogmatics: The Doctrine of Reconciliation*, vol. IV/4, ed. G. W. Bromiley and T. F. Torrance, trans. T. H. L. Parker et al. (Edinburgh: T&T Clark, 1956), 130 (hereafter cited as CD IV/4).
25. Ibid., IV/4, 102.
26. Ibid., IV/4, 188.
27. Alexander Schmemann, *For the Life of the World: Sacraments and Orthodoxy* (Crestwood, NJ: St. Vladimir's Seminary Press, 1998), 20.
28. Ibid., 21.
29. *Baptism, Eucharist, and Ministry*, Faith and Order Paper No. 111 (Geneva: World Council of Churches, 1982).

15

John and Charles Wesley

PAUL W. CHILCOTE

John Wesley (1703–91) and Charles Wesley (1707–88) were co-founders of the Methodist movement, the former a noted preacher and the latter a hymn-writer poet. Sons of the Anglican clergyman Samuel Wesley and the incomparable Susanna, both were educated at Christ Church, Oxford, and ordained to the priesthood of the Church of England. They spearheaded a movement of renewal in the life of the eighteenth-century church combining a warm-hearted evangelical piety and a dynamic Eucharistic fervor. Often falling under the shadow of his brother, John, the younger Charles led the way in many of the personal and institutional developments that revolved around the rising revival. Charles founded the so-called "Holy Club" while a student at Oxford, the leadership of which was taken over by John. The younger brother first experienced God's unconditional love in a "religious experience" on 21 May 1738 that preceded the famous "Aldersgate Experience" of his brother three days later. John traveled over 250,000 miles on horseback during his lifetime, preaching a message of faith working by love across the British Isles. Charles wrote some 9,000 hymns—about 180 hymns per year over the course of half a century—through which the vast majority of people called Methodists learned the theology of the movement. In 1745 the brothers jointly published *Hymns on the Lord's Supper*, a collection of 166 hymns that expound their Eucharistic theology. The spirituality of both brothers revolved around the concept of perfect love, or Christian perfection. John Wesley's *A Plain Account of Christian Perfection*, often considered his magnum opus, summarizes his teaching on the subject. His *Journal*, letters, sermons, and treatises are available in many editions. Charles Wesley left his hymns as a legacy to the wider Christian family. His most important publication was the 1780 *Collection of Hymns for the People Called Methodist*. For many years this hymn book was the standard reference point for every dimension of Methodist spirituality and Christian practice.

* * *

John and Charles Wesley directed a movement of spiritual renewal within the Church of England during the eighteenth century best described as an evangelical and sacramental revival.[1] While this revival entailed a rediscovery of the Christian life as a way of devotion—a life empowered by the Spirit and rooted in God's grace experienced in Jesus Christ—it also reclaimed the central place of the sacraments in this spiritual journey. At a time when sacramental devotion was at low ebb in the life of their church, the Wesleys resituated their movement around the life-giving and grace-offering sacraments. They asserted that through the Sacrament of Baptism, God initiates the work of grace, and through the Sacrament of Holy Communion, God sustains believers in their grace-filled pilgrimage of faith. John and Charles Wesley's theology and practice of sacraments emerged out of their larger vision of the Christian life as an act of worship—a life to be sung to the glory of God. Their theology maintained a vital synthesis of sacramental grace and evangelical experience.

Sacraments within the Context of the Worship of God

The Wesleyan revival, like nearly all other movements of renewal in the history of the church, was characterized by liturgical revolution. Worship shapes theology and theology shapes worship. The Wesleys conceived worship as the grateful surrender of all one is and all one has, a living sacrifice of praise and thanksgiving to the God of love who created all things and bears witness with one's spirit that one is a child of God. Once this essential discovery is made, all of life becomes an act of genuine worship, and all can sing with Charles Wesley:

> Thee I shall then forever praise,
>   In spirit and in truth adore,
> While all I am declares thy grace,
>   And born of God I sin no more,
> The pure and heavenly treasure share,
> And fruit into perfection bear.[2]

Baptism signals this new birth; Holy Communion provides the nourishment that leads to a life of perfect love. Worship, in general, and the sacraments, in particular, orient one's life around the pillars of authentic discipleship, a way of redemption characterized by faith, love, and holiness.[3] Orthodoxy (literally, the proper praise of God) means quite simply (1) to believe in God by faith, (2) to desire nothing but God's love, and (3) to glorify God by following in the path of righteousness. It is interesting that John Wesley's first definition of Methodism revolved around the life of a worshiping community. A society, he wrote, "is no other than 'a company of men [and women] "having the form and seeking the power of godliness," united in order to pray together, to receive the word of exhortation, and to watch over one another in love, that they may help each other to work out their salvation.'"[4] Authentic Christian worship is worship in spirit and truth that enables the Christ follower to believe, and love, and serve God. In the context of a worshipping community, the sacraments anchor all who have been called to follow Jesus in this way of life.

The Wesleys constructed their theology of the sacraments, therefore, around several critical doxological premises drawn from the worship of God.[5]

1. God is more important than the way God is worshipped

    If the authenticity of worship is rooted in a relationship, then the object of faith, love, and holiness is much more important than the individual, peculiar, and culturally shaped means of entering into relationship with God. In their own age, and particularly under the shadow of the generations that immediately preceded them, the Wesleys lamented the way in which concerns about sacramental practice fractured the community of faith. Questions as to whether one stood or knelt when receiving Holy Communion and was sprinkled or immersed in Baptism led to deep divisions in the life of the church. For the Wesleys, God was more important than the methods or means of engaging God's presence.

2. God reveals Godself through means as well as apart from them

    God can be known immediately (literally "without any means"). But God also uses material, physical things to reveal the divine. Through the Incarnation, for example, God entered the physical world in the person of Jesus Christ. "The Word," as John's account of the Gospel declares, "became flesh and made his home among us" (John 1:14 CEB). Building on this fundamental reality, in a Wesleyan perspective, the sacraments reveal that a bit of common bread can be the medium of the presence of God and that water can be the instrument of God's life-giving grace. Through the sacramental elements of water, bread, and wine, God uses material or physical things to reveal the spiritual. God transforms common, ordinary elements into sacred instruments of love.

3. God not only offers grace to individuals, but locates grace within the Church

The Wesley brothers built a religious revival upon this simple foundation—the personal and transforming experience of the love of God in Christ. The church (the body of Christ or fellowship of believers), they claimed, is composed of those persons who share this experience. Christians are, by the very nature of their faith, drawn into community; their faith is social as well as personal, and the sacraments amplify this dynamic reality. John Wesley spent much of his ministry redressing the neglect of this social dimension. "Holy solitaries," he exclaimed on one occasion, "is a phrase no more consistent with the gospel than holy adulterers. The gospel of Christ knows of no religion, but social [religion]."[6] The sacraments, therefore, are not only means of grace for individuals; they are also important social symbols.

4. God uses actions in addition to words to communicate the gospel

It was impossible for the Wesleys to think about the spoken word (preaching) apart from the Word made visible (Holy Communion). Both brothers frequently mention word and sacrament together. "The Lord gave us, under the word, to know the power of His resurrection," Charles wrote on Easter 1747, "but in the sacrament he carried us quite above ourselves and all earthly things."[7] Actions do speak louder than words, a principle the Wesley's had learned early in their lives. Thus, in similar fashion, the act of baptism declares the need for all to die to self in order to be born anew in ways more powerful than words alone. The sacraments proclaim God's claim upon every life and the Lord's death until he comes. They proclaim the nature of authentic existence as a rhythm that moves ineluctably from death to life—dying to self the believer is raised with Christ—and of one's perennial need of spiritual sustenance as the believer "feeds on him by faith with thanksgiving." The sacraments faithfully proclaim the Word through sign-acts of love.

The purpose of worship, according to the Wesleys, was to cultivate personal, religious experience in the context of a supportive community of love. They assumed that God's love was potent enough to transform both individual lives and the life of the world. They held the individual and the community together, concerned equally about the parts as for the whole of God's design. The sacraments in the context of authentic worship became a powerful means in their effort to renew the church. As Ole Borgen concludes, "Baptism is *initiatory*; its function is to commence what the Lord's Supper (with other means of grace as well) are basically ordained to *preserve* and *develop*: a life in faith and holiness."[8]

The Wesleys' Definition of "Sacrament"

As devout Anglican priests, the Wesleys defined a sacrament on the basis of the Church of England *Catechism* as "an outward sign of inward grace, and a *means* whereby we receive the same."[9] Historians of doctrine trace this classic definition to St. Augustine. This definition included the philosophical distinction between *signum* (sign) and *res* (the thing signified). While the sign is outward and visible, the thing signified is inward and spiritual. In the sacraments, water, bread, and wine, the outward washing, and the meal signify respectively the inward cleansing and the spiritual nourishment of the soul. For the Wesleys, the sign and thing signified are distinct, but never separate. While the one is outward, visible, and material, the other is inward, invisible, and spiritual; but both must always be held together—the one goes inextricably with the other.

The Church of England also provided a more extended definition of the sacraments in the 39 *Articles of Religion*. When John Wesley edited these *Articles* and published his twenty-four revisions in *The Sunday Service* in 1784, he left the article pertaining generically to the sacraments virtually unaltered. In conformity to standard Protestant practice, the original article and the Wesleys' redaction omitted confirmation, penance, orders, matrimony, and extreme unction from the status of sacraments, counseled against an unbiblical veneration of any sacrament, and commended a worthy reception of the sacraments. The opening paragraphs of the article identify and describe the two dominical ordinances:

Article XVI—Of the Sacraments

Sacraments ordained of Christ, are not only badges or tokens of Christian Men's Profession; but rather they are certain Signs of Grace, and God's good Will toward us, by the which he doth work invisibly in us, and doth not only quicken, but also strengthen and confirm our faith in him.
There are two Sacraments ordained of Christ our Lord in the Gospel; that is to say, Baptism, and the Supper of the Lord.[10]

The Wesleys' Theology of Baptism

Baptism, unlike Holy Communion, was not a subject of primary concern for either of the Wesley brothers. Because of the dearth of material on the topic in their corpus, the Wesleys' theology of baptism is one of the most difficult doctrines to assess fully in their theological program.[11] Robert Cushman lamented the "large elements of uncertainty and, perhaps, ambiguity in the express utterances as well as exasperating silences of John Wesley himself regarding the means of baptism and its significance."[12] But John Wesley did edit and publish two small tracts on baptism, both highly dependent on their original authors. In 1751, he anonymously published a twenty-one-page redaction of William Wall's four-volume tome, *Thoughts upon Infant-Baptism*. John Wesley's *Treatise on Baptism*, an abridgement of his father's work of 1710, provides greater insight into his views. It also included an earlier publication, *Serious Thoughts Concerning Godfathers and Godmothers* (1752), with the obvious connections to baptismal theology.[13] His article on baptism (XVII), while reducing article XXVII of the *Book of Common Prayer* somewhat substantially, retained the essence of the Anglican view. "Baptism is not only a sign of profession, and mark of difference, whereby Christians are distinguished from others that are not baptized; but it is also a sign of regeneration, or the new birth. The baptism of young children is to be retained in the church."[14] While Charles Wesley left behind no definitive statement concerning his views on or practice related to baptism in his prose works, he produced many hymns specifically for use at both infant and adult rites.

Despite some twists and turns in John Wesley's early practice of baptism, once the Wesleyan revival was in full swing, an earlier dogmatic spirit seems to have given way to moderation, especially with regard to the mode of baptism. His *Thoughts upon Infant-Baptism* reveal what might be considered his mature thinking related to this particular issue:

> With regard to the mode of baptizing, I would only add, Christ no where, as far as I can find, requires *dipping*, but only *baptizing*; which word, many most eminent for learning and piety have declared, signifies to *pour on*, or *sprinkle*, as well as to *dip*. As our Lord has graciously given us a word of such extensive meaning, doubtless the parent, or the person to be baptized, if he be adult, ought to choose which way he best approves. What God has left *indifferent*, it becomes not *man* to make necessary.[15]

This trend away from rigid conformity to formal ecclesiastical standards and toward a more flexible pattern of practice seems to have typified the mature view of both brothers.[16] With regard to two particular issues, they reflected a fairly conventional Anglican view of the sacrament: the proper recipients and the benefits of baptism.

Throughout the course of his ministry, John Wesley endorsed infant baptism. The concluding sections of his *Treatise on Baptism* and the entirety of *Thoughts upon Infant-Baptism* provide arguments supporting this practice. He based his arguments on (1) the infant's need, (2) the desirability of the child's incorporation into the church, (3) the practice of the historic church, and primarily (4) the parallelism between circumcision in the old and Baptism in the new covenant. Charles Wesley's lyrical paraphrase of Matthew 19:13 identifies at least two primary functions of infant baptism: blessing and incorporation:

> Jesus, in earth and heaven the same,
> > Accept a parent's vow,
> To Thee, baptiz'd into thy name,
> > I bring my children now;

Thy love permits, invites, commands,
    My offspring to be blesst:
Lay on them Lord, thy gracious hands,
And hide them in thy breast.

To each the hallowing Spirit give
    Ev'n from their infancy,
And pure into thy church receive
    Whom I devote to Thee;
Committed to thy faithful care,
    Protected by thy blood,
Preserved by thine unceasing prayer,
And bring them all to God.[17]

According to Gayle Felton,

> infant baptism is the ordinary vehicle of regeneration; adult baptism is accompanied by rebirth only under certain circumstances and, instead, functions as a more general means of grace. The person who has been converted should receive baptism as a testimony to the faith experience and as a rite of admission into the church.[18]

But the baptism of an adult can convey regenerating grace as well, as can be seen in a Charles Wesley text:

Father, Son, and Holy Ghost,
    In solemn power come down!
Present with thy heavenly host,
    Thine ordinance to crown.
See a sinful worm of earth!
    Bless to him the cleansing flood!
Plunge him, by a second birth,
    Into the depths of God.

Let the promised inward grace
    Accompany the sign;
On his new-born soul impress

> The character divine!
> Father, all thy love reveal!
> Jesus, all thy name impart!
> Holy Ghost, renew, and dwell
> For ever in her heart![19]

The Wesleys conceived both infants and adults as the proper recipients of baptism because both needed to be born again. They denied the false polarities of sacramental grace and evangelical experience, affirming the validity and necessity of both. Attempting to adjudicate the tension between baptism and subsequent conversion in the thought of the Wesleys, Albert Outler asserts in his prefatory comments to Wesley's *Treatise on Baptism*:

> The obvious purpose of this "extract" was to re-enforce the wavering convictions of some of the Methodist people as to the validity of infant baptism and to re-emphasize the objectivity of divine grace in this sacrament. One ought, however, to compare this essay on baptism . . . with the sermon on "The New Birth" . . . where the stress falls heavily on conversion as a conscious adult experience of regeneration. The point is that Wesley held to both ideas.[20]

In his *Treatise on Baptism* John Wesley identified five benefits of the sacrament: (1) removal of the guilt of original sin, (2) entrance into covenant with God, (3) incorporation into the church, (4) restoration as children of God, and (5) initiation into the kingdom of God. Brian Galliers identifies four additional benefits from other sources within the Wesleyan corpus: (6) solidarity in the death of Christ, (7) admission to the Lord's Table, (8) reception of the gift of the Holy Spirit, and (9) physical healing.[21]

In addition to these sources, the journals, sermons, and hymns of the brothers clarify their theology of baptism. First, the Wesleys refused to accept a reductionism that makes baptism a purely symbolic act. Second, they viewed baptism as initiatory. Third, they conceived this sacrament as the ordinary means to salvation within the community of faith. God "makes Christians" through baptism. Fourth, baptism situates the child of God on a trajectory, the goal of which is genuine, living faith and holiness. The means cannot be separated from the goal, but the Wesleys focused attention on the end rather than the means. Fifth, all grace may be lost; but while possible, this loss is never inevitable. Their keen observation of Christian living taught the Wesleys that an experience of conversion subsequent to baptism was necessary in the lives of most, if not all, people. But such life-changing experiences did not negate the act of infant baptism. Neither did they empty baptism of its meaning. Rather, subsequent new birth simply culminated the work of the Spirit begun in baptism itself.

Many of these themes find poignant expression in one of Charles Wesley's hymns, "At the Baptism of a Child," from his *Family Hymns* collection:

> God of eternal truth and love,
>   Vouchsafe the promis'd grace we claim,
> Thine own great ordinance approve,
>   The child baptis'd into thy name
> Partaker of thy nature make,
> And give her all thine image back.
>
> Born in the dregs of sin and time,
>   These darkest, last, apostate days,
> Burthen'd with *Adam's* curse and crime
>   Thou in thy mercy's arms embrace,
> And wash out all her guilty load,
> And quench the brand in Jesus' blood.
>
> Father, if such thy sovereign will,
>   If Jesus *did* the rite injoin,
> Annex thy hallowing Spirit's seal,
>   And let the grace attend the sign;
> The seed of endless life impart,
> Seize for thy own our infant's heart.
>
> Answer on her thy wisdom's end
>   In present and eternal good;
> Whate'er thou didst for man intend,
>   Whate'er thou hast on man bestow'd,

> Now to this favour'd babe be given,
> Pardon, and holiness, and heaven.
>
> In presence of thy heavenly host
>   Thyself we faithfully require;
> Come, Father, Son, and Holy Ghost
>   By blood, by water, and by fire,
> And fill up all thy human shrine,
> And seal our souls for ever Thine.[22]

The Wesleys' Holy Communion Theology

Charles Wesley described the Sacrament of Holy Communion as the "richest legacy" that Jesus left the community of faith.[23]

> Fasting he doth and hearing bless,
> And prayer can much avail,
> Good vessels all to draw the grace
> Out of salvation's well.
>
> But none like this mysterious rite
> Which dying mercy gave
> Can draw forth all God's promised might
> And all God's will to save.
>
> This is the richest legacy
> Thou hast on us bestowed,
> Here chiefly, Lord, we feed on thee,
> And drink thy precious blood.
>
> Here all thy blessings we receive,
> Here all thy gifts are given;
> To those that would in thee believe,
> Pardon, and grace, and heaven.
>
> Thus may we still in thee be blessed
> 'Till all from earth remove,

> And share with thee the marriage feast,
> And drink the wine above.[24]

Scholars have documented the general neglect of the Eucharist in the Church of England during the Wesleys' day. In stark contrast to the norms of his age, John Wesley communed on average about once every four days throughout his lifetime and put the sacrament back at the very center of Christian spirituality and discipleship. When he sent his *Sunday Service* to the fledgling Methodist communities in North America, he advised them "to administer the Supper of the Lord on every Lord's day."[25] Both brothers viewed the Lord's Supper as the "chief means of grace."[26] Early Methodists flocked to the celebration of Holy Communion because they encountered God there. They received spiritual nourishment around the table. Locating the sacrament among other means of grace, Charles Wesley sang,

> The prayer, the fast, the word conveys,
>   When mixt with faith, thy life to me,
> In all the channels of thy grace,
>   I still have fellowship with thee,
> But chiefly here my soul is fed
>   With fullness of immortal bread.[27]

These "feasts of love," as the early Methodists often described them, shaped their understanding of God's love for them and their reciprocal love for God.

In his journal, John Wesley recorded every celebration of the sacrament in which he was involved and frequently commented on his sacramental theology. From a detailed comparison of Wesley's early and later diaries, John Bowmer came to two clear conclusions: (1) throughout the course of his life, Wesley's frequent participation in the sacrament and his practice, in general, remained remarkably consistent, and (2) he either celebrated or participated in Eucharist whenever the opportunity presented itself.[28] With regard to the place of the sacrament among the Methodist people under the Wesleys' direction, Bowmer drew similar conclusions:

> There can be little doubt that the high place which the Sacrament occupied in early Methodism was due to the precept and the example of the Wesleys, for it is not too much to say that, for them it was the highest form of devotion and the most comprehensive act of worship the Church could offer. As necessary as preaching was—and it would be unjust to attempt to minimize its place in the Methodist revival—a preaching service was not, to the Wesleys, the supreme spiritual exercise. On the other hand, the Lord's Supper was completely satisfying.[29]

Of the many sources from which to construct John Wesley's theology of Holy Communion, his sermon on "The Duty of Constant Communion," published late in his life, provides the most succinct statement of his Eucharistic doctrine and practice.[30] The primary purpose of this exposition of Luke 22:19 was to demonstrate the duty of every Christian to receive Holy Communion as often as possible. The primary reasons supporting this constancy included the fact that it is a plain command of Christ and that it is a blessing of God through which we receive the benefits of Christ's passion and love. In the sermon, Wesley identified and answered five common objections to the practice of constant Communion.

First, against those who lamented that their unworthiness disqualified their participation, he claimed that the root of this common attitude rests in a misinterpretation of St. Paul's purported prohibitions. Christ particularly welcomed the unworthy (i.e., all people) to the table. Second, whereas some claimed that an elevated esteem for the sacrament might unrealistically exaggerate their expectations concerning holiness in life, Wesley maintained that anything else would be a denial of their baptismal covenant. Third, Wesley argued that reverence for the command of proper preparation should never become a pretense for disobedience. Fourth, against those who expressed concern about the numbing effect of repetition, he argued that practices habituated within the community of faith need never lessen true religious reverence. Fifth, he bore testimony to the imperceptible strengthening often associated with the sacrament in response to those who "felt nothing" at the table. "No man can have any pretense to Christian piety," Wesley concluded, "who does not receive it (not once a month, but) as often as he can (II.21)."[31]

While the Wesley brothers jointly published *Hymns on the Lord's Supper*, Charles wrote virtually all of the 166 hymns in this unique volume. This collection of religious verse comprises his fullest possible expression of Eucharistic spirituality—a theology in hymns. "The eighteenth-century revival," Richard Heitzenrater has observed, "was to a great extent borne on the wings of Charles's poetry. Charles's hymns not only helped form the texture of the Methodist mind but also, perhaps more importantly, set the temper of the Methodist spirit."[32] This collection of Eucharistic hymns included John's abridged version of Daniel Brevint's *The Christian Sacrament and Sacrifice*, which functioned as a preface to the volume.[33] John, most likely, arranged the hymns under primary headings, closely following the pattern laid out by Brevint in his treatise:

1. As It Is a Memorial of the Sufferings and Death of Christ
2. As It Is a Sign and a Means of Grace
3. The Sacrament as a Pledge of Heaven
4. The Holy Eucharist as It Implies a Sacrifice
5. Concerning the Sacrifice of Our Persons
6. After the Sacrament

The first three sections closely parallel the dimensions of time and provide the outline for Charles's lyrical theological reflections on the sacrament as a memorial, a sign and means of grace, and a pledge of heaven.

First, *the Lord's Supper is a memorial of the passion of Christ.*[34] The opening hymn of Wesley's collection sets the somber tone of this section:

> In that sad memorable night,
>> When Jesus was for us betray'd,
> He left his death-recording rite.[35]

The sacrament proclaims "the Lord's death until he comes," St. Paul reminded the Corinthian community (1 Cor. 11:26). Charles's death imagery in these "past dimension hymns," therefore, should be no surprise. The fact that the redemptive suffering of Jesus procures eternal life for the believer, however, startles those who experience the power of this redemptive act of love:

> The grace which I to all bequeath
> > In this divine memorial take,
> And mindful of your Saviour's death,
> > Do this, my followers, for my sake,
> Whose dying love hath left behind
> Eternal life for all mankind.[36]

As critical as this memorial aspect is for the Wesleys, they recoil from a "bare memorialism" in their view of the sacrament. Rather, sacramental remembrance connotes *anamnesis*, that is, calling an event to mind in such a way as to make it real in the present. Memory functioned in this way for the Jewish community in the annual remembrance of Passover. The Hebrew people celebrated the Passover meal not simply to recall God's deliverance of the people of Israel from bondage in Egypt, but to experience liberation in the present moment as well. Charles's masterful use of imagery created what J. Ernest Rattenbury called a "Protestant Crucifix," poetry that continues to bring the event of the cross to the forefront of our consciousness and into our experience:

> Endless scenes of wonder rise
> > With that mysterious tree,
> Crucified before our eyes
> > Where we our Maker see:
> Jesus, Lord, what hast thou done!
> > Publish we the death divine,
> Stop, and gaze, and fall, and own
> > Was never love like thine!
>
> Never love nor sorrow was
> > Like that my Jesus show'd;
> See him stretch'd on yonder cross
> > And crush'd beneath the load!
> Now discern the deity,
> > Now his heavenly birth declare!
> Faith cries out, 'Tis he, 'tis he,
> > My God that suffers there![37]

Excursus on Sacrifice

The sacrificial metaphors applied by the Wesleys to the Lord's Supper are those that the writers of Hebrews and Revelation employ most frequently; the slaughtered Lamb who was also the Great High Priest. This Priest/Victim imagery brings out with unequivocal force their sense of the continuing power of sacrifice on the part of the ascended Christ. The earthly symbol represents this ongoing sacrifice of Christ on behalf of all. The Priest/Victim pleads the cause of sinful children for whom he died. The sacrifice on which God is asked to look is not our own but the one oblation for the sins of the world—the sacrifice of God's beloved Son. But the oblation offered in the sacrament also belongs to the faithful who join their sacrifice to Christ's. The sacrament not only refers to the dynamic sacrifice of Christ, but reminds the community of faith— the church—of its obligation to engage in self-sacrificing acts of love in imitation of Christ. The followers of Jesus offer up to God all their thoughts, words, and actions, "through the Son of his love, as a sacrifice of praise and thanksgiving."[38] Participation in the sacrament mandates that all take up the cross, thereby permitting God to form them into cruciform followers of the Lamb through the power of the Spirit.

Charles describes this sacrificial character of the Christian life, in which the worshiper participates repeatedly at the table of the Lord, and clarifies its relationship to the sacrifice of Christ:

> While faith th' atoning blood applies,
> Ourselves a living sacrifice
>   We freely offer up to God:
> And none but those his glory share
> Who crucified with Jesus are,
>   And follow where their Saviour trod.

> Saviour, to thee our lives we give,
> Our meanest sacrifice receive,
>   And to thy own oblation join,
> Our suffering and triumphant head,
> Thro' all thy states thy members lead,
>   And seat us on the throne divine.[39]

Second, *Holy Communion is a celebration of the presence of the living Christ.* The Wesleys associated this present dimension most closely with the sacrament as a "sign and means" of grace. Without any question, the earliest Eucharistic feasts of the Christian community, at which the disciples of Jesus "ate their food with glad and generous hearts" (Acts 2:46), were characterized by joy and thanksgiving. Charles Wesley captured that primitive spirit of *eucharistia* or thanksgiving:

> JESU, WE THUS OBEY
> Thy last and kindest word,
> Here in thine own appointed way
> We come to meet our Lord;
> The way thou hast injoin'd
> Thou wilt therein appear:
> We come with confidence to find
> Thy special presence here.
>
> OUR HEARTS WE OPEN WIDE
> To make the Saviour room:
> And lo! the Lamb, the crucified,
> The sinner's friend, is come!
> His presence makes the feast,
> And now our bosoms feel
> The glory not to be exprest,
> The joy unspeakable.[40]

Through faith, the Wesleys believed, the outward sign transmits the signified. Those who believe meet Jesus at the table, and the heights to which faith can move them are immeasurable:

> The joy is more unspeakable,
> And yields me larger draughts of God,
> 'Till nature faints beneath the power,
> And faith fill'd up can hold no more.[41]

Excursus on Presence

The sacrament, according to the Wesleys, effects what it represents. According to Rattenbury, "an examination of the hymns will result quite frequently in the discovery of allusions to the 'real Presence' of Christ, but it is always a *personal* Presence."[42] One of Charles's hymns illustrates this well:

> O thou who this mysterious bread
> Didst in Emmaus break,
> Return herewith our souls to feed,
> And to thy followers speak.
>
> Unseal the volume of thy grace,
> Apply the gospel-word;
> Open our eyes to see thy face,
> Our hearts to know the Lord.
>
> Of thee communing still, we mourn
> Till thou the veil remove;
> Talk with us, and our hearts shall burn
> With flames of fervent love.
>
> Inkindle now the heavenly zeal,
> And make thy mercy known,
> And give our pardon'd souls to feel
> That God and love are one.[43]

While advocating what could be described with integrity as a "real presence," the Wesleys denied any position approaching "transubstantiation."[44] Ole Borgen described this Wesleyan concept of real presence as a "dynamic" or "living presence," affirming that "wherever God acts, there God is."[45] Essentially beyond the possibility of rational explanation, Charles declared the depths of this holy mystery:

> O the depth of love divine,
> Th' unfathomable grace!

Who shall say how bread and wine
God into man conveys?
How the bread his flesh imparts,
How the wine transmits his blood,
Fills his faithful people's hearts
With all the life of God!

Let the wisest mortal shew
How we the grace receive:
Feeble elements bestow
A power not theirs to give:
Who explains the wondrous way?
How thro' these the virtue came?
These the virtue did convey,
Yet still remain the same.

Sure and real is the grace,
The manner be unknown;
Only meet us in thy ways
And perfect us in one,
Let us taste the heavenly powers,
Lord, we ask for nothing more;
Thine to bless, 'tis only ours
To wonder, and adore.[46]

Third, *Holy Communion is a pledge of the heavenly banquet to come.* The holy meal anticipates the glorious reunion of the faithful at the heavenly feast. As the writer to the Hebrews claims, "we are surrounded by a great cloud of witnesses" (Heb. 12:1), and at no time does the reality of this communion of saints forcefully impress itself upon the present church as in the celebration of Holy Communion. The Wesleys spoke often of the sacrament as a foretaste of this banquet, an earnest, or pledge, of things to come. Their rediscovery of "the communion of the saints" in relationship to this Holy Communion was a significant contribution they made to the sacramental theology of their own day. Hope became the keynote of this future dimension of the sacrament in John's preaching and Charles's poetry.

"By faith and hope already there," sings Charles, "Ev'n now the marriage-feast we share."[47] This is a "soul-transporting feast" that "bears us now on eagles' wings" and "seals our eternal bliss."[48] The amazing imagery in Charles's lyrical theology reflects his vision of the church as a community of hope:

> How glorious is the life above
>   Which in this ordinance we *taste*;
> That fulness of celestial love,
>   That joy which shall for ever last!
>
> The light of life eternal darts
>   Into our souls a dazling ray,
> A drop of heav'n o'erflows our hearts,
>   And deluges the house of clay.
>
> Sure pledge of extacies unknown
>   Shall this divine communion be,
> The ray shall rise into a sun,
>   The drop shall swell into a sea.[49]

The Wesleys employ these various dimensions in an effort to communicate the depth and breadth of meaning in the sacrament and to enrich the experience of the participants. In this sign-act of love, the past, present, and future—faith, hope, and love—are compressed, as it were, into a timeless, communal act of praise. The fullness of the Christian faith is celebrated in the mystery of a holy meal and the people of God are empowered to faithful ministry and service. As faithful disciples repeatedly participate in the Eucharistic actions of taking, blessing, breaking, and giving—the constitutive aspects of an authentic, sacrificial life—God conforms them to the image of Christ.

Conclusion

John Wesley's published letter of 6 January 1756 to William Law enunciated the central principle upon which the founders of Methodism constructed their theology of the sacraments:

All the externals of religion are in order to the renewal of our soul in righteousness and true holiness. But it is not true that the external way is one and the internal way another. There is but one scriptural way wherein we receive inward grace—through the outward means which God hath appointed.[50]

While the Wesleys wrote little about baptism, assuming both its centrality and importance for the Christian life, they affirmed the initiatory role of this sacrament. They viewed this sign-act of grace as the initial step in a process that shapes a beloved child into a disciple of Jesus. The Wesleyan movement of renewal was both an evangelical and a Eucharistic revival. Methodist spirituality revolved around the Sacrament of the Lord's Supper. The Wesleys believed that, in this sign-act of love, the Spirit meets disciples at their point of need and enables them to grow into the fullest possible love of God and others in this life.

NOTES

1. Some of the more recent works that touch upon this theme include Paul W. Chilcote, *The Wesleyan Tradition: A Paradigm for Renewal* (Nashville: Abingdon Press, 2002); Leon O. Hynson, *To Reform the Nation* (Grand Rapids, MI: Francis Asbury Press, 1984); Howard A. Snyder, *Signs of the Spirit: How God Reshapes the Church* (Grand Rapids, MI: Academic Books, 1989); and Howard A. Snyder, *The Radical Wesley and Patterns for Church Renewal* (Downers Grove, IL: InterVarsity, 1980).
2. John and Charles Wesley, *Hymns and Sacred Poems* (Bristol: Farley, 1742), 79–80 ("Groaning for Redemption," pt. 3, hymn 10).
3. See John Wesley's sermon "Upon the Lord's Sermon on the Mount IV," in *The Works of John Wesley*, ed. Albert C. Outler (Nashville: Abingdon Press, 1984), 1:531–49 (hereafter cited as Wesley, *Works*).
4. Wesley, *Works*, 9:69, quoted from Wesley's *The Nature, Design, and General Rules, of the United Societies*.
5. On the Wesleys' general sacramentology, see Ole Borgen, *John Wesley on the Sacraments* (Nashville: Abingdon Press, 1972); John Parris, *John Wesley's Doctrine of the Sacraments* (London: Epworth Press, 1963); Rob Staples, *Outward Sign and Inward Grace: The Place of Sacraments in Wesleyan Spirituality* (Kansas City: Beacon Hill, 1991); and Geoffrey Wainwright, "The Sacraments in Wesleyan Perspective," *Doxology* 5 (1988): 5–20.
6. In his "Preface to the *Hymns and Sacred Poems*" of 1739, in *The Works of John Wesley*, ed. Thomas Jackson (London: Wesleyan Methodist Book Room, 1872), 14:321.
7. Thomas Jackson, ed., *The Journal of Charles Wesley* (London: John Mason, 1849), 1:450.

8. Borgen, *Wesley on the Sacraments*, 122.
9. Wesley, *Works*, 1:381, from Wesley's sermon "The Means of Grace (II.1)." The classic statement is "an outward and visible sign of an inward and spiritual grace."
10. John Wesley, *The Sunday Service of the Methodists in North America* (London: [William Strahan], 1784), 311. He reproduced article XXV of the *39 Articles of Religion* from the *Book of Common Prayer* (1662) nearly verbatim. Of the six articles that deal with the sacraments, Wesley omitted articles XXVI, "Of the Unworthiness of the Ministers, Which Hinders Not the Effect of the Sacrament," and XXIX, "Of the Wicked Which Eat Not the Body of Christ in the Use of the Lord's Supper."
11. On the Wesleys' theology of baptism, see Gayle C. Felton, *This Gift of Water: The Practice and Theology of Baptism among Methodists in America* (Nashville: Abingdon Press, 1992); Bernard Holland, *Baptism in Early Methodism* (London: Epworth Press, 1970); Brian Galliers, "The Theology of Baptism in the Writings of John Wesley" (MA thesis, Leeds University, 1957); and Paul Sanders, "John Wesley and Baptismal Regeneration," *Religion in Life* 23 (1953–54): 591–603.
12. Robert E. Cushman, "Baptism and the Family of God," in *The Doctrine of the Church*, ed. Dow Kirkpatrick (Nashville: Abingdon Press, 1964), 82.
13. In addition, Wesley's *Sunday Service* contains liturgical texts for both sacraments, but this work provides little additional guidance in these matters.
14. The full text of the original Anglican article XXVII, "Of Baptism," reads, "Baptism is not only a sign of profession, and mark of difference, whereby Christians are discerned from others that are not christened, but it is also a sign of regeneration, or the new birth, whereby, as by an instrument, they that receive Baptism rightly are grafted into the Church; the promises of the forgiveness of sin, and of our adoption to be the sons of God by the Holy Ghost, are visibly signed and sealed; Faith is confirmed, and Grace increased by virtue of prayer unto God. The Baptism of young children is in any wise to be retained in the church, as most agreeable with the institution of Christ."
15. Quoted in Felton, *This Gift of Water*, 19.
16. See Felton's discussion of Wesleyan baptismal practice in *This Gift of Water*, 13–25.
17. Charles Wesley, MS Matthew, 221. The text of this hymn is cited from "Wesley and Methodist Texts and Research Resources" of the Center for Studies in the Wesleyan Tradition, Duke Divinity School, as is the case for all other Charles Wesley texts in this chapter.
18. Felton, *This Gift of Water*, 44–45.
19. Wesley, *Works*, 7:647–48, originally published in *Hymns and Sacred Poems* (1749), II, 246 (hymn 418).
20. Albert C. Outler, ed., *John Wesley* (New York: Oxford University Press, 1964), 318.
21. Brian Galliers, "The Theology of Baptism in the Writings of John Wesley," *Proceedings of the Wesley Historical Society* 32 (1960): 123.
22. Charles Wesley, *Hymns for the Use of Families* (Bristol: Pine, 1767), 63–64 (hymn 62).

23. On the Wesleys' Eucharistic theology, see John Bowmer, *The Sacrament of the Lord's Supper in Early Methodism* (London: Dacre Press, 1951); Egil Grislis, "The Wesleyan Doctrine of the Last Supper," *Duke Divinity School Review* 28 (1963): 99–110; J. Ernest Rattenbury, *The Eucharistic Hymns of John and Charles Wesley* (London: Epworth Press, 1948; and Paul Sanders, "Wesley's Eucharistic Faith and Practice," *Doxology* 5 (1988): 21–34.
24. John and Charles Wesley, *Hymns on the Lord's Supper* (Bristol: Printed by Felix Farley, 1745), 31 (hymn 42:2–6).
25. Wesley, *Sunday Service*, ii.
26. See John Wesley's sermon "On the Means of Grace," in Wesley, *Works*, 1:376–97.
27. Wesley and Wesley, *Hymns on the Lord's Supper*, 39 (hymn 54:4).
28. See Bowmer, *Sacrament of the Lord's Supper*, 55–61.
29. Ibid., 188–89.
30. Wesley, *Works*, 3:427–39. This sermon was a distillation of at least two earlier tracts on the sacrament, published by the Anglican divines Robert Nelson ("The Great Duty of Frequenting the Christian Sacrifice") and Arthur Bury ("The Constant Communicant") in the seventeenth century, but extensively edited, expanded, and adapted by Wesley to make them his own.
31. Wesley, *Works*, 3:439.
32. Quoted in S. T. Kimbrough, Jr., *Lost in Wonder: Charles Wesley, the Meaning of His Hymns Today* (Nashville: Upper Room Books, 1987), 11–12.
33. This collection of hymns, properly described as a liturgical classic, went through nine editions during the lifetime of the brothers and was one of their primary means to revive the Eucharistic life of the Church of England. In addition to the full reprinting of the hymns in Rattenbury, *Eucharistic Hymns*, 195–249, see the facsimile reprint of the first edition, published by the Charles Wesley Society (Madison, NJ) in 1995 to mark its 250th anniversary, introduced by Geoffrey Wainwright. Daniel Brevint, dean of Lincoln Cathedral during the Restoration, emphasized a high view of the sacramental presence of Christ, the sacrificial (albeit anti-Catholic) character of the sacrament, and the benefits of Holy Communion.
34. Wesley's article XVI, drawn with only minimal changes from the *Book of Common Prayer*, maintained that "the Supper of the Lord is not only a sign of the love that Christians ought to have among themselves one to another, but rather is a sacrament of our redemption by Christ's death; insomuch, that to such as rightly, worthily, and with faith receive the same, the bread which we break is a partaking of the body of Christ; and likewise the cup of blessing is a partaking of the blood of Christ" (Wesley, *Sunday Service*, 311).
35. Wesley and Wesley, *Hymns on the Lord's Supper*, 1 (hymn 1:1).
36. Ibid., 2 (hymn 1:5).
37. Ibid., 16 (hymn 21:2, 3).
38. Wesley, *Works*, 3:76, from Wesley's sermon "On Perfection (I.11)."
39. Wesley and Wesley, *Hymns on the Lord's Supper*, 110 (hymn 128:3).

40. Ibid., 69 (hymn 81:1, 2).
41. Ibid., 39 (hymn 54:5).
42. Rattenbury, *Eucharistic Hymns*, 59.
43. Wesley and Wesley, *Hymns on the Lord's Supper*, 22–23 (hymn 29).
44. John Wesley left the statement on this issue untouched in his edited *Articles of Religion* from the *Book of Common Prayer*: "Transubstantiation, or the change of the substance of bread and wine in the Supper of our Lord, cannot be proved by Holy Writ, but is repugnant to the plain words of Scripture, overthroweth the nature of a sacrament, and hath given occasion to many superstitions" (article XVIII, Wesley, *Sunday Service*, 311).
45. See Borgen, *Wesley on the Sacraments*, 58–69.
46. Wesley and Wesley, *Hymns on the Lord's Supper*, 41 (hymn 57:1–2, 4).
47. Ibid., 82 (hymn 93:4).
48. Ibid., 82–83 (hymn 94:1, 3, 4).
49. Ibid., 87 (hymn 101:1, 3, 4).
50. John Wesley, *The Letters of the Rev. John Wesley, A.M.*, ed. John Telford (London: Epworth Press, 1931), 3:366–67.

16

Friedrich Schleiermacher

PAUL T. NIMMO

Friedrich Schleiermacher (1768–1834) was born in Breslau in Silesia (now Wrocław in Poland). His father was a Reformed pastor with a strong connection to the Moravian community, thus the young Schleiermacher was educated at Pietist institutions in Niesky and Barby (both now in eastern Germany). However, Schleiermacher became increasingly dissatisfied with the restricted Moravian curriculum, and desired to continue his education at a more progressive institution. He enrolled in 1787 at the University of Halle, a stronghold of Enlightenment thinking, where he studied Plato, Aristotle, and Kant. He spent some years thereafter in a combination of personal study, ordination training, and private tutoring, before taking his first pastoral charge in 1796 as the Reformed preacher at the Charité hospital in Berlin. Schleiermacher flourished in the vibrant Prussian capital, finding friends within its cultured salon society and its creative, Romantic circles. In 1799, he published his famous apologetic work *Speeches on Religion to the Cultured among Its Despisers*. After a brief period in a further pastoral charge in Stolp in Pomerania (now Słupsk in Poland), he was appointed extraordinary professor and university preacher at the University of Halle in 1804, but the university was closed in 1806 following the city's occupation by Napoleon. Returning to Berlin, where he spent the remainder of his days, Schleiermacher was active in three principal domains. First, from 1809 he was a minister at the Dreifaltigkeitskirche (Trinity Church). He preached weekly, and was heavily involved in the conversation and controversy surrounding the union of Lutheran and Reformed churches in Prussia, a union he advocated and defended. Second, in 1810 he became a founding professor of the University of Berlin. Within the Faculty of Theology, he lectured on dogmatics, ethics, exegesis, hermeneutics, church history, and practical theology, and served as dean of the faculty and as rector of the university. In this connection, he produced two editions of his landmark dogmatic work, *Christian Faith*. Third, he was actively interested in political matters, particularly in the areas of education policy and constitutional matters. At times the Prussian state sought to capitalize upon this interest, but at other times viewed it with suspicion. In 1834, while still deeply active on all fronts, Schleiermacher died of pneumonia, five years after the death of his only son. Thousands attended his funeral procession.

Introduction

Friedrich Schleiermacher is one of the most significant theologians of the post-Enlightenment period. His work exhibits the marks of his Pietist upbringing, his rationalist education, and his Romantic connections, and also reflects his training as a Reformed theologian and his vocation as a Reformed preacher. But above all, his work signals him as one of the most original and creative thinkers of his era—a scholar-preacher seeking to locate and explain the importance of Christian faith and Christian theology in the context of an increasingly skeptical era. His work would strongly influence later generations of scholars not only within the subject of theology but also within the disciplines of exegesis, hermeneutics, ethics, philosophy, and pedagogy.

Central—foundational, even—to the theology of Schleiermacher is the Christian community's experience of redemption in Jesus Christ. Formally, this experience relates principally not to the human faculties of knowing or doing, such that the discipline of theology could proceed along the lines of metaphysics or ethics, but to the human capacity for feeling: it is the immediate self-consciousness that is the seat of piety and thus of the human consciousness of being in relation to God. Materially, this experience relates exclusively to the historical person of Jesus Christ and the living influence that he continues to exert over the community of the church. In redemption, Christians are assumed into the power of Christ's perfect God-consciousness and the communion of Christ's unclouded blessedness. For Schleiermacher, Christian doctrines do not derive from Scripture or tradition, but offer an account of the religious affections of the Christian community that correspond to this redemption in Christ. It is from this starting point that Schleiermacher develops his major work *Christian Faith*.[1]

The purpose of this chapter is to explore the way in which, on the basis of this highly innovative starting point, Schleiermacher conceives of the sacraments of the Christian community. Though his sacramental theology has been somewhat overlooked in much of the secondary literature,[2] Schleiermacher offers substantive and sustained presentations of both baptism and Eucharist.[3]

Before embarking on such a detailed study, however, it is important to draw attention to two important contextual considerations that shape his sacramental thinking. First, Schleiermacher self-consciously locates himself within the magisterial Protestant tradition of Luther and Calvin. On the one hand, then, he is keen to avoid any view of the sacraments that would resemble Roman Catholic teaching, for example an automatic efficacy of the sacraments or a transubstantiation of the Eucharistic elements. On the other hand, however, he is keen to avoid any view of the sacraments that would echo sacramentarian teaching; for example, in undervaluing or rejecting the significance of the sacraments. These divergent conceptions he respectively describes as "magical" and "empirical"; and as will be seen, Schleiermacher seeks a middle ground. Second, Schleiermacher lived in an era of great change for the Protestant churches in Prussia: the king decreed a controversial union of Reformed and Lutheran churches in 1817, and mandated a common liturgy for use in the newly united churches in 1822. These moves caused much tension and dissent.[4] The sacraments, a source of division between Reformed and Lutheran perspectives, posed a significant obstacle to the union on both doctrinal and liturgical grounds. Schleiermacher, a firm supporter of the union, thus sought to present a theology of the sacraments that demonstrated to both parties within the newly united church the lack of justification for any separation of the church community.

With this contextual background in mind, this chapter proceeds by focusing on sections 127 and 136–43 of Schleiermacher's *Christian Faith* in order to offer a close reading of his doctrine of baptism and his doctrine of the Eucharist. The chapter concludes with a consideration of the significant features and constructive potential of Schleiermacher's work on the sacraments for contemporary theology.

The Essential and Invariable Features of the Church

In *Christian Faith*, the doctrines of baptism and the Eucharist are found within the doctrine of the church, making their initial appearance in a paragraph introducing the "essential and invariable features" of the church.[5] Six such features are identified: Scripture, the ordained ministry, baptism, the Eucharist, church authority, and prayer.[6] These features ensure that, despite all the changes that affect it in its relation to the world, the Christian community in its "relation to Christ and to [the holy] Spirit is always and everywhere self-identical."[7]

This emphasis upon the constancy of the church and its preservation by these essential and invariable features stems from Schleiermacher's insistence that the Christian faith be the same across time and space. For Schleiermacher, it is crucial that "our Christianity should be the same as that of the Apostles."[8] In the time of the Gospels, the beginning and the growth of Christian faith took place as individuals came into direct contact with Jesus Christ. Recognizing, however, that "we have nothing more to expect from direct personal influences of Christ," Schleiermacher posits that in the present time, "the establishment and renewal of the communion of life with Christ must come from the church and be traced back to its actions."[9]

It is at this point that the sacraments find their place: the actions that establish and preserve communion of life with Christ in the present day are, respectively, baptism and the Eucharist. In respect of the *establishment* of this communion, Schleiermacher recognizes that baptism as originally instituted was not always the first point of contact between the church and an individual. Nevertheless, he contends that it is only through baptism that everything that precedes it is confirmed in such a way that a continuity of communion of life with Christ begins. In respect of the *preservation* of this communion, Schleiermacher recognizes that the Eucharist is not the only possible means. Nevertheless, he contends that it is the highest of its kind, and that every other kind of participation in Christ merely approximates or continues this communion.[10] The result is that the church will remain always and everywhere self-identical, according to Schleiermacher, "in so far as the establishment and preservation of communion of life with Christ is founded on [these] ordinances of Christ."[11]

Though baptism and the Eucharist are clearly activities of the Christian community, Schleiermacher insists that they are not simply human activities: instead, the sacraments "are to be regarded as activities of Christ," such that "Christ in no way behaves passively in this connection or stands in the shade of the church."[12] There is thus no conflict necessary, for Schleiermacher, between understanding the sacraments as acts of the Christian community and understanding the sacraments as acts of Christ; indeed, such a dual perspective is central to his understanding of their role in the Christian life.

The Doctrine of Baptism

In the thesis with which Schleiermacher opens his doctrine of baptism, he neatly rehearses this dual concept of the sacraments. On the one hand, he describes baptism "as an act of the church [which] identifies the act of will by means of which the church receives the individual into the community."[13] On the other hand, he states that "at the same time, in so far as the effective promise of Christ rests upon it, it is the medium of the justifying divine activity, by which the individual is taken up into communion of life with Christ."[14] The outward form and the inward purpose of the act are united by the fact that baptism arises in the church as an institution of Jesus Christ. For this reason, Schleiermacher notes, "every such reception [of an individual in baptism] is an act of Christ himself, if it is performed in the manner instructed by him and in accordance with his command," and, in such cases, "[Christ's] promise will be fulfilled that with this reception there begins the blessedness of the individual."[15] This is true even if, as Schleiermacher contends, "no information can be demanded or given as to whether and how the external content and purpose of this action is connected with the inner content and purpose of the same."[16]

This seems to be a very robust view of baptism, equating the external, church act of baptism with the internal, spiritual event of conversion. But Schleiermacher quickly acknowledges that this view represents the ideal of the sacrament and not necessarily its reality. The *ideal* situation presupposes that the whole, undivided church agrees to baptize the individual, and that the individual is as spiritually mature and ready for communion of life with Christ as the apostles at their calling. The *real* situation of baptism, by contrast, is that the church is divided in its administration and imperfect in its activity, and that the exact moment of individual regeneration may not coincide with the event of baptism.[17]

There are two important consequences for Schleiermacher of this distinction between the ideality and the reality of baptism. First, as Schleiermacher notes, "what would be an absolutely simple [thing] under the presupposition of the perfection of the church now disintegrates into two series, which also finish in two different moments."[18] The external event of baptism in the church and the internal event of regeneration by the Spirit may not coincide; indeed, the New Testament witnesses to many instances of this. However this does not mean, for Schleiermacher, that the connection between the two is severed: by contrast, if the Spirit works first, there exists an "imperative demand" to have baptism—as reception into the community—follow immediately, and if baptism occurs first, this is legitimated only by the assured belief, on the basis of activity of the church, that the "regeneration of the one received [in baptism] will follow from the influences of the community."[19] Second, as Schleiermacher observes, "the simple result is how widely views of the value and efficacy of baptism can vary," without any of these views legitimately being described as "unchristian."[20] At one extreme of the range of views, then, it is quite acceptable to claim that the event of baptism effects no inward change in the individual, on the basis that there is no necessary temporal coincidence of baptism and regeneration. This would represent a rather low view of baptism, and Schleiermacher here provides a quotation from Zwingli in the footnotes. However, Schleiermacher continues, it would be wrong to conclude from the (imperfect) state of affairs that such a position represents a complete statement of Christian baptism: "baptism should . . . be evoked by the activity of the Spirit and should always be intimately connected with the same."[21] At the other extreme of the range of views, moreover, it is quite acceptable to claim that regeneration and baptism are "essentially connected with each other and mutually conditioned," such that "one and the same series of church activities has the dual end of baptism and regeneration."[22] Such would represent a rather high view of baptism, perhaps with affinities to Lutheran and Roman Catholic views, though Schleiermacher cites no sources here. However, he continues, this position holds only for the ideal state of affairs; furthermore, the idea that God must of necessity justify one who has been baptized Schleiermacher calls "monstrous."[23]

At this point in his presentation, Schleiermacher has indicated the limits of acceptable church teaching on baptism. In what follows, he proceeds to develop a more precise exposition of baptism within these two limits by way of advancing two propositions. It is noticeable that in the case of each proposition, he proceeds by prefacing his discussion with a series of relevant quotations from various Protestant confessional documents.

The first proposition is that "baptism bestows both citizenship in the Christian church and blessedness in connection with the divine grace in regeneration."[24] The connection between reception into the church, justification/regeneration, and baptism has already been noted above: it is only within the church that the communion of life with Christ finds (its full) realization, and only in baptism in the church that the communion with Christ and the communion with the church find (their full) confirmation. But Schleiermacher immediately observes that in the Lutheran and Reformed confessional statements, which preface this discussion, there is disagreement on how much efficacy to ascribe to baptism at this point. Here, Schleiermacher aligns himself with the "side ascribing most to baptism."[25] First, he posits that the efficacy of baptism is not dependent upon the morality or orthodoxy of the one baptizing, because the act is ultimately an act of the church (or at least intends to be such), and thus any baptism is valid for all churches. Second, he posits that the efficacy of baptism is not dependent upon a particular form of liturgy or ritual being used, though all acts of baptism should include a presentation of the Word of God to those being baptized and their acknowledgment of the same: without these, the baptism would be incomplete.[26] This last point indicates that, for Schleiermacher, faith is presupposed in baptism; indeed, he declares that "baptism is received wrongly if it is received without faith—it is also not given rightly."[27] By contrast, when baptism is given and received rightly, that is, in faith, then it can indeed be said to "effect blessedness . . . in so far as it fulfils the reception [of the believer] into the community."[28] Schleiermacher posits clearly at this point that the inception of the Christian life embraces aspects—such as faith, conversion, regeneration, and baptism—that can be separated in concept but cannot be separated in practice. Depending then, upon the *way* in which these interrelated aspects are conceived, different theological positions can be advanced. In this light, Schleiermacher revisits the Lutheran and Reformed statements cited previously, which on first inspection appear to break into two antithetical camps, and suggests that "our paragraph [on baptism] is the reconciliation of both types of confessional expression."[29]

The second proposition is that "infant baptism is only a complete baptism if one considers the confession of faith which arrives after education is completed as the final act belonging to it."[30] Again, he introduces this paragraph with a series of relevant statements from Protestant confessions. In light of his earlier insistence on the necessity of faith in baptism, it is no surprise that Schleiermacher finds it difficult to defend the practice. This difficulty is enhanced given that he finds there to be no New Testament evidence for the practice, and considers the Protestant defenses in the confessions to proceed "in an inadequate manner and on grounds which cancel each other out."[31] Ultimately, Schleiermacher can justify infant baptism only on the grounds that in the case of the children of Christian parents, "there is reason to count on their future faith and on the confession of the same."[32] For this reason, then, infant baptism is similar to any other baptism given "early," before regeneration has taken place; for this reason also, infant baptism must be completed by confirmation in later life for it to satisfy Christ's institution. Correspondingly, the church is to pay close attention to the importance of the education and confirmation of its young people. Yet it is clear that Schleiermacher remains uneasy, writing, "at the time of the Reformation, one could very reasonably have abandoned infant baptism . . . and we could do this even now without thereby seceding from the community in that period."[33]

The Doctrine of the Eucharist

Schleiermacher then moves to consider the doctrine of the Eucharist. He begins his reflections with the following thesis: "Christians experience in participation in the Eucharist a particular strengthening of the spiritual life, as in it—according to the institution of Christ—His body and His blood are offered to them."[34] The reference to the experience of the Christian relates back to Schleiermacher's emphasis on the Christian religious affections as the source of church doctrines. He explains that "we must start here with the experience which we ourselves have of this action and . . . which we also expect all believers to have."[35] It is evident right from the outset, therefore, that for Schleiermacher the Eucharist has a very profound corporate dimension.

For Schleiermacher, the relationships of the individual with Christ and with the church that are begun in baptism require "to be periodically supported and strengthened."[36] It is clear that the former, the communion with Christ, can be nourished by devout meditation on Christ with the aid of Scripture, while the latter, the communion with the Christian community, can be nourished by powerful and moving demonstrations of Christian love in the common life.[37] However, according to Schleiermacher, what public worship in general, and the Eucharist in particular, effect is both a strengthening and a uniting of these two communions. And thus Schleiermacher writes of the Eucharist that "Christ instituted it as a corporate action, and if at the same time as a making-present of himself, so also certainly as a strengthening of both communions."[38]

Two points of investigation immediately follow for Schleiermacher. First, Schleiermacher explores how the Eucharist relates to public worship as a whole. Here, he observes that the whole tradition has from the start "considered the Eucharist as the highest pinnacle of public worship," and that the circle of our gathered worship would appear "incomplete" to us without the Eucharist taking its place as the most intimate bond of both communions.[39] Here alone, the relationship of the two communions—of the believer with Christ and of the believers as a community—is perfectly in balance, with neither the community nor the individual dominating. The result, Schleiermacher asserts, is that "we are directed simply to the complete redeeming love of Christ," and find ourselves "in the state of the most open receptivity for the influences of Christ."[40] Far from the Eucharist simply being an activity of the church, then, or even of the presiding celebrant, there is here a real activity of Christ. Schleiermacher explains,

> Every effect proceeds . . . immediately and indivisibly from the Word of institution, in which the redeeming and community-founding love of Christ not only represents itself but always stirs itself powerfully anew,

and in confident obedience to which the action [of the community] itself is performed every time.[41]

The power of the Eucharist is thus not the power of the community, although it is mediated by the community: the power of the Eucharist is the power of the Word that instantiates and communicates the love of Christ afresh for the community. The difference in this view between the Eucharist and the other aspects of public worship is certainly one of degree only; nevertheless, on account of its "indivisible and exclusive immediacy" and of the "consequent independence of its efficacy from changing personal circumstances and relations," the Eucharist retains here a particular significance over other aspects of public worship.[42] Second, Schleiermacher explores how our spiritual participation in the body and blood of Christ relates to the material participation in bread and wine in the Eucharist. He first acknowledges readily once again that "spiritual participation in the body [of Christ] can take place more generally in all kinds of ways."[43] At the same time, however, he once again asserts firmly that the Eucharist is distinct insofar as the result—spiritual participation in the body of Christ—"is bound to [a] particular action that is blessed and sanctified by the Word of Christ."[44] The difficulty lies in offering an account of the relationship between the two actions. This issue, Schleiermacher observes, is not merely exegetical: if it were, he notes, "the teaching of doctrine could wait the end of hermeneutical negotiations and then accept the result."[45] The issue is also historical, for it involves the need to ascertain the actual words Christ used to institute the Eucharist.[46] And finally, the issue is also theological, as is evidenced by the variety of different opinions extant among Protestants as to how to express this Eucharistic relationship.

In respect to the diversity of Protestant views of the Eucharist— evidenced by the quotations from various Protestant confessional documents with which he once again prefaces his discussion—Schleiermacher observes that his task is to "present the conviction underlying the union [of Lutheran and Reformed churches in Prussia] . . . that the differences [in Eucharistic doctrine] cannot hinder the commonality of participation."[47] His reflections on the Eucharist are thus, once again, marked by generosity of spirit, seeking not to ignore Protestant disunity on the

Eucharist, but rather to explore this disunity critically, to indicate that it has limits, and to posit that it should not be church dividing.

Schleiermacher proceeds by way of indicating the legitimate extent of positions within the Protestant church. His basic criterion in view is as follows: "any explanation [of the words of institution] which is able to prove itself hermeneutically can be correct for us, in so far as it does not endanger for the believer the connection between the action and the result."[48] This last clause is crucial, for whenever this connection between the Eucharistic action and the spiritual result is severed, Schleiermacher will object. On the one hand, then, Schleiermacher writes that the Protestant church categorically opposes those "who view the relationship [of material and spiritual participation] as independent of the act of participation."[49] Explicitly in view here, for Schleiermacher, is Roman Catholic teaching, and not so much the doctrine of transubstantiation per se but the perdurance of the transubstantiated elements outside the Eucharistic act. To separate the Eucharistic elements from the Eucharistic action is, he writes, "to attach magical spiritual effects to the bodily [effects]."[50] On the other hand, however, Schleiermacher writes that the Protestant church categorically opposes those "who . . . do not desire to admit any connection [between material and spiritual participation]."[51] Explicitly in view here, for Schleiermacher, is sacramentarian teaching—teaching that, in all its varieties, rejects the sacrament and/or the connection between taking bread and wine materially in the Eucharist and participating spiritually in the body and blood of Christ. In opposition to such,[52] Schleiermacher writes, "we trust the Word of Christ, that . . . by His power . . . every believer dependably finds spiritual participation in the sacramental action."[53] All the theological ground between these two extremes—between "ascribing a magical value to the Eucharist . . . [and] reducing it to a mere sign"[54]—is left to the Protestant church.

It is on this middle ground that Schleiermacher locates the historic positions of the Protestant church: the Lutheran, tending toward the Roman Catholic view; the Zwinglian, running closer to the sacramentarian view; and the Calvinist, offering a mediating view. Schleiermacher recognizes that these different positions persist, and that, resting on different interpretations of the institution of the Eucharist in Scripture, they offer different views of the relationship between the material action of the Eucharist and the spiritual action of participation. However, he considers that not one of them is able to explain fully the relationships involved in the Eucharist.[55] Instead, Schleiermacher optimistically concludes that "it is to be expected that, on the basis of the continued unprejudiced work of the interpreters, a still further [conception] will develop, which will not be shipwrecked on all these cliffs."[56]

Alongside their disagreements, the three classic Protestant positions—at least according to Schleiermacher—all agree as to "the effects of the Eucharist."[57] Schleiermacher briefly deals in turn with both the positive and the negative dimensions of these shared views. The first (positive) doctrine that Schleiermacher explores is that "participation in the body and blood of Christ in the Eucharist redounds to all believers in the strengthening of their communion with Christ."[58] For all their diversity of language, according to Schleiermacher, the various Protestant confessions emphasize that "in the sacrament there is renewed and strengthened the forgiveness of sins, . . . [and] that we then experience an advance of the powers of sanctification."[59] Schleiermacher is broadly content with this view, although he explicitly laments the way in which the Protestant confessions deal with the issue by considering "every individual participant only as [an individual]."[60] It is by way of addition, then, that Schleiermacher includes a communal perspective in his modification of this position. He observes explicitly that the strengthening of our communion with Christ in the Eucharist includes "the strengthening of Christians in their union with one another," for "the union of the individual with Christ is not to be thought without her union with believers."[61] The second (negative) doctrine that Schleiermacher explores is that "unworthy participation in the Eucharist redounds to the partaker as judgement."[62] About this idea Schleiermacher is more hesitant, observing that "it is difficult to have a specific idea of where the unworthiness should arise."[63] The best that he can do is to posit that participation is unworthy when it takes place "without the desire for this participation being stimulated . . . by consciousness of [an] imperfect spiritual state."[64] Nevertheless, Schleiermacher refuses to allow that such unworthy participation be connected in any way with eternal damnation.[65]

The Sacraments as a Category

In a final appendix, Schleiermacher considers the term "sacrament" itself. He posits that "one might foster the wish even more unconditionally than Zwingli that this term would better not have been taken up into the language of the church, and consequently [the wish] that it might be removed once again."[66] Methodologically, however, Schleiermacher observes that "we have treated baptism and the Eucharist in themselves and without any special relation to the term [sacrament]."[67] Such a procedure evidently differs markedly from one that starts out with a conception of the sacrament and then seeks to derive a theology of the individual sacraments from this prescriptive framework. Schleiermacher concludes that "if the term is still to be used, nothing more is left to us than to mark it in a purely arbitrary way and without any further consideration for its original sense as a communal description for both these institutions."[68]

Conclusion

For all that Schleiermacher fails to accord any material significance to the overarching notion of a sacrament, his treatments of the doctrines of baptism and of the Eucharist share numerous similarities. The most significant of these are identified here by way of recapitulation, with a view to indicating their constructive potential for contemporary sacramental theology.

First, it is important to return to the question of Schleiermacher's intentions. On the one hand, he clearly seeks to identify and align himself with the traditions of the magisterial Protestant Reformers in respect of the sacraments. This is evident in the way he cites a series of Lutheran and Reformed documents and in the way they provide him with his most earnest conversation partners—albeit conversation partners not above reproach. But it is also demonstrated in the way he positions himself against the alternatives to magisterial Protestant views of the sacraments—the "magic" of the Roman Catholic view and the "bareness" of the sacramentarian view. On the other hand, when dealing with views of the sacraments falling within the parameters of the magisterial Reformation, Schleiermacher displays an extraordinary generosity of spirit. Although he is ready to question the adequacy of the works of Luther, Calvin, and Zwingli, he is happy to embrace them all as acceptable alternatives and refuses to see their differences as church dividing. Toward the end of his treatment of the Eucharist, for example, he writes that "it is worth . . . looking back from this point once again at the difference between the Lutheran and the Calvinist conception of the Eucharist, in order to convince ourselves how little it is suited to justifying a separation of the church community."[69] This view is clearly related to his unwavering support for Prussian Church Union. But his generous orthodoxy extends even to those views that he rejects outright: even these are not described as being unchristian but rather have their virtues recognized. This willingness of Schleiermacher to identify with a tradition in an irenic yet not uncritical manner is worthy of admiration and emulation today. The way in which he engaged carefully on the sacraments with Protestant confessions—Reformed and Lutheran—is a feature not only of his Eucharistic theology in particular but of his dogmatic theology in general. Over and against more polemic and aggressive detractors of the Prussian Church Union, Schleiermacher advocated practical unity in the face of doctrinal differences that he acknowledged but did not consider sufficient to jeopardize church community.

Second, it is important to recognize the heart of Schleiermacher's sacramental theology. In eschewing both a "magical" and an "empirical" approach to the sacraments, Schleiermacher sets forth what one might best call a "mystical" view of baptism and the Eucharist.[70] It is a conception rooted in the religious affections of the Christian community in its encounter with the Word of Jesus Christ as witnessed in Scripture. Within this conception, attention is paid in the sacraments not only to the material activity of the church, but also to the spiritual activity of the Redeemer. Though there is certainly no simple identity between the two, nor is there any absolute diastasis: the Christian community is, after all, the community of Christ, and its animating spirit is the Spirit of Christ. Within this conception also, attention is paid in the sacraments not only to the communion of the individual with Christ, but also to the communion of the individual with other believers. Eschewing any individualistic understanding of baptism or the Eucharist, the sacraments are seen, administered, and effective in the context of the Christian community. While baptism pertains to the entering of the individual into the communion of the church and the entering of the individual into communion with Christ, the Eucharist pertains to the preserving and strengthening of these two communions.

This willingness of Schleiermacher to foreground the communal dimension of the sacraments is also worthy of identification and adoption today. For all its reference to the church as the locus of the correct administration of the sacraments, the Protestant tradition in particular has not fared well in the quest to maintain the significance of the horizontal dimension of the sacraments. There is a tendency in Lutheran and Calvinist thought for the community to fade from view at the summit of our sacramental participation, but it is here that Schleiermacher—ironically in company with Zwingli—is able to retain a suitable emphasis on the corporate nature of baptism and the Eucharist.

Finally, it is important to recognize the acknowledged limitations of this view of the sacraments. In respect to both baptism and the Eucharist, Schleiermacher situates his doctrine clearly in relation to particular boundaries and particular confessions, counseling peace with other views that claim the same position. But once there, it seems that Schleiermacher has little by way of a position of his own to advance. On the one hand, he looks forward in hope to progress in scriptural exegesis, historical criticism, and theological understanding of the sacraments paving the way toward greater doctrinal agreement and ecclesial unity in future. On the other hand, he expresses profound reservations about the extent to which it is possible to provide precise information about the connection between the external and physical and the internal and spiritual dimensions of the sacraments.[71] The result is, then, that he moves beyond the Protestant sacramental impasse not so much by ignoring the problem, nor by invoking ineffable mystery, but simply by recognizing the issue, contending that there is more work to be done, and expressing the hope that it will be done and—one day—done successfully. His position is, in one sense, not a position. The boundaries of his theological procedure mean that at this point and at this time, no more can be said. Precisely here, sacramental theology is not all worked out: there remains scope for the legitimate pursuit of questions of exegesis, history, and doctrine. Instead, what is central, for Schleiermacher, is the clear insistence upon the significance of the sacraments at the beginning and in the continuation of the life of Christian discipleship, and in the maintenance of the constancy of the Christian church.

This willingness of Schleiermacher to draw something of a dogmatic veil at a certain point in his elucidation of the sacraments poses a real challenge to theological reflection today. There is implied in it an acknowledgment that at some points in reflecting upon the religious affections of the Christian there may be no discursively elegant and conceptually precise answer. Instead, there may be simply an ongoing and questing drive to explore ever further the ways and means of communion of life with Christ. Perhaps here, then, is his greatest lesson of all: that Christian theology is and remains a provisional and incomplete venture, in which one must sometimes desist from hubris and strive for humility in the attempt to attest and express the mystical nature of the Christian life.

NOTES

1. Friedrich Schleiermacher, *Der christliche Glaube nach den Grundsätzen der evangelischen Kirche im Zusammenhange dargestellt: 2. Auflage* (1830/31), commonly *Glaubenslehre*, 2 vols., ed. Rolf Schäfer (Berlin: Walter de Gruyter, 2008). This (heavily revised) second edition originally appeared in 1830–31, just shy of a decade after the publication of the first edition of the material in 1821–22. The English translation is *The Christian Faith*, ed. H. R. Mackintosh and J. S. Stewart, translated by various (Edinburgh: T&T Clark, 1999). References to this work in what follows are denoted "GL" and include the relevant paragraph and section number, the volume and page number in the German edition, and the corresponding page number in the English translation; the present chapter, however, offers its own translations.
2. For a notable exception, see Martin Ohst's exploration of the Eucharist in *Schleiermacher und die Bekenntnisschriften* (Tübingen: Mohr, 1989), 245–60.
3. The term "Eucharist" is used throughout this chapter as a neutral term of reference.
4. For an excellent English-language account of the process of the Prussian Church Union, see Anette I. Hagan, *Eternal Blessedness for All? A Historical-Systematic Examination of Schleiermacher's Understanding of Predestination* (Eugene, OR: Wipf & Stock, 2013), 27–50.
5. GL §127.Titel, II:309/[ET] 586.
6. GL §127.Lehrsatz, II:309/[ET] 586.
7. GL §126.Lehrsatz, II:303/[ET] 582.
8. GL §127.2, II:311/[ET] 587.
9. GL §127.2, II:312/[ET] 588.

10. GL §127.2, II:312–13/[ET] 589.
11. GL §127.Lehrsatz, II:309/[ET] 586.
12. GL §127.2, II:312/[ET] 587. Correspondingly, Schleiermacher considers baptism and the Eucharist to be related to the priestly office of the Redeemer, GL §127.3, II:315/[ET] 590.
13. GL §136.Lehrsatz, II:353/[ET] 619.
14. Ibid.
15. GL §136.1, II:354/[ET] 620.
16. Ibid.
17. GL §136.3, II:356–57/[ET] 622.
18. GL §136.3, II:357/[ET] 622–23.
19. GL §136.3, II:358/[ET] 623.
20. GL §136.3, II:359/[ET] 623.
21. GL §136.3, II:359/[ET] 624. This noted, Schleiermacher states that not even a position that rejects baptism entirely can be labeled "absolutely unchristian," for "it belittles baptism as something external only to extol the unique value of what is internal, namely regeneration." GL §136.3, II:359/[ET] 625.
22. GL §136.3, II:360/[ET] 625.
23. GL §136.3, II:361/[ET] 626. Though, once again, Schleiermacher states that not even this position can be labeled "absolutely unchristian," because it "always traces the power ascribed to the church back to Christ." GL §136.3, II:361/[ET] 626.
24. GL §137.Lehrsatz, II:362/[ET] 626. For support from Scripture, Schleiermacher here alludes to Matt. 28:19–20 and Acts 2:41 and 47.
25. GL §137.1, II:363/[ET] 627.
26. GL §137.1, II:364–66/[ET] 627–29.
27. Schleiermacher draws attention here to Matt. 28:19–20 and Mark 16:16.
28. GL §137.2, II:369/[ET] 631.
29. GL §137.2, II:371/[ET] 632. The result is that if baptism is rightly administered, "there is no reason present either to attach magical effects to it or to denigrate it as a merely external custom." GL §137.3, II:371/[ET] 632.
30. GL §138.Lehrsatz, II:373/[ET] 633.
31. GL §138.1, II:374/[ET] 635. Schleiermacher tries to offer some reasons for why the practice may have arisen in history, but confesses that it is difficult to explain. GL §138.1, II:374, [ET] 635.
32. GL §138.1, II:375/[ET] 635.
33. GL §138.1, II:377/[ET] 637.
34. GL §139.Lehrsatz, II:378/[ET] 638.
35. GL §139.1, II:378/[ET] 638. As Schleiermacher observes, "If, however, it is only by faith in what others extol as their experience that every individual can come to have this experience also themselves, then this leads us by way of an uninterrupted tradition to the beginning of the church and to the very meal which Christ held with His disciples." GL §139.1, II:379/[ET] 639.
36. GL §139.1, II:378, [ET] 638.

37. GL §139.1, II:378–79, [ET] 639.
38. GL §139.1, II:379/[ET] 639.
39. GL §139.2, II:379–80/[ET] 640.
40. GL §139.2, II:380–81/[ET] 640.
41. GL §139.2, II:381/[ET] 640–41.
42. GL §139.2, II:381/[ET] 641.
43. GL §139.2, II:382/[ET] 641. Indeed, Schleiermacher observes that the discourse in John 6—in which Jesus speaks of eating His flesh and blood—is *not* connected with the sacrament, but is rather an indication of how "He must become and prosper our being." GL §139.2, II:381/[ET] 641.
44. GL §139.2, II:382/[ET] 641. On the interesting question of the relation of the dominical command instituting the Eucharist to that mandating mutual foot-washing, Schleiermacher writes, "as it is evident that [the apostles] did the one and not the other, so we can abide by what they have established." GL §139.3, II:384/[ET] 643.
45. GL §140.1, II:386/[ET] 644. Even then, for Schleiermacher, the result could not be received uncritically, for the basic criterion for dogmatic statements remains the immediate self-consciousness of the Christian, and not the text of Scripture. GL §140.1, II:386/[ET] 644.
46. GL §140.1, II:386/[ET] 645. It is worth noting that Schleiermacher is not sanguine about the prospect of any agreement being reached on this matter.
47. GL §140.1, II:387/[ET] 645.
48. Ibid.
49. GL §140.Lehrsatz, II:385/[ET] 644.
50. GL §140.2, II:389/[ET] 646. No Roman Catholic source is cited.
51. GL §140.Lehrsatz, II:385/[ET] 644.
52. Schleiermacher here (GL §140.2, II:389/[ET] 647) references the Racovian Catechism of 1605, and it is instructive (and correct) that he does not consider Zwingli to subscribe to this position.
53. GL §140.2, II:389/[ET] 647.
54. GL §140.4, II:390/[ET] 648.
55. For details, see GL §140.4, II:390–93/[ET] 648–50.
56. GL §140.4, II:393/[ET] 650–51.
57. GL §140.4, II:393/[ET] 651.
58. GL §141.Lehrsatz, II:394/[ET] 651.
59. GL §141, II:395/[ET] 652.
60. GL §141, II:395/[ET] 651. He cites 1 Cor. 10:17 and 12:27 to support his view.
61. GL §141, II:394–95/[ET] 651. For Schleiermacher, the practical consequences of this view are manifold: there is to be no participation in the Eucharist for the unconfirmed, for the underage, or for those with mental health conditions; the Eucharist must take place in the church; and there is no sense of any ongoing sacrifice of Christ in the Eucharist. GL §141.2, II:397–98/[ET] 654.
62. GL §142. Lehrsatz, II:400/[ET] 655.

63. GL §142.1, II:400/[ET] 655.
64. GL §142.1, II:401/[ET] 655.
65. GL §142.2, II:401/[ET] 656.
66. GL §143.1, II:404/[ET] 658.
67. Ibid.
68. GL §143.1, II:405/[ET] 659.
69. GL §142.3, II:402/[ET] 657.
70. The term "mystical" must here be understood according to Schleiermacher's qualified use of the term: see GL §100.3, II:109/[ET] 428–29.
71. See GL §136.1, II:354/[ET] 620 and GL §140.4, II:393/[ET] 651.

17

Karl Barth

JOHN YOCUM

Karl Barth (1886–1968) is considered to be one of the greatest Protestant theologians of the twentieth century. Born in Basel, Switzerland, he began his theological studies at Berne and then continued his education under the direction of many of the prominent liberal theologians of the period, including Adolf von Harnack and Wilhelm Herrmann, at universities in Berlin, Tübingen, and Marburg. In the years before and during World War I, Barth held several Swiss pastorates. While serving as a pastor in the industrial town of Safenwil, he composed his *Römerbrief*, a commentary on Romans, in which he challenged the liberal theology of his earlier training by calling for a radically transcendent view of God. The publication of this work, the first edition in 1919 and the more influential second edition in 1921, has been seen as a turning point in the history of modern theology. In 1921 Barth became a professor in Göttingen, moving to the University of Munster in 1925 and to Bonn in 1930. When Hitler came to power, Barth became one of the founders of the Confessing Church, which resisted the capitulation of the "German Christians" to Nazi propaganda, and he helped to draft the Barmen Declaration of 1934, which affirmed the sovereignty of the Word of God in Christ over against all political ideologies. In 1935, having refused to take a loyalty oath to Nazism, Barth was dismissed from his university chair and forced to flee from Germany. He returned to Basel, where he lived and taught until his retirement in 1962. Barth's massive *Church Dogmatics*, the first volume of which appeared in 1932, is regarded as one of the masterpieces of twentieth-century theology. His other well-known works include *Anselm: Fides Quaerens Intellectum*, *The Word of God and the Word of Man*, and *The Humanity of God*.

Introduction

There is a certain irony about a chapter on Karl Barth in a volume on Christian sacramental theologies. What Barth is best known for in relation to sacraments is his denial in the final volume of his great *Church Dogmatics* of any sacrament, save Jesus Christ. This was a position, however, that Barth reached only in the last phase of his career. In the preface to *Church Dogmatics*, Barth says,

> It will perhaps have been noted that in Volume II and III I made less and less use—and finally none at all—of the general term "sacrament," which was so confidently bandied about in Volume I. . . . Here, if anywhere, I have learned to regard a cautious and respectful "demythologising" as expedient and practicable.[1]

He promises to give Baptism and the Lord's Supper their due place at the end of Volume IV, in elaborating the ethics of the Doctrine of Reconciliation.

Barth enunciated a "radically new view" of baptism in his lectures in 1959–60.[2] This new view of baptism distinguished baptism with the Spirit from baptism with water. "Baptism with the Spirit and fire" relates to "the commencement of liberation for . . . Christian and churchly responsibility," and baptism with water to entering upon the discharge of that responsibility in the shape of living hope in God, service to the world, free confession, and prayer.[3] "In the one event of the foundation of the Christian life we have the wholly different action of two inalienably distinct subjects."[4]

In 1967, Barth published a slim volume (slim by Barthian standards at least), a fragment of the projected treatment of the ethics of reconciliation, on the doctrine of Baptism. The *Church Dogmatics* had seemed to come to an unfinished close eight years earlier, but Barth's concern with contemporary developments on the theological scene prompted him to bring out his non-sacramental interpretation of baptism.

This chapter follows the course of Barth's thinking on Baptism and the Lord's Supper from the first volume of the *Church Dogmatics* through the final part-volume, often referred to as "the Baptism fragment." I conclude with some brief comments on the reception of Barth's work.

Sacrament in *Church Dogmatics* I–II

The context of Barth's discussion of Baptism and the Lord's Supper in the first volume of the *Dogmatics* is his doctrine of the Word of God. Here Barth lays the foundation for his dogmatic project. Nineteenth-century Protestant theology was in the habit of beginning theological works with a prolegomena consisting of general observations on human epistemology, which conditioned the possibility of theological knowledge and therefore speech about God.[5] Barth determined to begin with the object of theological enquiry itself: Jesus Christ. The task of theology is to subject the Church's speech about God to critical assessment by the criterion of its own existence, Jesus Christ, the Word of God who assumed flesh.[6] God is known by us in an encounter with Him in his Word in threefold form: as God revealed in Jesus Christ's incarnate life; in the attestation of that Word in Scripture; and in the preaching of the Word in the Church's proclamation of the gospel.

On Barth's account, each of these three forms of the Word of God has the character of an event. Revelation for Barth is a "success word;"[7] it occurs only where and when the divine act reaches its goal in human knowledge of God. Though the objective side of revelation occurs in the Incarnation of the uncreated Word of God,[8] the human nature of Jesus Christ in and of itself serves only to veil God.[9] Revelation takes place only by the power of the Holy Spirit, whose illuminating act in the believer constitutes the subjective possibility of revelation.[10] In and of itself the human words of the Bible, which attests Jesus Christ in the present, have no capacity to bear the Word of God.[11] The Bible becomes the Word of God again and again, only in the event of God making use of this human testimony to reveal Jesus Christ.[12] Similarly, Church proclamation becomes the Word of God only as God makes use of signs and human preaching to make the one Word of God known.[13]

Barth emphasizes that Church proclamation has an essentially human character, with all the "ambiguity, vulnerability to misunderstanding, and contestability" of a creaturely event. Nonetheless, Church proclamation in the event of the Word of God is not just the will and act of the human being, "It is also and indeed it is primarily and decisively the divine willing and doing. Precisely for this reason, the human element is not set aside."[14]

This event character of the Word of God is the foundation of Barth's declaration in the first volume of the *Church Dogmatics* that the Church's proclamation itself consists of two elements: preaching and sacrament.[15] Preaching is "the attempt by someone called thereto in the Church . . . to express in his own words and to make intelligible to the men of his own generation the promise of the revelation, reconciliation and vocation of God as they are to be expected here and now."[16] But preaching must be accompanied by sacrament. In affirming the place of sacraments in Church proclamation, Barth takes up the "unusually clear and exhaustive definition of the term" offered by the *Heidelberg Catechism*. "They are visible, sacred signs and seals appointed by God" to "better give us to understand the promise of the Gospel, and seal the same, namely, that for the sake of the one sacrifice of Christ accomplished on the cross He graciously grants us remission of sins and eternal life."[17]

While the subjective reality of revelation occurs in human beings by the power of the Holy Spirit, there is also a special determination of "definite signs," of the objective reality of revelation. "By them the word which entered the world objectively in revelation, which was spoken once for all into the world, now wills to speak further into the world, to be received and heard in further areas and ages of this world."[18] Indeed, the manifestation of Christ Himself can be heard and understood only in the form of signs.[19] The utility of these signs, Barth adds, rests not upon any capacity immanent in them, but on "the divine foundation and institution."[20]

> They are the instruments by which [the Word] aims at becoming a Word which is apprehended by men and therefore a Word which justifies and sanctifies men, by which it aims at executing upon men the grace of God which is its content. And their instrumental function is to veil the objective of revelation under a creaturely reality; and yet to unveil it, i.e., in the actual form of such creaturely reality to bring it close to men, who are themselves also a creaturely reality. They point to revelation. They attest it. No, the Word of God made flesh attests by them that it was not made flesh in vain.[21]

Note here that Barth does not see these signs as simply cognitive aids. They are that as well, but they function as a word that justifies and sanctifies human beings. They are instruments, Barth explicitly says, which execute grace upon human beings. Under the New Testament dispensation, according to Barth, these divinely founded and instituted signs are reduced to the apostles, the *kerygma* of the Church, Baptism, and the Lord's Supper. They will cease when He comes again, but for now the Church is marked by preaching of the pure gospel and administration of Baptism and the Lord's Supper.[22]

The "general concept" of sacrament, according to Barth, is equivalent to that of a sign. Under this general concept, the whole objective side of the Church could be included. Two aspects of this general sacramentality are particularly important in Barth's treatment in the first volume. First, a sacrament is a sensible sign, and only in the narrower sense, comprising Baptism and the Lord's Supper, are sacraments necessarily visible. Thus, the preaching of the Church falls under this sacramental category. Second, a sacrament is an *actio sacra*, a holy action. In both these respects preaching fits under the general concept of a sacrament.[23] The sacraments in the narrower sense, as visible signs, external symbols, and actions that involve the elements of the creaturely world, assert "clearly and with relatively greater eloquence than the word in the narrower sense can ever do, that the *iustificatio*, or *sanctificatio hominis*, which is the meaning of all divine sign-giving, does not rest upon an idea but upon reality, upon an event."[24]

Barth takes John 3:5, Ephesians 5:26–27, Titus 3:5, and John 6:52–56 as strongly realistic passages bearing upon the sacramental nature of God's revealing and saving action. The inner working of the Spirit and the visible action of Baptism and the Lord's Supper are to be taken together, such that these passages speak *pars pro toto*.[25] That is to say, Barth takes these passages, linking bread and water with the divine life-giving action, as indicative of the dynamics of sign-giving in general. Barth does not delineate here a clear sacramental theory, whether instrumental or occasional.[26] Barth asserts repeatedly that the sacraments are instruments, but he does not unambiguously articulate the relation of the inner working of the Spirit and the external sign. Nonetheless, the life of the children of God

> is ordered and maintained in the way indicated by the sacraments. For that reason and in that sense we have to say in all seriousness that sac-

raments are an indispensable "means of grace." ... And no complaints about "Roman sacramentalism" will prevent us from declaring that on its objective side the Church is sacramental.[27]

Barth is adamant that revelation, and therefore Jesus Christ,[28] comes to the human being by means of sign giving, and that God actually uses these signs. At the same time, Barth is equally adamant that we cannot attribute anything to "man's side."[29] If revelation occurs in connection with the use of such signs, it is entirely a matter of the free grace of God.[30] We cannot make human beings "autonomous partners or workmates of God co-operating in the work of revelation."[31] This principle is consistent from beginning to end in Barth's theology. It appears in his dialogue with Hans Urs von Balthasar, in which Barth refuses secondary causality in the event of grace, either in preaching or in sacrament. It appears in his desire to head off any possibility that human action might set divine action in motion.[32] It appears in his concern that Catholic theology binds Christ to ecclesiastical office.[33] Barth stoutly refuses, from beginning to end, an *ex opere operato* understanding of Baptism or the Lord's Supper, or any other form of ecclesial activity.

In *Church Dogmatics* I, Barth does not employ a clearly elaborated sacramental theory of action; indeed, he rejects the idea that the relation of divine and human action can be neatly systematized.[34] He seems, however, in this volume of the *Dogmatics* to represent the sacraments as in some mysterious way, a "communion of action," to borrow a phrase from George Hunsinger.[35] In this volume, Barth speaks of the Church as active in a manner that looks almost like a communication of idioms. For example, he is able to speak of the assurance that the individual Christian receives through the promise of God given to the Church and communicated in sacramental action.

> In holy baptism I am placed by the Church under the promise of the Holy Ghost. I am instructed and comforted and led by the Church. In the Lord's Supper I am nourished by the Church on the true body and blood of Christ to eternal life. And it is in this sacramental positing and ordering of my existence that I lay hold of that assurance and put it into action. It is as I accept this sacramental determination of my existence in all its concreteness that I have the concrete courage for that assurance, and

therefore for the obedience whose result I cannot foresee, and therefore for the love of my neighbor.[36]

Barth carries forward his understanding of the importance of signs in the following volume, "The Doctrine of God," speaking about the place of signs and—sign giving in the knowledge of God. By this time, Barth has already conceived, on the basis of some stimulus from Pierre Maury, his doctrine of election, and so he likely wrote CD II/1 with his basic convictions on this doctrine in place.[37] In his full elaboration of this conception in CD II/2, he reworks the Reformed doctrine of the divine "double decree," by which some are elected to rejection and some to salvation. In Barth's doctrine, Jesus Christ is both electing God and electing man.[38] Jesus Christ elects to take on the rejection of the human race for the sake of its election to covenant with God. Barth speaks of the covenant as executed in Jesus Christ.[39] Jesus Christ Himself is the covenant; God and humanity are reconciled in His own person. By means of an *enhypostatic* Christology, in which the Word of God takes human nature to himself, Barth interprets the history of Jesus Christ as involving every human being, as enclosing within itself the being of all men and women of all times.[40]

Barth insists here on the sacramental nature of knowledge of God, built on a notion of the "secondary objectivity" of God. The "primary objectivity" of God is His objectivity to Himself, in which He knows Himself immediately, as Father, Son, and Holy Spirit. In secondary objectivity, "God gives Himself to the human being to be known in the revelation of his Word through the Holy Spirit."[41] God makes Himself knowable to the human being through some creaturely reality, "made and used by God as his clothing, temple, or sign," which attests the objectivity of God. Barth uses not the term *Objekt*, but *Gegenstand*. The latter term denotes someone or something standing over against another. God makes Himself objective not in the manner of a passive object, but as a subject standing before the human being, and thereby making knowledge of Him possible.[42] God never relinquishes His position as a subject in this encounter. The knowledge of God comes "through God and God alone."[43] Not only does He act by means of a secondary object taken from the created world of the human being's environment, but also the Holy Spirit acts within the human subject.[44]

At the heart of Barth's account is the Incarnation, the preeminent and unique occurrence of God's revelation through secondary objectivity.[45] The humanity of Jesus Christ is "the supreme and outstanding work and sign of God,"[46] and the "first sacrament."[47] He is the "basic reality and substance of the highest possibility of the creature as such."[48] The humanity of Christ is a veiling for the sake of unveiling; God assumes a created form that, in and of itself, has no capacity to reveal God. The Incarnation is unique, and as Barth says elsewhere, there are no extensions, or prolongations of this.[49] "But attestation [of God] through the existence of the man Jesus is a beginning of which there are continuations; a sacramental continuity stretches backwards into the existence of the people of Israel . . . and forwards into the existence of the apostolate and the Church founded on the apostolate."[50] Barth hastens to add that revelation in this sacramental form is a veiling as well as an unveiling, and can be rejected. It occurs only in faith.[51] For all that, however, "Revelation means sacrament."[52] More precisely, in the age following the resurrection, Barth says, the apostles, the visible Church, audible preaching, and the operative sacraments become instances of the secondary objectivity of God.[53]

For all this, Barth's depiction of revelation, which is never a mere cognition, but an empowerment to act, has a strongly "sacramental" character, that is, by means of creaturely media. These creaturely media include human actions, such as immersion in the baptismal water or human utterance in preaching. In God's use of the created things, the creature remains a creature. Barth's objection to the Roman Catholic doctrine of transubstantiation is not principally that it involves a certain realism about the presence of Christ in the Eucharist. What Barth objects to is any annihilation of the creaturely forms themselves. It is precisely in their "creatureliness" that God makes use of these elements of the human world. The manner in which Barth depicts this divine use in these volumes may reasonably be called "instrumental."[54]

The 1941 Seminar with Balthasar and the Teaching of the Church Regarding Baptism

In the summer of 1941, Barth hosted a graduate seminar about "the canons on the sacraments in general" from the Council of Trent, with Hans Urs von Balthasar participating.⁵⁵ On Canon 5, which rejects the statement "that the sacraments were instituted for the nourishing of faith alone,"⁵⁶ the seminar agreed that the sacraments not only nourish faith, but also communicate grace by creating faith. The seminar rewrote the canon to express both agreement and disagreement: "The sacraments are actions in which God places Jesus Christ before us and through that creates faith in us. We have thus avoided the appearance as if sacraments worked by their own laws. God remains the Subject of the sacramental event, even if the Church is the acting subject."⁵⁷ Admittedly, one cannot simply attribute the seminar's position to Barth, but one might expect that he would have a decisive influence against anything that he found unacceptable. It is striking, then, that in 1941, Barth affirms the sacraments as means of grace, specifically the creation of faith, in which both the Church and God act.

Perhaps most intriguing of all the exchanges between Barth and Balthasar in this seminar is over the term frequently used by medieval theologians to speak about the nature of sacraments, *significando causant*: they cause by signifying. They agreed that sacraments both signify and cause, though Barth thought that Trent erred in distinguishing the two. Barth concluded, "The Protestants did not understand that the Catholics spoke of a *significando* causare, whereas the Catholics had not paid attention that the Protestants said significando *causare*."⁵⁸ In other words, the Protestants missed the importance of signification in Catholic sacramental theology, and Catholics missed the causal aspect of Protestant sacramental theology. Balthasar's rejoinder is that Barth should concede that there is a place for an expression of human causal agency in the covenant of grace. Barth is not convinced.⁵⁹

In 1943, Barth delivered a lecture to a group of theological students at Gwatt, later published as *The Teaching of the Church Regarding Baptism*.⁶⁰ While objecting to infant baptism, at this point Barth still held baptism to be an effective act, "the event in which God in Jesus Christ makes a man his child and a member of his covenant, awakening faith through his grace and calling a man to life in the Church."⁶¹ The lecture highlights important aspects of Barth's sacramental thinking at the time.

First, in keeping with the central place of the doctrine of election, baptism does not affect salvation, but rather effectively attests, as a visible word, that salvation has already occurred in the history of Jesus Christ.[62] "In baptism he calls and engages a man to be what he is in Him."[63] Baptism is "a living and expressive" representation, one that shows to the human being "that objective reality to which he himself belongs."[64] Thus, there is a "sacramental dimension and form" to the work and word of Jesus Christ. It extends to the sense and experience of a human being. The absence of this, Barth says, makes the teaching of Zwingli on baptism and the Lord's Supper "strangely flat and cold, and so unsatisfactory in relation to the New Testament references."[65]

Second, Barth interprets baptism as a declaration over the baptized that he or she belongs to Christ and is called to Him. It makes the baptized "a marked man." That, Barth says, is baptism's power.[66] And though baptism is a cognition of salvation, not a cause of salvation, it is no less the act of Jesus Christ.[67] Because of that, Barth holds, imperfect reception does not nullify the sacrament's power, even in the case of an infant.[68] Baptism's special work is a "sealing," like the sealing of a letter Christ has written in His Person and work. As long as it is thus understood, it can be said that "it saves, sanctifies, purifies, mediates, and gives the forgiveness of sins and the grace of the Holy Spirit, it effects new birth, it is the admission of man into the covenant of grace and into the Church."[69]

Third, on its human side, "Baptism is part of the Church's proclamation. But manifestly and inevitably it also concerns the one baptized."[70] As far as the Church is concerned, "She administers it [baptism] as instituted by her Lord. She obeys his command. By word and deed she serves those who are His, in hope and expectation that through the power of her words and deeds His Word and His deed will find expression." So far, Barth remains consistent with his placement of Baptism in the first volume of the *Dogmatics*, squarely under the rubric of proclamation. He also affirms the action of Christ in baptism "through the instrumentality of human words and works."[71]

But he even more strongly insists here that baptism is the human act of the baptized, in conscious and free response to Jesus Christ, to whom he has already responded in faith.[72] Thus, the one baptized is not a passive object, but an active partner.[73] This makes infant baptism problematic, to say the least.[74] In baptism, individuals "publicly proclaim themselves as saved and are publicly acknowledged as such."[75] Part of the concern that Barth evinces in this lecture is with the Volkskirchen, the National Churches of Germany, Switzerland, and other countries, and the diminution of the Church's witness through the unwilling baptism of whole populations.[76]

Church Dogmatics IV/4

Barth lectured on baptism in 1959–60, enunciating a "radically new view" of Baptism and the concept of sacrament in comparison with the 1943 lecture, and from those lectures emerged the fragment of what would have been the section of *Church Dogmatics* IV on ethics.[77] In this fragment, Barth distinguishes the human act of baptism with water from the divine act of baptism with the Spirit. "Baptism with the Spirit and fire" relate to "the commencement of liberation for . . . Christian and churchly responsibility," and baptism with water to entering upon the discharge of that responsibility in the shape of living hope in God, service to the world, free confession, and prayer.[78] "In the one event of the foundation of the Christian life we have the wholly different action of two inalienably distinct subjects."[79] What is radical here cannot be the rejection of infant baptism; that was in place in 1943. What is radical here is the rejection of a notion of "sacrament" by means of a strong distinction of actions and agents. One can reject infant baptism as improper, and yet *also* reject the strong distinction of baptism with water and baptism with the Spirit.[80]

Barth credits the exegetical work of his son, Markus, with convincing him to lay aside the "sacramental" view of baptism that he held in 1943.[81] He explains his decision to publish the fragment of his uncompleted section on ethics to a practical and current concern. "Today there is much ready talk (too much and too ready) about the world which is supposed to have come of age in relation to God. . . . My own concern is with the man who ought to come of age in relation to God and the world, i.e., the mature Christian and mature Christianity, its thought, speech and action in responsibility to God, in living hope in Him, in service to the world, in free confession and unceasing prayer."[82]

The first section of Barth's part-volume treats "Baptism with the Holy Spirit." This is the "divine change" that enables the freedom, willingness, and ability to become the responsible subjects of their own history, which is not a history of salvation.[83] "In the work of the Holy Spirit the history manifested to all men in the resurrection of Jesus Christ is manifest and present to a specific man as his own salvation history."[84] This is an exclusively divine work: "He neither needs nor will He tolerate other factors or redeemers in this work of his. There is no place for such." He cannot allow even his community to represent Him.[85] Baptism with the Spirit is a form of grace; indeed, it is the grace of the self-attestation and self-impartation of Jesus Christ.[86] "Here if anywhere, one might speak of a sacramental happening in the current sense of the term."[87] This wholly divine, invisible act demands the fully human, public, and visible act of baptism with water.

Barth gives about 80 percent of CD IV/4 to treating baptism with water. He divides the exposition under three headings: the basis, goal, and meaning of Christian baptism. Its basis is the baptism of Jesus in the Jordan in which Jesus obeys the call of the Father, confesses God and solidarity with human beings in confessing their sins as His own, and takes up His mission.[88] This becomes the pattern for those who follow Him.[89] The goal of baptism with water is baptism with the Spirit, not as an act that mediates or effects, but as an act oriented to it, as a prayer for the ever-repeated divine act of baptism with the Spirit. As prayer, it is obedience and confident hope.[90]

What baptism certainly is not and cannot be, according to Barth, is a sacrament. Sacrament is derived from the Latin translation of μυστήριον, which Barth says is used in the New Testament only of God's work and revelation in history.[91] His analysis of the New Testament in testing the possibility for a particular reference to baptism being sacramental becomes the question of whether the passage speaks of an action as such or its basis, or its goal.[92] The result of the exegetical enquiry about baptism as a sacrament concedes that some passages might be taken sacramentally, but in others that interpretation is ruled out. Barth concludes, "Until better instructed both as a whole and in detail, we must regard these findings as proved and binding."[93] As for the Lord's Supper, of course, we have no full treatment in the *Dogmatics*. We have some indications from scattered comments Barth made, and he himself tells us intelligent readers can surmise what he would have said. The Lord's Supper would be an act of confession, of gratitude and hope, but not a means of grace in any sense.[94]

Conclusion

For the most part, Barth's late doctrine of baptism and its implications for sacraments in general have not been greeted with unambiguous support. Even those generally favorable to Barth have stood aloof from him or sought to modify his conclusions in some way—Alasdair Heron,[95] T. F. Torrance,[96] George Hunsinger,[97] John Webster,[98] Kimlyn Bender,[99] and, most recently, W. Travis McMaken.[100] The most common complaint is that Barth has too sharply distinguished the two moments of baptism, and misplaces baptism under the category of ethics.

Barth's exegesis, like that of his son Markus, has not gained the day either. His elimination of some passages from consideration as not speaking directly of baptism,[101] his sharp distinction of basis, goal, and meaning in interpreting various passages,[102] and his positing of an invisible and wholly divine baptism in the Spirit, based on Mark 1:8,[103] have all been the basis for critique. Surveys of New Testament teaching on baptism most commonly conclude that baptism with water is, in fact, the occasion of a divine work.[104]

Still, Barth never fails to stimulate, or to advance discussion on difficult issues. It's interesting that Roman Catholic commentators often voice the most appreciation for Barth's protest. He acts as a healthy foil to those tempted to inflate the role of human institutions and practices. Even when he fails to convince, Barth manages to unsettle easy assumptions and challenge dogmatic complacency.

NOTES

1. *Church Dogmatics*, 2nd ed., 4 vols., ed. Geoffrey Bromiley and T. F. Torrance (Edinburgh: T&T Clark, 1956–75), xi (hereafter cited as CD). Vol. I: *The Doctrine of the Word of God*; vol. II: *The Doctrine of God*; vol. III: *The Doctrine of Creation*; vol. IV: *The Doctrine of Reconciliation*.
2. CD IV/4, ix.
3. Ibid., x.
4. Ibid., 41.
5. CD I/2, 5.
6. CD I/1, 3.
7. "A word whose application entails the truth of an embedded clause, or the achievement of some result, e.g., I remember, I know. . . ." *Oxford Dictionary of Philosophy*, 2nd rev. ed., ed. Simon Blackburn (Oxford: Oxford University Press, 2008). For use of this term in relation to revelation, see Colin Gunton, *A Brief*

Theology of Revelation (Edinburgh: Bloomsbury T&T Clark, 2005), 113. Barth's equivalent notion is that revelation is "not only an event proceeding from God, but an event that reaches man." CD I/2, 204. Revelation, that is, must reach its goal. CD I/2, 236.
8. CD I/1, 158.
9. CD I/2, 36.
10. Ibid., §16.
11. Ibid., 463.
12. Ibid., 462.
13. CD I/1, 88.
14. Ibid., 94. The English translation softens the German to "vulnerability to misunderstanding."
15. Ibid., 56.
16. Ibid., 56.
17. Ibid., quoting the *Heidelberg Catechism*, 1563, question 66.
18. CD I/2, 223.
19. Ibid., 226.
20. Ibid.
21. Ibid. NB: I have quoted the published English translation. "Durch," which the published English translation translates as "by," could be translated as "through," in keeping with the instrumental language Barth employs here.
22. Ibid., 226–27.
23. Ibid., 230.
24. Ibid., 230.
25. Ibid., 231.
26. "When we are asked how objective revelation reaches man, we can and must reply that it takes place by means of the divine sign-giving. In this sign-giving objective revelation is repeated in such a way that it can come to man in genuinely human form. All that we know is that God really does avail Himself of this medium, and that therefore objective revelation is actually shown to man by the signs."
27. CD I/2, 232.
28. Ibid.
29. Ibid., 235.
30. Ibid., 234.
31. Ibid., 235.
32. Karl Barth, "An Outing to the Bruderholz," in *Fragments Grave and Gay* (London: SCM, 1971), 88.
33. CD I/1, 96–98.
34. CD I/2, 861.
35. George Hunsinger, "Baptism and the Soteriology of Forgiveness," *International Journal of Systematic Theology* 2 (2000): 247–69.
36. CD I/2, 453.

37. See the account in Bruce L. McCormack, *Karl Barth's Critically Realistic Dialectical Theology: Its Genesis and Development, 1909–1936* (Oxford: Clarendon, 1997), 454–63.
38. CD II/2, 94.
39. Ibid., 116.
40. Ibid., §33, esp. 175–94.
41. Ibid., 9.
42. CD II/1, 21.
43. Ibid.
44. Ibid., 10.
45. Ibid., 19–20.
46. Ibid., 53.
47. Ibid., 54.
48. Ibid., 54.
49. W. Travis McMaken is quite right to point out that in one instance I carelessly misspeak on this score in my *Ecclesial Mediation in Karl Barth* (Aldershot: Ashgate, 2004), 174, when I speak of secondary objectivity as an "extension— though not repetition—of the Incarnation" (McMaken, *The Sign of the Gospel: Toward an Evangelical Doctrine of Infant Baptism after Karl Barth* [Minneapolis: Fortress, 2013], 214). In my main treatment of secondary objectivity in the same book, I make Barth's affirmation of the utter uniqueness of the Incarnation clear (*Ecclesial Mediation*, 35–45). Elsewhere I say explicitly that Barth would not agree to language about a "prolongation" of the Incarnation (*Ecclesial Mediation*, 183). Nevertheless, even in the statement McMaken cites, I affirm, as Barth does in CD II/1, 54, that there is no *repetition* of the Incarnation; McMaken excises that clause from his quotation. He attributes my misstatement to a reflex reaction rooted in my "ecclesiastical commitments." On the contrary, nowhere in the book do I approve of the expression. Indeed, in registering concerns about Barth's theologoumenon of the Church as the worldly historical form of Christ's existence, I make clear the importance of acknowledging the sin that still besets the Church throughout this present age (*Ecclesial Mediation*, 118–19). Barth's own language on these matters can be loose and variable. Barth denies any "repetition" of the Incarnation when he speaks about secondary objectivity in CD II/1. In CD I/2, however, Barth says that one meaning of the term Body of Christ in the New Testament is that

> the existence of the Church involves a repetition of the incarnation of the Word of God in the person of Jesus Christ in that area of the rest of humanity which is distinct from Jesus Christ. The repetition is quite heterogeneous. Yet for all its heterogeneity it is quite homogeneous too (although the uniqueness of the objective revelation forbids us to call it a continuation, prolongation, extension, or the like).

50. CD II/1, 54.
51. Ibid., 55.

52. Ibid., 52.
53. Ibid., 20.
54. In his review of my *Ecclesial Mediation in Karl Barth*, John G. Flett asserts that there is no instrumental relation and no sacramental mediation at all in Protestantism (Flett, "Yocum's *Ecclesial Mediation in Karl Barth*," *Zeitschrift für dialektische Theologie* 20 [2005]: 147–51). In Protestant sacramental theology, divine and human actions are parallel, Flett claims. This understanding, Flett alleges, is directly counter to the Thomistic sacramental conception, in which the priest mediates—in the sense of "handing over"—grace. Flett thinks I could easily have learned as much by reading Brian Gerrish. (Flett supplies no more specific reference.) Gerrish, however, corrects the sharp Catholic-Protestant distinction Flett lays out by drawing a parallel between Calvin's theology of the Eucharist and the instrumental language of the medieval schoolmen! (see Brian Gerrish, *Grace and Gratitude: The Eucharistic Theology of John Calvin* [Eugene, OR: Wipf & Stock, 1993], 168nn32–33). Furthermore, Flett seems confused about the history of sacramental theology on which he bases his critique. Thomas does not think of the priest as "handing over" grace; the point of his theory of instrumental causality is that God alone gives grace. (For a good summary of the range of positions on sacramental causality taken by various schools at the time of Aquinas, see Bernhard Blankenhorn, "The Place of Romans 6 in Aquinas's Doctrine of Sacramental Causality," in *Ressourcement Thomism: Sacred Doctrine, the Sacraments and the Moral Life: Essays in Honor of Romanus Cessario, O.P.*, ed. Reinhard Hütter and Matthew Levering [Washington, DC: Catholic University of America Press, 2010], 136–49.) Finally, Flett attributes my blindness in all these matters to my being an "Anglican of High Church sympathies." I am, in fact, not an Anglican at all. For a better analysis of the variety of approaches to instrumentality, see McMaken, *Sign of the Gospel*, 240–44.
55. The protocols from this seminar have yet to be published, but there is a good account of them in D. Stephen Long, *Saving Karl Barth: Hans Urs von Balthasar's Preoccupation* (Minneapolis: Fortress, 2014), 243–65. I am completely dependent upon Long's account of this event.
56. See Heinrich Denzinger, *Enchiridion symbolorum*, Latin-English ed., ed. Peter Hünermann (San Francisco: Ignatius, 2013), art. 1605.
57. Long, *Saving Karl Barth*, 246.
58. Ibid., 255. Barth's reading of Catholic tradition is correct. Aquinas, for example, defines sacraments as signs, and distinguishes new covenant sacraments from old covenant sacraments by their differing relations to Christ. New covenant sacraments derive their efficacy entirely from the passion of Christ, while old covenant sacraments can only look forward to Christ and are not efficacious in grace. See my "Sacraments in Aquinas," in *Aquinas on Doctrine: A Critical Introduction*, ed. Thomas Weinandy, Daniel Keating, and John Yocum (Edinburgh: T&T Clark, 2004).

59. Long, *Saving Karl Barth*, 255–56. See Hans Urs von Balthasar, *The Theology of Karl Barth: Exposition and Interpretation* (San Francisco: Ignatius Press, 1992), 135. This is a point I press in *Ecclesial Mediation in Karl Barth*, 83–92.
60. *The Teaching of the Church Regarding Baptism*, trans. Ernest A. Payne (Eugene OR: Wipf & Stock, 2006).
61. Ibid., 14.
62. Ibid., 15. Barth appeals to Calvin (John Calvin, *The Institutes of the Christian Religion*, IV.15.2), but clearly with his Christological reworking of the Reformed doctrine of election in place.
63. *Teaching of the Church Regarding Baptism*, 29.
64. Ibid., 15–16.
65. Ibid., 28.
66. Ibid., 15–16.
67. Ibid., 29.
68. Ibid., 35–36.
69. Ibid., 29.
70. Ibid., 34.
71. Ibid., 32–33.
72. Ibid., 42.
73. Ibid., 41.
74. Ibid., 54.
75. Ibid., 31–32.
76. Ibid., 52–54.
77. CD IV/4, ix.
78. Ibid., x.
79. Ibid., 41.
80. See, for example, G. R. Beasley-Murray, *Baptism in the New Testament* (London: Macmillan, 1962), 275–79. Beasley-Murray rejects infant baptism. Yet he takes an occasionalist view of baptism, holding on the basis of the New Testament that the Holy Spirit is indubitably at work in baptism.
81. Markus Barth, *Die Taufe: ein Sakrament? Ein exegetischer Beitrag zum Gespräch über die kirchliche Taufe* (Zürich: Evangelischer Verlag, 1951).
82. CD IV/4, x.
83. Ibid., 26–27.
84. Ibid., 27.
85. Ibid., 33.
86. Ibid.
87. Ibid., 34.
88. Ibid., 58–59.
89. Ibid., 68.
90. Ibid., 210.
91. Ibid., 109.
92. Ibid., 110.

93. Ibid., 127–28.
94. For a large-scale attempt at such a surmise, see Paul Molnar, *Karl Barth and the Theology of the Lord's Supper: A Systematic Investigation* (New York: Peter Lang, 1966).
95. Alasdair Heron, *Table and Tradition: Toward an Ecumenical Understanding of the Eucharist* (Philadelphia: Westminster, 1983), 156–58.
96. T. F. Torrance, *Karl Barth: Biblical and Evangelical Theologian* (Edinburgh: T&T Clark, 1990), 134–35; Torrance, "The One Baptism Common to Christ and His Church," in *Theology in Reconciliation: Essays toward Evangelical and Catholic Unity in East and West* (Eugene, OR: Wipf & Stock, 1996), 82–105.
97. Hunsinger, "Baptism and the Soteriology of Forgiveness," 247–69; Hunsinger, *The Eucharist and Ecumenism* (Cambridge: Cambridge University Press, 2008), 15–18.
98. John Webster, *Barth's Ethics of Reconciliation* (Cambridge: Cambridge University Press, 1995), 168–73.
99. Kimlyn Bender, *Karl Barth's Christological Ecclesiology* (Burlington, VT: Ashgate, 2005), 223–24.
100. McMaken, *Sign of the Gospel*, 209–74. McMaken is trying to mount a defense for the possibility of legitimate infant baptism while accepting Barth's premises. I am not convinced that he fully acknowledges or appreciates that by placing baptism with water back in the category of Church proclamation, rather than the ethics of individual response, he has made a very substantial revision of Barth's doctrine.
101. E.g., Titus 3:5 (CD IV/4, 115); Eph. 5:26 (CD IV/4, 113). For arguments that these passages are "baptismal," see Beasley-Murray, *Baptism in the New Testament*, 200–204, 209–16; Lars Hartman, *Into the Name of the Lord Jesus* (Edinburgh: T&T Clark, 1997), 105–6, 108–13; Everett Ferguson, *Baptism in the Early Church: History, Theology and Liturgy in the First Five Centuries* (Grand Rapids, MI: Eerdmans, 2009), 161–64.
102. Erich Dinkler, "Die Taufaussagen des neuen Testaments: neu untersucht in Hinblick auf Karl Barths Tauflehre," in *Zu Karl Barths Lehre von der Taufe*, ed. F. Viering (Gütersloh: Gerd Mohn, 1971), 111.
103. Ibid., 149; Henry Mottu, "Les sacrements selon Karl Barth et Eberhard Jüngel," *Foi et Vie* 88 (1989): 43; Richard Schlüter, *Karl Barths Tauflehre: ein interkonfessionelles Gespräch* (Paderborn: Verlag Bonifacius-Drückerei, 1973), 102. The most common view among commentators, whether they find continuity or contrast, is that Mark 1:8 applies to the relation between John's baptism and Christian baptism, not to forms or "moments" of Christian baptism. See, for example, Hugh Anderson, *The Gospel of Mark*, The New Century Bible Commentary (London: Marshall, Morgan & Scott, 1976), 73–74; C. E. B. Cranfield, *The Gospel according to St. Mark*, Cambridge Greek New Testament Commentary (Cambridge: Cambridge University Press, 1959), 49–51; Morna Hooker, *The Gospel according to St. Mark*, Black's New Testament Commentaries (London: A&C Black, 1991), 37–43.
104. Hartman, *Into the Name of the Lord Jesus*:

All our authors [Matthew, Mark, Luke, John, Paul, the disputed Paulines, Hebrews, 1Pt] take baptism for granted. In different ways they represent a conviction that it means an encounter between the divine and the human. An earthly concrete event mediates divine actions and conveys spiritual gifts. (168)

Both Paul and other theologians in his milieu seem to have regarded baptism as a cultic actualization of the salvific work of Jesus. Thus, according to Romans 6, those who were baptised died "with Christ" in baptism, and "with" him they also received a life which they should now live "for God," but which also had a future, a definitive life "with Christ." (164)

See also Ferguson, *Baptism in the Early Church*, 162–63.

18

Edward Schillebeeckx and Louis-Marie Chauvet

JOSEPH C. MUDD

The Belgian-born Dominican Edward Schillebeeckx (1914–2009) spent most of his teaching career at the University of Nijmegen, where he became one of the most influential Catholic theologians of the second half of the twentieth century. Schillebeeckx arrived in Nijmegen in 1957 after spending ten years at Louvain, where he taught the full range of theology courses for young Dominicans. He would remain teaching in Nijmegen until his retirement in 1983. As a student studying at the French Dominican house of studies at Le Saulchoir, Schillebeeckx was influenced by Marie-Dominique Chenu, a leading figure in a movement known as "ressourcement Thomism." Schillebeeckx undertook his own work of returning to the sources in his dissertation on the sacraments *De sacramentele heilseconomie* in 1952. Many of the ideas developed in the dissertation were eventually published for a wider audience in 1963 as *Christ, the Sacrament of the Encounter with God*. Very soon thereafter the Second Vatican Council began its work of bringing the church up to date, or *aggiornamento*. Schillebeeckx played a significant role in moving the reforming agenda of the council forward through his work with the Dutch bishops, and he joined other leading theologians in continuing to push for reform after the council by establishing the theological journal *Concilium*. Schillebeeckx went on to publish major studies in Christology, including *Jesus: An Experiment in Christology* (1974) and *Christ: The Experience of Jesus as Lord* (1983), as well as in ecclesiology, including *The Church with a Human Face* (1987) and *Church: The Human Story of God* (1990). His later works, grounded in historical and biblical studies, consistently emphasize the ethical and political demands of Christian life in the contemporary world. Schillebeeckx's works were not without controversy. He was called to Rome on three occasions to defend his positions before the Congregation for the Doctrine of the Faith, however he was never formally censured. He is widely regarded as one of the most prolific and influential theologians of his generation.

* * *

Louis-Marie Chauvet (1942–) hails from Vendée along the Atlantic coast of France. Chauvet was educated in the seminary at Luçon and ordained to the priesthood in 1966. Animated by a concern to make theology speak on the level of the time, he undertook historical and biblical studies in the hope that these might help him better address contemporary theological questions. He defended a thesis on the priesthood of Christ in the Letter to the Hebrews in 1967, earning his licentiate in theology. While at seminary Chauvet developed an interest in Martin Heidegger and his critique of metaphysics. In 1973, having completed a dissertation on the role of penance in the thought of John Calvin at the Sorbonne, Chauvet returned to parish life. Not long after he was contacted by Pierre-Marie Gy to teach in the Superior Institute of Liturgy, and in 1974 he began his teaching career at the Institut Catholique in Paris. Chauvet published his initial research on symbol and sacrament in *Du symbolique au symbole. Essai sur les sacrements* in 1979. His dissertation, *Symbol et Sacrement: une relecture sacramentelle de l'existence chrétienne*, attracted international attention when it was published in 1987. With the publication of an English translation, *Symbol and Sacrament: A Sacramental Reinterpretation of Christian Existence*, in 1995, interest in Chauvet's work among North American theologians increased significantly. Chauvet's other major work available in English translation, *Sacraments: The Word of God at the Mercy of the Body*, makes his ideas available to a broader, nonspecialist audience. His most recent work is a series of four essays on the understanding of mediation in sacramental theology published in Italian under the title *Della Mediazione. Quattro studi di teologia sacramentaria fondamentale* (2006). He has authored dozens of articles, regularly contributing to the French theological journal *La Maison Dieu*. Throughout his career Chauvet served the church as a parish priest. He retired from teaching in 2007. Chauvet's work has earned both praise and criticism for its content, but his unique contribution to a contemporary sacramental theology is universally recognized.

Introduction

At the turn of the twentieth century Catholic theology was dominated by a Neo-Scholastic theology derived from Pope Leo XIII's 1879 encyclical *Aeterni Patris*. While Neo-Scholastic thought, coming on the heels of Vatican I, promoted the Pope's vision of a perennial philosophy and theology able to combat the errors of modernity, it also adopted a rationalist approach to theology and a meticulous separation of nature and supernature. Over time, however, Leo's promotion of Thomas Aquinas would lead to a revitalization of Catholic sacramental theology. By returning to the patristic and medieval sources, leaders of *ressourcement* Thomism (a movement its opponents called "the new theology," or *la nouvelle théologie*) began to develop a sacramental ontology that would repair the breach opened between nature and supernature, theology and life, by Neo-Scholasticism.[1]

Representatives of the *nouvelle théologie* like Jean Danielou (1905–74), Henri de Lubac (1896–1991), and Marie Dominique Chenu (1895–1990) were concerned that the Neo-Scholastic tendency to separate nature and supernature ended up embracing an Enlightenment view of nature as an autonomous and purely secular sphere. This posed a problem for sacramental theology insofar as the sacraments seem to transgress the boundary set up between nature and supernature. The Catholic theological manuals used to train seminarians treated the sacraments in strictly supernatural terms as "containers" of grace given to human beings by church officials. As a result, sacramental theology in the Neo-Scholastic mode was primarily concerned with matters of validity and efficacy, and the ancient notion that one encountered divine mysteries in the sacraments receded into the background. From the perspective of *nouvelle théologie*, on the other hand, nature was God's creation and therefore already sacramental. Furthermore, the incarnation reveals that God is intimately involved with human history, transforming it through concrete, historical human expressions of divine love, first in the life of Christ and then in his body the church. These developments provided the foundations for major developments in Catholic sacramental theology in the second half of the twentieth century.

In introducing *Christ, the Sacrament of the Encounter with God*, Edward Schillebeeckx laments the state of Catholic sacramental theology under the influence of Neo-Scholasticism, noting that the emphasis on objectivity common to the theological manuals led to a "purely impersonal, almost mechanical" theology in which sacraments "were considered chiefly in terms of physical categories."[2] The sacraments wound up being subsumed under the rationally demonstrable laws of cause and effect. The net result was that the faithful "appeared to be merely passive recipients of sacramental grace, which seemed to be 'put into us' automatically."[3] In order to counter this prevalent view promoted by the manuals, Schillebeeckx, building on his interpretation of Thomas Aquinas, emphasized that sacraments are instances of personal encounter grounded in the saving work of God in the incarnation and therefore proper to a distinctly human world. Throughout his work on the topic, Schillebeeckx reorients sacramental theology in order to take the human world of history and subjectivity seriously.

Louis-Marie Chauvet also felt that the prevailing Neo-Scholastic theology of the sacraments failed to address the symbolic character of the human world shaped by language and culture. He was concerned that "the insistence on the objective efficacy of the sacraments is done at the expense of the concrete existential subjects, who are not taken into account."[4] Chauvet describes this theology as "objectivist."[5] It was a theology concerned with the objective effects of sacraments in terms of the production of grace in the individual recipient. In his major work *Symbol and Sacrament: A Sacramental Reinterpretation of Christian Existence*, Chauvet criticizes the metaphysical presuppositions of classical sacramental theology and proposes a fundamental theology of sacramentality grounded in contemporary explorations into the nature of language and culture.

Though certainly not the only theologians to make major contributions to the reorientation of Catholic sacramental theology during the twentieth century, Schillebeeckx and Chauvet are two of the most innovative, and sometimes controversial, voices in Catholic sacramental theology in the past fifty years. Although separated by nearly thirty years, they share a common concern that contemporary sacramental theologies take the concrete historicity of human subjects seriously rather than rely on abstract philosophical categories. Both Schillebeeckx and Chauvet (1) employ theological methods that intend to take human subjectivity and culture seriously; (2) stress encounter with the paschal mystery of

Christ in the sacraments; (3) emphasize the ecclesial dimension of sacramental life; and (4) underscore the connection between sacrament and ethics in the lived practice of the Christian community in imitation of Christ and anticipation of the Kingdom of God. Taking each thinker in turn, we will explore their methodological, Christological, ecclesiological, and ethical concerns and thereby develop a clearer understanding of the major themes of contemporary Catholic sacramental theology.

Edward Schillebeeckx

Method

In *Christ, the Sacrament of the Encounter with God*, Schillebeeckx explains that he intends to take "the concept of human, personal encounter as the basis of our consideration."[6] The notion of personal encounter, echoing developments in existentialist criticisms of rationalism, animates Schillebeeckx's treatment of the sacraments. He derives his notion of sacramentality from this emphasis on personal encounter. Grace is a matter of personal encounter with God in history, not simply a quality attached to a soul. For Schillebeeckx, the "sacramental" refers to the way in which personal encounter with God in the sacraments "makes history." The sacraments are those events where supernatural reality is realized in history.[7] Sacramentality therefore derives from the fact that we exist "in an I-Thou relationship, in a situation of dialogue with God" who enters into history.[8] Because our being as human subjects is a process of becoming, we are historical beings whose becoming occurs through encounter with other persons in time. For Schillebeeckx history is the site of revelation. Participation in the sacraments is not an escape from history, but a transformation of history through personal encounter. By attending to the historical context of sacramental encounter, Schillebeeckx argues that sacramental grace is better understood in terms of a developing relationship with God, rather than an automatic infusion of holiness. Furthermore, to be human is to be an embodied being living in a material world.

Human embodiment and materiality are fundamental to contemporary sacramental theology. The symbol-making capacity of the human is due precisely to our lives as embodied beings, because symbols mediate between the interior and the exterior lives of human beings. In his earlier work, Schillebeeckx holds to the Thomist notion that human symbol making is an expression of interiority such that our bodies mediate our interior being.[9] Developing this notion further in *The Eucharist*, Schillebeeckx complicates the picture through increasing attention to phenomenological approaches to embodiment. There he notes that developments in phenomenology offer an understanding of the human person that is nondualist, in which interior and exterior exist in a dialectical tension in the human subject. Schillebeeckx explains, "According to this anthropological conception, man is not, in the first instance an enclosed interiority which, later, in a second stage as it were, becomes incarnate in the world through bodiliness."[10] Our being as embodied is fundamental to our being as human. Schillebeeckx resists any depiction of the subject as an "enclosed interiority" that mediates itself to the outside world by way of signs. Instead, the human subject is present to herself only through encounter with what is other than the self. Unlike matter, however, other persons not only appear to us but also speak.[11] They make demands. Consequently, Schillebeeckx suggests that "on the basis of these anthropological considerations, then, the sacraments can be dissociated from the material sphere of 'things' and taken up into the personal sphere. They are interpersonal encounters between the believer and Christ."[12] Sacraments are not simply encounters with brute matter, but words addressed to the recipient by Christ. The Christian subject becomes aware of herself, indeed becomes herself, through these bodily encounters with Christ in the sacraments.

Thinking in terms of interpersonal encounter liberates sacramental theology from reliance on categories related to material things that had been common in the Neo-Scholastic method. If sacraments are personal encounters, an entirely new series of questions emerges for theological reflection. Rather than be concerned primarily with cause and effect in terms of validity, for example, one might more closely attend to the conditions for fruitful reception of sacraments in terms of the transformed living of a person. While such questions were not simply foreign to the mind of Thomas Aquinas, their importance can easily be diminished by a strictly apologetic and juridical approach to sacramental theology focused on matters of validity. Basing his sacramental theology on the notion of encounter, Schillebeeckx turns his attention to the person

Christians encounter in the sacraments. The grace mediated by the sacraments is ultimately an experience of personal encounter with Christ.

Christology

For Schillebeeckx, Jesus is the way one encounters God. Christ is the sacrament of encounter with God because he reveals the fully human attitude of "existence toward God."[13] To encounter Jesus is also therefore to encounter redemption. We can talk about Jesus as sign and cause of grace because "the human acts of Jesus are the divine bestowal of grace itself realized in human form."[14] In this sense one can say, using scholastic categories, that sacraments cause what they signify. Schillebeeckx explains that it is through the life of Christ that human beings encounter and experience redemption in history, and in the sacraments, the life, death, and resurrection of Christ presented in ritual symbolic form continue to mediate the grace of redemption in history.[15]

Schillebeeckx elaborates his position by attending to the ascending and descending aspects of this understanding of Christ as the sacrament of encounter. Ascending from below upward, by attending to the historical life of Jesus, Schillebeeckx interprets the human actions of Christ as the perfection of human living toward God the Father: "Jesus became the redeemer in actual fact by freely living his human life in religious worship of and attachment to the Father."[16] This total fidelity to God is Jesus's true worship of the Father. Moving from above down, Schillebeeckx interprets Jesus's life as the revelation of the Father's love in a human way. Jesus therefore acts as a mediator insofar as he is both the "offer of divine love to man made visible" and "the supreme realization of the response of human love to this divine offer."[17] Schillebeeckx concludes, "In the Hypostatic Union we are confronted with a divine way of being human and a human way of being God."[18] Both the divine way of being human and the human way of being God involve the cross.

At the center of Christian ritual life we find the cross. This is the event Christians proclaim until the Lord comes again.[19] Therefore, if the sacraments are understood in terms of encounter with Christ, Schillebeeckx suggests that this encounter begins with the cross.[20] Through the cross Christ intervenes with the Father for the grace of redemption and makes "reparation for our disobedience" and failure to render proper worship to God.²¹ Schillebeeckx interprets the cross here in terms of the total self-dispossession of Jesus to the Father. Insofar as it is an act of pure fidelity, the cross puts sin to death, with the result that Jesus becomes the head of a redeemed humanity, the new creation. Schillebeeckx goes on to interpret the cross as a historical manifestation of the eternally active redemptive work of the Son. The sacraments derive their power from the Cross, indeed "the sacraments are that very sacrifice made visible."²² The sacraments are "the face of redemption turned visibly toward us, so that in them we are truly able to encounter the living Christ. The heavenly saving activity, invisible to us, becomes visible in the sacraments."²³ But the sacraments become visible only within a historical community Christians call "church."

Church

In his groundbreaking research into the notion of the Church as the "mystical body" in the Middle Ages, Henri de Lubac found that over time theologians had reversed the titles given to the Church and the Eucharist.²⁴ While the patristic tradition referred to the Church as the *verum corpus*, or true body of Christ, and called the Eucharist the "mystical body of Christ," the medieval Eucharistic controversies led to a reversal. In order to remove any doubt about the presence of Christ in the Eucharist, medieval theologians employed a term that had referred to the Church to describe the consecrated host. Shaped by de Lubac's research, Schillebeeckx concludes that "the Church is a prolongation primarily of the heavenly Christ, and therefore it prolongs the function of the earthly body of Jesus."²⁵ Like the humanity of Jesus, the Church is the body of Christ in history.

The Church is integrally involved in the saving work of God in history made human in the incarnation. As a sacrament, the Church makes the salvation accomplished by Christ visible throughout history.²⁶ The Church is embedded in history, not an escape to an otherworldly plane, so it makes the saving work of God in history explicit in word and sacrament. In his later works, Schillebeeckx affirms that the Church participates in the saving work of Christ whenever it lives out a liberative practice of justice and mercy in solidarity with the suffering.[27] The Church mediates salvation both to the individual and to the world.

Ethics

In his earlier works, Schillebeeckx reflects on the ethical dimension of sacraments in terms of personal holiness. Sacraments issue in the theological virtues of faith, hope, and love expressed in the "moral behavior" of persons who have encountered God in the sacraments.[28] He notes, "moral virtue comes to depend on personal communion with God; it becomes the embodiment of our divine communion on every plane of human living."[29] The church makes the saving work of Christ visible in history, both in its liturgical and sacramental life, but also in the daily living of each person formed by the church. Holiness in daily life is never simply personal. For Schillebeeckx, by living holy lives the faithful become sacraments of grace for others.[30] Citing the prophet Amos, Schillebeeckx warns that until Christians make holiness a reality in the world, they are obscuring the purpose of the sacraments in history.[31]

In his later work, Schillebeeckx increasingly connects sacraments with a liberative praxis of the reign of God in history.[32] In *Church: The Human Story of God*, he writes,

> Confession and word, sacrament and praxis of faith, action which heals and opens up communication, following Jesus, do not make the experience of the world superfluous, while events in the so-called outside world in turn necessitate talking in the language of faith and Christian praxis. Precisely for that reason, historical and indeed social and political praxis in the world cannot be separated from the action of the church in proclamation, pastoral work and the sacraments. Anyone who severs this connection damages the internal structure of religion and being the church.[33]

That is to say that for Schillebeeckx there is an integral connection between the church and the world; the church exists in dialogue with the world. This is perhaps the most consistent emphasis of his entire corpus. The constant temptation to separate faith from daily life undermines the

Gospel call to transform history and reduces the sacraments to private channels of an "automatic" grace.

Conclusion

Building on his research into the sacramental theology of Thomas Aquinas, Schillebeeckx reaches out to the contemporary believer through the phenomenological language of encounter. While he normally avoids scholastic jargon throughout his discussion of sacraments as encounter, he remains committed to the notion that sacraments are infallible works of grace, and in that sense instances of efficient causality. The sacraments are the grace-giving encounter with the love of Christ incarnate in the words and gestures of the Church. They are effective signs (*signum efficax*) because, like Christ's human love, they are able "to effect an answering love."[34]

Louis-Marie Chauvet

Method

Unlike Schillebeeckx, who remains in dialogue with Aquinas, Chauvet seeks a new way forward in sacramental theology that departs from the metaphysical commitments of classical sacramental theology. Chauvet grounds his approach to sacraments in an analysis of the symbolic order. To be human is to live in a symbolic order.[35] By "symbolic order" Chauvet means the convergence of meanings and values in which human identity is formed and through which human experience of the world occurs. Our experience of the world and of ourselves is mediated, and indeed constructed, by that order through language. For Chauvet, following Martin Heidegger, reality comes to be through the evocative power of language.[36] Classical metaphysical categories on the other hand attempt to shoehorn all of reality into a totalizing theoretical construct using terms like causality and presence.[37]

Chauvet finds the notions of causality and presence employed by classical sacramental theology particularly problematic. First, the notion of causality, which he argues is inevitably involved in a productionist view of reality, seems incompatible with the understanding that sacraments are signs.[38] Talking about sacramental signs as causes ignores the complex context of human becoming in which sacraments participate. The language of cause and effect may help us to understand the interactions of billiard balls, but can it have anything to say about the life of grace? Second, Chauvet maintains that the conception of divine presence in classical sacramental theology ultimately leads to an idolatry in which God is conceived as a permanent, static presence. Therefore, Chauvet urges us to consent to "the presence of the absence of God."[39] The absence of God is revealed on the cross where God "'crosses himself out' in the crushed humanity of the crucified One."[40] Consenting to symbolic mediation involves a conversion, in both our theologizing and our worship, to a God beyond any human conception of "God."[41] Within this horizon, grace refers to a way of thinking and being, neither an objective divine presence nor a thing to be earned or hoarded, but a gratuitous gift that comes without any reason other than the sheer graciousness of a God fully revealed in Christ's kenotic self-giving.[42]

Christology

Chauvet takes the paschal mystery as his point of departure for understanding the connections between the Christ event and the sacraments. The paschal mystery refers to the entire drama of salvation.[43] Chauvet opposes any attempt to separate elements of the drama, including the incarnation, historical life, death, and resurrection, ascension, Pentecost, church, and Parousia.[44] Each of these elements can be understood only in relation to the others. Attempts to isolate one moment can have major theological and pastoral consequences. For example, many Christians, preferring to focus on the moment of incarnation, find in the nativity their preferred way to imagine Jesus. This popular image can easily be domesticated, enabling whole cultures to project onto the Christ child their own sets of meanings and values. But Chauvet reminds us that whatever we say about Jesus, including about his birth, we say, following the biblical witnesses, from the perspective of the resurrection, and therefore also the death of Christ. At the center of the paschal mystery is the cross, which provides the hermeneutical key for interpreting all the other events of the drama, because only the cross fully reveals who God is.

The cross challenges whatever preconceived or parochial notions of "god" we might have and reveals the true God "in the disfigured human being on the cross."[45] The self-effacing God made known in Jesus Christ crosses out "god." In Christ, God enters into solidarity with the human condition even to the point of death—even to the point of not being God—and finally reveals the fullness of divinity in the poverty of Christ's broken humanity.[46] The flesh and bone of the incarnation are destined for death. From the perspective of the cross the nativity already reveals the human poverty of the kenotic God. But to know God in this way, as wholly other, is the fruit of the Holy Spirit.

Chauvet argues that the Christological pole of sacramental theology must necessarily be accompanied by a Pneumatological pole. Chauvet explains, "the Spirit is the third term which works to subvert in us every idolatrous attempt at manipulating God (whether at the conceptual, ethical or ritual level . . .), and to keep perpetually open, as 'the question of questions,' the question of God's identity: God crossed out, never so divine as in God's erasure in the disfigured humanity of the Crucified."[47] The Spirit that raised Christ from the dead also raises up the body of the Church in whom the Word is made flesh in history, concretely in the ethical praxis of Christians.[48] Sacraments inscribe in the faithful the Word to which they testify with their bodies.

Church

The Church is the fundamental sacrament of the risen Christ. In order to make this point, Chauvet turns to the story of the supper at Emmaus. The disciples recognize Jesus in the ritual performance of blessing and breaking bread. Like those disciples, all who live in the time of the Church encounter Christ in the proclamation, liturgy, and life of the Church. Whenever the Church proclaims his death and resurrection, blesses and breaks bread in his name, lives in his justice and mercy, Christ is present. This presence is a symbolic presence, a presence of absence, and therefore also an eschatological presence calling the Church forward in history toward the Parousia. In this sense, the Church is not a privileged place in which one is granted special access to God, but the body of believers who consent to the presence of the absence of God in order to give God a body in history.

Ethics

Without the ethical moment of verification, a sacrament is easily reduced to idolatry—an idolatry of the self.[49] Chauvet engages the social sciences to develop a way of thinking about the sacramental economy that integrates the ethical. He calls his theory "symbolic gift exchange."[50] Unlike market exchange, which functions according to a logic of value and calculation (how much for how many?), symbolic exchange operates according to a logic of gift wherein having received a gift, one incurs an obligation to give to some other in turn. As opposed to the binary transaction of market exchange, symbolic exchange includes a third, setting up a cycle of gift, reception (obligation), and return gift (other).[51] Chauvet uses this model to think about the Eucharist. The gift of God's love is neither coerced nor constrained according to the logic of value and calculation, it is radically gratuitous. If it is received graciously, the Eucharist inspires a loving response of thanksgiving manifest in the desire to freely share this same love with another. Chauvet interprets the relationship between the "three moments" of Scripture, sacrament, and ethics through this theory of symbolic exchange.[52] The moment of Scripture tells the story of God's gift of salvation in history culminating in Christ's self-offering in death of his life to the Father. In the moment of sacrament, human beings gratefully receive the gift of salvation mediated by the memorial of Christ's passion. In gratitude for the gift they have received, Christians offer a return gift of love for others made concrete in practices of justice and mercy in imitation of Christ.

Conclusion

Chauvet's larger goal is not a sacramental theology per se, but what he calls a "foundational theology of sacramentality." He argues that traditional approaches to the sacraments that employ metaphysical categories have been discredited and that what is needed today is a theology of the sacramental.[53] Chauvet's goal is to compose a "theology which opens up a *sacramental reinterpretation*, initially modest but ultimately global in its potential extension, of what it means to *lead a Christian life*."[54] He proposes that the change in language regarding sacraments "constitutes a *fundamental revision of the terms with which we approach the problem*: those of language and symbol, and no longer those of cause and instrument."[55] Chauvet proposes a new method as reflection on the "arch-sacramentality" of embodied Christian existence. In the process, he deconstructs the theology that makes the sacraments into something Christians do, rather than enactments of who Christians are.

Conclusion

Schillebeeckx and Chauvet have dramatically reoriented contemporary Catholic sacramental theology over the past fifty years. Learning from developments in twentieth-century philosophy and social sciences, they tried to help contemporary Christians think about sacraments in a new way. Schillebeeckx urges his readers to see sacraments as the way to encounter God's saving grace in daily life. Chauvet invites his readers to a conversion to the presence of the absence of God made known through symbolic mediation. Both ask that we take the sign character of sacraments seriously and avoid talking about them in terms borrowed from physics like cause and effect. As signs, sacraments operate in the world of language in which Christian identity takes shape and the life of grace is lived in response to the gift of God's saving love manifest on the cross of Christ.

Schillebeeckx and Chauvet both follow Thomas Aquinas in affirming that the power of the sacraments comes from Christ's passion, but they interpret the paschal mystery in distinct ways.[56] For Schillebeeckx, the cross and resurrection reveal the reign of God in history, and the promise of its eschatological fulfillment. The cross, which he interprets in his earlier work as Christ's proper worship of the Father, is the symbol par excellence of the reign of God in the life and ministry of Jesus. Jesus's prophetic and liberative confrontation with the powers of the world leads ineluctably to the cross, and yet the resurrection confirms that this praxis of the reign of God, to which all Christians are called, is grounded in the hope of a world transformed and fully alive in God. For Chauvet, the cross reveals the humanity of the kenotic God of Jesus Christ. The cross liberates us from subservience to an idolatrous image of God that is really no more than a projection of our desire for mastery of what is other. The cross calls into question all our speaking about God, and asks us to undertake a work of mourning the presence of the absence of

God.[57] Taking Chauvet and Schillebeeckx together on these points we might think about sacraments as encounters with the presence of the absence of God that ask the faithful to give God a body in history.

The body of Christ in history, for both Schillebeeckx and Chauvet, is found in the Church. The Church is the fundamental sacrament because it is only through the witness of the Church that one comes to know the risen Christ in faith. The ecclesial mediation of sacramental encounter is fundamental to both thinkers, but not for reasons of canon law. Both freely admit that the Church regularly fails to be God's body, because it is a collection of fallible human beings. But this does not require that we abandon the Church for some more pristine, extra-ecclesial way of living. Instead, both Schillebeeckx and Chauvet call for an evangelization of the Church. This does not mean, as Schillebeeckx puts it, mere propaganda.[58] Rather it is a call to reinvigorate the sacramental life with an ethical practice.

Attention to the ethical is fundamental to the sacramental life. Both Schillebeeckx and Chauvet were concerned with the implications of earlier sacramental theologies that spoke about the mediation of sacramental grace in purely private and automatic ways. Is there any need to live a holy life if one is already made holy by the mediation of sacramental grace? What is our proper response to the gift of grace? Is grace something for me alone? Schillebeeckx was particularly concerned that today many people "pass Christianity by" because the grace of Christ is hidden by the counterwitness of so many Christians.[59] Chauvet, for his part, calls for an ethical verification of one's gracious reception of divine love in the sacraments in a gratuitous sharing of love with others.

Catholic sacramental theology after Vatican II unfolds in two stages represented by the protagonists of this chapter. The 1950s and 1960s produced a number of developments in sacramental theology based on developments in phenomenology and existentialism. Increasing attention to the place of the sacraments in the daily life and self-understanding of Christians expanded on the renewed emphasis on active participation among the laity in the liturgical life of the Church. These theologies often employed methods of correlation to talk about the relationship between the faith tradition and contemporary daily life. From the horizon of Vatican II, "the world" was not to be held in suspicion, rather it was the place where one meets God in nature and culture. Lieven Boeve notes, however, that theologies of correlation like that of Schillebeeckx suffered "when the still-existing overlap between Christianity and culture progressively disappeared."[60] Schillebeeckx's global and compact claim that everything is "grace made visible"[61] seems an inadequate description of the fragmentation and ambiguity of contemporary human experience. Schillebeeckx intended to return to sacramental theology toward the end of his life. His recently published collected works include a final essay, "Towards a Rediscovery of the Christian Sacraments: Ritualising Religious Elements in Daily Life," in which Schillebeeckx acknowledges Chauvet's developments and begins to chart a new development in sacramental theology with special attention to theories of ritual performance.[62]

While he rarely refers to Schillebeeckx explicitly, Glenn Ambrose suggests, "Chauvet's fundamental project, to provide a sacramental reinterpretation of the Christian life, can be seen as the continuation of Schillebeeckx's work."[63] And in many ways it is, as we have seen. Where Chauvet departs from Schillebeeckx is on the questions of foundations. Chauvet is rigorously antifoundationalist in his method in a way that Schillebeeckx never was. Nevertheless, Chauvet's postmodern method may be more adequate to twenty-first-century concerns.[64]

Like all important thinkers, both Schillebeeckx and Chauvet have received some share of criticisms. Boeve has drawn attention to a residual premodern religious horizon in Schillebeeckx's Thomist commitments, which may be foreign to many contemporary readers.[65] Bernard Blankenhorn probed Chauvet's interpretation of Thomas Aquinas on the question of causality and found it wanting.[66] He clarifies that for Thomas grace is, indeed, not a thing, but a quality. He also shows that Thomas's understanding of causality is not properly understood on the model of production Chauvet tries to force on him. Vincent Miller, on the other hand, questions whether Chauvet's work of deconstruction has been radical enough, especially as it regards the received tradition of liturgical practice.[67] Miller wonders whether one should really allow oneself to be formed by the symbolic mediation of the Church when the Church and its liturgies reflect deep-seated prejudices. My own criticism of Chauvet targets his Heideggerian method.[68] Criticisms notwithstanding, Schillebeeckx and Chauvet established themselves as leaders in the ongoing transformation of Catholic sacramental theology following Vatican II.

The twentieth century witnessed epochal developments in religion and culture that are still working themselves out. In the domain of religion, one of those developments was a fundamental reorientation of the way modern Christians relate to the sacred through symbols. Twentieth-century theologians confronted a sacramental crisis. If the enchanted world of the premodern horizon had disappeared, would sacraments go with it? In the midst of the Second Vatican Council, Romano Guardini wondered aloud whether "modern man" could celebrate the liturgy.[69] Schillebeeckx and Chauvet urge contemporary theologians to talk about the sacramental life of the church in a way that reaches contemporary people. Their legacy is a permanent part of ongoing conversations in sacramental theology today.

NOTES

1. Hans Boersma, *Nouvelle Theologie and Sacramental Ontology: A Return to Mystery* (London: Oxford University Press, 2009), 5. See Henri de Lubac, *Corpus Mysticum: The Eucharist and the Church in the Middle Ages*, trans. Gemma Simmonds, Richard Price, and Christopher Stephens, ed. Laurence Paul Hemming and Susan Frank Parsons (Notre Dame, IN: University of Notre Dame Press, 2006) and *The Mystery of the Supernatural*, Milestones in Catholic Theology, trans. Rosemary Sheed (New York: Crossroad, 1998). For a critical response to de Lubac, see Ralph McInerny, *Preambula Fidei: Thomism and the God of the Philosophers* (Washington, DC: Catholic University of America Press, 2006). See also Joseph Komonchak, "Returning from Exile: Catholic Theology in the 1930s," in *The Twentieth Century: A Theological Overview*, ed. Gregory Baum (Maryknoll, NY: Orbis Books, 1999).
2. Edward Schillebeeckx OP, *Christ, the Sacrament of the Encounter with God* (Kansas City, MO: Sheed and Ward, 1963), 3.
3. Ibid.
4. Ibid.
5. See Louis-Marie Chauvet, *The Sacraments: The Word of God at the Mercy of the Body*, trans. Madeliene Beaumont (Liturgical Press, 2001), xv.
6. Schillebeeckx, *Christ, the Sacrament*, 3.
7. Ibid., 5.
8. Ibid., 9.
9. Ibid., 16. See also ibid., 64.
10. Edward Schillebeeckx OP, *The Eucharist*, trans. N. D. Smith (New York: Sheed and Ward, 1968), 99–100.

11. See Emmanuel Levinas, *Totality and Infinity: An Essay on Exteriority*, trans. Alphonso Lingis (Pittsburgh: Duquesne University Press, 1969).
12. Schillebeeckx, *Eucharist*, 101.
13. Schillebeeckx, *Christ, the Sacrament*, 15–16.
14. Ibid., 17.
15. Ibid.
16. Ibid., 18.
17. Ibid., 18.
18. Ibid., 57.
19. 1 Cor. 11:26.
20. Schillebeeckx, *Christ, the Sacrament*, 62. These three aspects derive from Thomas Aquinas's discussion of sacraments at *Summa Theologiae*, book III, question 60, article 3.
21. Schillebeeckx, *Christ, the Sacrament*, 30.
22. Ibid., 61.
23. Ibid., 44.
24. Lubac, *Corpus Mysticum*, 9.
25. Schillebeeckx, *Christ, the Sacrament*, 47.
26. Ibid. See Edward Schillebeeckx, *The Mission of the Church*, trans. N. D. Smith (New York: Crossroad, 1973), 45.
27. Edward Schillebeeckx, *Church: The Human Story of God*, trans. John Bowden (New York: Crossroad, 1990), 184–85.
28. Schillebeeckx, *Christ, the Sacrament*, 183.
29. Ibid.
30. Ibid., 208.
31. Ibid.
32. See Susan A. Ross, "Church and Sacraments," in *The Praxis of the Reign of God: An Introduction to the Theology of Edward Schillebeeckx*, ed. Mary Catherine Hilkert and Robert Schreiter (New York: Fordham University Press, 2002), 134.
33. Schillebeeckx, *Church*.
34. Schillebeeckx, *Christ, the Sacrament*, 78.
35. See Louis-Marie Chauvet, *Symbol and Sacrament: A Sacramental Reinterpretation of Christian Existence*, trans. Patrick Madigan and Madeleine Beaumont (Collegeville, MN: Liturgical Press, 1995), 84.
36. Ibid., 88.
37. See Glenn P. Ambrose, *The Theology of Louis-Marie Chauvet: Overcoming Onto-Theology with the Sacramental Tradition* (Burlington, VT: Ashgate, 2012), 35.
38. Chauvet, *Symbol and Sacrament*, 21.
39. Ibid., 74.
40. Ibid.
41. Ibid., 265.
42. Chauvet, *Sacraments*, 88.
43. Ibid., 159.

44. Ibid., 160.
45. Ibid., 163.
46. Chauvet, *Symbol and Sacrament*, 493.
47. Ibid., 517.
48. Ibid., 526–29.
49. Timothy M. Brunk, *Liturgy and Life: The Unity of Sacrament and Ethics in the Theology of Louis-Marie Chauvet* (New York: Peter Lang, 2007).
50. Chauvet, *Sacraments*, 117.
51. Ibid., 121.
52. Chauvet, *Symbol and Sacrament*, 278.
53. Ibid., 1.
54. Ibid.
55. Ibid., 2.
56. Thomas Aquinas, *Summa Theologiae*, book III, question 62, article 5.
57. Chauvet, *Symbol and Sacrament*, 74.
58. Schillebeeckx, *Christ, the Sacrament*, 207.
59. Ibid.
60. Lieven Boeve, "Theology in a Postmodern Context and the Hermeneutical Project of Louis-Marie Chauvet," in *Sacraments: Revelation of the Humanity of God: Engaging the Fundamental Theology of Louis Marie Chauvet*, ed. Philippe Bordeyne and Bruce T. Morrill (Collegeville, MN: Liturgical Press, 2008), 5–23, here 18.
61. Schillebeeckx, *Christ, the Sacrament*, 215.
62. Edward Schillebeeckx, "Towards a Rediscovery of the Christian Sacraments: Ritualising Religious Elements in Daily Life," in *The Collected Works of Edward Schillebeeckx: Volume 11, Essays. Ongoing Quests*, ed. Ted Mark Schoof and Carl Sterkens, trans. Marcelle Manley (New York: Bloomsbury, 2014), 183–210.
63. Ambrose, *Theology of Louis-Marie Chauvet*, 153.
64. See, for example, Conor Sweeney, *Sacramental Presence after Heidegger: Onto-Theology, Sacraments and the Mother's Smile* (Eugene, OR: Wipf & Stock, 2015).
65. Lieven Boeve and Lambert Leijssen, eds., *Sacramental Presence in a Postmodern Context* (Leuven, Belgium: Peeters Press, 2001), 12.
66. See Bernard Blankenhorn, "The Instrumental Causality of the Sacraments: Thomas Aquinas and Louis-Marie Chauvet," *Nova et Vetera*, English ed. 4, no. 2 (2006): 255–94.
67. Vincent J. Miller, "An Abyss at the Heart of Mediation: Louis-Marie Chauvet's Fundamental Theology of Sacramentality," *Horizons* 24, no. 2 (1 September 1997): 230–47.
68. Joseph C. Mudd, *Eucharist as Meaning: Critical Metaphysics and Contemporary Sacramental Theology* (Collegeville, MN: Liturgical Press, 2014).
69. See Frank C. Senn, *New Creation: A Liturgical Worldview* (Minneapolis, MN: Augsburg Fortress, 2000), 85.

19

Feminism and Womanism

MARY VEENEMAN

Feminist Approaches to Sacraments in the Catholic Tradition

It is hard to consider the sacraments without considering them in the context of the Catholic tradition. The "sacramental principle" found in the Catholic tradition affirms that God's grace is pervasive throughout creation. Because it is fundamentally analogical, it also affirms points of continuity between God and creation and the ways in which creation reveals the Creator.[1] Sacraments are events in the church in which God's grace is made present to the community.[2]

Susan Ross argues that it is not enough to take current sacramental theology and discuss ways in which feminism might influence it. Rather, she argues, the entire meaning of the Christian sacramental vision must be reworked in light of women's experience.[3] In order to think about how sacramental theology experiences a radical shift in light of feminist thought, it is important to know the current state of sacramental thought.

Two significant thinkers for twentieth-century sacramental thought were Karl Rahner and Edward Schillebeeckx. Schillebeeckx, who was deeply influenced by phenomenology, published *Christ, the Sacrament of the Encounter with God*, in which he argued that human life with God is rooted in human experience in this world. Because of this, Schillebeeckx argued that the sacraments provide human beings with encounter with God. They are not simply those things that convey grace to the human being, but rather anticipatory signs of salvation and places where human beings live out the gospel.[4]

Karl Rahner connected the idea of symbol to the sacraments. He argued that the use of symbolic language for the sacraments had been considered problematic for centuries, largely because there was a growing separation between the symbol and the "real." This separation or distance should not be, Rahner argued. Rather, sacramentality is fundamentally rooted in the Incarnation and symbolic expression is central to how human beings know and love things.[5] In other words, to talk about the symbolic is not to assume some separation between symbol and reality.

Ross argues that the importance of Schillebeeckx and Rahner on sacramental theology is crucial; the work of both theologians incorporated more personal terms into the discussion of sacraments, which resulted in a closing of the sacred/secular divide, a reintroducing of symbolic language, and an emphasizing of the importance of the laity and the clergy into sacramental theology.[6] Ross also points out that many of the changes made in this area at the Second Vatican Council are directly indebted to Rahner and Schillebeeckx.[7]

Sacraments and Ordination

The issue of sacraments in the Catholic tradition is directly tied to Catholic views of ordination and in that, to Catholic views of Christ himself. Elizabeth Johnson makes this clear in her treatment of Christ in *Freeing Theology*. The problem with Christology as historically understood in the Catholic tradition, she argues, is that it has been interpreted within a "partriarchal framework," which has served to undergird male privilege in the church.[8] According to Johnson, some of the groundwork for this came from the earliest period of Christianity.

In the Greco-Roman world, Johnson argues, the early church built its structures in the image of both the patriarchal household and the Roman Empire. Because of this, Christ took on the image of head of household or absolute ruler in the early Christian imagination. According to Johnson, "He was seen as the Pantocrater, the absolute king of glory whose heavenly reign sets up and legitimizes the earthly rule of the head of family, empire, and church."[9] With the adoption of this imagery, Johnson claims, the image of Christ the liberator lost its "subversive significance."[10]

Johnson takes great care to stress that Jesus of Nazareth was historically male and that feminists do not have any interest in disputing that fact. At the same time, the ways in which the church has interpreted that maleness have been problematic. She writes,

> [Jesus's] maleness is constitutive for his personal identity, part of the perfection and limitation of his historical reality, and as such it is to be respected. His sex is as intrinsic to his historical person as are his race, class, ethnic heritage, culture, Jewish religious faith, his Galilean village roots, and so forth.[11]

To be clear, then, this is not a problem for feminist thinkers; rather, of all theologians, it should be liberation theologians (which includes feminist theologians) that affirm the overarching significance of one's context be that of ethnicity, gender, socioeconomic status, nationality, and so on.

To return to the question of ordination, it is important to point out that not all Catholic feminists see the ordination of women as the ultimate goal. Some argue that ordaining women as priests in the Catholic Church will not actually result in women gaining full partnership in the church. Elisabeth Schüssler Fiorenza views calls for women's ordination within the Catholic Church as being aimed at gaining women's full and equal participation in the church; but, given the current hierarchical structure of the church, she does not view it as possible.[12] In order for true equality to be a reality, according to Schüssler Fiorenza and others, the fundamental structure of the church must change. Without that change, the ordination of women will not lead to the "discipleship of equals" for which Schüssler Fiorenza and others call.

Anne Clifford argues that any genuine change must go beyond simply ordaining a few women to the priesthood. She argues that adding some female priests will not change the ministerial priorities of dioceses, which will remain male dominated. It will not result in major changes to canon law. Having women celebrate the Eucharist by itself will not change the language and imagery used to describe God. Clifford writes, "Women leading prayers in which 'man' supposedly includes women and God is imaged as always male will not advance the cause of women's full equality."[13] Clifford argues that the language must change, because if women are ordained and act in the place of Christ in offering the sacraments, the current male-dominated language would not fit the experience of the church, which would at that point include women in the sacrament of Holy Orders.[14]

The Nature of Christ and Human Salvation

The problem is how Jesus's maleness is interpreted within the church. First, Jesus is interpreted as the incarnation of the Word. Greek philosophy dictates that the Word, or Logos, is directly connected to maleness due to its inherent connection to rationality. This means that any understanding of the incarnate Word is connected to an anthropology that sees maleness as normative and femaleness as a nonnormative or secondary expression of humanity. What this means, according to Johnson, is that Christology ends up serving to undergird an understanding of male humanity as superior.[15]

Ultimately, the problem with this is that maleness becomes an essential part of Christ's humanity and an essential part of who he is as the redeemer of creation. This blocks women, because of their sex, from fully participating in the image of Christ, and it insinuates that maleness is an essential characteristic of the divine being. In addition, according to Johnson, the argument that the Logos chose to take on male humanity legitimizes the superiority of men over women in the gender of Jesus as a male. A final problem with this view is that it suggests that "sexist Christology" (to use Johnson's words) could potentially call women's salvation into question.[16]

What does any of this have to do with the sacraments? There is a closer connection than might initially meet the eye. The Catholic Church makes a number of arguments against the ordination of women to the priesthood (or the diaconate). One of the key arguments it makes involves the inability of women to image Christ. *Inter Insigniores* (1976) states that a fundamental element of the priestly role is the representation of Christ. When a bishop or a priest carries out his ministry, he acts not on his own behalf, but on behalf of Christ, who is the true actor.[17] This is true across the whole of priestly ministry, but it is particularly true in the celebration of the Eucharist, and it is here that the connection to the sacraments is clear. The Eucharist, according to *Inter Insigniores*, is

> the source and centre of the Church's unity, the sacrificial meal in which the People of God are associated in the sacrifice of Christ: the priest, who alone has the power to perform it, then acts not only through the effective

power conferred on him by Christ, but *in persona Christi*, taking the role of Christ, to the point of being his very image.[18]

In other words, when the priest celebrates the Eucharist, he stands in for Christ. It is truly Christ offering the sacrament to the congregation, and the priest serves as the image of Christ for the people of God. Although many might ask how this connects to the question of women serving as priests, *Inter Insigniores* makes it quite clear. The priest is a sign of the sacramental nature of the priesthood. The sign must be one that is "perceptible and which the faithful must be able to recognize with ease."[19] Citing Thomas Aquinas's claim that "sacramental signs represent what they signify by natural resemblance,"[20] *Inter Insigniores* declares that the one signifying Christ must have a "natural resemblance" to him, in order to be understood by the faithful. This is something that men, according to *Inter Insigniores*, are able to do, and that women cannot do.[21] Because of this, the church, claims *Inter Insigniores*, is not authorized to confer ordination of women. This was a position that was reaffirmed in John Paul II's *Ordinatio Sacerdotalis*.[22]

How does this potentially call the salvation of women into question? Johnson makes this clear when she refers to the early Christian maxim, "What is not assumed is not redeemed, but what is assumed is saved by union with God."[23] What Johnson alludes to here is the Apollinarian controversy. Apollinaris lived in the latter part of the fourth century. He considered himself to be a disciple of Athanasius and a vehement opponent of Arius. Because he wanted to counter Arius's theological claim that Christ was a creature higher above human beings but not divine, Apollinaris wanted to articulate an understanding of Christ that would protect his divinity. To do this, Apollinaris stated that Christ had a human body, with the soul or intellect coming directly from the Son. In other words, Jesus had a human body and a divine mind.[24]

The Church Fathers argued that anything that was not assumed by Christ was not actually redeemed by Christ. In other words, if Christ's soul or intellect was only divine, then the human soul or intellect is not actually redeemed by Christ. Apollinaris's views were condemned numerous times between the late fourth century and the Council of Chalcedon.[25]

What does any of this have to do with the sacraments or Elizabeth Johnson's view? If the Catholic Church argues that women fundamentally cannot image Christ in offering the Eucharist, it raises the question of whether or not one's sex is an essential component of humanity. If it is (and the claim that men alone can represent/image Christ implies that it is), then it raises the question of whether or not women can be fully redeemed by Christ if their humanity is in some way fundamentally different from Christ's humanity. If sex is such a fundamental part of humanity that women cannot image a male savior in celebrating the Eucharist, then it raises the question of whether or not a male savior can redeem all of their humanity. Johnson puts it this way: "Christ's solidarity with all of humanity is what is crucial for salvation." She argues that if the words in the Nicene Creed referring to Christ becoming human actually refer to him becoming a man—in that maleness is essential—then, since Christ did not take up female sexuality, female humanity is not saved.[26]

The question of ordination is central to the larger understanding of sacraments in Catholic thought. A true sacrament cannot happen without a person ordained in apostolic succession, and according to the Vatican, women cannot serve in this role because they do not "naturally resemble" Christ.

What is interesting about the relationship between women and the Eucharist historically, though, is that it is the very physicality of the sacrament that appealed to women. Ross points out that there was an important distinction in the way in which the Eucharist was discussed among theologians in the medieval period and the way in which laypeople, including women, understood it. Women, she claims, had been told for centuries that they were more physical and less spiritual, and so the sacrament in which Christ is bodily present took on great significance for them.[27]

The continuing centrality of the Eucharist in the Catholic tradition leaves women with a difficult choice. The maleness of Christ, as Johnson discussed, was seen as essential to the priesthood, and the church is "not free" to change its position. Ross argues that there are not many feminist theologians who argue for the inclusion of women in the current structures of the church.[28] This may be more readily workable in some Christian traditions, but Catholic feminists, according to Ross, are left with the question of the sacramental system. If they leave the current structures of the church, then they leave behind the sacramental system as they know it; but if they remain within the sacramental system, as it now exists, they are continuing to participate in a male-dominated system.[29] While a number of feminist theologians have offered suggestions on how worship might be changed, or how women might think differently about their participation in the sacramental system, the problem remains, and Ross raises the question of whether or not the sacramental system is intrinsically sexist and whether a feminist sacramental theology is possible or even necessary.[30]

If women are to stay within the context of the Catholic Church (and many Catholic feminists decide to do so), a feminist sacramental theology is necessary. Ultimately, Ross argues that a feminist sacramental theology must begin with the basic assumption of the full humanity of women and the recognition that complementarity is inherently problematic.[31] Complementarity is the assumption that there are fundamental differences between men and women and that these differences imply different roles and abilities. It is most clearly seen in John Paul II's *The Genius of Women*, where he argues that women's "nature" is primarily oriented toward tasks and skills associated with the home, such as raising children. Ross further points out that John Paul II makes connections between vowed religious women and the maternal role. As a result, even when women have a role in the church, it is connected to their essential nature.[32]

A feminist sacramental theology would call complementarity into question and would adequately take into account the experiences of women. Ross argues that the strength of women's experience is the connection between the body and soul and the physical and the spiritual. There is a clear connection to nature of the sacraments: spiritual realities made present in physical ways.[33]

Ross discusses ways in which feminist theology would nuance all seven of the sacraments, but the two that are most important for this discussion are holy orders and the Eucharist. Ross argues that since Vatican II, the emphasis in conversations about the priesthood has been around the priest as a servant of the believing community. Emphasis has tended to play down the importance of the hierarchy, which was a critical element of the training of priests. Jesus, Ross argues, should be the model for ministry in the Catholic Church. His ministry was inclusive, destabilizing, and nonhierarchical, which calls into question the relevance of human structures within the church. Human structures and institutions are useful only insofar as they serve the message of the gospel. Ross writes, "This ministry is critical of hierarchy for its tendency to concentrate power in a few. A feminist theology of ministry is one of empowerment, serving to energize the community, not to rule over it."[34]

This new way of thinking about ministry is already operant in some places. Ross cites women who preach, lead base communities, and fill leadership roles in the church to argue that women have taken up ministerial roles. At the same time, without the acceptance of women in ordained ministry in the Catholic Church, women will not experience the truest form of ministry, because the church is fundamentally sacramental.[35]

As has already been made clear in the discussions of Ross and Johnson, the Eucharist is essentially inseparable from questions about ordained ministry. Groups of women, even vowed religious women, cannot celebrate the Eucharist on their own. Because women are barred from ordination, the presence of a priest is necessary for any celebration of the Eucharist, and this simply serves to underscore the hierarchical nature of the church. Thus, a sacrament that emphasizes unity is also a symbol of inequality.[36]

The Eucharist at its core is a celebration of the presence of Christ in the local community. Here Ross relies on the example of medieval women who found their own understandings of and relationships to the Eucharist, which can be helpful in the contemporary context. In finding their own understandings of the Eucharist, these women did not allow the Eucharist to be fully encompassed by the hierarchy of the church. They instead found ways in which the Eucharist coincided with their own experiences. A feminist critique of the Eucharist that holds that it has become a symbol of power could point to this earlier precedent and think of fresh ways to discuss the Eucharist. Ross argues that at its heart, the Eucharist "symbolizes the extravagant self-gift of Christ and the unity of the community in all its diversity and ambiguity."[37] A feminist understanding of the Eucharist looks chiefly to the people of God who partake in the sacrament rather than the male priest who presides over the sacrament.[38]

Ross makes one final point, which is crucial for this discussion. She notes that the Eucharist must be seen in connection to hunger and poverty in the world (and here she cites liberation theology as the source for this claim). Physical hunger and spiritual hunger, she argues, cannot fully be separated. It is noteworthy that women in the Catholic Church have frequently taken on the role of feeding the poor.[39] It is with this glimpse of the oppressed that Ross gives us a good point at which to segue to another set of religious experiences.

Womanism and the Sacraments

One of the most significant problems with second-wave feminism is its perceived context versus its actual context. The women's movement of the 1960s and 1970s primarily represented the interests of white, upper-middle-class, well-educated women from North America and Western Europe. As a result, this was the type of audience to which second-wave feminists spoke, but some of these feminists did not readily see the many diverse backgrounds from which women actually hail or acknowledge that those diverse backgrounds can lead to diverse experiences.

The third wave of feminism has paid attention to diverse backgrounds and has created space for feminisms emerging from many different contexts. As a result, no treatment of feminism and the sacraments would be complete without acknowledging other streams of feminist thought. One other prominent stream of feminism within the context of the United States is that of womanism.

To quote Alice Walker's famous definition, "Womanist is to feminist as purple is to lavender."[40] What Walker means is that feminism does not adequately speak to or represent the experiences of African American women. Delores Williams cites Walker in her own explanation of womanism, writing that for Walker (and thus other womanists), a womanist is committed to survival and wholeness.[41] Williams writes that the two key concerns of womanist theology should be survival and community building. The goal of community building is to establish flourishing life for African American men, women, and children. Williams goes on to emphasize that Walker stresses that womanists are not to separate themselves, except for health, and that this should serve as a reminder to Christian womanist theologians that their concern for community building must ultimately extend to the whole community. Further, while womanists are clear that they are not guided by what white feminists have identified as "women's issues," they avoid divisions that separate groups of women. Womanists love other women regardless of color or sexual orientation.[42]

In thinking about the theological task itself, Williams writes that womanist methodology must look toward dialogue with many other groups, but it must also have a "liturgical intent." In other words, it must also be relevant to the life and work of the black church. While it does this, though, it also seeks to challenge elements of the black church with the "discordant and prophetic messages" that come out of womanism's engagement in dialogue with other groups. In other words, the womanist will challenge the black church to employ "justice principles" to select the sources that will shape the liturgy.[43] Williams writes,

> The question must be asked: "How does this source portray blackness/darkness, women, and economic justice for non-ruling class people?" A negative portrayal will demand omission of the source or its radical reformation by the black Church. The Bible, a major source in black church liturgy, must also be subjected to the scrutiny of justice principles.[44]

Womanist theology is ultimately seeking to bring the experiences of African American women into the work of theology. Williams argues that the appropriateness of womanist theological language will be judged insofar as it is able to bring the history, culture, and religious experience of African American women into the theological conversation.[45]

One of the most interesting womanist considerations of the sacraments comes in the context of biblical hermeneutics. Mitzi Smith looks to the gospel accounts of the feeding of the crowd and discusses the ways in which Jesus brings about "holistic transformation."[46] In the moment of being told to feed the crowd and seeing the way in which they cannot fully respond to the needs of the crowd, Jesus's disciples move from a mode of inadequacy to one of ability where they are able to respond to the crowd. Smith writes that the disciples "[recognize] that in and with them is the breath of life, or as we shall see below, the Son of God. The disciples respond to God (through Jesus) by feeding the hungry crowd out of their own poverty."[47] This event involves the sharing of food with a large multitude. Smith writes, "In the Matthean feeding story we witness what happens when human need intersects with divine mandate and what occurs when a human faith response to the divine mandate engenders human transformation. Through the feeding miracle, Jesus taught the disciples the art of 'radical sharing.'"[48]

Smith argues that this very moment with Jesus and the disciples is sacramental. Sacraments occur when human beings are connected to God. Because Christians experience God through Jesus, Jesus constitutes the ultimate sacrament. Smith writes, "In sacramental events, lives that have touched, experienced, and encountered God are changed. Lives are transformed not just for themselves but for others."[49]

This is an interesting approach to the idea of sacrament, because it directly connects back to the idea of community building that is so central to both Alice Walker's and Delores Williams's understandings of womanism. Here the disciples make a move that requires them to draw upon God and feed others out of their own poverty, thus embodying the new community of Jesus's followers.

This is not the only place Westfield's definition appears in womanist literature. Deborah Buchanan draws on Westfield's definition and the imagery of sacrament to discuss her approach to pedagogy. Buchanan writes, "Attentiveness to student voices and narratives fosters sacramental moments in the classroom. . . . Sacramental moments in the classroom are often an invitation to engage what Walker names as 'the least glamorous stuff' with which the black revolutionary artist must concern herself in the African American community."[50] Buchanan connects Westfield's location of sacrament within the realm of hospitality with her own practice of hospitality within her classroom. She notes that Westfield discusses storytelling, praying, making no assumptions, planning and designing lessons, listening actively, being attentive to emotions, responding, and claiming one's own personhood as important elements of this hospitality that creates sacramental moments in the classroom.[51]

These ideas directly connect to Melanie Harris's vision of the transformative community. She writes,

> Designed to both empower and instruct, transformative pedagogy is an act of justice itself in which all involved—learners, leaders, teachers, students—form a community in which they can be both transformed in the experience of learning together and act as transforming agents in work of partnership, mutuality, and grace.[52]

This communal atmosphere is formed through story. Harris stresses the importance of looking to the life experiences and contexts of students to move away from a model of teaching that looks at the instructor as the sole source of knowledge that is to be imparted to and taken in by the students.[53]

While the term "sacrament" is not frequently found in womanist literature, the emphasis on community in womanist thought seems to be fundamentally sacramental. Westfield's definition of sacrament is that which puts human beings in touch with God.

At their core, sacraments are physical things that, in some way, make spiritual realities present. While there is significant debate about exactly how the physicality of the sacraments relates to the spiritual realities, sacraments play an important role in the life of the church across the Christian tradition. Feminist and womanist theologies ask questions about both the role of sacraments in the church and the participation of women in the administration of the sacraments. These conversations get at the heart of the feminist and womanist project: to ask about the place of women in the contemporary church.

NOTES

1. Susan Ross, "God's Embodiment and Women," in *Freeing Theology: The Essentials of Theology in Feminist Perspective*, ed. Catherine Mowry LaCugna (San Francisco: Harper, 1993), 186.
2. Ibid., 186.
3. Ibid.
4. Ibid., 190–91.
5. Ibid., 191.
6. Ibid.
7. Ibid.
8. Elizabeth A. Johnson, "Redeeming the Name of Christ," in LaCugna, *Freeing Theology*, 118.
9. Ibid., 118.
10. Ibid.
11. Ibid., 118–19.
12. Anne Clifford, *Introducing Feminist Theology* (Maryknoll, NY: Orbis, 2001), 146. She quotes Schüssler Fiorenza on this point: "To think feminist and priesthood [together] is to construct an oxymoron. According to Webster's dictionary an oxymoron is a 'combination of contradictory or incongruous words.' 'Feminist priesthood' not only combines contradictory words but also incongruous realities and incompatible spiritual visions: the radical democratic equality of the disciple-

ship of equals stands in contradiction to the essential religious state of hierarchical office which is conferred in and through ordination in exchange for the promise of obedience and submission." Elisabeth Schüssler Fiorenza, "Feminist/Womanist Priests—An Oxymoron?," *New Women, New Church* 18 (Fall 1995): 10.
13. Clifford, *Introducing Feminist Theology*, 146.
14. Ibid.
15. Ibid., 118.
16. Ibid., 119.
17. *Inter Insigniores*, 5, in *Women and the Vatican: An Exploration of Official Documents*, ed. Ivy A. Helman (Maryknoll, NY: Orbis, 2012), 83.
18. Ibid., 84.
19. Ibid.
20. Ibid.
21. The extended statement is important: "Christ is of course the firstborn of all humanity, of women as well as men: the unity of which he re-established after sin is such that there are no more distinctions between Jew and Greek, slave and free, male and female, but we are all one in Christ Jesus (Gal. 3.28). Nevertheless, the incarnation of the Word took place according to the male sex: this is indeed a question of fact, and this fact, while not implying an alleged natural superiority of man over woman, cannot be disassociated in the economy of salvation: it is indeed in harmony with the entirety of God's plan as God himself has revealed it, and of which the mystery of the Covenant is the nucleus." *Inter Insigniores*, 84.
22. *Ordinatio Sacerdotalis*, 1, in Helman, *Women and the Vatican*, 176.
23. Johnson, "Redeeming the Name of Christ," 119.
24. Justo L. Gonzalez, *A History of Christian Thought: From the Beginnings to the Council of Chalcedon* (Nashville: Abingdon Press, 1987), 349, 351.
25. Ibid.
26. Johnson, "Redeeming the Name of Christ," 120.
27. Ross, "God's Embodiment and Women," 189. She cites Caroline Walker Bynum's *Holy Feast and Holy Fast* (Berkeley: University of California Press, 1988) here.
28. Ross, "God's Embodiment and Women," 192.
29. Ibid., 192–93.
30. Ibid., 193–94.
31. Ibid., 189.
32. Ibid., 198.
33. Ibid., 199.
34. Ibid., 203.
35. Ibid., 203–4. Here Ross writes, "This new vision of ministry has already begun to take shape: in the voices of women who preach, in the small base communities of men and women, in the exercise of women's leadership in nonpriestly capacities. But the vision will remain unfulfilled as long as women are excluded from ordination. For in the deeply sacramental tradition that is Catholicism, the message

remains that women cannot fully represent Christ and that although women's bodies may bear the Incarnation, women cannot serve as priests."
36. Ibid., 204.
37. Ibid. She cites Mary Collins on this point.
38. Ibid., 204–5.
39. Ibid., 205.
40. This definition is found in Alice Walker, *In Search of Our Mothers' Gardens: Womanist Prose* (New York: Mariner Books, 2003).
41. Delores S. Williams, "Womanist Theology: Black Women's Voices," in *Feminist Theology from the Third World: A Reader*, ed. Ursula King (Maryknoll, NY: Orbis, 1994), 77–78.
42. Ibid., 81–82.
43. Ibid., 83–84.
44. Ibid., 84.
45. Ibid.
46. Mitzi J. Smith, "Give Them What You Have: A Womanist Reading of the Matthean Feeding Miracle," in *I Found God in Me: A Womanist Biblical Hermeneutics Reader*, ed. Mitzi J. Smith (Eugene, OR: Cascade Books, 2015). She sites Yung Suk Kim on this term.
47. Ibid., 288.
48. Ibid., 289.
49. Ibid., 289. She cites N. Lynne Westfield on the definition of sacrament. Westfield, *Dear Sisters: A Womanist Practice of Hospitality* (Cleveland: Pilgrim, 2001), 81.
50. Deborah Buchanan, "Vocational Journeys: Moving toward a Creative and Disruptive Womanist Pedagogy," in *Faith, Feminism, and Scholarship: The Next Generation*, ed. Melanie L. Harris and Katie M. Ott (New York: Palgrave Macmillan, 2011), 184.
51. Ibid.
52. Melanie L. Harris, "Womanist Wholeness and Community," in Harris and Ott, *Faith, Feminism, and Scholarship*, 129.
53. Ibid.

20

Liberation Theology

MARIO I. AGUILAR

Liberation theology arose as a theological reflection on human and Christian experience within the enormous changes faced by the Church and society in the 1960s and in the context of Latin America. Within such period the majority of Latin Americans lived in poverty and most of them were Christians and Roman Catholics. The Catholic Church led by Pope John XXIII had, since 1959, asked seminal questions about herself regarding her role in God's plan of salvation, her involvement with the world, and her work of evangelization within societies in which the poor were the majority of churchgoers. In order to discuss those questions within the Church, and within the context of "a Church of the poor," John XXIII called the Second Vatican Council (1962–65). The Council's understandings of the Church in the modern world and the sacramental life within the Church were to be central in preparing a Latin American response to the Council that eventually became known as liberation theology.

This chapter explores (1) the historical and theological developments that led to the beginnings of liberation theology as a reflection on Christian experience, as a "second step" within the theological method, with the experience of God through the poor and the marginalized as "the first step"; and (2) the central role that the celebration and renewed understanding of the sacraments played within the prophetic work of liberation theologians and the Latin American Church as exemplified in the Eucharist celebrated by Ernesto Cardenal and the Nicaraguan peasant communities of Solentiname.

Historical Developments

Following the completion of Vatican II in 1965, the Latin American Bishops' Conference headed by the progressive Chilean Bishop Manuel

Larraín scheduled a general meeting of Latin American Bishops at Medellín (Colombia) that took place in 1968. The meeting coincided with a time of questioning about poverty and injustice in Latin America and with the start of a period in which military regimes became more the norm rather than the exception.[1] The preparations at the local diocesan level for the Medellín conference were intense, and those leading the deliberations at continental level were not the theologians but the pastoral bishops who in the case of Brazil were already experiencing a systematic violation of human rights since the military had taken charge of the Brazilian government in 1964. Within the post–Vatican II deliberations, the renewal of the liturgical celebrations of the sacraments became central to the renewal of the sacramental life of the Christian communities all over Latin America (the new rites became available in 1972). The restoration of the sacraments of initiation (Baptism, Eucharist, Confirmation) and the sacraments of penance, marriage, anointing of the sick, and ordination within a liturgy that emphasized the people of God's participation in the vernacular language became crucial for the ecclesial reflections that led to the development of a Latin American liberation theology by 1968.

Within this difficult and changeable political period within the Latin American countries, the newly created Episcopal Conferences responded to the implementation of Vatican II with enthusiasm and were fully supported by a committed Catholic laity that were influenced by John XXIII's *Pacem in Terris* (1963) and Paul VI's *Populorum Progressio* (1967). The ideas contained in both encyclicals spoke of the possibility of a just order in society but an order that had to consider social development rather than armed struggle as its core value for an economic stability that provided the possibility of restoring dignity to all nations and to all human beings. The chore for such reflection was the celebration of the sacraments, particularly the Eucharist, in which the values of peace and justice of the Kingdom of God were already actualized. If societies were marked by class and injustice, all those who celebrated the Eucharist celebrated the justice of God in which all were invited to proclaim the values of the Kingdom of God and to share bread and wine together as equals around the table of God.

The genesis of Latin American liberation theology coincided with Christian reflections on development and the Church's involvement with the world that extended to the search for a theology of inculturation in Africa and the Christian dialogue with world religions in Asia.[2] However, within those globalized developments a Peruvian priest, Gustavo Gutiérrez, became the face of liberation theology and helped other priests' reflections vis-à-vis the implementation of Vatican II. Those priests were trying to develop a systematic framework that connected the life of the Latin American poor, development theory, and a divine sense of history, all under an umbrella of theological and material liberation.[3] *A Theology of Liberation* (1971) became the classic theological monograph; however, many other theologians started working on Christology, ecclesiology, soteriology, the history of the Church, and the role of the basic Christian communities.[4] The final document of Medellín supported that theological program by reiterating the materiality of God's salvation and by encouraging an ecclesial immersion in the life of the materially poor, the marginalized, and those who were the victims of social injustice due to the fact that societies had created unjust structures included by the Latin American bishops under the umbrella of "structural sin."[5] All those ecclesial involvements with the poor and the marginalized found their genesis in the celebration of the Eucharist by those who by the nature of their Baptism and the affirmation of the sacrament of Confirmation had been given Christ's prophetic characteristics.

The development of Latin American theology has an enormous complexity, but its genesis can be traced to the European reflection by Gustavo Gutiérrez and Juan Luis Segundo SJ in France, where both studied at the time when John XXIII (1959) had called the Council and had spoken of "a church of the poor."[6] Segundo and Gutiérrez had a different pastoral experience, and that experience shaped what Segundo called "two kinds of liberation theology."[7] Thus, for Gutiérrez and his life in the slums, the poor and the marginalized were at the center of God's work because they represented the incarnation of God while theology as a reflection was a "second act." The option for the poor, a theological option proclaimed by the Latin American Bishops at their Puebla meeting (1979), meant for Gutiérrez that Jesus in his life expressed a real closeness to the poor. Thus, liberation theology arose out of "our better understanding of the depth and complexity of the poverty and oppression experienced by most of humanity; it is due to our perception of the economic, social, and cultural mechanisms that produce that poverty;

and before all else, it is due to the new light which the word of the Lord sheds on that poverty."[8]

For Segundo, who had experienced pastoral work with the Uruguayan educated elites, liberation theology remained within the realm of the educated theologians who through their pastoral ministry passed some fresh ideas about the implementation of Vatican II to the laity and to the Catholic faithful in parishes. Those ideas reflected Segundo's own work with reflection groups, university students, and young professionals and his own commitment to a systematic investigation of theological themes at the service of the Church.

There is no contradiction between the role of the theologian in Gutiérrez and Segundo's work, but certainly Gutiérrez's work triggered numerous theological writings that used Marxist historical analysis as a hermeneutical tool in order to explore social realities. Within the context of Latin America in the 1970s Christians and Marxists had encountered each other in the same project of challenging unjust social structures, Christians following the values of the Kingdom of God, Marxists following the ideals of a revolution in which the people and the masses would be equal through further revolutions inspired by the Cuban Revolution (1959). The radicalization of the Latin American theologians coincided with the rising of Christians who equated the Gospel with a socialist political project, the so-called Christians for Socialism, and the consequent persecution of pastoral agents by the military in Brazil, Chile, Argentina, Uruguay, Paraguay, El Salvador, and Guatemala.

The optimism of the Council Fathers at the end of Vatican II, and the rich documents that reincorporated the Church into the contemporary world, created an optimistic and exciting atmosphere in Latin America. However, there was no way in which all the different pastoral agents were going to act and think in the same way. There was the need to renew the Christian communities, but there was also the need to outline economic development and a better distribution of wealth within society. In this sense, the complexity of the task of the bishops' reflection in Medellín was enormous and the dissemination of their own pastoral ideas necessary and much wanted by religious sisters, laypeople, and particularly the grassroots communities. All those reflections at a local level took place within the daily Eucharist and the communal reflection on the Gospels undertaken by each Christian community in Latin America.

The means to achieve that social and economic change were of concern to Christians and to Marxists alike, and therefore within a post–Cuban Revolution period a few Christian communities and a few priests understood the "signs of the times" as calling them to join Latin American groups that wanted to foster violent revolutions. That was the case of Fr. Camilo Torres Restrepo, a Colombian priest who was to become a symbol of a possible Christian commitment to Latin American revolutions. Already at the time of the Council Camilo Torres had developed the idea that the revolutionary struggle could be a Christian and a priestly activity. His influence was large in Colombian society because he himself came from a well-to-do family but also because he was involved with students at the National University of Colombia. Cardinal Luis Concha moved him from the university to a suburban parish, where he started attacking the hierarchy of the Church by suggesting that they were part of the Colombian oligarchy, a group that according to him impeded the formation of a more just society in Colombia. In June 1965 he asked to be relieved from his priestly duties, and in November 1965 he joined the Colombian guerrilla, the Ejército de Liberación Nacional. Torres was killed on 15 February 1966 and became an icon for many other Christians in Latin America. The main priestly duty of every priest engaged with change and development in Latin America was to preside over the communal celebration of the Eucharist.

Within that context of ongoing change and political challenges Paul VI traveled to Bogotá, Colombia, in 1968 in order to open the Thirty-Ninth International Eucharistic Congress. The first visit by a pope to Latin America was seen as a great moment for a growing Church within the context of a communal reflection on the Eucharist. Thus, leading Latin American bishops such as Cardinal Silva Henríquez of Chile felt excitement about the Pope's visit to Latin America and saw the visit as a service to all.[9] The "continent of hope" was the best ground for the implementation of Vatican II, and Silva Henríquez felt that finally the "servant of the servants of God" was arriving to visit the poor of Latin America as the leader of a servant Church. The meeting of Latin American bishops in Colombia was to set the guidelines for the implementation of Vatican II in Latin America, and the final document of Medellín was to vindicate the demands by those protesting against the Pope's visit rather than to crush their pastoral dreams. It is possible to argue that without the arrival of Paul VI the meeting of all Latin American bishops at Medellín would not have had the same strength and the same impact on the pastoral life of the Church in Latin America.

Thus, on 21 August 1968, Silva Henríquez traveled to Colombia in order to await the Pope's arrival on the following day. During his visit to Colombia, Paul VI ratified the winds of change given by Vatican II, offered the support of the Church to the poor and their just causes, and condemned any advocacy of violence in order to achieve a just society in Latin America. The visit coincided with the celebration of the International Eucharistic Congress in Bogotá between 18 and 25 August 1968. Unlike previous Eucharistic Congresses in Buenos Aires and Sao Paulo, the Colombian one was a celebration of the Christian communities under the motto *Vinculum Caritatis*.[10] During the Eucharistic Congress Paul VI, addressing peasants, stressed his commitment and that of the whole Church to defend the plight of the poor, to proclaim human and Christian dignities, to denounce injustices and abuses against peasants, and to foster initiatives and programs that supported people and their development.[11] In summary, Paul VI reaffirmed an ongoing ecclesial understanding in Latin America: the theme of the poor as a sacramental presence of Christ.[12] The Pope warned those attending the celebrations about the danger of putting their trust in violence or revolution.[13] The importance of the facts that this was the first time that a pope visited Latin America and that no other pope had journeyed outside Europe in order to physically be with the sick and the orphans cannot be underestimated.[14]

Paul VI inaugurated the second general meeting of Latin American bishops at Medellín at the cathedral in Bogotá on 24 August and returned to Rome. Those attending the Medellín conference were 137 bishops with the right to vote and 112 delegates and observers.[15] Thus, the Medellín conference was a fruitful opportunity for renewal, and many of the concepts outlined in the final document were new additions to the social doctrine of the Church, including, "a truly human economics," "institutionalized violence," and "sinful structures." At the center of all those deliberations there was a new understanding of the celebration of the sacraments to become communal, active, and participative celebrations of faith in order to challenge injustice, poverty, and underdevelopment within Latin American nations.

The Impact of Medellín

Thus, it was at Medellín in 1968 that the theological movement of a Latin America driven by lay unpublished theologians began.[16] The Church in Latin America had to ask questions about their religious and sacramental practices within difficult political circumstances, and aided by the theological reflection of Gutiérrez the bishops did not separate religion and politics, but provided a political response of commitment to political change and the defense of human rights. Virgilio Elizondo has argued, for example, that the transformative impact of the Medellín conference on the Church's pastoral practice and theology was far greater than that exercised by any other council of the Church. No particular dogmas or confessions of faith—Reformed or Catholic—were questioned or challenged. Instead, the whole edifice of Constantinian Christian thought, imagery, and symbolism was radically challenged in the name of Christianity itself. What was initiated was not a new academic or philosophical theology, but the transformation of the very structures and methods of doing theology out of a sacramental practice and reflection. To be faithful and authentic, Christian theology would have to emerge out of the spiritual experience of the believing community grappling with its history and responding to its contemporary situation within a daily celebration of the Eucharist.

The subsequent pastoral implementation of Medellín was very different in the various Latin American countries, but with the exception of Argentina and Colombia created the necessary pastoral and theological reflection as to challenge state oppression understood as "structural sin." In the case of Chile, for example, the bishops, whenever needed, challenged the military regime of General Pinochet, while in neighboring Argentina there was an avoidance of any prophetic denunciation in the name of the Gospel.[17] The Argentinean Church where Pope Francis (then Fr. Jorge Bergoglio SJ) was teaching and leading retreats supported the military for the most part, while the Jesuits followed the directives of their congregation to lead a more simple life and to embrace poverty in the spirit of St. Ignatius of Loyola, their founder.[18]

Among the groups that were going through a renewal and a Latin American reformation were consecrated men and women who already had been encouraged by the reflections of Medellín. Among them the

Jesuits played a significant role through their 1968 public declaration on their lifestyle and their pastoral work throughout Latin America. That declaration by the Jesuit Provincials preceded the conference of Medellín. When the Provincials of all the Jesuit provinces of Latin America met in Rio de Janeiro, Brazil, 6–14 May 1968, they reflected on their view of mission and their positioning within Latin America. As a result of their deliberations they decided to reiterate their involvement "in the temporal life of humankind."[19] However, within the particular context of Latin America their statement for a larger involvement within a movement that could change unjust structures and to be with the people was very strong and very down to earth. There was no high theology within the document but a challenge to personal lives and community activities with an added social and religious utopia. In a central passage of that document they asserted,

> In all our activities, our goal should be the liberation of humankind from every sort of servitude that oppresses it: the lack of life's necessities, illiteracy, the weight of sociological structures which deprive it of personal responsibility over life itself, the materialistic conception of history. We want all our efforts to work together toward the construction of a society in which all persons will find their place, and in which they will enjoy political, economic, cultural, and religious equality and liberty.[20]

Within the document and in later educational practices the Jesuits addressed a usual criticism toward their academic institutions, particularly schools and universities: that Jesuit schools educated the children of the rich and that their universities reiterated that social paradigm. The document argued that all Jesuit institutions should foster the social gospel and that all students should be involved in practical activities in which they would experience different social realities.[21] The Jesuit Provincials called for a formation of consciences among those they taught and for using the media to foster those aims. However, the final call was aimed at all Jesuit superiors to implement those changes as soon as possible, even when some of those changes would take some time. Moreover, there was also a call for a personal conversion with deep questions to each individual Jesuit working in Latin America outlined in the following paragraph of the Jesuit document:

> Are we capable of responding to the world's expectations? Are our faith and charity equal to the anxiety-ridden appeals of the world around us? Do we practice self-denial sufficiently, so that God is able to flood us with light and energy? Does personal prayer have its proper place in our life, so that we are united with God in this great human task that cannot succeed without God? Can the Society keep within its ranks those members who do not want to pray or who do not have a real and personal prayer in life?[22]

The response to the tenants of Medellín by the Jesuit communities in Latin America was swift and sometimes unsettling for parents and teachers of those students involved. Parents were told about the revised Jesuit aims within their schools and were asked to adhere to them despite conservative parents' apprehensions toward the formation of their children outside the academic classroom. Despite the large number of Jesuits who left the Society of Jesus after Vatican II, Jesuit secondary schools maintained their academic excellence with the addition of summer work or activities of a social nature for pupils in their last years of secondary school. Within universities it was easier to comply with practical activities of a social nature, as most university students were affected by a political climate of change, political awareness, and political questioning. Thus, the Jesuits not only affected the developments of theologies, pastoral or otherwise, but also became involved in many activities related to the defense of indigenous minorities, political refugees, and migrants. All those pastoral activities came out of the refreshed rites of celebration of the Eucharist and the increased use of Bibles and reflection on the Word of God by members of school, parish, and Christian communities.

In the case of El Salvador, where over the years the prominent theologian Jon Sobrino SJ worked, the Jesuits decided to build and implement a university that was to be a reflection of the open spirit of Vatican II and at the same time became a model institution for a deep commitment to the poor and the marginalized. The challenges of Medellín assured the Jesuit community in El Salvador that Medellín was not only a *kairos* but also a movement that could not be stopped easily. A short outline of the influential educational Jesuit enterprise arising out of Medellín is in order here, particularly the contribution of the Jesuit University of Central America (UCA). For it is a fact that the educational reform and tertiary education led by the Jesuits in El Salvador was the cause of the assassination of several Jesuits by the Salvadorian Army and the death squads paid by Salvadorian landowners. The new reformation had a strong stance among Jesuits, and the Jesuits, together with Monsignor Oscar Romero, shaped the application of such reformation within Central America in general and El Salvador in particular. The center of all those projects and changes was the daily celebration of the Eucharist at the Cathedral and by the UCA community.

Construction of the UCA campus began in 1970 through financial loans from the Inter-American Development Bank (Banco Interamericano del Desarrollo). The UCA under Román Mayorga Quirós as rector moved quickly into a progressive line following changes within the Jesuits, and by 1976 professor Ignacio Ellacuría SJ attracted the animosity of El Salvador's President Arturo Armando Molina after he wrote an editorial in the university's magazine criticizing the halting of the Salvadorian agrarian reform. The government withdrew educational subsidies to the UCA, and the attacks on the Jesuits started with the assassination of the Jesuit Rutilio Grande in March 1977. From that moment the UCA supported all pastoral plans by Archbishop Romero through its department of theology, headed by Jon Sobrino. In 1979, Ellacuría became rector of the UCA and moved the university into research programs related to the national realities of El Salvador while immersing students, staff, and the university community in the social realities of the poor of El Salvador. As the Salvadoran Civil War continued, Ellacuría became very prominent within the mediation of peace accords and spoke strongly against injustice and human rights abuses on television, on UCA radio, and in UCA publications.

Ignacio Ellacuría SJ, at the time of his assassination rector of the university, articulated this particular ministry in the following words: "the university should be present intellectually where it is needed: to provide science for those who have no science; to provide skills for the unskilled; to be a voice for those who have no voice; to give intellectual support for those who do not possess the academic qualifications to promote and legitimate their rights."[23] Jon Sobrino SJ was less romantic about the possibilities of a university due to past experiences whereby Jesuit universities became top educational institutions, but in doing so they compromised their possibilities of challenging unjust and sinful structures within society.

Sobrino advocated the inclusion of the poor within a Christian university by arguing that it was unrealistic to suggest that a university should be located among the poor but that all activities and the central activities of a Christian university should look toward the poor. For him, one of the central activities within this kind of university was the dialogue between faith and science and therefore the importance of the teaching and research of theology as a discipline and as a reflection on the life of the poor and marginalized from a Christian perspective. Sobrino's statement about theology within a university became central to understanding the challenges that the Jesuits posed to the powerful in El Salvador and the inspiration they provided to many of the communities linked to their extramural courses and training of leaders of Christian communities within El Salvador. Sobrino argued very strongly that "theology must be turned, then, towards the people of God; it should be inserted effectively among them, draw its agenda from them and accompany them. In this sense, university theology should be a moment of theo-praxis for the whole people of God and should be considered as a theo-culture, a Christo-culture, an ecclesio-culture—that is, an instrument that cultivates and nurtures faith, hope, and love of God's people."[24]

The impact of the 1968 Conference of Bishops on Latin America cannot be underestimated. The conclusions of the conference followed a deep reflection on the role and existence of the Catholic Church in Latin America and triggered change within the Church and also within the spheres of ecclesial influence in Latin America. The Jesuit response to Medellín was crucial because the Jesuits were in charge of the best schools and best universities of Latin America; as a result, they had a timely influence on the Latin American intellectuals and professionals. The Jesuit response to the Medellín document was a communitarian act of love arising out of the celebration of the Eucharist in which a theological response to liberation also entailed the possibility of questioning the Jesuit way of life at that time. Thus, the Jesuits reformed themselves as well as triggering challenges and winds of reform to the local churches in Latin America where the Jesuits played a central role in religious and political circles. Other religious congregations followed the same example, and an exodus from well-to-do places of ministry took place whereby religious women in numbers left their jobs teaching in well-to-do public schools, moving to where the poor lived and worked, mainly in shantytowns and deprived areas of Latin American cities. Missionary orders with foreign personnel also took very seriously the conclusions of Medellín and opened new parishes in locations where previously only Marxist activists and left-wing ideologists had any access. Within all those places the celebration of the sacraments and their pastoral understanding triggered a challenge toward the nation-state and the unjust social structures within Latin American society.

It is a fact that the role of religious communities and the celebration of the sacraments have been generally underplayed in the assessment of changes that took place in 1968 and after. Therefore, it is particularly important to remember that religious congregations and communities with expatriate missionaries from Ireland, Spain, France, and the United States expressed their own search for a closer follow-up of the Gospel within a movement from their convents and their religious houses to the periphery, to the shantytowns, and to places where they were most needed. This movement toward the periphery and the involvement of Christians within movements of liberation led to a golden pastoral moment for Latin America. The period of the 1970s and 1980s could be called a true *kairos* and at the same time the formation of a movement for liberation that was to shape the pastoral development of the universal church.

In conclusion, the year 1968 provided the beginning of a new reformation in and for Latin America. The third conference of Latin American Bishops in Puebla (Mexico, 1979) reiterated this movement toward the poor in society and proclaimed God's preferential option for the poor. The fourth conference of Latin American Bishops in Santo Domingo (Dominican Republic, 1992) reflected on the five hundred years since the arrival of Christianity in Latin America and stressed the central role of indigenous populations in the decision making and future of the Church in Latin America. The fifth conference of Latin American Bishops in Aparecida (Brazil, 2007) reflected on the role of the Church in a more secularized and democratic Latin American society, emphasizing under the guidance of Cardinal Jorge M. Bergoglio (currently Pope Francis) the mission of the Church to the marginalized in society; the final document highlighted the service and mission of the Church and gave a secondary role to the expansion or self-reflection of the Church upon herself.

The Sacraments and Prophetic Liberation

Liberation theology as a "second step" within the theological thinking reflected the first step of prophetic action in learning from the poor and the marginalized. For the most part the reflection on praxis, on a liberating praxis with the poor, was carried out during the celebration of the Eucharist. Communal reflections on the Gospel read as the third reading of the Liturgy of the Word became central to the action-reflection-action carried out by the Latin American Christian communities. There are very few of those reflections transcribed. However, one of the most important transcriptions was collected and edited by Ernesto Cardenal, priest, theologian, and poet, and included reflections carried out in the archipelago of Solentiname in Nicaragua, within a peasant community, in the years before the triumph of the Nicaraguan Revolution (1979).

Cardenal identified his community with a lay monastery under the name of Our Lady of Solentiname. Members of the Christian community included William Agudelo and Teresita, a couple who had two children named Irene and Juan, and they were joined by some local young men, Alejandro, Elbis, and Laureano. They lived on the produce of the land, and while from the start they cultivated the earth, in order to survive financially they were forced to work on objects that could be sold and indeed were later sold all over the world. Their work included the making of ashtrays, candle sticks, and souvenirs in the shape of local fauna. They shared their profits in a common purse and supplied for the needs of each individual community member. The utopian nature of the community was summarized by Cardenal's wish that one day there would be no money in the world and that everybody would be filled with love for each other.

When the monastic experiment ended because of the bombardment of the islands by the Armed Forces of Somoza, some of the transcripts of those conversations that took place after the reading of the Gospel at the Sunday Mass in Solentiname were published. The two published volumes became important testimonies to Cardenal's creativity and to the driving force of contemplation into the life of a priest who became identified with the politics of the Nicaraguan Revolution and with the involvement of Latin American priests in politics. However, as Cardenal expressed it during the moments in which he found the life of a government minister tough after he was appointed minister of culture within the first Nicaraguan revolutionary government (1979), he was interrupting his contemplative life only in order to serve the people, and he was looking forward to the day when he would cease to be a politician and return to celebrate the Eucharist in a Christian community.

In the two volumes published as *The Gospel in Solentiname*, Cardenal explained through a short introduction that the *Sitz im Leben* of the commentaries collided.[25] Cardenal stressed the fact that there were different personalities involved in the commentaries that at the end were the work of the Spirit in an isolated archipelago in which not everybody had access to a boat to reach Cardenal's community. Those reflections took place within a Sunday Eucharistic celebration in which copies of the New Testament were distributed to all participants, some of whom, particularly the elderly, could not read the text.[26] After the Mass, all participants shared a simple but communal lunch.

The communal commentary spoke of the involvement of Christians within Nicaraguan society in which social injustice and the oppression of those who had land was their ordinary reality. For example, the community discussed the Gospel passage taken from Matthew 22:15–22 where Jesus is challenged on his allegiance to Caesar and/or God and in which at the end he told those present "Give to Caesar what is Caesar's and to God what is God's."[27] Cardenal commented that those questions were a trap against Jesus to see what he would say. Laureano commented that Jesus told them to build the kingdom of love and to wait for a confrontation with Rome that would take place only later; in other words the emperor loved his image on the coins, and Jesus was asking his disciples to love God first and not the selfishness of money.[28] Alejandro expanded that idea by reminding the group that at that time the emperor was considered God and Jesus challenged the possibility of paying taxes to a foreign ruler who was not the God of the Jews or the God whom Jesus was speaking about. Alejandro reflected on the passage, suggesting that Jesus was speaking against Roman imperialism and that he speaks against any imperialism today.[29] Every Sunday, Cardenal linked the different comments in one long conversation, and after Alejandro had spoken Cardenal argued that Jesus was acting like a politician as a leader of the people who does not change his opinion because he is pushed to do so; Jesus not only spoke to the Jews about the politics of that time but speaks to all peoples as well. For Cardenal, there is still imperialism today associated with the service to money, however for him to give to God what is God's is to take part in a revolution. Indeed, for Cardenal God liberates because he is always pushing for change, for a revolution; that is the message of all prophets.[30] After Cardenal's comments, all those present agreed that money in itself was good but that selfishness because of money was not.

The celebration of the Eucharist in Solentiname was a common occurrence in Latin America at the time when liberation theology as a theological reflection was emerging. Those who became known as theologians of liberation of the first generation celebrated the Eucharist with a Christian community daily and reflected on what was happening around them in the context of the communal celebration of the sacraments.

Liberation theology cannot be understood without understanding the sacraments, particularly those of initiation: Baptism, Eucharist, and Confirmation. These three sacraments were taken very seriously by Christian Communities in Latin America after Vatican II in order to provide a response to the challenges of the Council. Those challenges were taken up by the Latin American bishops meeting in Medellín in 1968 by providing the reflections brought to them previously by all Christian communities. The process that followed was of an intense Christian involvement in the world of the poor, the majority of Latin Americans, from the point of view of the Gospel. Liberation theology arose after the conference of Medellín as a theological method coming out of that community experience, the experience of celebrating together the sacraments, especially the Eucharist, within the world of the poor and the marginalized.

NOTES

1. For a detailed analysis of the relation between church and state at the period and within different Latin American countries, see Jeffrey Klaiber SJ, *The Church, Dictatorships, and Democracy in Latin America* (Maryknoll, NY: Orbis, 1998).

2. At the theological level African and Latin American theologians encountered each other through the Ecumenical Association of Third World Theologians (EATWOT), and the first period of their work was coordinated by Enrique Dussel and François Houtart. See a useful historical overview in Enrique Dussel, "Theologies of the 'Periphery' and the 'Centre': Encounter or Confrontation?," in *Different Theologies, Common Responsibility, Babel or Pentecost?, Concilium* 171 (1984), ed. Claude Geffré, Gustavo Gutiérrez, and Virgil Elizondo (Edinburgh: T&T Clark, 87–97); see also EATWOT, *The Emergent Gospel* (Maryknoll, NY: Orbis Books, 1976). For a theological overview, see Theo Witvliet, *A Place in the Sun: An Introduction to Liberation Theology in the Third World* (London: SCM Press, 1985). An Asian Christianity as a Christian project was more problematic; numbers of Christians in Asia, with the exception of the Philippines, remain small, and the post–Vatican II discussions on salvation within the world religions created more than an impasse between those who adhered to a Christ-centric option (exclusivists) and those who understood the world religions as places where God could save (inclusivists). See Paul F. Knitter, *No Other Name? A Critical Survey of Christian Attitudes towards the World Religions* (London: SCM Press, 1985).
3. For historical data on his life, see Sergio Torres, "Gustavo Gutiérrez: A Historical Sketch," in *The Future of Liberation Theology: Essays in Honor of Gustavo Gutiérrez*, ed. Marc H. Ellis and Otto Maduro (Maryknoll, NY: Orbis, 1989), 95–101.
4. Gustavo Gutiérrez, *Teología de la liberación: Perspectivas* (1971; 16th ed., Salamanca: Ediciones Sígueme, 1999); for a full review of the theological works of eighteen Latin American theologians, see Mario I. Aguilar, *The History and Politics of Latin American Theology*, vols. 1–2 (London: SCM Press, 2007).
5. See Second General Conference of Latin American Bishops 1968, *The Church in the Present-Day Transformation of Latin America in the Light of the Council II Conclusions* (Washington, DC: United States Catholic Conference, 1970).
6. For a comprehensive history of liberation theology and of some of the most prominent theologians of liberation, see Mario I. Aguilar, *The History and Politics of Latin American Theology*, 3 vols. (London: SCM Press, 2007–8).
7. Juan Luis Segundo SJ, "Two Theologies of Liberation" (Toronto, 22 March 1983), in *Liberation Theology: A Documentary History*, ed. Alfred T. Hennelly (Maryknoll, NY: Orbis, 1990), 353–66.
8. Gustavo Gutiérrez, "Option for the Poor," in *Mysterium Liberationis: Fundamental Concepts of Liberation Theology*, ed. Ignacio Ellacuría SJ and Jon Sobrino SJ (Maryknoll, NY: Orbis, 1993), 235–50, at 250.
9. Silva Henríquez gave the following thoughts in an interview with *U.S. News & World Report*: "Este proceso, válido para toda la Iglesia, se singulariza y reviste de connotación particular en América Latina. Continente en vías de desarrollo, el servicio eclesial a América Latina se concreta en un servicio al desarrollo, entendido en la acepción de Populorum Progressio: de condiciones menos humanas, hacia un humanismo integral, que incluye el don de la fe." Ascanio Cavallo, ed.,

Memorias: Cardenal Raúl Silva Henríquez (Santiago: Ediciones Copygraph, 1991), 2:137.
10. Josep-Ignasi Saranyana, director, and Carmen-José Alejos Grau, coordinator, *Teología en América Latina*, vol. 3: *El siglo de las teologías latinoamericanistas 1899–2001* (Madrid: Iberoamericana, 2002), 124.
11. Ibid., 124.
12. Ibid., 125.
13. Ibid., 126.
14. Ibid.
15. Ibid.
16. "Emergence of a World Church and the Irruption of the Poor," in *The Twentieth Century: A Theological Overview*, ed. Gregory Baum (Maryknoll, NY: Orbis, 1999), 108.
17. See Mario I. Aguilar, *A Social History of the Catholic Church in Chile, vol. I: The First Period of the Pinochet Government 1973–1980* (Lewiston, NY: Edwin Mellen, 2004).
18. While Bergoglio supported the poor and the persecuted, this was not a national pastoral guideline by the Argentinean Episcopal Conference, a fact that gives Bergoglio's actions much more weight as he was not following the general trend of ignoring the political realm and certainly ignoring the violence that abounded in Argentina in the period before and during the military regime.
19. Provincials of the Society of Jesus, "The Jesuits in Latin America" (May 1968), in Hennelly, *Liberation Theology*, 77–83.
20. Ibid., § 3.
21. Ibid., § 7.
22. Ibid., § 10.
23. Ignacio Ellacuría SJ, "The Task of a Christian University," in *Companions of Jesus*, ed. Jon Sobrino, Ignacio Ellacuría, et al. (Maryknoll, NY: Orbis, 1990), 150.
24. Jon Sobrino SJ, "The University's Christian Inspiration," in Sobrino et al., *Companions of Jesus*, 170–71.
25. Ernesto Cardenal, *El Evangelio en Solentiname* (Salamanca: Ediciones Sígueme, 1976) and *El Evangelio en Solentiname: Volumen Segundo* (Salamanca: Ediciones Sígueme, 1978).
26. Ernesto Cardenal, "Introducción," in *El Evangelio en Solentiname*, 9–10.
27. Cardenal, *El Evangelio en Solentiname: Volumen Segundo*, 143–47.
28. Ibid., 143–44.
29. Ibid., 144–45.
30. Ibid., 145–46.

ABOUT THE CONTRIBUTORS

THE EDITORS

Justin S. Holcomb is Affiliate Professor of Theology at Gordon-Conwell Theological Seminary. Previously, he taught at the University of Virginia. He is the author or editor of numerous books, including *Christian Theologies of Scripture*, *Christian Theologies of Salvation*, *Know the Heretics*, and *Know the Creeds and Councils*.

David A. Johnson is Rector of Christ Episcopal Church in Valdosta, Georgia. He is the author of *Grace upon Grace*, *The Good News of God's Grace*, *The Grace of God Has Appeared*, and *By Grace You Have Been Saved*.

THE CONTRIBUTORS

Mario I. Aguilar is Professor of Divinity (Religion and Politics) and Director of the Centre for the Study of Religion and Politics (CSRP) at the University of St. Andrews, Scotland, UK. His books include *The History and Politics of Latin American Theology* (three volumes), *A Social History of the Catholic Church in Chile* (nine volumes), *Church, Liberation and World Religions: Towards a Christian-Buddhist Dialogue*, *Pope Francis: His Life and Thought*; and *Religion, Torture and the Liberation of God*.

Paul W. Chilcote is Dean and Professor of Historical Theology & Wesleyan Studies at Ashland Theological Seminary in Ohio. He has published more than twenty books, including *Recapturing the Wesleys' Vision*, *John & Charles Wesley*, *Praying in the Wesleyan Spirit*, *Early Methodist Spirituality*, and *The Wesleyan Tradition*. He is a Unit Editor in the Works of John Wesley Project and is former President of the Charles Wesley Society.

Richard Cross is the Rev. John A. O'Brien Professor of Philosophy and Chair of the Department of Philosophy at the University of Notre Dame. He has written numerous articles and books on Duns Scotus, including *Duns Scotus on God*, *The Physics of John Duns Scotus*, *John Duns Scotus*, and *The Metaphysics of the Incarnation: Thomas Aquinas to Duns Scotus*.

Bruce Gordon is the Titus Street Professor of Ecclesiastical History at Yale Divinity School. His research focuses on European religious cultures of the late medieval and early modern periods, with a particular interest in the Reformation in German-speaking lands.

Bruce has written and edited numerous books, including *Calvin*, *The Swiss Reformation*, *Protestant History and Identity in Sixteenth-Century Europe*, and *Shaping the Bible in the Reformation: Books, Scholars and Their Readers in the Sixteenth Century*.

James R. Gordon is a Guest Professor of Biblical and Theological Studies and Philosophy at Wheaton College. He is the author of *The Holy One in Our Midst: An Essay on Christ's Flesh*. He has published essays in the *International Journal of Systematic Theology* and the *Heythrop Journal*.

Michael S. Horton is J. G. Machen Professor of Systematic Theology and Apologetics at Westminster Seminary California. His books include a four-volume dogmatics series (*Covenant and Eschatology*, *Lord and Servant*, *Covenant and Salvation*, and *People and Place*) and *The Christian Faith: A Systematic Theology for Pilgrims on the Way*. He has written articles for *Pro Ecclesia*, the *International Journal of Systematic Theology*, and *Christianity Today*.

Thomas L. Humphries, Jr. is Assistant Professor of Philosophy, Theology, and Religion at Saint Leo University in Florida. He is the author of *Ascetic Pneumatology from John Cassian to Gregory the Great* and helped to edit the *Oxford Handbook of Catholic Theology*.

Robert Kolb is Missions Professor of Systematic Theology Emeritus at Concordia Seminary, Saint Louis. He is the author of *Martin Luther and the Enduring Word of God: The Wittenberg School and Its Proclamation of Scripture*; *Luther and the Stories of God*; *Martin Luther: Confessor of the Faith*; with Charles P. Arand, *The Genius of Luther's Theology*; with Arand and James A. Nestingen, *The Lutheran Confessions*; and other books and articles. With Irene Dingel and Lubomir Batka, he edited *The Oxford Handbook of Martin Luther's Theology*, and with Timothy J. Wengert, the newest translation of *The Book of Concord*.

Matthew Levering is James N. and Mary D. Perry, Jr. Chair of Theology at Mundelein Seminary, and Co-Director of the Chicago Theological Initiative. He is the author or editor of over thirty books, including *Proofs of God*; *Paul in the Summa Theologiae*; *Engaging the Doctrine of Revelation*; *Mary's Bodily Assumption*; and *The Oxford Handbook of Sacramental Theology* (co-edited with Hans Boersma). He is the co-editor of two quarterly journals, *Nova et Vetera* and *International Journal of Systematic Theology*. Since 2007 he has served as Chair of the Board of the Academy of Catholic Theology.

Scot McKnight is the Julius R. Mantey Professor of New Testament at Northern Seminary (Lombard, Illinois). He is the author of *Jesus and His Death: Historiography, the Historical Jesus and Atonement Theory*; *The Letter of James*; *A Community Called Atonement*; *The King Jesus Gospel*; *Kingdom Conspiracy*; and the forthcoming *Paul's Letter to the Colossians* and *Paul's Letter to Philemon*. He is co-editor of *Jesus Is Lord, Caesar Is Not* and *Paul and the Christian Life*, and he serves on the editorial board for *Currents in Biblical Studies*.

Joseph C. Mudd is Assistant Professor in the Department of Religious Studies at Gonzaga University. He is the author of *Eucharist as Meaning: Critical Metaphysics and Contemporary Sacramental Theology*.

Paul T. Nimmo is the King's Chair of Systematic Theology at the University of Aberdeen. He is the author of *Being in Action: The Theological Shape of Barth's Ethical Vision*, which won a John Templeton Award for Theological Promise, and has written a series of research articles and essays on the work of Karl Barth and Friedrich Schleiermacher. He is an Editor of the *International Journal of Systematic Theology* and serves on the AAR Reformed Theology and History Steering Committee.

Ashley Null is a German Research Council Fellow at Humboldt-Universität zu Berlin and a Visiting Fellow of the Divinity Faculty, Cambridge University, and St. John's College, Durham. He has written numerous articles and books on Thomas Cranmer, including *Thomas Cranmer's Doctrine of Repentance: Renewing the Power to Love* and *Divine Allurement: Cranmer's Comfortable Words*. He is currently preparing a critical edition—a five-volume project—of Cranmer's private theological notebooks.

Donald S. Prudlo is Associate Professor of Ancient and Medieval History at Jacksonville State University in Alabama. He is the author of *The Martyred Inquisitor: The Life and Cult of Peter of Verona (†1252)*; *The Origin, Development, and Refinement of Medieval Religious Mendicancies*; and *Certain Sainthood: The Origins of Papal Infallibility in Canonization*, in addition to many articles and chapters on such topics as hagiography, scriptural theology, and Church history. He is currently writing on the history of the early Dominican Order.

Ryan M. Reeves is Associate Professor of Historical Theology and Dean of the Jacksonville Campus of Gordon-Conwell Theological Seminary. He is author of *Political Obedience and Resistance in Tudor England: 1528–1570* and *The Story of Creeds and Confessions*.

Philipp W. Rosemann is Professor and Chair of Philosophy at the University of Dallas. His publications on Peter Lombard include *Peter Lombard* (2004) and *The Story of a Great Medieval Book: Peter Lombard's "Sentences"* (2007). He has also edited volumes 2 and 3 of *Mediaeval Commentaries on the "Sentences" of Peter Lombard* (2010 and 2015), a handbook that brings together research on the influence of the *Sentences* in medieval and early modern theology. He edits the Dallas Medieval Texts and Translations series, in which twenty-one volumes have appeared to date.

Jacob N. Van Sickle received his doctorate in Historical Theology from Saint Louis University in 2017. He is the author/translator of *St. Basil the Great: On Christian Ethics*. He was ordained a priest in 2016 and serves at St. Theodosius Orthodox Cathedral in Cleveland, Ohio. He also teaches at Cleveland State University and the St. Macrina Institute for Diakonia and Catechesis.

Mary Veeneman is Associate Professor of Biblical and Theological Studies at North Park University. She is the author of *Introducing Method of Theology*.

John Yocum has taught at Greyfriars, Oxford; Loyola School of Theology, Manila; and Sacred Heart Major Seminary, Detroit. He is the author of *Ecclesial Mediation in Karl Barth*, and co-editor of two volumes on Aquinas.

Randall C. Zachman is Professor of Reformation Studies at the University of Notre Dame. His most recent book is *Reconsidering John Calvin*, and he is also author of *Image and Word in the Theology of John Calvin*; *John Calvin as Teacher, Pastor and Theologian*; and *The Assurance of Faith: Conscience in the Theology of Martin Luther and John Calvin*.

INDEX

Page numbers for biblical references are in boldface.

Abelard, Peter, 59, 61; *Sic et non*, 63; *Theologia*, 62
Acts 2:38, **182, 244**
Acts 2:46, **287**
Aguilar, Mario, 9, 366
Aquinas, Thomas, 3, 9, 21, 65, 76, 81, 94, 102–103, 105, 186, 244, 335, 338, 346; Christ's Passion and sacraments, 87–88, 90, 92; Christ's prophetic mission, 86; Christ's revelatory mission, 86; Christ's salvific mission, 86, 90–91; Christ's sanctifying mission, 87, 92; concomitance, 110; Council to Lyons, 82; definition of sacraments, 87, 91, 329n58; Doctor of Universal Church, 82; eschatological perspective of sacraments, 91–93; "grace perfects nature," 21; Mystical body, 85; reason for sacraments, 83; sacraments connected to Christ's mission of reconciliation, 5, 83–84; sacraments and perfection, 88; sacrament of baptism, 89; sacrament of Eucharist, 88–91; sacrament of extreme unction, 90; sacrament of holy orders, 88; sacrament of marriage, 88; sacrament of penance, 90; scholastic approach to sacraments, 4; sacraments as a gift of grace, 5, 87; sacraments as unified organism, 82; salvific Pasch, 82–83, 91; *Summa Contra Gentiles*, 82; *Summa Theologiae*, 82; theology of salvation, 83; theology of sacraments, 93

Anabaptist, 7, 119–120, 136, 140, 154, 159, 169, 175, 184, 188; definition of, 177; ethical separation, 120; Lord's Supper, 120, 184–188; Menno Simons, 7, 175–190; perfection, 120; rejection of magisterial justification, 120; theology of baptism, 120; theology of the sacraments, 7, 121, 176, 188
Aristotle, 107
Apollinarianism, 221
Asketikon, 24–25
Augsburg Confession, 122, 124, 199, 210, 215
Augustine of Hippo, 1, 4, 17–18, 22, 33, 41, 46, 60, 62, 65, 158, 182, 191, 209, 251, 275; Christ as agent in sacraments, 48; *Confessions*, 41, 56; difference between sign and thing signified, 17; Donatists, 49; infant baptism, 4, 48; marriage as sign of eschatological fulfillment, 53; mystery of God, 4, 43–45, 50, 54; ordination as sacrament, 4; sacrament of baptism, 47–51; sacrament of chrism, 48; sacrament of confirmation, 48; sacrament of Eucharist, 53–55; sacrament of marriage, 51–53; sacrament of monogamous marriage, 53; sacrament of polygamous marriage, 53; sacraments as kind of language, 49; sacraments as visible signs, 43–44; sacraments bear fruit and fulfill love, 43; *sacramentum*, 17, 43–44, 49, 54, 56; *Sermons*, 41; theological concept of mystery, 43–44;

387

Augustine of Hippo (*cont.*)
   theology of baptism, 4, 47, 50; theology of marriage, 4, 46, 51; theology of the sacraments, 4, 43; *Tractates*, 41; understanding the sacraments, 45
"Augustine's sacramental theology," 43, 50, 52, 55

Balthasar, Urs van, 8, 187, 267, 319, 321–322
Baptism, 2, 4, 15, 47, 119, 122, 263; efficacy of, 6, 123
Barth, Karl, 8–9, 267, 314; baptism, 315, 321–324; *Church Dogmatics*, 9, 314, 316–317; definition of sacraments, 317; denial of sacraments, 9, 315; doctrine of reconciliation, 315; Incarnation, 321, 328n49; "means of grace," 319; rejection of infant baptism, 322–323; rejection of baptism as a sacrament, 324–326; rejection of transubstantiation, 321; "revelation means sacrament," 321; sacraments as instruments, 318; sacraments as proclaiming Jesus Christ, 9; "secondary objectivity of God," 9, 320–321, 328n49; theology of the sacraments, 9, 315, 318
Basil the Great, 3, 4, 16–17, 24, 33; *Asketikon*, 24–25; connection between rite and Word, 30; defense of unwritten tradition, 26–27; defense of Nicene orthodoxy, 26; Dread mysteries, 33; *Ethics*, 27; Heavenly mysteries, 30–31; infant baptism, 33, 39n36, 40n51; *On Baptism*, 25, 34; *On the Holy Spirit*, 25; presence of Holy Spirit, 31–32; relationship between faith in Christ and participation in rituals, 29; rituals of salvation, 31; role of the Trinity in sacraments, 4; Scriptures as first principle of Christian thought, 26; theology of Baptism, 4, 29, 31–32, 34–36; theology of the Eucharist, 4, 16, 25, 29–30, 32, 36; theology of the sacraments, 25–26;
Trinitarian theology, 31, 37; view of Scripture, 28; "word of doctrine," 29
Berengar of Tours, 20; rejection of materialist language in the sacraments, 20
Bernard of Clairvaux, 59
Book of Common Prayer, 1
Book of Sentences, 4

Calvin, John, 5, 6, 126, 127, 154, 184, 191, 241 251, 334; definition of sacraments, 196–197; distinction between sacraments and Christ, 197; efficacy of the sacraments, 192, 200, 201; infant baptism, 201, 203; *Institutes of the Christian Religion*, 191, 204; "ladder ascending to heaven," 7, 205–206; Law and Gospel, 7, 192, 199–200; reality of Christ portrayed in the sacraments, 192, 198; rejection of Zwingli's view of sacraments, 122, 126; representation of Christ in the sacraments, 192, 197, 198; sacrament and the Law, 7, 199–200; sacrament of baptism, 199, 202–203; sacrament of the Lord's Supper, 204–205; self-manifestation of Christ in the sacraments of the Law, 199–202; self-manifestation of God in creation and Christ, 7, 192–196; self-revelation of Christ in the sacraments of the Gospel, 202; self-revelation of Christ in Word and sacrament, 196–199; theology of the sacraments, 7, 192–199, 206
Cardenal, Ernesto, 9
Carolingian dynasty, 18, 73
Catholic Counter Reformation, 5, 8, 117, 119, 233, 248, 252n1; baptism, 238–240, 246, 256n33; Baroque movement, 248–249; Catholic education, 233; Catholic liturgy, 233, 248; concomitance, 242; confirmation, 238–240, 246; contrition, 244; Council of Trent, 233, 234, 236–238, 247, 250–252, 256n34; Eucharist and the Mass, 240–243, 245,

257n40; Holy orders, 245–246; Jesuit order, 233; marriage, 245–246; missionary efforts, 233; private confession, 244–245; sacramental absolution, 244; sacraments in Catholicism, 234–236, 252; sacrament of confession, 243–245; sacraments of initiation, 238–240; sacraments of vocation, 245; *Tametsi*, 247, 252; transubstantiation, 241, 248–249

Catholic Reform, 5, 8, 117, 119, 233

Catholic sacramental theology, 9, 124, 233–250, 255n10

Chauvet, Louis-Marie, 8, 333; against Neo-Scholasticism, 9, 336; Christology, 343–344; Church, 344; ethics, 344–345; "presence of the absence of God," 343, 346–347; problems with classical sacramental theology, 342; sacraments as "objectivist," 9; sacramental theology, 9, 336, 342; "symbolic gift exchange," 345

Chilcote, Paul W., 8, 271

Church Dogmatics, 9, 267, 314, 316–317

Colossians 2:11–12, **182**

Colossians 2:11–15, **137**

Colossians 3:1–2, **85**

Constantine, 33

Consubstantiation, 143, 234, 241

Council of Nicea, 4

Council of Trent, 8, 64, 111, 124, 125, 233, 234, 236–238, 247, 250–252, 255n9, 264, 321; affirmation of the seven sacraments, 8, 119; Eucharist as true propitiatory sacrifice, 119, 124; impact on Catholic culture, 8, 236–238; theology of the sacraments, 8; transubstantiation, 119

Cranmer, Thomas, 5, 6, 127, 209; Archbishop of Canterbury, 209; *Articles of Religion*, 210; baptism, 219, 220; *Book of Homilies*, 210, 216; *Book of Common Prayer*, 210, 217, 227; *communicatio idimatum*, 221, 225 232n75; communion, 220, 222, 223–227; confirmation as a sacrament, 214–215; Cyril of Alexandria, 221–227, 228, 231n66; definition of sacrament, 211; efficacy of sacraments, 211–212, 219; *eucharistia*, 215–216; justification by faith, 210, 213, 216, 219; mutual indwelling, 221–222, 228; rejection of transubstantiation, 212; sacramental theology, 7, 213, 214, 225; solifidianism, 213–214, 227, 229; understanding of the sacraments, 216–221; view of penance, 214–215

Cross, Richard, 5, 100

Cyril of Alexandria, 221

Deuteronomy 6:5, **42**

Donatists, 49, 235

Edwards, Jonathan, 8

Efficacy of Sacraments, 6, 263

Ephesians 2:6, **195**

Ephesians 3:14, **25**

Ephesians 3:17, **88**

Ephesians 4:10, **85**

Ephesians 4:11–13, **85**

Ephesians 4:15–16, **86**

Ephesians 4:32–32, **44**

Ephesians 5:26, **86**

Ephesians 5:26–27, **318**

Ephesians 5:31, **75**

Ephesians 5:31–32, **89**

Ephesians 6:17, **138**

Eutychianism, 125

ex opere operato, 49, 119, 133, 142, 198, 210, 214, 217, 319

Exodus 20:2, **161**

Feminist Theology, 8, 352; theology of the sacraments, 9

First Corinthians 1:16–2:16, **141**

First Corinthians 6:20, **84**

First Corinthians 10:1–3, **55**

First Corinthians 10:1–4, **92**

First Corinthians 11, **169**

First Corinthians 11:23–25, **241**

First Corinthians 13:2, **44**

First Corinthians 13:12, **92**
First Corinthians 15:28, **42**
First Great Awakening, 263
First Peter 1:16, **158**
First Peter 2:21, **83**
First Vatican Council, 8, 264
Fourth Lateran Council, 4, 19–20, 68, 106, 241, 264; impact on sacramental theology, 4

Genesis 1, **133**
Genesis 2:24, **51, 75, 89**
Gordon, Bruce, 6, 152
Gordon, James R., 8, 261
Gutierrez, Gustavo, 9

Hebrews 1:3, **194**
Hebrews 7:25, **85**
Hebrews 7:27, **88**
Hebrews 10:1, **92**
Hebrews 12:1, **289**
Heidelberg catechism, 120–121, 317
Holcomb, Justin S., 1
Horton, Michael, 5, 119
Hugh of Saint-Victor, 59, 62, 65, 68
Humphries, Thomas L., 4, 41
Hus, Jan, 4, 242; rejection of medieval sacramental teachings, 21–22

Incarnation, 44, 53–54
Infant Baptism, 4, 33, 39n36, 40n51, 48, 141, 238, 267
Irenaeus of Lyon, 32
Isidore of Seville, 19; *Etymologiae*, 19; *Trivium*, 19; *Quadrivium*, 19

James 5:4–15, **245**
Johnson, David A., 1
Johnson, Elizabeth, 9
John 1:14, **274**
John 1:16, **1**
John 3, **28**
John 3:5, **318**

John 6, **28, 30, 186, 241**
John 6:47, **63, 169**
John 6:51, **161**
John 6:52–56, **318**
John 6:53–54, **89**
John 6:53–58, **28**
John 6:56, **220**
John 6:63, **146, 166**
John 6:69, **165**
John 8:36, **135**
John 8:44, **138, 183**
John 10:19, **146**
John 11:25, **135**
John 14–17, **126**
John 14:3, **85**
John 16:7, **126**
John 16:28, **51**
John 16:29, **85**
John 20:22–23, **243**
John 21:25, **86**

Kolb, Robert, 6, 132

Levering, Matthew, 5, 81
Leviticus 20:21, **209**
Liberation theology, 9, 366; celebration of the Eucharist, 370, 372, 374, 375, 376, 378, 380; definition of liberation theology, 380; Jesuit, 372–374, 376; Jesuit University of Central America, 374–376; Marxists, 369–370; impact of Medellín, 368, 371-; poor as sacramental presence of Christ, 371; sacraments and prophetic liberation, 378; social gospel, 373; Society of Jesus, 374
Lombard, Peter, 3, 4, 20, 46, 59, 101, 113n5; *Book of Sentences*, 4, 20, 60–65, 70, 72, 74, 76–77, 81; confession (penance) as unique aspect of sacramental theology, 5, 68–71, 77; definition of sacraments, 4, 65–66; efficacious sign of God's grace, 67; general traits of sacraments, 65; *Magna Glosatura*, 59; marriage as

unique aspect of sacramental theology, 5, 72–77; Master, 61; *On Christian Doctrine*, 62–63; *res*, 71, 75; *sacrae paginae tractatum*, 62; sacrament of baptism, 67; sacraments of the New Law, 67; sacraments resemble God's grace, 66; sexuality as "tinder of sin" and quintessence of incontinence, 76

Lubac, Henri de, 8, 267, 340
Luke 16:29, **139**
Luke 22:14–20, **241**
Luke 22:19, **283**
Luke 22:20, **161**
Luke 24:49, **89**
Luther, Martin, 5, 6, 65, 126, 132, 136, 152, 153, 154, 155, 176, 184, 191, 196, 234, 250; baptism, 137–142, 148; definition of sacraments, 6, 136; engagement with Scripture, 133; hypostatic union, 146; infant baptism, 141; justification, 134, 137; *Large Catechism*, 133, 140, 148; Lord's Supper, 136, 142–148; Ockhamist school, 135, 142, 148; real presence of Christ, 121; rejection of transubstantiation, 6, 143; resurrection, 134; role of Holy Spirit, 138, 145, 147; *Small Catechism*, 133, 136; theology of the cross, 6, 141; theology of the sacraments, 6, 124, 136, 147–148; Trinity as baptizing tool, 141

Mark 1:8, **326, 331n103**
Mark 10:14, **183**
Mark 14:17–25, **241**
Matthew 3:2, **244**
Matthew 4:4, **135**
Matthew 7:29, **86**
Matthew 10, **169**
Matthew 16:19, **166**
Matthew 18:20, **126**
Matthew 19:6, **89, 246**
Matthew 19:13, **277**
Matthew 22:15–22, **379**
Matthew 22:34–40, **42**
Matthew 26:20–29, **241**
Matthew 27:46, **195**
Matthew 28:19, **35, 159**
Matthew 28:20, **126**
Mass, 6, 127, 202; as real sacrifice of Christ, 8
McKnight, Scot, 7, 175
Merovingian dynasty, 18
Modernity, 261, 264
Mudd, Joseph C., 333
Mysteries of God, 3, 16, 25–26

Neo-Scholastic theology, 335, 336
Nestorianism, 125, 221
Nicene Creed, 27
Nimmo, Paul T., 9, 295
Null, Ashley, 7, 209

Oxford Movement, 8, 266

Patristic witness, 16
Pelagianism, 94, 238, 250
Petrarch, 18
Philippians 2:8–11, **84**
Protestant Christians, 47; definition of sacrament, 47
Prudlo, Donald, 8, 233
Psalm 22:1, **195**
Psalm 41:4, **90**
Psalm 113, **170**

Reeves, Ryan, 3, 15
Reformation, 4, 5, 16, 117, 119, 125, 152, 154, 234, 235, 238, 254n1, 262–263; baptism and circumcision, 123; covenant of grace, 121–122; efficacy of sacraments from external Word, 120, 123, 124; efficacy of sacraments as work of God, 121; glorification, 120; Heidelberg catechism, 120–121; justification, 119, 120; sacraments as God's means of grace, 121; sacraments versus Catholic Counter-Reformation, 5, 121; sanctification, 120; *Westminster confession*, 123

392 | INDEX

Reformers, 111, 120, 124
Regeneration, 263, 278, 300, 302
Renaissance, 18, 61, 250, 268n1
res, 275
res tantum, 49
Roman Catholic, 175; reflection on the sacraments, 22
Romans 1:16, **133, 139**
Romans 3:24–25, **88**
Romans 6, **137, 332n104**
Romans 6:3, **88**
Romans 6:3–4, **137**
Romans 12:1, **156**
Rosemann, Philipp W., 4, 59

Sacramentalism, 263
Sacramentalist, 18, 177, 186, 265
sacramentum tantum, 49
Sacramental theology, 2, 25, 54, 177, 282, 289, 297, 306, 308, 309, 321, 334, 336; impact of Fourth Lateran Council on, 4; overlap with other theologies, 10
Sacraments, 1, 15, 47, 153; administration of, 2; as "channels of grace," 8, 198; as mysteries, 16; as related to conversion and regeneration, 8; definition of, 2, 76, 196; during the Medieval period, 18; function of, 1; ministering grace of God, 1, 5, 10; Scholasticism and, 7, 19, 21; the earliest church and, 16
Sanctification, 2, 243
Schillebeeckx, Edward, 8, 333, 352–353; against Neo-Scholasticism, 9, 335; Christology, 339–340; *Christ, the Sacrament of the Encounter with God*, 337; church, 340–341, 347; ethics, 341–342; Neo-Scholastic method, 338; sacramental grace, 337, 347; sacraments as personal encounter, 9, 336, 337, 339; sacramental theology, 9, 338; Thomist view, 338, 348
Schleiermacher, Friedrich, 8–9, 264–266, 269n5, 295; baptism, 265–266, 297, 299–302; *Christian Faith*, 297, 298; definition of sacraments, 299; disagreement with Luther and Zwingli, 9; efficacy of the sacraments, 297, 301, 304; essential features of the Church, 298–299; eucharist, 265–266, 297, 302–306; infant baptism, 265, 302; mystical approach to sacraments, 9, 308, 313n70; sacramentarian, 265, 297, 305, 306; *Speeches on Religion to the Cultured about Its Despisers*, 295; theology of the sacraments, 9, 297, 306, 308, 309; transubstantiation, 305
Schmemann, Alexander, 8, 267–268
Scholasticism, 7, 19, 21; impact on discussion of sacraments, 20
Scotus, Duns, 3; against Aquinas, 104, 105, 106, 110; baptism, 105; Bonaventure and sacramental theology, 101, 102, 103; concomitance, 110, 111, 115n65; consubstantiation, 108; definition of sacrament, 102; doctrine of Eucharistic sacrifice, 111; efficacious significance of sacraments, 102, 105, 106, 112; Franciscan order, 100; instrumental cause of grace, 102–103; Mass and the Eucharist, 104, 111, 112; metaphysics, 101; occasionalist option, 104; penance, 105; role of priest in sacraments, 111–112, 114n43; sacramental causality of grace, 102, 103, 104, 112; sacramental theology, 101; sacraments as signs of God's salvific activity, 5, 102; theology of the Eucharist, 102, 104–105, 106–107, 109; transubstantiation, 5, 101, 106, 107, 108, 109; use of sameness and identity in theology, 101
Second Timothy 1:6, **246**
Second Vatican Council, 8, 246, 266, 333, 349, 353, 366
Segundo, Juan Luis, 9
Seven sacraments, 4, 5, 93, 113n5, 237, 265; affirmation of, 8, 119

Simons, Menno, 5, 7, 175–190; Anabaptist heritage, 178–179; baptism and circumcision, 182; baptism as act of obedience, 7; believer's baptism versus infant baptism, 7, 179, 180–184, 190n21; definition of Anabaptism, 177; Eucharist as expression of God's love, 7; opposition to Martin Luther, 181; rejection of transubstantiation, 7, 186; sacramentalist, 177, 186, 188; theology of baptism, 179–184; theology of the Lord's Supper, 184–188

Titus 3:5, **89, 122, 139, 318**
Titus 3:5–8, **136**
Theology of the sacraments, 3, 15, 21, 273
Tractarians, 266
Transubstantiation, 5, 124, 143, 264; the Fourth Lateran Council and, 19, 241

Van Sickle, Jacob N., 4, 23
Veeneman, Mary, 9, 352; definition of sacraments, 363; feminist and womanist theologies, 9, 352; feminist sacramental theology, 358; holy orders and the eucharist, 358; Johnson, Elizabeth, 353–360; nature of Christ and human salvation, 355; Ross, Susan, 352, 353, 357, 358; sacraments and ordination, 353–360; second-wave feminism, 360; third-wave feminism, 360; womanism and the sacraments, 360–363

Wesley, Charles and John, 8, 263, 271; baptism, 272, 273, 275, 276–280, 291; Christian perfection, 271; definition of sacraments, 8, 275–276; excursus on presence, 288–290; excursus on sacrifice, 286–287; grace-focused sacramental theology, 9, 274, 282; Holy Communion, 272, 273, 274, 281–285, 291; *Hymns on the Lord's Supper*, 271, 284; infant baptism, 276–277, 280; Methodist, 271, 282, 284; rejection of transubstantiation, 288, 294n44; regeneration, 278; relationship to worship and theology, 9; theology of the sacraments, 8–9, 273; work of grace, 9; worship and the sacraments, 272
Womanist theology, 8, 352; theology of the sacraments, 9
World Council of Churches, 8, 268; *Baptism, Eucharist, and Ministry*, 8, 268
Wycliffe, John, 4, 242; against medieval sacramental teachings, 21–22; rejection of transubstantiation, 22

Yocum, John, 9, 314

Zachman, Randall C., 7, 191
Zwingli, Ulrich, 5, 6, 125, 146, 152, 178, 212, 241, 269n4, 300, 306, 323; baptism as sign of, 6, 157, 158, 160, 169, 171; baptism equal to circumcision, 159; *Baptism, Rebaptism, and Infant Baptism*, 158–159; confrontation with Luther, 165–167; definition of sacraments, 6, 155, 168; disagreements with Luther, 6, 121; Eucharist a sign of, 6; *fidei contemplation*, 163; *Fidei Ratio*, 153–154; final years, 167–168; infant baptism, 157–160; Lord's Supper, 155, 157, 160–165, 166, 170; nature of sacraments, 155, 166; *On True and False Religion*, 153–154, 157, 159, 160, 166; real presence of Christ, 121, 161, 166; rejection of priesthood and the Mass, 156, 163, 166; rejection of transubstantiation, 6, 153, 160, 162; Resurrection, 156; sacramentarians, 165; sacraments as signs of work of grace, 6; *sacramentum*, 164; theology of the sacraments, 6, 122, 154, 155, 156, 162, 163; visualization of sacraments, 168–171